Maria W. Stewart

OXFORD NEW HISTORIES OF PHILOSOPHY

Series Editors
Christia Mercer, Melvin Rogers, and Eileen O'Neill (1953–2017)

*

Advisory Board
Lawrie Balfour, Jacqueline Broad, Marguerite Deslauriers, Karen Detlefsen, Bachir Diagne, Don Garrett, Robert Gooding-Williams, Andrew Janiak, Marcy Lascano, Lisa Shapiro, Tommie Shelby

*

Oxford New Histories of Philosophy provides essential resources for those aiming to diversify the content of their philosophy courses, revisit traditional narratives about the history of philosophy, or better understand the richness of philosophy's past. Examining previously neglected or understudied philosophical figures, movements, and traditions, the series includes both innovative new scholarship and new primary sources.

*

Published in the series

Mexican Philosophy in the 20th Century: Essential Readings
Edited by Carlos Alberto Sánchez and Robert Eli Sanchez, Jr.

Sophie de Grouchy's Letters on Sympathy: *A Critical Engagement with Adam Smith's* The Theory of Moral Sentiments
Edited by Sandrine Bergès and Eric Schliesser. Translated by Sandrine Bergès.

Margaret Cavendish: Essential Writings
Edited by David Cunning

Women Philosophers of Seventeenth-Century England: Selected Correspondence
Edited by Jacqueline Broad

The Correspondence of Catharine Macaulay
Edited by Karen Green

Mary Shepherd's Essays on the Perception of an External Universe
Edited by Antonia Lolordo

Women Philosophers of Eighteenth-Century England: Selected Correspondence
Edited by Jacqueline Broad

Frances Power Cobbe: Essential Writings of a Nineteenth-Century Feminist Philosopher
Edited by Alison Stone

Korean Women Philosophers and the Ideal of a Female Sage: Essential Writings of Im Yungjidang and Gang Jeongildang
Edited and Translated by Philip J. Ivanhoe and Hwa Yeong Wang

Louise Dupin's Work on Women: *Selections*
Edited and Translated by Angela Hunter and Rebecca Wilkin

Edith Landmann-Kalischer: Essays on Art, Aesthetics, and Value
Edited by Samantha Matherne. Translated by Daniel O. Dahlstrom

Mary Ann Shadd Cary: Essential Writings of a Nineteenth-Century Black Radical Feminist
Edited by Nneka D. Dennie

Slavery and Race: Philosophical Debates in the Eighteenth-Century
Julia Jorati

Maria W. Stewart: Essential Writings of a Nineteenth-Century Black Abolitionist
Edited by Douglas A. Jones

Maria W. Stewart

Essential Writings of a Nineteenth-Century Black Abolitionist

Edited by

DOUGLAS A. JONES

OXFORD
UNIVERSITY PRESS

Oxford University Press is a department of the University of Oxford. It furthers
the University's objective of excellence in research, scholarship, and education
by publishing worldwide. Oxford is a registered trade mark of Oxford University
Press in the UK and certain other countries.

Published in the United States of America by Oxford University Press
198 Madison Avenue, New York, NY 10016, United States of America.

© Oxford University Press 2024

All rights reserved. No part of this publication may be reproduced, stored in
a retrieval system, or transmitted, in any form or by any means, without the
prior permission in writing of Oxford University Press, or as expressly permitted
by law, by license, or under terms agreed with the appropriate reproduction
rights organization. Inquiries concerning reproduction outside the scope of the
above should be sent to the Rights Department, Oxford University Press, at the
address above.

You must not circulate this work in any other form
and you must impose this same condition on any acquirer.

Library of Congress Cataloging-in-Publication Data
Names: Stewart, Maria W., 1803–1879, author. | Jones, Douglas A., editor.
Title: Maria W. Stewart : essential writings of a Nineteenth-century Black abolitionist /
edited by Douglas A. Jones Jr.
Other titles: Essential writings of a Nineteenth-century Black abolitionist
Description: New York, NY : Oxford University Press, [2024] |
Series: Oxford new histories philosophy | Includes bibliographical references and index.
Identifiers: LCCN 2023042505 | ISBN 9780197612965 (paperback) |
ISBN 9780197612958 (hardback) | ISBN 9780197612989 (epub)
Subjects: LCSH: African Americans—History—To 1863. | African Americans—Social
conditions—To 1964. | Antislavery movements—United States—History—19th century. |
United States—Race relations—History—19th century.
Classification: LCC E185.97.S84 A25 | DDC 973.0496/073009034—dc23/eng/20231124
LC record available at https://lccn.loc.gov/2023042505

DOI: 10.1093/oso/9780197612958.001.0001

Paperback printed by Marquis Book Printing, Canada
Hardback printed by Bridgeport National Bindery, Inc., United States of America

For Cheryl A. Wall: scholar, teacher, mentor, and friend

Contents

Series Editors' Foreword ix
Introduction xi

PART I: GENDER THEORY

Contextual Works 3

1. Thomas Jefferson, *Notes on the State of Virginia*, Query XIV 5
2. Angelina Grimké, *Appeal to the Christian Women of the South* (selections) 23
3. Louisa Piquet and Hiram Mattison, *Louisa Picquet, the Octoroon, or, Inside Views of Southern Domestic Life* (selections) 31
4. Alexander Crummell, "The Black Woman of the South: Her Neglects and Her Needs" 44
5. Anna Julia Cooper, "Womanhood: A Vital Element in the Regeneration and Progress of a Race" 59

Stewart's Works 79

6. "Lecture Delivered at Franklin Hall" 81
7. "An Address Delivered Before the Afric-American Female Intelligence Society of Boston" 87
8. "Mrs. Stewart's Farewell Address to Her Friends in the City of Boston" 93

PART II: RACIAL ETHICS

Contextual Works 105

9. David Walker, *Walker's Appeal, in Four Articles: Together with a Preamble, to the Coloured Citizens of the World, but in Particular, and Very Expressly, to Those of the United States of America* (selections) 107

10. "Zillah" (Sarah Mapps Douglass) Writings Published in *The Liberator* — 125

11. Hosea Easton, *A Treatise on the Intellectual Character, and Civil and Political Condition of the Colored People of the U. States; And the Prejudice Exercised Towards Them; With a Sermon on the Duty of the Church to Them* (selections) — 136

12. Mary Ann Shadd Cary, "Open Letter to Frederick Douglass," "Adieu," "Speech, to the Judiciary Committee," and "Letters to the People—No. 1" — 150

Stewart's Works — 161

13. "Religion and the Pure Principles of Morality, the Sure Foundation on Which We Must Build" — 163

14. "Cause for Encouragement" — 177

15. "An Address Delivered at the African Masonic Hall" — 180

16. "The Proper Training of Children" — 188

PART III: LITERARY PRODUCTIONS

Contextual Works — 195

17. Jarena Lee, *The Life and Religious Experience of Jarena Lee* (selections) — 197

18. William J. Wilson ("Ethiop"), "From Our Brooklyn Correspondent" — 209

19. Frances Ellen Watkins (Harper), "Two Offers" and "Aunt Chloe's Politics" — 213

20. Charlotte Forten, "Life on the Sea Islands" — 224

Stewart's Works — 257

21. Meditation VI and Meditation XII — 259

22. "The Negro's Complaint" — 263

23. "The First Stage of Life" — 266

24. "Sufferings During the War" — 273

Selected Bibliography — 285
Index — 287

Series Editors' Foreword

Oxford New Histories of Philosophy (ONHP) speaks to a new climate in philosophy.

There is a growing awareness that philosophy's past is richer and more diverse than previously understood. It has become clear that canonical figures are best studied in a broad context. More exciting still is the recognition that our philosophical heritage contains long-forgotten innovative ideas, movements, and thinkers. Sometimes these thinkers warrant serious study in their own right; sometimes their importance resides in the conversations they helped reframe or problems they devised; often their philosophical proposals force us to rethink long-held assumptions about a period or genre; and frequently they cast well-known philosophical discussions in a fresh light.

There is also a mounting sense among philosophers that our discipline benefits from a diversity of perspectives and a commitment to inclusiveness. In a time when questions about justice, inequality, dignity, education, discrimination, and climate (to name a few) are especially vivid, it is appropriate to mine historical texts for insights that can shift conversations and reframe solutions. Given that philosophy's very long history contains astute discussions of a vast array of topics, the time is right to cast a broad historical net.

Lastly, there is increasing interest among philosophy instructors in speaking to the diversity and concerns of their students. Although historical discussions and texts can serve as a powerful means of doing so, finding the necessary time and tools to excavate long-buried historical materials is challenging.

Oxford New Histories of Philosophy is designed to address all these needs. It contains new editions and translations of significant historical texts. These primary materials make available, often for the first time, ideas and works by women, people of color, and movements in philosophy's past that were groundbreaking in their day, but left out of traditional accounts. Informative introductions help instructors and students navigate the new material. Alongside its primary texts, ONHP also publishes monographs and collections of essays that offer philosophically subtle analyses of understudied topics, movements, and figures. In combining primary materials and astute philosophical analyses, ONHP makes it easier for philosophers, historians, and instructors to include in their courses and research exciting new materials drawn from philosophy's past.

ONHP's range is wide, both historically and culturally. The series includes, for example, the writings of African American philosophers, twentieth-century Mexican philosophers, early modern and late medieval women, Islamic and Jewish authors, and non-western thinkers. It excavates and analyses problems and ideas that were prominent in their day, but forgotten by later historians. And it serves as a significant aid to philosophers in teaching and researching this material.

As we expand the range of philosophical voices, it is important to acknowledge one voice responsible for this series. Eileen O'Neill was a series editor until her death, December 1, 2017. She was instrumental in motivating and conceptualizing ONHP. Her brilliant scholarship, advocacy, and generosity made all the difference to the efforts that this series is meant to represent. She will be deeply missed, as a scholar and a friend.

We are proud to contribute to philosophy's present and to a richer understanding of its past.

Christia Mercer and Melvin Rogers
Series Editors

Introduction

At 8 Smith Court on Boston's Beacon Hill stands the African Meeting House. "The Black Faneuil Hall," as it was often called, was the hub of antebellum black Boston. Organizations such as the African Society and the Massachusetts General Colored Association held meetings there. Abolitionists rallied on behalf of the enslaved from its lecterns, and reformers spoke on the virtues of caring for orphans and widows on its stages. Primus Hall, son of black freemasonry founder Prince Hall, ran his school for black youth for over a quarter of a century in its basement. At the center of it all was the African Baptist Church, the lifeblood of the black community and the governing body of the African Meeting House.

The African Baptist Church emerged from the protestations of a few dozen African Americans who attended the city's white Baptist churches. These congregants were subjected to racially segregated sacraments, confined to sit in "nigger pews," and denied the franchise in church governance. Fed up, they left to form their own church and tapped a young exhorter from New Hampshire named Thomas Paul to pastor them. With official recognition from the regional denominational association in 1805, the African Baptist Church erected the African Meeting House in 1806. Paul shepherded his flock from its pulpit and performed baptisms, funerals, and marriage ceremonies at its altar. One of the weddings he officiated was that of James and Maria Stewart on August 10, 1826.[1] Three year later, James Stewart was dead; all Maria Stewart had to fall back on were the social networks she established at the African Meeting House. Those relationships did more than sustain her as a new widow: they became the foundation for the groundbreaking political thought she cultivated over the next five decades.[2]

---

[1] Details of Stewart's marriage are available in the Register of Marriages in Boston. Records indicate they were "people of colour" married by "Rev. Thomas Paul."

[2] James O. Horton and Lois E. Horton, *Black Bostonians: Family Life and Community Struggle in the Antebellum North* (1979; New York: Holmes and Meier, 1999), 1–55; George A. Levesque, *Black Boston: African American Life and Culture in Urban America, 1750–1860* (New York: Garland, 1994), 266–292; 338–344.

xii INTRODUCTION

Stewart moved to Boston in 1826 when she was still Maria Miller, an unwed woman in her early twenties from Hartford, Connecticut. There is no record of her having previously visited Boston. But the allure of New England's preeminent city, its fabled history, and the charisma of its residents whom she met in Hartford were an immense draw. Travelers from Boston en route to New York or other points south regularly stopped in Connecticut's city capital. Thomas Paul, like other African Americans who took that trip, lodged with members of its tight-knit black community. Stewart may have heard Paul preach or even met him in 1824 when he passed through on his way to New York City to celebrate his brother's instillation as pastor of what is now Abyssinian Baptist Church in Harlem.[3]

Boston offered black women like Stewart more opportunities for intellectual growth and social mobility than Hartford ever could. She became an orphan at age five in 1808, was indentured to a white Congregationalist minister for the next decade, and then attended a sabbath school until she was twenty. The degree of her literacy across different stages of her life is an unresolved question, but there is no doubt she received little to no formal education, academic or vocational, before she settled in Boston. Once there, she immersed herself in black institutional life and friendship circles that proved crucial to her activism and intellectual pursuits in social criticism, gender theory, and Africana philosophy, especially black nationalism.

Maria W. Stewart: Essential Writings of a 19th-Century Black Abolitionist offers the most comprehensive volume of her incredible corpus to date.[4] All of Stewart's known essays, lectures, and fiction, including recently discovered texts, are in this collection.[5] Its editorial apparatus situates Stewart's political philosophy in its rich intellectual contexts: abolitionism, feminism, sentimentalism, and black nationalism. Key works by other thinkers that shaped or were shaped by Stewart's writings are included.

Three core sections organize the book. "Gender Theory" illuminates Stewart's philosophy of the meanings, history, and uses of gender and

---

[3] Abyssinian Baptist Church worshipped in several downtown locations before it moved to Harlem in the early twentieth century. John Dowling, "Sketches of New-York Baptists—No. IV," Enoch Hutchinson and Stephen Remington, eds., *The Baptist Memorial and Monthly Record* Vol. 8 (New York: Hatch, 1849), 298. Hartford was one of the state's two capital cities, but the General Assembly always met there.

[4] This volume builds on the only other collection of Stewart's writings and speeches, Marilyn Richardson's *Maria W. Stewart, America's First Black Woman Political Writer: Essays and Speeches* (Cambridge: MIT Press, 1987).

[5] In the "Literary Productions" section, this volume includes a few of Stewart's religious devotions from the lengthy *Meditations from the Pen of Mrs. Maria W. Stewart* (1832; 1879).

womanhood. "Racial Ethics" organizes her ideas about racial identity, black history, solidarity, liberation, and uplift. "Literary Productions" showcases her aesthetic flexibility to emphasize the interdependence of formal prose and other genres in (black) philosophical discourse of this period. These sections, along with an extended introduction that includes new research into her biography, trace the evolution of Stewart's thought as it tracked developments in American politics and society. In so doing, *Maria W. Stewart: Essential Writings* positions Stewart as a major thinker whose contributions reveal the complexity of nineteenth-century African American political philosophy, especially in terms of thinking beyond commitments, duties, and obligations against race-based oppression.

***

Maria Stewart did not know the city in which she was born. In all her autobiographical accounts she names Hartford, Connecticut, as her birthplace, but Kristin Waters has recently determined that Stewart was born in Greenwich.[6] Stewart's error tells us at least two major aspects about free black life in early America. The first is that details about ancestry, origins, and familial life were and remain difficult to pin down, even for the individual or family in question, because of the often-haphazard modes authorities used to keep vital records for black people. The other is that it registers African Americans' dominant migration pattern in the era: resettling in cities or in bigger cities. The move to more urban locales was especially characteristic of those newly freed.

Stewart's parents "Caesar & Lib (negro)" fit that profile.[7] They were from the small coastal Connecticut town of Greenwich. It was among the scores of locales in the north and upper south that experienced a wave of manumissions following the American War of Independence. The democratic zeal that animated revolutions across the Atlantic world also hit slave owners and lawmakers in those regions. The manner of manumission from place to place was not uniform: some enslaved persons were set free immediately, while others had to serve a period of years or reach a certain age, among other conditions, before they were granted freedom. Precisely how Caesar

---

[6] Kristin Waters, *Maria W. Stewart and the Roots of Black Political Thought* (Jackson: University Press of Mississippi), 20–21.
[7] Greenwich Vital Records 1640–1848, Barbour Collection, and Index Book.

and Lib gained their freedom remains unknown, but they left Greenwich for Hartford sometime before Stewart, who was born free, turned five.

Hartford offered Caesar and Lib more economic opportunities than Greenwich did. But greater possibilities for self-definition may have been the strongest impetus for their move. As Barbara Fields explains, "For the manumitted slave, [the city] offered greater independence and a greater sense of responsibility for his own life than the rural community, where the round of work, leisure, and associations remained closely encircled by the regime of slavery" and its legacies.[8] Hartford would be the place for Caesar, Lib, and young Maria to take advantage of their new freedom to the fullest extent possible.

The Hartford they relocated to had a very small black population relative to the whole. But the increase in African Americans in both raw numbers and racial proportionality over the first decade of the century was steady and somewhat auspicious, considering the residential and commercial restrictions on black people. From 1800 to 1805, the percentage of black residents increased over 50 percent from a little over 3 percent to nearly 5 percent of the city's total number of inhabitants.[9] Caesar and Lib were part of this population growth, but they did not experience Hartford for long: Stewart became an orphan in 1808 and was indentured to a minister for the next ten years of her life.[10] Although the minister and his family for whom she worked were white, Stewart was part of Hartford's fledgling black community as it began to establish itself as an appreciable presence in the state capital.

Early black Hartford's first major institutional achievement occurred in 1819, when black members of the First Congregational Church protested segregated seating and left the church to create their own. The African Religious Society of Hartford, as they called themselves, founded their own Sunday School in 1820 and opened its meetinghouse in 1827, the Talcott

---

[8] Barbara J. Fields, *Slavery and Freedom on Middle on the Middle Ground: Maryland during the Nineteenth Century* (New Haven, CT: Yale University Press, 1986), 34. Although Fields's interest is Maryland, her point holds as a general principle.

[9] Barbara J. Beeching, *African Americans and Native Americans in Hartford 1636–1800: Antecedents of Hartford's Nineteenth Century Black Community Antecedents of Hartford's Nineteenth Century* (Hartford, CT: Trinity College, 1993), 5.

The census lists "Whites," "Negroes," and "Indians." Although it only delineates five Indians over the fifty years it covers, beginning in 1800 they were counted as Negroes.

[10] Indenturing black orphans to families was a customary practice in the era. Throughout the long nineteenth century, fears of black idleness of any sort led to a raft of so-called anti-vagrancy laws for free and enslaved black persons across states and municipalities.

Street Congregationalist Church.[11] Stewart ended her indenture in 1818 and attended "sabbath schools" thereafter until 1823.[12] One of those sabbath schools was very likely the African Religious Society's. Her post-indenture years in Hartford coincided with the black community achieving a real foothold in the city, despite never topping 5 percent of the total population.

When Stewart arrived in Boston in 1826, she found among the city's black Baptists institutional cultures and histories that were principally the same as those she was part of in Hartford. Boston's Black Baptists may have appealed to Stewart because the first pastoral leader of the African Religious Society of Hartford was an ordained Baptist minister, Asa Goldsborough.[13] Stewart almost certainly worshipped and attended sabbath school under his leadership. Goldsborough was the first in a line of ministers who led Hartford's Black Congregationalists but pastored cross-denominationally.

Another minister of that line was Hosea Easton. He crossed paths with Stewart in Boston in the late 1820s before he moved to Hartford. Easton pastored the Talcott Street Church from 1833 to 1836, when he left to lead the newly built Colored Methodist Episcopal Zion Church (CMEZ). Easton's tenure at Talcott Street was marked by tremendous internal and external conflicts: disputes over doctrine and modes of worship caused a split within the membership, which resulted in the formation of the CMEZ congregation, while a spate of anti-abolitionist race riots wracked black Hartford.[14]

Easton deemed himself responsible for the protection of the black community. Alongside on-the-ground ministrations, Easton dedicated himself to the production of an intellectual response to the daily assaults on African

---

[11] Barbara Beeching, *Hopes and Expectations: The Origins of the Black Middle Class in Hartford, Connecticut* (New York: SUNY Press, 2016), 19–28.

[12] Maria W. Stewart, "Religion and the Pure Principles of Morality" (1831), 161. (Unless noted otherwise, all citations to her work come from this volume.) Stewart rehearsed this biography in several of her publications. The plural on "schools" suggests she may have attended multiple sabbath schools.

[13] Beeching, *Hopes and Expectations*, 20.

[14] The English social reformer Edward Strutt Abdy singled out Hartford's antiblack violence as the most ruthless and unrelenting he witnessed during his travels across the United States from 1833 to 1834. He wrote:

Throughout the Union, there is, perhaps, no city containing the same amount of population, where the blacks meet with more contumely and unkindness than at this place. Some of them told me it was hardly safe for them to be in the street alone at night. One man assured me that he never ventured out after day-light, without some weapon of defence about him. No young woman of that race, if she would avoid insult, dare pass through the town, in the dusk of the evening, without a man to protect her. To pelt them with stones, and cry out nigger! nigger! as they pass, seems to be the pastime of the place. I had seen and heard so much of the indignities and cruelties heaped on the heads of this persecuted race, that I had ceased to feel surprised at anything I was told on the subject. (Abdy, *Journal of a Residence and Tour in The United States of North America, From April, 1833, to October, 1834* Vol. III [London: John Murray, 1835], 206–207)

Americans in Hartford and beyond. The result is one of the era's most blistering condemnations of the racist cant of American democracy, *Treatise on the Intellectual Character, and the Civil and Political Condition of the Colored People of the U. States; and the Prejudice Exercised towards Them: With a Sermon on the Duty of the Church to Them* (1837).

Easton's *Treatise*, selections of which are included in this volume, is a cornerstone text of early African American political theory. It stands alongside David Walker's *Appeal to the Coloured Citizens of the World* (1829) as one of the two most sustained, unflinching treatments of race, politics, and American society published before 1840. Easton opens the *Treatise* with a disquisition on humans' constitutional uniformity and the historical similarities between European and African civilizations. He then moves to consider how the plight of black people in the United States belies human anatomy and these histories. Their lives are the consequence of "the most corrupt policy which ever ... has been adopted by both church and state, for the avowed purpose of withholding the *inalienable rights* of one part of the subjects of the government."[15]

The hypocrisy of race in America is the dominant theme of early African American political thought, but Easton's analysis is unique in its exploration of the sociocultural pedagogies that teach and transmit those hypocrisies across generations. In a remarkable chapter called "On the Nature of the Prejudice of the White Population of the United States, in its Malignant Exercise Toward the Colored People," he outlines three modes by which racism's "baneful seed" is "sown in the tender soil of youthful minds, and there cultivated by the hand of a corrupt immoral policy."

1. *Blackness as spectral danger.* If a white child does not do what he is told, he hears he will be seized by a horrid black fiend. "Go to sleep, if you don't the old *nigger* will carry you off."
2. *Blackness as impending personal deformity.* If a white child does not do what he needs to develop in one way or another, he hears he will turn into a black person. The child "will be poor or ignorant as a nigger; or that they will be black as a nigger; or have no more credit than a nigger," if he or she does not follow directions.

---

[15] Hosea Easton, *A Treatise on the Intellectual Character and Civil and Political Condition of the Colored People of the U. States; And the Prejudice Exercised toward Them: With a Sermon on the Duty of the Church to Them* (Boston: Knapp, 1837), 33.

3. *Blackness as social alienation.* If a white child does not behave, he hears he will have to socialize with black people as punishment. The child is "frequently instructed in school rooms by referring them to the nigger-seat, and are sometimes threatened with being made to sit with the niggers, if they do not behave. The same or similar use is made of nigger pews or seating in meeting-houses."[16]

Easton argues that a network of cultural texts reinforces these lessons beyond the home, school, and church. Such "display[s] of American civility" are inescapable and constitutive of the American public sphere.[17] The *Treatise* instantiates a collective consciousness among African Americans that they were a national community united by a national struggle for emancipation and full black citizenship.

No event signaled the advent of a black national consciousness more than the publication of *Freedom's Journal* in 1827. The first black-owned newspaper in the United States, *Freedom's Journal* aimed to redress the fact that no periodical had "been devoted exclusively to [black people's] improvement . . . and more important still, that this large body of our citizens have no public channel."[18] While editor-proprietors Samuel Cornish and John Russworm devoted the newspaper to abolitionism and other political concerns, they reserved space for cultural and social matters that were vital to building free black communities within slave and post-slave societies.

The contemporaneous formation of the Boston-based Massachusetts General Colored Association (MGCA) is another clear indication of the emergence of a national black consciousness in the era. Founding member David Walker deemed organizing black people across the country into a politicized corporate body the MGCA's "primary object." As he proclaimed in an 1828 address before the MGCA, "It is necessary to remark here, at once, that the primary object of this institution, is, to unite the colored population, so far, through the United States of America, as may be practical and expedient."[19] The creation of associations like the MGCA gave African Americans embodied outlets to press for sociopolitical change nationally,

---

[16] Easton, *A Treatise on the Intellectual Character*, 40–41.
[17] Easton, *A Treatise on the Intellectual Character*, 42.
[18] Samuel Cornish and John Russworm, "To Our Patrons," *Freedom's Journal* 1., no. 1 (March 1827): 16.
[19] David Walker, "Address—Delivered before the General Colored Association at Boston," *Freedom's Journal*, December 19, 1828.

while publications like *Freedom's Journal* revitalized and reinforced their campaigns virtually.

To those who wondered how the "*General Colored Association* (or the Institution) [will] unite the colored population" throughout the country, Walker insisted that the common "miseries and degradations" black persons endured would be motivation enough.[20] He marshaled a series of incisive rhetorical questions about black life that aimed to convert skeptics of MGCA's organizational efforts into true believers. "Ought we not to form ourselves into a general body, to protect, aid, and assist each other to the utmost of our power, with the before mentioned restrictions?" he concluded.[21] This section of his MGCA address exemplifies the stylistic bravura that distinguishes Walker's *Appeal to the Coloured Citizens of the World*, selections of which are included in this volume.

Walker's communicative gifts endeared him to black Bostonians from the time he moved there in 1825.[22] Within two years of his arrival from Charleston, South Carolina, he opened a relatively successful used clothing store, was initiated into Prince Hall Freemasonry, helped found the MGCA, and served as *Freedom's Journal*'s primary subscription agent in the region.[23] Along with his marriage in 1826 to Eliza Butler, who belonged to one of the city's most prominent black families, Walker swiftly ascended black Boston's social ranks.[24]

Like Walker, Maria Stewart married not long after her arrival in Boston. Such similarities run deep in their respective biographies: both were born free even though at least one of their parents was at some point enslaved; both were transplants who quickly found themselves at the center of black Boston's social scene; both were married in 1826, the Walkers in February and the Stewarts in August; and both lived in the same building, what is now 81 Joy Street in Boston.[25] Walker was Stewart's mentor and the single greatest influence on her political and intellectual development.

---

[20] Walker, "Address."

[21] Walker, "Address."

[22] David Walker is listed in the Boston Directory of 1825 as a "clothes dealer, City Market" in the "People of Colour" section.

[23] David Walker and Peter P. Hinks, *David Walker's Appeal to the Coloured Citizens of the World* (University Park: Pennsylvania State University Press, 2000), xxiii–xxiv.

[24] Boston's Register of Marriages lists David Walker and Eliza Butler as married on February 23, 1826 by Rev. Isaac Bonner.

[25] Walker was born in Wilmington, North Carolina, to a free mother and formerly enslaved father. For a fine biographical treatment on Walker's early years, Peter P. Hinks, *To Awaken My Afflicted Brethren: David Walker and the Problem of Antebellum Slave Resistance* (University Park: Pennsylvania State University Press, 1997), 1–62.

At the core of their friendship was a shared spiritual foundation. Even though Walker remained a steadfast Methodist his entire life and Methodism was not of the several denominations Stewart embraced, both came of age in Second Great Awakening (c. 1795-1840). The Second Great Awakening emphasized sociomoral reformation beyond theology and the church.[26] Participants were caught up in a religionism that linked fiery revivalist worship with a millenarian ethos that projected a thoroughgoing transformation of the whole of society. This vision was especially attractive to figures like Walker and Stewart because it revealed to them the need for black and female voices in American life. Both were moved to understand the work of prophecy as simultaneously sacred and temporal. For them, changes in who spoke were required to reveal what God ordained for this world in preparation for the next.

Consider Jarena Lee's call to ministry. A trailblazing preacher of black Methodism, Lee is an icon of the democratizing impulses of the Second Great Awakening. In her autobiography *The Life and Religious Experience of Jarena Lee* (1849), selections of which are included in this volume, Lee describes how in 1807 she heard God's voice command her to "'Preach the Gospel; I will put words in your mouth, and will turn your enemies to become your friends.'"[27] Lee then went to Richard Allen, leader of the black Methodists in Philadelphia and future founding bishop of the African Methodist Episcopal Church, and told him what she heard from God. Allen's evangelizing had affected Lee deeply, and she believed it was under his leadership that she should preach. Allen told her another woman, a "Mrs. Cook," also believed she received the same call from God but "as to women preaching, our Discipline knew nothing about it—that it did not call for women preachers."[28] After submitting to his decision, Lee eventually reverted to her initial desire to preach. She offered a reading of the Gospel that insisted on women preachers: "Did not Mary *first* preach the risen Saviour, and is not the doctrine of the resurrection the very climax of Christianity—hangs not all our hope on this, as argued by St. Paul?"[29] She developed a feminist

---

[26] It bears noting that the Second Great Awakening was also marked by ecclesiastical authorities' attempts to consolidate their power within the church itself. See Nathan O Hatch, *The Democratization of American Christianity* (New Haven, CT: Yale University Press, 1989).

[27] Jarena Lee, *The Life and Religious Experience of Jarena Lee, Giving an Account of Her Call to Preach the Gospel* (Philadelphia, 1849), 10.

[28] Lee, *The Life and Religious Experience of Jarena Lee*, 11.

[29] Lee, *The Life and Religious Experience of Jarena Lee*, 11.

hermeneutics to legitimate her preaching. Allen ultimately relented, but she refused ordination.

Stewart regarded her voice in the same way.[30] She believed God called on her to enjoin audiences to (re)discover the political and personal morality He demanded. Her writing and activism were secular prophecy. The work of prophecy here is not divination but, as George Shulman puts it, "the public role of those who address a community by mediating its relationship to the larger realities conditioning its existence and choices." Such prophets "are called" to mount "performances [that] incite audiences to self-reflection and action."[31] In Stewart, prophecy is an evaluative genre, a way of assessing the world and speaking its ills, that she learned from the example of the Hebrew prophets. The prophetic is the dominant genre in Stewart's political philosophy, and she regularly located herself, albeit humbly, within genealogies of religious prophets.

She began an 1832 speech at Boston's Franklin Hall by telling the audience she "heard a spiritual interrogation" that asked her, " 'Who shall go forward and take off the reproach that is cast upon the people of color? Shall it be a woman?' And my heart made this reply—'If it is thy will, be it even so, Lord Jesus!' "[32] Later in the speech she made another claim to prophecy, but in far more oblique terms: "It is upon you [men] that woman depends; she can do but little besides using her influence; and it is for her sake and for yours that I have come forward and made myself a hissing and reproach among the people; for I am also one of the wretched and miserable daughters of the descendants of fallen Africa."[33] Stewart's diction here alludes to Jeremiah's letter to the Israelites deported to Babylon after the fall of Jerusalem in sixth century BCE (Jeremiah 29); in the letter he writes to assure them of imminent retribution for their plight. Like Jeremiah, Stewart's office was to bring word of (divine) deliverance to a defeated, suffering people living in a land not of their choosing: her politics were the fulfillment of God's will, never her own.

Stewart was an American Jeremiah. She mastered the rhetorical form of the jeremiad, a founding idiom of American sociopolitical discourse. Very often mournful and withering in tone, the jeremiad "narrate[s] conduct

---

[30] See Valerie C. Cooper, *Word, Like Fire: Maria Stewart, the Bible, and the Rights of African Americans* (Charlottesville: University of Virginia Press, 2011).

[31] George Shulman, *American Prophecy: Race and Redemption in American Political Culture* (Minneapolis: University of Minnesota Press, 2008), 2, 3, 6.

[32] Stewart, 79. In an earlier essay, she said the condition of free black life in the United States was in as "miserable and wretched a state as was the house of Israel in the days of Jeremiah" (165).

[33] Stewart, 83.

as a decline from origins, to address a community about its constitutive commitments and current difficulties, to make its future contingent on a 'decision' about its conduct."[34] Stewart frequently lamented the condition of black American populations as one of declension, as a self-induced fall from a glorious, if sometimes notional, past they have the capacity to recover but only after they eschew those behaviors that caused the fall in the first place. "History informs us that we have sprung from one of the most learned nations of the whole earth; from the seat, if not the parent, of science," she acclaimed before an audience at Boston's African Masonic Hall in 1833.

> Yes, poor despised Africa was once the resort of sages and legislators of other nations, was esteemed the school for learning, and the most illustrious men in Greece flocked thither for instruction. But it was our gross sins and abominations that provoked the Almighty to frown thus heavily upon us, and give our glory unto others. Sin and prodigality have caused the downfall of nations, king, emperors; and were it not that God in wrath remembers mercy, we might indeed despair; but a promise is left us; "Ethiopia shall again stretch for her hands unto God."[35]

As much as Stewart believed in the certainty of a latter-day Ethiopia's ascension, she maintained such a rise was contingent upon black people choosing to rectify their own moral shortcomings. Virtuous acts and attitudes were always the "means to bring about [God's] purposes," and Stewart never conceived any political project as viable without probity as a first principle.[36]

Many in attendance at Stewart's Boston addresses in the early 1830s would have expected the tenor and substance of her message because of their personal interactions. But she primed a much broader audience with her groundbreaking essay "Religion and the Pure Principles of Morality, the Sure Foundation on Which We Must Build" (1831). William Lloyd Garrison published and sold the essay in pamphlet form out of the offices of the radical abolitionist newspaper *The Liberator*, which he had founded with Isaac Knapp only a few months prior. Nearly fifty years after they first met, Garrison recalled his initial impressions of Stewart and astonishment

---

[34] Shulman, *American Prophecy*, 8.
[35] Stewart, 180.
[36] Stewart, 88. The full quote is instructive: "But God has said, that Ethiopia shall stretch forth her arms unto him. True, but God uses means to bring about his purposes, and unless the rising generation manifest a different temper and disposition towards each other from what we have manifested, the generation following will never be an enlightened people."

at the brilliance of her writings. He wrote, "Soon after I started the publication of *The Liberator* you made yourself known to me by coming into my office and putting into my hands, for criticism and friendly advice, a manuscript embodying your devotional thoughts and aspirations, and also various essays.... I not only gave you words of encouragement, but in my printing office put your manuscript [i.e., "Religion and the Pure Principles of Morality"] into type, an edition of which was struck off, in tract form, subject to your order. I was impressed by your intelligence and excellence of character."[37] The work of devotions and prayers he published became *Meditations from the Pen of Mrs. Maria W. Stewart* (1832).

Stewart wrote this book as she mourned the death of her husband who died in December 1829 and moved toward her "public profession of [her] faith in Christ."[38] She "presented" *Meditations* to the "First African Baptist Church and Society of Boston, Mass." as a token of gratitude for the intellectual and spiritual nourishments it provided in the wake of tremendous loss.[39] (David Walker died in August 1830, only eight months after James's death.) Like Garrison, readers of *Meditations* and "Religion and the Pure Principles" were impressed by Stewart's expressive authority and the clarity of her discernment.[40] Her early writings announced the arrival of a distinctive, indispensable new voice in the antislavery and social reformist public spheres.

"Religion and the Pure Principles of Morality" was a remarkable debut. It established the dominant theme of Stewart's politics during her Boston years: self-determination through strict moral virtue, personal accountability, and black institution building. In the essay, she recognized there were but "few to promote [black people's] cause, none to encourage their talents." But she insisted they should "not let [their] hearts be any longer discouraged; it is no use to murmur nor to repine; but let us promote ourselves and improve our talents.... But '*I can't*,' is a great barrier in the way. I hope it will soon be removed, and '*I will*,' resume its place."[41] However fanciful this notion might seem, antebellum black critics like Stewart regularly advocated such an approach; they believed it was the most direct way to better their

---

[37] William Lloyd Garrison, "Mrs. Maria W. Stewart," in *Meditations from the Pen of Mrs. Maria W. Stewart* (Washington, 1879), 6.
[38] Stewart, 161.
[39] Stewart, *Meditations*, n.p.
[40] Despite her somewhat forced exit from Boston, "Friends of Freedom and Virtue" in the city published a new collection of her writings, *Productions of Mrs. Maria W. Stewart* in 1835.
[41] Stewart, 167.

lives and, as a result, foster the conditions that would make substantive structural changes possible.[42]

Although Stewart was severe in her censure of those extra-communal forces that inhibited African Americans' ambitions, she was even more relentless in her insistence there were actions black households and communities refused to perform that would drastically improve their material conditions and elevate their standing in the broader polity.[43] She told black mothers it was their task to "create in the minds of [their] little girls and boys a thirst for knowledge, the love of virtue, the abhorrence of vice and the cultivation of a pure heart."[44] To ensure the continued development of black children beyond "good housewifery" in the home, Stewart called on them to raise money for schools for their community. "Let every female heart become united, and let us raise a fund ourselves," she wrote in "Religion and the Pure Principles of Morality," and "at the end of one year and a half, we might be able to lay the corner stone for the building of a High School, that the higher branches of knowledge might be enjoyed by us."[45] The black-established school is one of the two institutional pillars of Stewart's conception of the most excellent black community.

The other pillar is the black-owned and black-operated business. She writes, "Unite and build a store of your own. . . . Fill one side with dry goods, and the other with groceries. Do you ask where is the money? We have spent more than enough for nonsense, to do what building we want."[46]

---

[42] For example, David Walker was often unsparing in his reproofs of African Americans who, to his mind, moderated their ambitions owing to dominant race relations: "I met a coloured man in the street a short time since, with a string of boots on his shoulders; we fell into conversation, and in course of which, I said to him, what a miserable set of people we are! He asked, why?—Said I, we are so subjected under the whites, that we cannot obtain the comforts of life, but by cleaning their boots and shoes, old clothes, waiting on them, shaving them &c. Said he, (with the boots on his shoulders) 'I am completely happy!!! I never want to live any better or happier than when I can get a plenty of boots and shoes to clean!!!' Oh! how can those who are actuated by avarice only, but think, that our Creator made us to be an inheritance to them for ever, when they see that our greatest glory is centered in such mean and low objects? Understand me, brethren, I do not mean to speak against the occupations by which we acquire enough and sometimes scarcely that, to render ourselves and families comfortable through life. I am subjected to the same inconvenience, as you all.—My objections are, to our *glorying* and being *happy* in such low employments; for if we are men, we ought to be thankful to the Lord for the past, and for the future. Be looking forward with thankful hearts to higher attainments than *wielding the razor* and *cleaning boots and shoes*. The man whose aspirations are not *above*, and even *below* these, is indeed, ignorant and wretched enough" (Walker and Hinks, *David Walker's Appeal to the Coloured Citizens of the World*, 30–31).

[43] For Stewart's rebukes of the race-based domination and oppression African Americans endured, see 89–90, 163–167, 181–182.

[44] Stewart, 168.

[45] Stewart, 169.

[46] Stewart, 170.

Not only would these businesses become the foundation for black economic prosperity, but also they would provide African Americans with dignified, self-affirming employment that Stewart argued was virtually impossible in contemporaneous labor markets. She urged her Franklin Hall audience to "look at our young men, smart, active, and energetic, with souls filled with ambitious fire. . . . They can be nothing but the humblest laborers, on account of their dark complexion; hence many of them lose their ambition, and become worthless."[47] Young black women were even more vulnerable to the negative consequences of "continual drudgery and toil" because the best they could ask for were "lives as house-domestics, washing windows, shaking carpets, brushing boots, or tending upon gentlemen's tables." Unlike their "fairer sisters, whose hands are never soiled, whose nerves and muscles are never strained," young black women never had occasion "to improve [their] moral and mental faculties."[48] So rather than wait for white Americans to welcome their black counterparts into all segments of the workforce, black communities should create work opportunities that would propel their members to "rise above the condition of servants and drudges."[49] Establishing their own schools and businesses formed the core of her vision.

Stewart was fully aware of the perilous risks such ventures entailed. Large-scale race riots against black persons and institutions like those in Hartford mushroomed in the early 1830s. But she maintained *racial solidarism* was most essential to withstand the onslaught of violence and calumny that thriving black communities would surely face. But in her view, racial solidarity was anathema to African Americans whom she lambasted as "meddlers" who took pains to undermine each other's efforts.

> It appears to me that there are no people under the heavens so unkind and so unfeeling towards their own, as are the descendants of fallen Africa. I have been something of a traveller in my day; and the general cry among the people is, "Our own color are our greatest opposers"; and even the whites say that we are greater enemies towards each other, than they are

---

[47] Stewart, 83. Not only the young, but older demographics suffered these same indignities, Stewart argued: "Look at our middle-aged men, clad in their rusty plaids and coats; in winter, every cent they earn goes to buy their wood and pay their rents; their poor wives also toil beyond their strength, to help support their families. Look at our aged sires, whose heads are whitened with the front of seventy winters, with their old wood-saws on their backs. Alas, what keeps us so? Prejudice, ignorance and poverty" (83).
[48] Stewart, 82.
[49] Stewart, 81.

towards us. [...] No gentle methods are used to promote love and friendship among us, but much is done to destroy [them].[50]

Stewart adduced other groups in recent world history whose solidarism helped fend off oppressors; she said one need only consider "the suffering Greeks," "the French in the late revolution," "the Haytians," "the Poles, a feeble people," and "even the wild Indians of the forest" for proof of the effectiveness of racial solidarity. "Insult one of them, and you insult a thousand" was the organizing principle of these groups' ethical mores, she argued, and by this principle they "have contended for their rights and privileges, and are held in higher repute than we are."[51]

Stewart's theories of, and commitments to, racial solidarism are some of the most important contributions to early black nationalism. Black nationalism in this period was a complex of discursive (i.e., race language) and moral-hermeneutical (i.e., race-based obligations) paradigms that did not aim for lives apart from white people. Unlike later and better-known iterations that called for race-based separatism or emigration schemes to West Africa or elsewhere in the Americas, black nationalism before the 1850s "captured the distinctiveness of the oppressed condition of African Americans[,] did not extend beyond the political and social relations that gave it meaning [, and] merely expressed the solidarity necessary to confront the reality of race in the United States."[52] For Stewart, racial solidarism would enact the "spirit of independence ... of men, bold and enterprising"—the very spirit that would prove to the world and themselves that black people were nothing if not American.[53]

According to Stewart, the problem was that antebellum African Americans spurned racial solidarity because their "fathers" had done the same. Precisely who were these "fathers" is unclear—did she mean previous generations of black people in colonial America or earlier ancestors in Africa who in some way helped facilitate the transatlantic slave trade? But she ascribed her generation's refusal to dispense with this regrettable legacy to the idea that her contemporaries in Boston and throughout the United States were too

---

[50] Stewart, 88–89.
[51] Stewart, 88–89.
[52] Eddie S. Glaude, Jr., *Exodus!: Religion, Race, and Nation in Early Nineteenth-Century Black American* (Chicago: University of Chicago Press, 2000), 15.
[53] Stewart, 170. Stewart was a staunch anti-colonizationist and once boasted, "I can but die for expressing my sentiments; and I am as willing to die by the sword as the pestilence; for I and a true born American; your blood flows in my veins, and your spirit fires my breast" (81).

fearful. As she told an audience at the African Masonic Hall in 1833, "We have suffered ourselves to be considered dastards, cowards, mean, fainthearted wretches."[54] Stewart went on to explicate how and why fear was the overriding emotion among African Americans, and it must have been particularly wounding for the Prince Hall Masons of Boston to listen to a woman castigate them for lacking the requisite courage to defend their families and enrich their communities. Nevertheless, she called on these men, indeed all African Americans, to come to grips with their cowardice then overcome it by developing the mettle necessary to act in the interests of black people's collective aims, come what may. Without fear, she argued, they would finally embrace racial solidarity and build thriving, self-sustaining communities that would make "prejudice . . . gradually diminish" and "whites say, unloose those fetters!"[55] Stewart's prioritization of economic and social self-sufficiency above all does not mean she minimized or underappreciated the importance of abolitionism and full citizenship to improving the conditions of black life. Rather, she believed African Americans could never succeed in these broader struggles until they waged substantive struggles among themselves, out of which they would emerge as a fearless and united people.

Stewart's work from her Boston years is rife with blistering criticism for African Americans. The language she used to diagnose the problems of free black communities, and to rally them to corrective action, was consistently abrasive, harsh, and pointed. Invective thus emerged as the chief linguistic instrument for her politics. Very often personal in nature, Stewart's invective did not work toward resolution or consensus that conventional modes of political speech propose; rather, it aimed for subsequent discourse and contestation, which is to say toward more politics. Stewart never sought leadership over her audiences but wanted to persuade them to perform specific actions that would prepare them for broader, more difficult political struggles. Her use of invective was critical to this effort: without recourse to denunciatory language, Stewart most likely would not have achieved standing in the political arenas within which she fought.

Consider Stewart's contentious address to Boston's Prince Hall Freemasons. She questioned whether black men were indeed men who possess the spirit of men. . . . Have the sons of Africa no souls? Feel they no ambitious desires? Shall the chains of ignorance forever confine them?"[56] Stewart

[54] Stewart, 178.
[55] Stewart, 80.
[56] Stewart, 179.

used invective of this sort because she did not want these men, or any of her audiences, to dismiss her as an oratorical curiosity or frivolity. She demanded they take her seriously and see beyond the novelty of a woman intervening so directly in public affairs. Elsewhere, she deemed black women "busy bodies" and "meddlers in other men's matters," and argued black youth did not "care to distinguish themselves either in religious or moral improvement.... [T]he greater part of our community follow the vain bubbles of life with so much eagerness, which will only prove to them like the serpent's sting upon the bed of death."[57] These pronouncements are representative of Stewart's stinging candor, and the ubiquity of invective across her corpus compelled African Americans to grapple with her charges in both word and deed. She surmised that without insult her activism would be nothing more than a blip.

By the time Stewart delivered her invective-laden censures in her speeches and writings, she always made sure to establish herself as a humble messenger compelled to speak by God. That positioning certainly redoubled the sting of her rebukes. Such self-effacing moves were neither ruse nor contrivance, however: they were attempts to legitimate the prophetic authority of her politics. Stewart began this practice in her very first essay, "Religion and Pure Principles," and it recurs throughout her oeuvre. Its opening sentence launches Stewart's entire career as a social critic and political philosopher: "Feeling a deep solemnity of soul, in view of our wretched and degraded situation, and sensible of the gross ignorance that prevails among us, I have thought proper thus publicly to express my sentiments before you."[58] Such exordia recur in Stewart's corpus, and over time she became more assured of the need for her voice in the day's political affairs. "The frowns of the world shall never discourage me, nor its smiles flatter me; for with the help of God, I am resolved to withstand the fiery darts of the devil, and the assaults of wicked men," she proclaimed in an 1832 speech before Boston's Afric-American Female Intelligence Society. "[T]he God in whom I trust is able to deliver me from the rage and malice of mine enemies, and from them that rise up against me."[59] In this and similar occasions, Stewart drew on her deep religious convictions to defy critics who objected to her participation in the public sphere—after all, she was very possibly the first American-born woman, black or white, in recorded history to have "mounted a lecture

[57] Stewart, 166–167; 165.
[58] Stewart, 161.
[59] Stewart, 162.

xxviii   INTRODUCTION

platform and raised a political argument before a 'promiscuous' audience, that is one composed of both men and women," as one biographer writes, and "likely the first black American to lecture in defense of women's rights."[60] Stewart's embrace of her singularity was the opening gambit in her effort to prevail upon the public the validity and ineluctability of her judgments.

Stewart's modesty may have emerged from more than the distinctiveness of her positionality: there is a real possibility that she could barely write. Alexander Crummell wrote about the "surprise" of learning about Stewart's literacy during her time in Boston. She was "a person who had received but six weeks' schooling, who could not even pen her own thoughts, who had to get a little girl ten years old to write every word of [*Meditations* and her other Boston-era writings]—that *such* a person could compose essays of this kind, and give expression to such thoughts and be the author of such" an oeuvre.[61] He offered this assessment in a prefatory commendation to a collection of Stewart's writings that she published late in her life. The two scholars who have worked most on Stewart's biography, Marilyn Richardson and Kristin Waters, have rejected Crummell's claim. Richardson argues that Stewart's "failure to correct or contradict him might have been a diplomatic gesture" because she was a member of the church he pastored.[62] Waters's dismissal is even more brusque, calling Crummell's assertion regarding Stewart's lack of literacy "a case of a sympathetic romantic notion of a benighted frail woman—sadly false."[63] Both Waters and Richardson adduce Stewart's signature on legal documents as proof she could write well enough to produce her own manuscripts—that is, she "wrote [with] a steady hand."[64]

The evidence suggests their repudiations of Crummell are too swift insofar as they brush past Stewart's education and ignore her approval of his broader account. The many documents Stewart signed throughout her life do show a constant and assured script, but one's ability to sign one's name does not signify she can put down on paper essays of the quality of Stewart's. (It bears noting that we have yet to locate any of the manuscripts of her work to compare to the signature.) She may have perfected her signature in sabbath schools, but they did not provide her the training necessary to compose

---

[60] Maria W. Stewart and Marilyn Richardson, *Maria W. Stewart, America's First Black Woman Political Writer: Essays and Speeches* (Bloomington: Indiana University Press, 1987), xiii.
[61] Alexander Crummell in Stewart, *Meditations*, 10.
[62] Stewart and Richardson, *Maria W. Stewart, America's First Black Woman Political Writer*, 130, n.22.
[63] Waters, *Maria W. Stewart and the Roots of Black Political Thought*, 196.
[64] Stewart Richardson, *Maria W. Stewart, America's First Black Woman Political Writer*, 130, n.22.

an essay like "Religion and the Pure Principles of Morality."[65] Crummell noted Stewart had a ten-year-old girl produce her manuscripts while she was in Boston. Why would Stewart allow this remarkable detail to appear in her book if untrue? Neither Richardson nor Waters deals with the case of the child amanuensis.

Further, the bulk of Stewart's work during her Boston years was lectures and addresses. She only published one short piece, "Cause for Encouragement" (1832), after "Religion and the Pure Principles of Mortality" and *Meditations*. All things considered, the evidence suggests Crummell's claim is closer to truth than a fanciful or "romantic" memory. His comments on how she finally acquired full literacy lend even greater credence: after resettling in New York City in 1833, he says, teachers "gladly met" Stewart's "eagerness for instruction," and she joined a circle of black women "who willingly aided her in the study of arithmetic, geography, grammar, and other branches. Ere long she became a member of a 'Female Literary Society.'"[66]

Stewart had left Boston in a fit of pique. Fewer than two years after she began her career as a lecturer and political essayist, she chose to leave Boston "perhaps never to return." As she declared in a "Farewell Address" in September 1833, "It is no use for me as an individual to try to make myself useful among my color in the city."[67] Stewart said black Bostonians "despitefully used and persecuted" her because they could not stomach the upbraiding criticisms that organized her politics; she included many in her "circle of friends" in this charge.[68] The "Farewell Address" was a concession speech, and she accepted the ramifications of her political defeats without condition. However undue or overblown Stewart's assessment of her public career in Boston was, her relocation to New York City was her way of acceding to the will of the people: she lost the battle and therefore had to go. Leaving Boston was crucial to her prophecy, and the recognition of it as such, because it enacted the "embodied form of symbolic action" that complements the prophet's "rhetorical act[s]."[69]

---

[65] What Garrison wrote of his amazement upon receiving her manuscript is instructive: "You will recollect, if not the surprise, at least the satisfaction I expressed on examining what you had written—far more remarkable in those early days that it would be now, when there are so many educated persons of color who are able to write with ability" (Garrison in Stewart, *Meditations*, 6).

[66] Crummell in Stewart, *Meditations*, 10.

[67] Crummel in Stewart, X.

[68] Stewart, 99; William Cooper Nell, "Letter from William Cooper Nell," *The Liberator*, February 19, 1852.

[69] Shulman, *American Prophecy*, 6.

The New York City she found was well on its way to becoming a global metropolis. Major advances in transportation, maritime trade and migration, and infrastructure (e.g., the Erie Canal) supercharged the city's development. Stewart entered a bustling urban landscape that was a hub of the Atlantic world. Writers such as Charles Dickins (*American Notes*, 1842), E. Z. C. Judson (*The Mysteries and Miseries of New York*, 1848), and George G. Foster (*New York by Gas-Light and Other Urban Sketches*, 1850) enthralled readers with observations of New York City life and culture, especially its veiled seedier elements. Among the most incisive of this cohort was William J. Wilson. Wilson was a correspondent for *Frederick Douglass' Paper* (*FDP*) who wrote under the pseudonym "Ethiop." He dedicated his writing to the creation of new ways of rendering black subjectivity in print. For an 1853 *FDP* column he wrote, "We must begin to tell our own story, write our own lecture, paint our own picture, chisel our own bust, (I demand not caricatures but correct emanations,) acknowledge and love our own peculiarities if we have any."[70] Vital to that project was theorizing new critical perspectives and modalities. His essays spearheaded that effort.

One of Ethiop's primary methods was to assume the role of the urban flâneur. He offered some of the most compelling portraits of street life and urban stylings in antebellum (African) American letters. He was especially interested in how of sociology of race, gender, and class emerged from city scenes, one very much determined by the observer's positionality and vista. In one of his most captivating *FDP* columns, which is included in this volume, Ethiop wrote about how crossing Atlantic Avenue leaves one awash with so many different types of people. (The essay's many nautical metaphors are incredibly witty.) He focuses on the personal creativity of young black men over against their white monied counterparts' debauched lack of style. He writes, "Wealth may be found at your Astor, and your Irving, but easy negligence, careless abandonment and refined freedom may be studied here. . . . Most of the whites of your Astor, Irving, Howard, and like resorts, are fresh from the country. Money they may have, but good judges of these luxuries, never."[71] His readings here and elsewhere throughout his oeuvre expose the lie of the nation's sociocultural order: money does *not* connote human value, but ingenuity does, which black people had in abundance. Despites its race-based strictures, antebellum New York City offered African Americans

---

[70] William J. Wilson, "From Our Brooklyn Correspondent," *Frederick Douglass' Paper*, March 11, 1853.

[71] Wilson, "From Our Brooklyn Correspondent," February 26, 1852.

opportunities for personal fulfillment and collective action that very few, if any, American cities could. Ethiop documented how their efforts took shape in quotidian activities, errands, and interactions on city streets.

It is unclear precisely how Stewart initially reacted to New York's hustle and bustle, which dwarfed anything she experienced in Boston or Hartford. But we do know that she took great advantage of the city's unparalleled intellectual culture. Alexander Crummell provides the most detailed account of Stewart's time in New York. He recalls first meeting her as a young man after he had just returned from studying at the Oneida Institute.[72] Of Stewart, Crummell "remembered very distinctly of the great surprise of both my friends and myself at finding in New York a young woman of my own people full of literary aspiration and ambitious of authorship."[73] She addressed her deficiencies as a reader and writer by working with city teachers. There is no evidence to determine if Stewart enrolled in public school (she would have been in her early thirties) or if the teachers acted as tutors. In any case, she "advanced to sufficient fitness to become a public school teacher, and served as such in New York and Brooklyn" for the next decade.[74] One history of the Brooklyn school in which she taught, Colored School No. 3 in Williamsburg, notes that "by 1845 more than sixty Black scholars were taught by a Maria W. Stewart," and in 1847 she became assistant to the principle.[75] Teaching became the primary means by which Stewart supported herself for the rest of her life, although she supplemented that work with menial labor when she fell on especially hard times.

Stewart refined what she learned from her teachers in the women's literary society she joined. Black women established these societies throughout the country, especially in the mid-Atlantic. The societies offered intellectual, social, and sometimes economic resources that were otherwise lacking in their lives. As Elizabeth Henry writes, "Although deprived of the advantages of formal schooling, black women had a desire to educate themselves. Evidence suggests that women's literary societies from 1830 to 1850 may have outnumbered men's, even though they did not exceed them in size or prominence. Whereas men's literary societies typically consisted of a large

---

[72] Oneida offered a robust classical education and a culture of radical abolitionism. Among its black alumni are several leading abolitionists, ministers, and writers from the era, including Henry Highland Garnet, Samuel Ringgold Ward, William G. Allen, and Julia Williams, probably its only female student.
[73] Crummell in Stewart, *Meditations*, 10.
[74] Crummell in Stewart, *Meditations*, 10.
[75] Stewart and Richardson, *Maria W. Stewart, America's First Black Woman Political Writer*, xvi.

membership and sponsored public lectures and debates, women's societies were more likely to assemble in small groups in a member's home."[76] Stewart was very familiar with these societies before she arrived in New York. She addressed one in 1832, the Afric-American Female Intelligence Society of Boston (AAFI); there is no evidence she was a member. The AAFI was one of the most formalized black women's literary societies in the era. The preamble to its constitution offers a good sense of the work that the collective of antebellum black women's voluntary associations intended to perform.

> Whereas the subscribers, women of color of the Commonwealth of Massachusetts, actuated by a natural feeling for the welfare of our friends, have thought fit to associate for the diffusion of knowledge, the suppression of vice and immorality, and for cherishing such virtues as will render us happy and useful to society, sensible of the gross ignorance under which we have too long labored, but trusting by the blessing of God, we shall be able to accomplish the object of our union—we have therefore associated ourselves under the name of the Afric-American Female Intelligence Society and have adopted the following Constitution.[77]

For groups like the FFAI, moral development was as high a priority as intellectual growth. But the bulk of its constitution is concerned with fundraising and appropriations. One of the more fascinating of its articles spells out the assistance the AAFI would provide its financially struggling members: "Any member of this Society of one year's standing having regularly paid up her dues who may be taken sick shall receive one dollar per week out of the funds of the Society as long as consistent with the means of the institution."[78] Black women's associations, literary or otherwise, often provided material aid to their members and their families.

The Ladies Literary Society of New York that Stewart joined was formed in 1834. It emerged out of the groundbreaking work of the African (Female) Dorcas Association, a women's group dedicated to making and procuring

---

[76] Elizabeth McHenry, *Forgotten Readers: Recovering the Lost History of African American Literary Societies* (Durham, NC: Duke University Press, 2022), 57.

[77] "Constitution of the Afric-American Female Intelligence Society of Boston," *Liberator,* January 7, 1832.

[78] "Constitution of the Afric-American Female Intelligence Society of Boston," *Liberator,* January 7, 1832.

clothes for indigent students at the city's African Free Schools.[79] There was considerable overlap between the leadership and membership of both groups, but their primary missions were very different. The Ladies Literary Society was focused on "the improvement of the mind," as one of its members put it in an anniversary address.[80] Crummell writes that these women, which included his sister Lucy, numbered the "few young women in New York who thought of these higher [i.e., intellectual and literary] things."[81] Stewart declaimed original texts for the members and the public; unfortunately, none of those have works seems to have survived. She wrote encomiums, dialogues, poetry, orations, and/or expository essays; she may have also participated in their musical programs. A visitor to one of the society's public events in 1837 called its offerings a *"mental feast,"* going on to "recommend our young female friends to enroll their names in this useful institution, if they wish to improve themselves and set an example to the rising generation. We would also say to parents and guardians, encourage those entrusted to your care to unite with this praiseworthy institution."[82] If Stewart came to New York City "full of greed for literature and letters," as Crummell described her, the Ladies Literary Society sated her yearning.[83]

Although none of Stewart's compositions for the society are extant, we can get a sense of the form, substance, and tone of what she might have written by examining the writings of black women from similar literary associations. The most well-known of this cohort is Sarah Mapps Douglass. Born into one of Philadelphia's leading abolitionist families, Douglass was a pioneering educator who operated several schools for black students and helped establish the interracial Philadelphia Female Anti-Slavery in 1833. She was also a founding member of the Female Literary Association (FLA). Founded in 1831, the FLA's aim, structure, and programs were like those of the Ladies Literary Society of New York. Its members met weekly for "recitation and reading." Although they read works from established authors, their most distinctive feature was how they shared their own: they wrote anonymous texts, placed them in a box, then at a later meeting someone drew a piece to

---

[79] *Freedom's Journal* published several articles on the African Dorcas Association's collection efforts and commendations of its work. An especially illustrative piece was a letter to the editor by a "Cato" published on November 21, 1828.
[80] "Third Anniversary of the Ladies' Literary Society of the City of New-York," *Colored American*, September 23, 1837.
[81] Crummell in Stewart, *Meditations*, 10.
[82] "Third Anniversary of the Ladies' Literary Society of the City of New-York."
[83] Crummell in Stewart, *Meditations*, 10.

read.[84] Much of what we know about their compositions comes from what is available in the abolitionist press, especially Garrison's *Liberator*, which covered the FLA's work within its ranks and the larger Philadelphia community. Douglass was a regular contributor to the *Liberator* and published under several pseudonyms, "Zillah" being the one she used most. Her writings, several of which are included in this volume, demonstrate how black women used literary society meetings to hone their interventions in discourses like abolitionism, sentimentalism, and women's rights—interventions born of their distinct experiences and perspectives. Although we remember names like Douglass and Stewart from these institutions, it was the collective of unnamed black women that led to the flowering of black women's philosophy, literary production, and social criticism at the turn of the twentieth century.

The Ladies Literary Society of New York and the city's budding public school system frame nearly everything we know about Stewart's life in Manhattan and Brooklyn. Beyond these institutions, only the 1850 federal census seems to offer additional insight into her personal life there. It lists a "Maria Stewart" who was thirty-six years old and "mulatto." She lived with a middle-class barber named "William Stewart" who was forty-three years old and "mulatto."[85] The name and residential area in Brooklyn suggests it is Maria W. Stewart; the racial designation of "mulatto" also indicates it is she because subsequent, more reliable federal censuses identify her as such. But a few elements point to someone else: the age is ten years too young, the place of birth is incorrect (Massachusetts), and the organizational logic of the listing intimates she and William were married. (Maria W. Stewart never remarried after James's death in 1829.) What is certain is that she was in New York at the time of the census because she left the city for good in 1852 to resettle in Baltimore, Maryland.

In an 1879 autobiographical sketch of her life during the US Civil War, Stewart says she left New York for Baltimore because she heard "the colored people were more religious and God-fearing in the South."[86] If communities of deeply religious black persons in the South were what Stewart desired, Baltimore was almost certainly the best location. The city boasted incredible denominational heterogeneity among its black populations, including black Catholicism which stretched back to the early national era. Black religious

---

[84] Marie Lindhorst, "Politics in a Box: Sarah Mapps Douglass and the Female Literary Association, 1831–1833," *Pennsylvania History: A Journal of Mid-Atlantic Studies* 65, no. 3 (Summer 1998): 270.
[85] 1850 Federal Census.
[86] Stewart, 271.

life in Baltimore was anchored by Bethel African Methodist Episcopal Church. The eminent Daniel Payne pastored Bethel from 1845 to 1850 and oversaw the church's incredible growth from one thousand to fifteen hundred members. He was elected a bishop in 1852; he shaped the AME's ecclesiastical structure more than any other bishop in the nineteenth century. Payne was adamant that the AME church tells its own story to the world—he was appointed its historiographer in 1850—and offered platforms for African Americans to do the same. The AME established an official organ in 1848, the *Christian Herald*, that became the much better-known *Christian Recorder* in 1852. For the *Recorder*'s initial issue, Payne wrote the poem "Dedicatory Lines to the Recorder."[87]

Payne saw literature as a crucial front in the campaigns for full black citizenship and moral uplift. As bishop, he was instrumental in establishing AME literary magazines such as *The Repository of Religion and Literature and of Science and Art*. He saw the *Repository* as part of a church-wide effort "to aid one another in training [parents'] children, especially their daughters. That such organizations are needed among us no thoughtful-minded person will deny. Perhaps the greatest curse which slavery inflicted upon us was the *destruction of the home*. No home, no mother; no mother, no home! But what is home without a cultivated intellect, and what the value of such an intellect without a cultivated heart?"[88] By the late 1850s, the *Repository* was produced out of Baltimore. In it, Stewart published the essay "The Proper Training of Children" and the short story "The First Stage of Life" in 1861.

Beyond the church, other cultural and institutional infiltrations made possible by Baltimore's proximity to the North made several aspects of the city extremely familiar to Stewart, especially compared to other southern locations. To be sure, the most shocking aspect of life in Baltimore that awaited Stewart was chattel slavery. She had never lived in a slaveholding society, although she left no indication of fear or consternation of living in such a world. But Baltimore offered a level of relative autonomy for free blacks that was unmatched throughout the South. As Barbara Fields writes, "Free blacks living and working in Baltimore stood the best chance of escaping the emblems of inferiority. There they congregated in sufficient numbers to sustain a network of churches, clubs, schools, and informal gathering places

---

[87] Daniel A. Payne, *History of the African Methodist Episcopal Church* (Nashville: Publishing House of the A.M.E. Sunday-School Union, 1897), 297.
[88] Daniel A. Payne, *Recollections of Seventy Years* (Nashville: Publishing House of the A.M.E. Sunday-School Union, 1897), 137.

outside the sponsorship of whites. The economic life of the city created need for services that, although generally of a humble, even menial, character, nevertheless ensured them a reasonably secure livelihood."[89] When Stewart arrived in 1852, for example, more than half of the free black population had achieved some level of literacy.[90] They formed debating clubs, readings rooms, and literary societies. These associations were generally reserved for free black persons, but enslaved persons sometimes became members. As an enslaved young man in pursuit of literacy, Frederick Douglass joined the East Baltimore Mental Improvement Society on Fell's Point. Douglass recalled the "several times" he was "assigned a prominent part in its debates."[91] He acknowledged a debt of gratitude to the members of the society for the early education in logic and rhetoric they provided him. The East Baltimore Mental Improvement Society was only the most well-known of a group of cultural associations that shaped antebellum black Baltimore.

Although Stewart names the religious character of Baltimore as her reason for moving to the city, possibilities for intellectual life for free black persons quickly attracted her. Upon arriving in Baltimore, she "found all was not gold that glistened." Her disappointment did not stem from a lack of religiosity in the city but, rather, for "the want of means for the advancement of the common English branches, with no literary resources for the improvement of the mind scarcely."[92] What Stewart recognized was a relatively high degree of literacy and semi-literacy among black Baltimoreans but a lack of literary knowledge and other higher intellectual pursuits. Recognizing such a market, Stewart she set about to open a school. She had "circulars" made that detailed her "programme": namely, "reading, writing, spelling, mental and practical arithmetic, and whatever other studies called for."[93] Her most extensive recollections of her time in Baltimore details the travails of establishing her school. She received a steady wage when she worked for New York City schools, but running her own private one often left her wanting. She bemoaned a "refined sentiment of delicacy" within herself by which she "could not bear to charge for the worth of my labor. If any loss was to be sustained the loss was always on my side, and not on the side of the

---

[89] Fields, *Slavery and Freedom on Middle on the Middle Ground*, 37.
[90] Fields, *Slavery and Freedom on Middle on the Middle Ground*, 39.
[91] Frederick Douglass, *Autobiographies* (New York: The Library of America, 1994), 338.
[92] Stewart, 271–272.
[93] Stewart, 272.

parent or the scholar."[94] Despite these struggles, Stewart seemed to have eked out some sort of financial stability over her first several years in Baltimore.

On the eve of the Civil War, things took a turn for the worst. Hard up and struggling to make ends meet, Stewart seems to have taken residence in the home of the wealthy merchant Frederick W. Brune. Brune immigrated to Baltimore from Bremen, Germany, in 1799. He was central in facilitating a long-standing trade relationship between the two cities, a relationship that helped fuel the large numbers of German immigrants to Baltimore over the course of the nineteenth century.[95] The 1860 census lists a "Maria Stewart," a "mulatto" aged fifty-six, living with the Brune family as a "domestic." Her place of birth is listed as Maryland, not Massachusetts. But the other four black domestics in the household have Maryland listed as their birthplace, very possibly a consequence of the census taker's lack of interest in the specificity of their demographics. (The other Brune domestic was Fanny Johnson, a white woman born in Ireland.[96]) Given the Brunes' wealth and prominence, it is highly unlikely that Stewart tutored any of the grandchildren in a formal capacity.[97] Stewart reports that she had difficulty paying rent during this period; so, if she lived with Brune, he would have been her landlord. Did she defray a portion of her rent by performing menial labor around the home? Or was "domestic" simply a convenient entry for the census? In any case, Stewart was so down and out in this period that her friends in the city held a "festival" to help her with her bills. She "consented" to their wish to describe her as "poor" on the program. Stewart had reached a level of privation she had not experienced any time before: she was so embarrassed by her condition that she refused to return to New York to visit friends because she was not "looking as well in appearance" as she did when she left for Baltimore nearly ten years prior.[98]

Besides friends, Stewart turned to reading original writings at public exhibitions to make ends meet. She left no indication how much money she made. At least one of these submissions led to publication and, most likely, more remuneration: the lecture "The Proper Training of Children" for the Ladies Literary Festival in November 1860 was published in the AME's

---

[94] Stewart, 272.
[95] Francis F. Beirne, *The Amiable Baltimoreans* (1951; Baltimore: Johns Hopkins University Press, 1994), 203–204.
[96] 1860 Federal Census.
[97] Brune's son and heir George William Brown and his wife, Clara, had five children who all lived in the home.
[98] Stewart, 273.

The Repository of Religion and Literature and of Science and Art. The essay rehearses several familiar themes in Stewart's oeuvre, but its unsparing criticisms of children's moral character sets it apart. She associates "wicked and insolent" children of her day with those of the Bible; deems lying "one of [their] grand characteristics"; and analogizes their "unruly tempers and passions" to the "ragings of a *bear*." Only "pious missionary labor . . . as there is among Hottentots or the wild Hindoo" would remedy this crisis, she argued.[99] Reinforced by her Christian chauvinism, Stewart deemed unreformed children outside the fold of salvation: the "lake that burns with fire and brimstone" awaits them.[100] After more than two decades of working with children as a teacher and private tutor, interactions with her students animated the essay's unflinching diction and strident tone.

Stewart left Baltimore a few months after "The Proper Training of Children" appeared in the January 1861 issue of *The Repository*. Following a rent moratorium for the poor at the onset of the US Civil War, she "took the money I had saved to pay my rent and paid my way to Washington [D.C.]."[101] The sociocultural dynamics of Washington were familiar to Stewart: a slave-holding city with a substantial free black population, a relative high level of literacy, and thriving institutions and sociocultural networks. "By 1860," one historian argues, "Washington had acquired something of a reputation as a favorable location for free blacks to live and work."[102] Churches anchored the black community, and Stewart oriented her first years in the city through various religious affiliations. She writes about how in 1864 Washington churches "issued an edict among themselves that they would establish their own schools and supply their own teachers." The government provided funding for these efforts but, according to Stewart, discriminated against the Episcopalians (her denomination by this point) and would "have nothing to do with [a] colored school."[103] Stewart spent the next several years establishing her school for black children in Washington, which she eventually expanded into a sabbath school.

Stewart's work with the Episcopal church brought her into contact with several leading lights in the struggle for full black citizenship, most notably Alexander Crummell. The Cambridge-educated Crummell was a founding

---

[99] Stewart, 187.
[100] Stewart, 187.
[101] Stewart, 271.
[102] Robert Harrison, *Washington during Civil War and Reconstruction: Race and Radicalism* (Cambridge: Cambridge University Press, 2011), 9.
[103] Stewart, 273–274.

father of Pan-Africanism and the leading African American intellectual between Reconstruction and the fin-de-siècle. He was the inaugural pastor of St. Luke's Church, the oldest black Episcopal congregation in Washington. The church held its first service on Thanksgiving in 1879. Stewart, who was one the church's first members, died only a few weeks later.

In Stewart's final year of life, she published a new edition of *Meditations from the Pen of Mrs. Maria W. Stewart*. Stewart financed the project from the money she received as pensioner from her late husband's service in the War of 1812.[104] She also discovered that year that acquaintances in Boston swindled her of significant assets from his estate during probate.[105] Stewart's friend Louise Hatton writes that had it not been for their efforts to secure the pension and investigate James's will, Stewart "might have died in ignorance of the existence of her book, as she had not seen a copy of it for over forty years."[106] Hatton's account is one of several short texts on Stewart's life that preface the 1879 *Meditations*. These accounts speak to her relationships and achievements, especially after moving to Washington, which lay the groundwork for the recovering efforts of Stewart's groundbreaking political philosophy to which this volume contributes.

---

[104] In 1878, Congress passed a law that extended military pension benefits to widows.
[105] Waters, *Maria W. Stewart and the Roots of Black Political Thought*, 195–198.
[106] Louise C. Hatton in Stewart, *Meditations from the Pen of Mrs. Maria W. Stewart*, 9.

PART I
GENDER THEORY

Contextual Works

1

Thomas Jefferson, *Notes on the State of Virginia*, Query XIV

QUERY XIV.

The administration of justice and description of the laws?

The state is divided into counties. In every county are appointed magistrates, called justices of the peace, usually from eight to thirty or forty in number, in proportion to the size of the county, of the most discreet and honest inhabitants. They are nominated by their fellows, but commissioned by the governor, and act without reward. These magistrates have jurisdiction both criminal and civil. If the question before them be a question of law only, they decide on it themselves: but if it be of fact, or of fact and law combined, it must be referred to a jury. In the latter case, of a combination of law and fact, it is usual for the jurors to decide the fact, and to refer the law arising on it to the decision of the judges. But this division of the subject lies with their discretion only. And if the question relate to any point of public liberty, or if it be one of those in which the judges may be suspected of bias, the jury undertake to decide both law and fact. If they be mistaken, a decision against right, which is casual only, is less dangerous to the state, and less afflicting to the loser, than one which makes part of a regular and uniform system. In truth, it is better to toss up cross and pile in a cause, than to refer it to a judge whose mind is warped by any motive whatever, in that particular case. But the common sense of twelve honest men gives still a better chance of just decision, than the hazard of cross and pile. These judges execute their process by the sheriff or coroner of the county, or by constables of their own appointment. If any free person commit an offence against the commonwealth, if it be below the degree of felony, he is bound by a justice to appear before their court, to answer it on indictment or information. If it amount to felony, he is committed to jail, a court of these justices is called; if they on examination think him guilty, they send him to the jail of the general court, before which court he is to be tried first by a grand jury of 24, of whom 13 must concur in opinion: if they find him guilty, he is then tried by a jury of 12 men of the county where the offence was committed, and by their verdict, which must be unanimous, he is acquitted or condemned without appeal. If the criminal be a slave the trial by the county court is final. In every case however, except that of high treason, there resides in the governor a power of pardon. In high treason, the pardon can only flow from the general assembly. In civil matters these justices have jurisdiction in all cases of whatever value, not appertaining to the department of the admiralty. This jurisdiction is twofold. If the matter in dispute be of less value than 4 1/6 dollars, a single member may try it at any time and place within his county, and may award execution on the goods of the party cast. If it be of that or greater value, it is determinable before the county court, which consists of four at the least of those justices, and assembles at the court-house of the county on a certain day in every month. From their determination, if the matter be of the value of ten pounds sterling, or concern the title or bounds of lands, an appeal lies to one of the superior courts.

There are three superior courts, to wit, the high-court of chancery, the general court, and court of admiralty. The first and second of these receive appeals from the county courts, and also have original jurisdiction where the subject of controversy is of the value of ten pounds sterling, or where it concerns the title or bounds of land. The jurisdiction of the admiralty is original altogether. The high-court of chancery is composed of three judges, the general court of five, and the court of admiralty of three. The two first hold their sessions at Richmond at stated times, the chancery twice in the year, and the general court twice for business civil and criminal, and twice more for criminal only. The court of admiralty sits at Williamsburgh whenever a controversy arises.

There is one supreme court, called the court of appeals, composed of the judges of the three superior courts, assembling twice a year at stated times at Richmond. This court receives appeals in all civil cases from each of the superior courts, and determines them finally. But it has no original jurisdiction.

If a controversy arise between two foreigners of a nation in alliance with the United States, it is decided by the Consul for their State, or, if both parties [choose] it, by the ordinary courts of justice. If one of the parties only be such a foreigner, it is triable before the courts of justice of the country. But if it shall have been instituted in a county court, the foreigner may remove it into the general court, or court of chancery, who are to determine it at their first sessions, as they must also do if it be originally commenced before them. In cases of life and death, such foreigners have a right to be tried by a jury, the one half foreigners, the other natives.

All public accounts are settled with a board of auditors, consisting of three members, appointed by the general assembly, any two of whom may act. But an individual, dissatisfied with the determination of that board, may carry his case into the proper superior court.

A description of the laws.

The general assembly was constituted, as has been already shewn, by letters-patent of March the 9th, 1607, in the 4th year of the reign of James the First. The laws of England seem to have been adopted by consent of the settlers, which might easily enough be done whilst they were few and living all together. Of such adoption however we have no other proof than their practice, till the year 1661, when they were expressly adopted by an act of the assembly, except so far as "a difference of condition" rendered them inapplicable. Under this adoption, the rule, in our courts of judicature was, that the common law of England, and the general statutes previous to the 4th of James, were in force here; but that no subsequent statutes were, *unless we were named in them,* said the judges and other partisans of the crown, but *named or not named,* said those who reflected freely. It will be unnecessary to attempt a description of the laws of England, as that may be found in English publications. To those which were established here, by the adoption of the legislature, have been since added a number of acts of assembly passed during the monarchy, and ordinances of convention and acts of assembly enacted since the establishment of the republic. The following variations from the British model are perhaps worthy of being specified.

Debtors unable to pay their debts, and making faithful delivery of their whole effects, are released from confinement, and their persons for ever discharged from restraint for such previous debts: but any property they may afterwards acquire will be subject to their creditors.

The poor, unable to support themselves, are maintained by an assessment on the titheable persons in their parish. This assessment is levied and administered by twelve persons in each parish, called vestrymen, originally chosen by the housekeepers of the parish, but afterwards filling vacancies in their own body by their own choice. These are usually the most discreet farmers, so distributed through their parish, that every part of it may be under the immediate eye of some one of them. They are well acquainted with the details and economy of private life, and they find sufficient inducements to execute their charge well, in their philanthropy, in the approbation of their neighbours, and the distinction which that gives them. The poor who have neither property, friends, nor strength to labour, are boarded in the houses of good farmers, to whom a stipulated sum is annually paid. To those who are able to help themselves a little, or have friends from whom they derive some succours, inadequate however to their full maintenance, supplement[a]ry aids are given, which enable them to live comfortably in their own houses, or in the houses of their friends. Vagabonds, without visible property or vocation, are placed in workhouses, where they are well cl[o]thed, fed, lodged, and made to labour. Nearly the same method of providing for the poor prevails through all our states; and from Savannah to Portsmouth you will seldom meet a beggar. In the larger towns indeed they sometimes present themselves. These are usually foreigners, who have never obtained a settlement in any parish. I never yet saw a native American begging in the streets or highways. A subsistence is easily gained here: and if, by misfortunes, they are thrown on the charities of the world, those provided by their own country are so comfortable and so certain, that they never think of relinquishing them to become strolling beggars.[1] Their situation too, when sick, in the family of a good farmer, where every member is emulous to do them kind offices, where they are visited by all the neighbours, who bring them the little rarities which their sickly appetites may crave, and who take by rotation the nightly watch over them, when their condition requires it, is without comparison better than in a general hospital, where the sick, the dying, and the dead are crammed together, in the same rooms, and often in the same beds. The disadvantages, inseparable from general hospitals, are such as can never be counterpoised by all the regularities of medicine and regimen. Nature and kind nursing save a much greater proportion in our plain way, at a smaller expence, and with less abuse. One branch only of hospital institution is wanting with us; that is, a general establishment for those labouring under difficult cases of [surgery]. The aids of this art are not equivocal. But an able [surgeon] cannot be had in every parish. Such a receptacle should therefore be provided for those patients: but no others should be admitted.

Marriages must be solemnized either on special licen[s]e, granted by the first magistrate of the county, on proof of the consent of the parent or guardian of either party under age, or after solemn publication, on three

---

[1] Jefferson's assertion of America's natural bounty is important for his theories of race and society. The state provides work, clothing, and shelter for free "vagabonds" in need, he writes. He ties this bounty and support to "native American" status, laying the foundation for the white supremacist claims that organizes his nativism.

several Sundays, at some place of religious worship, in the parishes where the parties reside. The act of solemnization may be by the minister of any society of Christians, who shall have been previously licensed for this purpose by the court of the county. Quakers and Menonists [i.e., Mennonites] however are exempted from all these conditions, and marriage among them is to be solemnized by the society itself.

A foreigner of any nation, not in open war with us, becomes naturalized by removing to the state to reside, and taking an oath of fidelity: and thereupon acquires every right of a native citizen: and citizens may divest themselves of that character, by declaring, by solemn deed, or in open court, that they mean to expatriate themselves, and no longer to be citizens of this state.

Conveyances of land must be registered in the court of the county wherein they lie, or in the general court, or they are void, as to creditors, and subsequent purchasers.

Slaves pass by descent and dower as lands do. Where the descent is from a parent, the heir is bound to pay an equal share of their value in money to each of his brothers and sisters.

Slaves, as well as lands, were entailable during the monarchy: but, by an act of the first republican assembly, all donees in tail, present and future, were vested with the absolute dominion of the entailed subject.

Bills of exchange, being protested, carry 10 percent interest from their date.

No person is allowed, in any other case, to take more than five percent per annum simple interest, for the loan of monies.

Gaming debts are made void, and monies actually paid to discharge such debts (if they exceeded 40 shillings) may be recovered by the payer within three months, or by any other person afterwards.

Tobacco, flour, beef, pork, tar, pitch, and turpentine, must be inspected by persons publicly appointed, before they can be exported.

The erecting iron-works and mills is encouraged by many privileges; with necessary cautions however to prevent their dams from obstructing the navigation of the water-courses. The general assembly have on several occasions shewn a great desire to encourage the opening the great falls of James and Patowmac [i.e., Potomac] rivers. As yet, however, neither of these have been effected.

The laws have also descended to the preservation and improvement of the races of useful animals, such as horses, cattle, deer; to the extirpation of those which are noxious, as wolves, squirrels, crows, blackbirds; and to the guarding our citizens against infectious disorders, by obliging suspected vessels coming into the state, to perform quarantine, and by regulating the conduct of persons having such disorders within the state.

The mode of acquiring lands, in the earliest times of our settlement, was by petition to the general assembly. If the lands prayed for were already cleared of the Indian title, and the assembly thought the prayer reasonable, they passed the property by their vote to the petitioner. But if they had not yet been ceded by the Indians, it was necessary that the petitioner should previously purchase their right. This purchase the assembly verified, by enquiries of the Indian proprietors; and being satisfied of its reality and fairness, proceeded further to examine the reasonableness of the petition, and its consistence with policy; and, according to the result, either granted or rejected the petition. The company also sometimes, though very rarely, granted lands, independ[e]ntly of the general assembly. As the colony increased, and individual applications for land multiplied, it was found to give too much occupation to the general assembly to enquire into and execute the grant in every special case. They therefore thought it better to establish general rules, according to which all grants should be made, and to leave to the governor the execution of them, under these rules. This they did by what have been usually called the land laws, amending them from time to time, as their defects were developed. According to these laws, when an individual wished a portion of unappropriated land, he was to locate and survey it by a public officer, appointed for that purpose: its breadth was to bear a certain proportion to its length: the grant was to be executed by the governor: and the lands were to be improved in a certain manner, within a given time. From these regulations there resulted to the state a sole and exclusive power of taking conveyances of the Indian right of soil: since, according to them, an Indian conveyance alone could give no right to an individual, which the laws would acknowledge. The state, or the crown, thereafter, made general purchases of the Indians from time to time, and the governor parcelled them out by special grants, conformed to the rules before described, which it was not in his power, or in that of the crown, to dispense with. Grants, unaccompanied by their proper legal circumstances, were set aside regularly by *scire facias*, or by bill in Chancery. Since the establishment of our new government, this order of things is but little changed. An individual, wishing to appropriate to himself lands still unappropriated by any other, pays to the public treasurer a sum of money proportioned to the quantity he wants. He carries the treasurer's receipt to the auditors of public accompts, who thereupon debit the treasurer with the sum, and order the register of the land-office to give the party a warrant for his land. With this warrant from the register, he goes to the surveyor of the county where the land lies on which he has cast his eye. The surveyor lays it off for him, gives him its exact description, in the form of a certificate, which certificate he returns to the land-office, where a grant is made out, and is signed by the governor. This vests in him a perfect dominion in his lands, transmissible to whom he pleases by deed or will, or by descent to his heirs if he die intestate.

Many of the laws which were in force during the monarchy being relative merely to that form of government, or inculcating principles inconsistent with republicanism, the first assembly which met after the establishment of the commonwealth appointed a committee to revise the whole code, to reduce it into proper form and volume, and report it to the assembly. This work has been executed by three gentlemen, and reported; but probably will not be taken up till a restoration of peace shall leave to the legislature leisure to go through such a work.

The plan of the revisal was this. The common law of England, by which is meant, that part of the English law which was anterior to the date of the oldest statutes extant, is made the basis of the work. It was thought dangerous to attempt to reduce it to a text: it was therefore left to be collected from the usual monuments of it. Necessary alterations in that, and so much of the whole body of the British statutes, and of acts of assembly, as were thought proper to be retained, were digested into 126 new acts, in which simplicity of stile was aimed at, as far as was safe. The following are the most remarkable alterations proposed:

To change the rules of descent, so as that the lands of any person dying intestate shall be divisible equally among all his children, or other representatives, in equal degree.

To make slaves distributable among the next of kin, as other moveables.

To have all public expences, whether of the general treasury, or of a parish or county, (as for the maintenance of the poor, building bridges, courthouses, &c.) supplied by assessments on the citizens, in proportion to their property.

To hire undertakers for keeping the public roads in repair, and indemnify individuals through whose lands new roads shall be opened.

To define with precision the rules whereby aliens should become citizens, and citizens make themselves aliens.

To establish religious freedom on the broadest bottom.

To emancipate all slaves born after passing the act. The bill reported by the revisors does not itself contain this proposition; but an amendment containing it was prepared, to be offered to the legislature whenever the bill should be taken up, and further directing, that they should continue with their parents to a certain age, then be brought up, at the public expence, to tillage, arts or sciences, according to their geniu[s]es, till the females should be eighteen, and the males twenty-one years of age, when they should be colonized to such place as the circumstances of the time should render most proper, sending them out with arms, implements of hous[e]hold and of the handicraft arts, feeds, pairs of the useful domestic animals, &c. to declare them a free and independ[e]nt people, and extend to them our alliance and protection, till they shall have acquired strength; and to send vessels at the same time to other parts of the world for an equal number of white inhabitants; to induce whom to migrate hither, proper encouragements were to be proposed. It will probably be asked, Why not retain and incorporate the blacks into the state, and thus save the expence of supplying, by importation of white settlers, the vacancies they will leave? Deep rooted prejudices entertained by the whites; ten thousand recollections, by the blacks, of the injuries they have sustained; new provocations; the real distinctions which nature has made; and many other circumstances, will divide us into parties, and produce convulsions which will probably never end but in the extermination of the one or the other race.[2]—To these objections, which are political, may be added others, which are physical and moral. The first difference which strikes us is that of colour. Whether the black of the negro resides in the reticular membrane between the skin and scarf-skin, or in the scarf-skin itself; whether it proceeds from the colour of the blood, the colour of the bile, or from that of some other secretion, the difference is fixed in nature, and is as real as if its seat and cause were better known to us. And is this difference of no importance? Is it not the foundation of a greater or less share of beauty in the two races? Are not the fine mixtures of red and white, the expressions of every passion by greater or less suffusions of colour in the one, preferable to that eternal monotony, which reigns in the countenances, that immoveable veil of black which covers all the emotions of the other race? Add to these, flowing hair, a more elegant symmetry of form, their own judgment in favour of the whites, declared by their preference of them, as uniformly as is the

---

[2] Jefferson's consolidation of contemporaneous racial theories shapes his proslavery ideology in this query and elsewhere. The race war he imagines as the inevitable result of emancipation is the main reason for his emigration solution.

preference of the Oranootan [i.e., orangutang] for the black women over those of his own species. The circumstance of superior beauty, is thought worthy attention in the propagation of our horses, dogs, and other domestic animals; why not in that of man? Besides those of colour, figure, and hair, there are other physical distinctions proving a difference of race. They have less hair on the face and body. They secrete less by the kidnies, and more by the glands of the skin, which gives them a very strong and disagreeable odour. This greater degree of transpiration renders them more tolerant of heat, and less so of cold, than the whites. Perhaps too a difference of structure in the pulmonary apparatus, which a late ingenious* experimentalist[3] has discovered to be the principal regulator of animal heat, may have disabled them from extricating, in the act of inspiration, so much of that fluid from the outer air, or obliged them in expiration, to part with more of it. They seem to require less sleep. A black, after hard labour through the day, will be induced by the slightest amusements to sit up till midnight, or later, though knowing he must be out with the first dawn of the morning. They are at least as brave, and more adventuresome. But this may perhaps proceed from a want of forethought, which prevents their seeing a danger till it be present. When present, they do not go through it with more coolness or steadiness than the whites. They are more ardent after their female: but love seems with them to be more an eager desire, than a tender delicate mixture of sentiment and sensation. Their griefs are transient. Those numberless afflictions, which render it doubtful whether heaven has given life to us in mercy or in wrath, are less felt, and sooner forgotten with them. In general, their existence appears to participate more of sensation than reflection. To this must be ascribed their disposition to sleep when abstracted from their diversions, and unemployed in labour. An animal whose body is at rest, and who does not reflect, must be disposed to sleep of course. Comparing them by their faculties of memory, reason, and imagination, it appears to me, that in memory they are equal to the whites; in reason much inferior, as I think one could scarcely be found capable of tracing and comprehending the investigations of Euclid; and that in imagination they are dull, tasteless, and anomalous. It would be unfair to follow them to Africa for this

---

[3] Adair Crawford (1748–1795) was a doctor and chemist whose most widely circulated work, *Experiments and Observations on Animal Heat, and the Inflammation of Combustible Bodies* (1779), Jefferson references here. Crawford imagined his observations as transferable into a "general law of nature," as the book's subtitle suggests, which Jefferson relies on for his extrapolation of Crawford's theories to African and African-descended bodies.

investigation.[4] We will consider them here, on the same stage with the whites, and where the facts are not apocryphal on which a judgment is to be formed. It will be right to make great allowances for the difference of condition, of education, of conversation, of the sphere in which they move. Many millions of them have been brought to, and born in America. Most of them indeed have been confined to tillage, to their own homes, and their own society: yet many have been so situated, that they might have availed themselves of the conversation of their masters; many have been brought up to the handicraft arts, and from that circumstance have always been associated with the whites. Some have been liberally educated, and all have lived in countries where the arts and sciences are cultivated to a considerable degree, and have had before their eyes samples of the best works from abroad. The Indians, with no advantages of this kind, will often carve figures on their pipes not destitute of design and merit. They will crayon out an animal, a plant, or a country, so as to prove the existence of a germ in their minds which only wants cultivation. They astonish you with strokes of the most sublime oratory; such as prove their reason and sentiment strong, their imagination glowing and elevated. But never yet could I find that a black had uttered a thought above the level of plain narration; never see even an elementary trait of painting or sculpture. In music they are more generally gifted than the whites with accurate ears for tune and time, and they have been found capable of imagining a small catch.** Whether they will be equal to the composition of a more extensive run of melody, or of complicated harmony, is yet to be proved. Misery is often the parent of the most affecting touches in poetry—Among the blacks is misery enough, God knows, but no poetry. Love is the peculiar oestrum of the poet. Their love is ardent, but it kindles the senses only, not the imagination. Religion indeed has produced a Phyllis Whately [sic]; but it could not produce a poet. The compositions published under her name are below the dignity of criticism. The heroes of the Dunciad[5] are to her, as Hercules to the author of that poem. Ignatius Sancho has approached nearer to merit in

---

[4] While Jefferson refused to compare across continents, philosophers like Alexander Crummell embraced that analytical method. They believed it would reveal that the forms of degradation of enslaved Africans and their descendants endured were the result of their condition rather than nature.

[5] Alexander Pope's *The Dunciad* (1728) is a mock-heroic satire that critiques what Pope viewed as the depravity and irrationality that defined life in Great Britain. Pope was one of Wheatley's most significant influences. By deeming her work as inferior to Pope's, Jefferson suggests that Wheatley's serious engagements with epic poetry fall short of humorous satires.

composition; yet his letters do more honour to the heart than the head.[6] They breathe the purest effusions of friendship and general philanthropy, and shew how great a degree of the latter may be compounded with strong religious zeal. He is often happy in the turn of his compliments, and his stile is easy and familiar, except when he affects a Shandean fabrication[7] of words. But his imagination is wild and extravagant, escapes incessantly from every restraint of reason and taste, and, in the course of its vagaries, leaves a tract of thought as incoherent and eccentric, as is the course of a meteor through the sky. His subjects should often have led him to a process of sober reasoning: yet we find him always substituting sentiment for demonstration. Upon the whole, though we admit him to the first place among those of his own colour who have presented themselves to the public judgment, yet when we compare him with the writers of the race among whom he lived, and particularly with the epistolary class, in which he has taken his own stand, we are compelled to enroll him at the bottom of the column. This criticism supposes the letters published under his name to be genuine, and to have received amendment from no other hand; points which would not be of easy investigation. The improvement of the blacks in body and mind, in the first instance of their mixture with the whites, has been observed by every one, and proves that their inferiority is not the effect merely of their condition of life. We know that among the Romans, about the Augustan age especially, the condition of their slaves was much more deplorable than that of the blacks on the continent of America. The two sexes were confined in separate apartments, because to raise a child cost the master more than to buy one. Cato, for a very restricted indulgence to his slaves in this particular,*** took from them a certain price. But in this country the slaves multiply as fast as the free inhabitants. Their situation and manners place the commerce between the two sexes almost without restraint. —The same Cato, on a principle of economy, always sold his sick and superannuated slaves. He gives it as a standing precept to a master visiting his farm, to sell his old oxen, old wa[g]ons, old tools, old and diseased servants, and every thing else become useless. "Vendat boves vetulos, plaustrum vetus, ferramenta vetera, servum senem, servum morbosum, & si quid aliud supersit vendat." Cato de re rusticâ. c. 2. The

---

[6] Ignatius Sancho was a significant figure in transatlantic abolitionism. His musical compositions, whose relative merit Jefferson acknowledges, were primarily for public and communal engagements. His letters, which Jefferson sees as unnecessarily sentimental, were published posthumously in 1782.
[7] The term derives from Laurence Sterne's 1759 novel *Tristram Shandy*. According to the *Oxford English Dictionary*, the term refers to "crack-brained" or "half-crazy" behavior.

American slaves cannot enumerate this among the injuries and insults they receive. It was the common practice to expose in the island of Aesculapius, in the Tyber, diseased slaves, whose cure was like to become tedious. The Emperor Claudius, by an edict, gave freedom to such of them as should recover, and first declared, that if any person chose to kill rather than to expose them, it should be deemed homicide. The exposing them is a crime of which no instance has existed with us; and were it to be followed by death, it would be punished capitally. We are told of a certain Vedius Pollio, who, in the presence of Augustus, would have given a slave as food to his fish, for having broken a glass.[8] With the Romans, the regular method of taking the evidence of their slaves was under torture. Here it has been thought better never to resort to their evidence. When a master was murdered, all his slaves, in the same house, or within hearing, were condemned to death. Here punishment falls on the guilty only, and as precise proof is required against him as against a freeman. Yet notwithstanding these and other discouraging circumstances among the Romans, their slaves were often their rarest artists. They excelled too in science, insomuch as to be usually employed as tutors to their master's children. Epictetus, Terence, and Phaedrus, were slaves. But they were of the race of whites. It is not their condition then, but nature, which has produced the distinction[9].—Whether further observation will or will not verify the conjecture, that nature has been less bountiful to them in the endowments of the head, I believe that in those of the heart she will be found to have done them justice. That disposition to theft with which they have been branded, must be ascribed to their situation, and not to any depravity of the moral sense. The man, in whose favour no laws of property exist, probably feels himself less bound to respect those made in favour of others. When arguing for ourselves, we lay it down as a fundamental, that laws, to be just, must give a reciprocation of right: that, without this, they are mere arbitrary rules of conduct, founded in force, and not in conscience: and it is a problem which I give to the master to solve, whether the religious precepts against the violation of property were not framed for him as well as his slave? And whether

---

[8] Jefferson references the story of Vedius Pollio, who threatened to feed a servant to his eels for breaking a goblet. Augustus orders goblets to be broken so that Pollio faces the moral dilemma of his punishment; as a consequence, he spares his servant the punishments. This story appears in Cassius Dio's *The Roman History: The Reign of Augustus*, book 54, chapter 23.

[9] David Walker references this passage in Article I of his *Appeal*. Jefferson uses Epictetus, Terence, and Phaedrus as proof that the inferiority of enslaved Africans is the result of their nature rather the condition of slavery. Abolitionists like Angelina Grimké repeatedly differentiated between Roman slavery and US chattel slavery to undermine claims that these systems of enslavement are comparable.

the slave may not as justifiably take a little from one, who has taken all from him, as he may slay one who would slay him? That a change in the relations in which a man is placed should change his ideas of moral right and wrong, is neither new, nor peculiar to the colour of the blacks. Homer tells us it was so 2600 years ago.

{'Emisy, gaz t' aretes apoainylai eyrythpa Zeys
Aneros, eyt, an min kata dolion emaz elesin.} Od. 17. 323.
    Jove fix'd it certain, that whatever day
    Makes man a slave, takes half his worth away.

But the slaves of which Homer speaks were whites. Notwithstanding these considerations which must weaken their respect for the laws of property, we find among them numerous instances of the most rigid integrity, and as many as among their better instructed masters, of benevolence, gratitude, and unshaken fidelity—The opinion, that they are inferior in the faculties of reason and imagination, must be hazarded with great diffidence. To justify a general conclusion, requires many observations, even where the subject may be submitted to the Anatomical knife, to Optical glasses, to analysis by fire, or by solvents. How much more then where it is a faculty, not a substance, we are examining; where it eludes the research of all the senses; where the conditions of its existence are various and variously combined; where the effects of those which are present or absent bid defiance to calculation; let me add too, as a circumstance of great tenderness, where our conclusion would degrade a whole race of men from the rank in the scale of beings which their Creator may perhaps have given them.[10] To our reproach it must be said, that though for a century and a half we have had under our eyes the races of black and of red men, they have never yet been viewed by us as subjects of natural history. I advance it therefore as a suspicion only, that the blacks, whether originally a distinct race, or made distinct by time and circumstances, are inferior to the whites in the endowments both of body and mind.[11] It is not against experience to suppose, that different species of the same genus, or varieties of the same species, may possess different qualifications. Will not a lover of natural history then, one who views the gradations in all the races

---

[10] This is the first point in the query in which Jefferson recognizes, however implicitly, the tension between the ideals in the United States' founding documents and how Americans practice them.

[11] Walker quotes this passage in his *Appeal*. He argues black people must actively refute and disprove such claims.

of animals with the eye of philosophy, excuse an effort to keep those in the department of man as distinct as nature has formed them? This unfortunate difference of colour, and perhaps of faculty, is a powerful obstacle to the emancipation of these people. Many of their advocates, while they wish to vindicate the liberty of human nature, are anxious also to preserve its dignity and beauty. Some of these, embarrassed by the question "What further is to be done with them?" join themselves in opposition with those who are actuated by sordid avarice only. Among the Romans emancipation required but one effort. The slave, when made free, might mix with, without staining the blood of his master. But with us a second is necessary, unknown to history. When freed, he is to be removed beyond the reach of mixture.

The revised code further proposes to proportion crimes and punishments. This is attempted on the following scale.

I. Crimes whose punishment extends to Life.
   1. High treason. Death by hanging.
      Forfeiture of lands and goods to the commonwealth.
   2. Petty treason. Death by hanging. Dissection.
      Forfeiture of half the lands and goods to the representatives of the party slain.
   3. Murder.
      1. by poison. Death by poison.
         Forfeiture of one-half as before.
      2. in Duel. Death by hanging. Gibbeting, if the challenger.
         Forfeiture of one-half as before, unless it be the party challenged, then the forfeiture is to the commonwealth.
      3. in any other way. Death by hanging.
         Forfeiture of one-half as before.
   4. Manslaughter. The second offence is murder.
II. Crimes whose punishment goes to Limb.
   1. Rape,} Dismemberment.
   2. Sodomy,}
   3. Maiming,} Retaliation, and the forfeiture of half the
   4. Disfiguring} lands and goods to the sufferer.
III. Crimes punishable by Labour.
   1. Manslaughter, 1st offence. Labour VII. years
      for the public.
      Forfeiture of half as in murder.

2. Counterfeiting money. Labour VI. years.
   Forfeiture of lands and goods to
   the commonwealth.
3. Arson.} Labour V. years.
4. Asportation of vessels.}
   Reparation three-fold.
5. Robbery.} Labour IV. years.
6. Burglary.}
   Reparation double.
7. Housebreaking.} Labour III. years.
8. Horse-stealing.}
   Reparation.
9. Grand Larcency. Labour II. years.
   Reparation. Pillory.
10. Petty Larcency. Labour I. year.
    Reparation. Pillory.
11. Pretensions to witch-craft, &c. Ducking. Stripes.
12. Excusable homicide.} to be pitied, not punished.
13. Suicide.}
14. Apostacy. Heresy.}

Pardon and privilege of clergy are proposed to be abolished; but if the verdict be against the defendant, the court in their discretion, may allow a new trial. No attainder to cause a corruption of blood, or forfeiture of dower. Slaves guilty of offences punishable in others by labour, to be transported to Africa, or elsewhere, as the circumstances of the time admit, there to be continued in slavery. A rigorous regimen proposed for those condemned to labour.

Another object of the revisal is, to diffuse knowledge more generally through the mass of the people. This bill proposes to lay off every county into small districts of five or six miles square, called hundreds, and in each of them to establish a school for teaching reading, writing, and arithmetic. The tutor to be supported by the hundred, and every person in it entitled to send their children three years gratis, and as much longer as they please, paying for it. These schools to be under a visitor, who is annually to [choose] the boy, of best genius in the school, of those whose parents are too poor to give them further education, and to send him forward to one of the grammar schools, of which twenty are proposed to be erected in different parts of the country, for teaching Greek, Latin, geography, and the higher branches of numerical arithmetic. Of the boys thus sent in any one year, trial is to be made at the grammar schools one or two years, and the best genius of the whole selected, and continued six years, and the residue dismissed. By this means twenty of the best geniu[s]es will be raked from the rubbish annually, and be instructed, at the public expence, so far as the gramm[a]r schools go. At the end of six years instruction, one half are to be discontinued (from among whom the grammar schools will probably be supplied with future masters); and the other half, who are to be chosen for the superiority of their parts and disposition, are to be sent and continued three years in the study of such sciences as they shall [choose], at William and Mary college, the plan of which is proposed to be enlarged, as will be hereafter explained, and extended to all the useful sciences. The ultimate result of the whole scheme of education would be the teaching all the children of the state reading, writing, and common arithmetic: turning out ten annually of superior genius, well taught in Greek, Latin, geography, and the higher branches of arithmetic: turning out ten others annually, of still superior parts, who, to those branches of learning, shall have added such of the sciences as their genius shall have led them to: the furnishing to the wealthier part of the people convenient schools, at which their children may be educated, at their own expence. —The general objects of this law are to provide an education adapted to the years, to the capacity, and the condition of every one, and directed to their freedom and happiness. Specific details were not proper for the law. These must be the business of the visitors entrusted with its execution. The first stage of this education being the schools of the hundreds, wherein the great mass of the people will receive their instruction, the principal foundations of future order will be laid here. Instead therefore of putting the Bible and Testament into the hands of the children, at an age when their judgments are not sufficiently matured for religious enquiries, their memories may here be stored with the most useful facts from Grecian, Roman, European and American history. The first elements of morality too may be instilled into their minds; such as, when further developed as their judgments advance in strength, may teach them how to work out their own greatest happiness, by shewing them that it does not depend on the condition of life in which chance has placed them, but is always the result of a good conscience, good health, occupation, and freedom in all just pursuits.—Those whom either the wealth of their parents or the adoption of the state shall destine to higher degrees of learning, will go on to the grammar schools, which constitute the next stage, there to be instructed in the languages. The learning

Greek and Latin, I am told, is going into disuse in Europe. I know not what their manners and occupations may call for: but it would be very ill-judged in us to follow their example in this instance. There is a certain period of life, say from eight to fifteen or sixteen years of age, when the mind, like the body, is not yet firm enough for laborious and close operations. If applied to such, it falls an early victim to premature exertion; exhibiting indeed at first, in these young and tender subjects, the flattering appearance of their being men while they are yet children, but ending in reducing them to be children when they should be men.[12] The memory is then most susceptible and tenacious of impressions; and the learning of languages being chiefly a work of memory, it seems precisely fitted to the powers of this period, which is long enough too for acquiring the most useful languages antient and modern. I do not pretend that language is science. It is only an instrument for the attainment of science. But that time is not lost which is employed in providing tools for future operation: more especially as in this case the books put into the hands of the youth for this purpose may be such as will at the same time impress their minds with useful facts and good principles. If this period be suffered to pass in idleness, the mind becomes lethargic and impotent, as would the body it inhabits if unexercised during the same time. The sympathy between body and mind during their rise, progress and decline, is too strict and obvious to endanger our being misled while we reason from the one to the other. —As soon as they are of sufficient age, it is supposed they will be sent on from the grammar schools to the university, which constitutes our third and last stage, there to study those sciences which may be adapted to their views.— By that part of our plan which prescribes the selection of the youths of genius from among the classes of the poor, we hope to avail the state of those talents which nature has sown as liberally among the poor as the rich, but which perish without use, if not sought for and cultivated.— But of all the views of this law none is more important, none more legitimate, than that of rendering the people the safe, as they are the ultimate, guardians of their own liberty. For this purpose the reading in the first stage, where they will receive their whole education, is proposed, as has been said, to be chiefly historical. History by apprising them of the past will enable them to judge of the future; it will avail them of the experience of other times and other nations; it will

---

[12] Jefferson's does not extend this belief about the effects of children's labor to enslaved Africans and their descendants. See Grimké (Stewart, 23–30) for a how an abolitionist did; she uses the image of the laboring child as "violent pressure" in her *Appeal to the Christian Women of the South*.

qualify them as judges of the actions and designs of men; it will enable them to know ambition under every disguise it may assume; and knowing it, to defeat its views. In every government on earth is some trace of human weakness, some germ of corruption and degeneracy, which cunning will discover, and wickedness insensibly open, cultivate, and improve. Every government degenerates when trusted to the rulers of the people alone. The people themselves therefore are its only safe depositories. And to render even them safe their minds must be improved to a certain degree. This indeed is not all that is necessary, though it be essentially necessary. An amendment of our constitution must here come in aid of the public education. The influence over government must be shared among all the people. If every individual which composes their mass participates of the ultimate authority, the government will be safe; because the corrupting the whole mass will exceed any private resources of wealth: and public ones cannot be provided but by levies on the people. In this case every man would have to pay his own price. The government of Great-Britain has been corrupted, because but one man in ten has a right to vote for members of parliament. The sellers of the government therefore get nine-tenths of their price clear. It has been thought that corruption is restrained by confining the right of suffrage to a few of the wealthier of the people: but it would be more effectually restrained by an extension of that right to such numbers as would bid defiance to the means of corruption.

Lastly, it is proposed, by a bill in this revisal,to begin a public library and gallery, by laying out a certain sum annually in books, paintings, and statues.

* Crawford.
** The instrument proper to them is the Banjar, which they brought hither from Africa, and which is the original of the guitar, its chords being precisely the four lower chords of the guitar.
*** Tos dolos etaxen orismeno nomismatos omilein tais therapainisin. — Plutarch. Cato.

2
Angelina Grimké, *Appeal to the Christian Women of the South* (selections)

"Then Mordecai commanded to answer Esther, Think not with thyself that thou shalt escape in the king's house, more than all the Jews. For if thou altogether holdest thy peace at this time, then shall there enlargement and deliverance arise to the Jews from another place; but thou and thy father's house shall be destroyed: and who knoweth whether thou art come to the kingdom for such a time as this? And Esther bade them return Mordecai this answer: — and so will I go in unto the king, which is not according to the law: and *if I perish, I perish.*" Esther IV. 13–16.

Respected Friends,

It is because I feel a deep and tender interest in your present and eternal welfare that I am willing thus publicly to address you. Some of you have loved me as a relative, and some have felt bound to me in Christian sympathy, and Gospel fellowship; and even when compelled by a strong sense of duty, to break those outward bonds of union which bound us together as members of the same community, and members of the same religious denomination, you were generous enough to give me credit, for sincerity as a Christian, though you believed I had been most strangely deceived.[1] I thanked you then for your kindness, and I ask you *now*, for the sake of former confidence, and former friendship, to read the following pages in the spirit of calm investigation and fervent prayer.[2] It is because you have known me, that I write thus unto you.

---

[1] Grimké frames her relationship to the wider public in relation to her own religious history. Over the course of her life, she was affiliated with the Society of Friends (Quakers) and Presbyterians. Notwithstanding denominational distinctions, she appeals to those relationships as the foundation for her arguments against slavery as an absolute sin that all Christians should recognize as such.

[2] This is part of a wider discourse on public participation. She draws the phrase "fervent prayer" from Colossians 4:12 ("Epaphras, who is one of you, a servant of Christ, saluteth you, always laboring fervently for you in prayers, that you may stand perfect and complete in all the will of God"; KJV) and James 5:16 ("Confess your faults one to another, and pray for one another, that ye may be healed. The effectual fervent prayer of a righteous man availeth much"; KJV). This approach is one of submission, rather than judgment. She invites her readers to participate in a process of religious reform or purification, one that is in line with nineteenth-century discourses of gender expectation. As the

But there are other Christian women scattered over the Southern States, a very large number of whom have never seen me, and never heard my name, and who feel *no* interest whatever in *me*. But I feel an interest in *you*, as branches of the same vine[3] from whose root I daily draw the principle of spiritual vitality—Yes! Sisters in Christ I feel an interest in *you*, and often has the secret prayer arisen on your behalf, Lord "open thou their eyes that they may see wondrous things out of thy Law"[4]—It is then, because I *do feel* and *do pray* for you, that I thus address you upon a subject about which of all others, perhaps you would rather not hear any thing; but, "would to God ye could bear with me a little in my folly, and indeed bear with me, for I am jealous over you with godly jealousy." Be not afraid then to read my appeal; it is *not* written in the heat of passion or prejudice, but in that solemn calmness which is the result of conviction and duty. It is true, I am going to tell you unwelcome truths, but I mean to speak those *truths in love*, and remember Solomon says, "faithful are the *wounds* of a friend." I do not believe the time has yet come when *Christian women* "will not endure sound doctrine," even on the subject of Slavery, if it is spoken to them in tenderness and love, therefore I now address *you*.

To all of you then, known or unknown, relatives or strangers, (for you are all *one* in Christ,) I would speak. I have felt for you at this time, when unwelcome light is pouring in upon the world on the subject of slavery; light which even Christians would exclude, if they could, from our country, or at any rate from the southern portion of it, saying, as its rays strike the rocky bound coasts of New England and scatter their warmth and radiance over her hills and valleys, and from thence travel onward over the Palisades of the Hudson, and down the soft flowing waters of the Delaware and gild the waves of the Potomac, "hitherto shalt thou come and no further;" I know that even professors of His name who has been emphatically called the "Light of the world" would, if they could, build a wall of adamant around the Southern

---

essay will later suggest, prayers are directly related to political petitioning, which was a maxim of the Anti-Slavery Society.

[3] With another reference to disparate Christian denominations in her reading audience, Grimke reframes their relationship as a single community growing from as single root. She takes the imagery from John 5:1–8. The idea is that one Christian community underpins her claims about black freedom and full sociopolitical inclusion.

[4] Rather than arguing against the constitutional legality of slavery, Grimké's essay focuses on religious legal history. Her adaptation of Psalm 119:18 ("Open thou mine eyes, that I may behold wondrous things out of thy law"; KJV) is the foundation of her argument against slavery: God's law is the standard against which she judges chattel slavery.

States whose top might reach unto heaven, in order to shut out the light which is bounding from mountain to mountain and from the hills to the plains and valleys beneath, through the vast extent of our Northern States. But believe me, when I tell you, their attempts will be as utterly fruitless as were the efforts of the builders of Babel; and why? Because moral, like natural light, is so extremely subtle in its nature as to overleap all human barriers, and laugh at the puny efforts of man to control it. All the excuses and palliations of this system must inevitably be swept away, just as other "refuges of lies" have been, by the irresistible torrent of a rectified public opinion. "The *supporters* of the slave system," says Jonathan Dymond in his admirable work on the Principles of Morality, "will *hereafter* be regarded with the *same* public feeling, as he who was an advocate for the slave trade *now* is."[5] It will be, and that very soon, clearly perceived and fully acknowledged by all the virtuous and the candid, that in *principle* it is as sinful to hold a human being in bondage who has been born in Carolina, as one who has been born in Africa. All that sophistry of argument which has been employed to prove, that although it is sinful to send to Africa to procure men and women as slaves, who have never been in slavery, that still, it is not sinful to keep those in bondage who have come down by inheritance, will be utterly overthrown. We must come back to the good old doctrine of our forefathers who declared to the world, "this self evident truth that *all* men are created equal, and that they have certain *inalienable* rights among which are life, *liberty*, and the pursuit of happiness." It is even a greater absurdity to suppose a man can be legally born a slave under *our free Republican* Government, than under the petty despotisms of barbarian Africa. If then, we have no right to enslave an African, surely we can have none to enslave an American; if it is a self evident truth that *all* men, every where and of every color are born equal, and have an *inalienable right to liberty*, then it is equally true that *no* man can be born a slave, and no man can ever *rightfully* be reduced to *involuntary* bondage and held as a slave, however fair may be the claim of his master or mistress through wills and title-deeds.

But after all, it may be said, our fathers were certainly mistaken, for the Bible sanctions Slavery, and that is the highest authority. Now the Bible is

---

[5] Grimké's reference is Johnathan Dymond's (1796–1828) *Essays on the Principles of Morality and on the Private and Political Rights and Obligations of Mankind* (1828). Grimké was drawn to Dymond's definition of "duty," a term that she uses several times throughout the "Appeal." Grimké references the chapter called "Slavery" from *Essays* in which Dymond argues that "he who simply applies the requisitions of the Moral Law finds no time for reasoning or for doubt" that the abolition of slavery is Christians' "duty" (241).

my ultimate appeal in all matters of faith and practice, and it is to this test I am anxious to bring the subject at issue between us. Let us then begin with Adam and examine the charter of privileges which was given to him. "Have dominion over the fish of the sea, and over the fowl of the air, and over every living thing that moveth upon the earth." In the eighth Psalm we have a still fuller description of this charter which through Adam was given to all mankind. "Thou madest him to have dominion over the works of thy hands; thou hast put all things under his feet. All sheep and oxen, yea, and the beasts of the field, the fowl of the air, the fish of the sea, and whatsoever passeth through the paths of the seas." And after the flood when this charter of human rights was renewed, we find *no additional* power vested in man. "And the fear of you and the dread of you shall be upon every beast of the earth, and every fowl of the air, and upon all that moveth upon the earth, and upon all the fishes of the sea, into your hand are they delivered." In this charter, although the different kinds of *irrational* beings are so particularly enumerated, and supreme dominion over *all of them* is granted, yet man is *never* vested with this dominion *over his fellow man*; he was never told that any of the human species were put *under his feet*; it was only *all things*, and man, who was created in the image of his Maker, *never* can properly be termed a *thing*, though the laws of Slave States do call him "a chattel personal;" *Man* then, I assert *never* was put *under the feet of man*, by that first charter of human rights which was given by God, to the Fathers of the Antediluvian and Postdiluvian worlds, therefore this doctrine of equality is based on the Bible.[6]

[. . .]

But perhaps you will be ready to query, why appeal to *women* on this subject? *We* do not make the laws which perpetuate slavery. *No* legislative power is vested in *us*; *we* can do nothing to overthrow the system, even if we wished to do so. To this I reply, I know you do not make the laws, but I also know that *you are the wives and mothers, the sisters and daughters of those who do*; and if you really suppose you can do nothing to overthrow slavery, you are greatly

---

[6] Grimke intimates the humanity of enslaved persons because they are rational rather than irrational beings. As rational beings, not things, Grimke argues they are not included as under human dominion. Grimké's argument refutes Jefferson's argument about black humanity in Query XIV that Africans are "in reason much inferior" (Stewart, 13) due to their constitutional inherence ("nature which has produced the distinction") (Stewart, 16).

mistaken. You can do much in every way: four things I will name. 1st. You can read on this subject. 2d. You can pray over this subject. 3d. You can speak on this subject. 4th. You can *act* on this subject. I have not placed reading before praying because I regard it more important, but because, in order to pray aright, we must understand what we are praying for; it is only then we can "pray with the understanding and the spirit also."

1. Read then on the subject of slavery. Search the Scriptures daily, whether the things I have told you are true. Other books and papers might be a great help to you in this investigation, but they are not necessary, and it is hardly probable that your Committees of Vigilance will allow you to have any other. The *Bible* then is the book I want you to read in the spirit of inquiry, and the spirit of prayer. Even the enemies of Abolitionists, acknowledge that their doctrines are drawn from it. In the great mob in Boston, last autumn, when the books and papers of the Anti-Slavery Society, were thrown out of the windows of their office, one individual laid hold of the Bible and was about tossing it out to the ground, when another reminded him that it was the Bible he had in his hand. "*O! 'tis all one,*" he replied, and out went the sacred volume, along with the rest. We thank him for the acknowledgment. Yes, "*it is all one,*" for our books and papers are mostly commentaries on the Bible, and the Declaration. Read the *Bible* then, it contains the words of Jesus, and they are spirit and life. Judge for yourselves whether *he sanctioned* such a system of oppression and crime.

2. Pray over this subject. When you have entered into your closets, and shut to the doors, then pray to your father, who seeth in secret, that he would open your eyes to see whether slavery is *sinful*, and if it is, that he would enable you to bear a faithful, open and unshrinking testimony against it, and to do whatsoever your hands find to do, leaving the consequences entirely to him, who still says to us whenever we try to reason away duty from the fear of consequences, "*What is that to thee, follow thou me.*" Pray also for that poor slave, that he may be kept patient and submissive under his hard lot, until God is pleased to open the door of freedom to him without violence or bloodshed. Pray too for the master that his heart may be softened, and he made willing to acknowledge, as Joseph's brethren did, "Verily we are guilty concerning our brother," before he will be compelled to add in consequence of Divine judgment, therefore is all this evil come upon us." Pray also for all your brethren and sisters who are laboring in the righteous cause of Emancipation in the Northern States, England and the world. There is great encouragement for prayer in these words of our Lord. "Whatsoever ye shall

ask the Father *in my name*, he *will* give it to you"—Pray then without ceasing, in the closet and the social circle.

3. Speak on this subject. It is through the tongue, the pen, and the press, that truth is principally propagated. Speak then to your relatives, your friends, your acquaintances on the subject of slavery; be not afraid if you are conscientiously convinced it is *sinful*, to say so openly, but calmly, and to let your sentiments be known. If you are served by the slaves of others, try to ameliorate their condition as much as possible; never aggravate their faults, and thus add fuel to the fire of anger already kindled, in a master and mistress's bosom; remember their extreme ignorance, and consider them as your Heavenly Father does the *less* culpable on this account, even when they do wrong things. Discountenance all cruelty to them, all starvation, all corporal chastisement; these may brutalize and *break* their spirits, but will never bend them to willing, cheerful obedience. If possible, see that they are comfortably and *seasonably* fed, whether in the house or the field; it is unreasonable and cruel to expect slaves to wait for their breakfast until eleven o'clock, when they rise at five or six. Do all you can, to induce their owners to clothe them well, and to allow them many little indulgences which would contribute to their comfort. Above all, try to persuade your husband, father, brothers and sons, that *slavery is a crime against God and man*, and that it is a great sin to keep *human beings* in such abject ignorance; to deny them the privilege of learning to read and write. The Catholics are universally condemned, for denying the Bible to the common people, but, *slaveholders must not* blame them, for *they* are doing the *very same thing*, and for the very same reason, neither of these systems can bear the light which bursts from the pages of that Holy Book.[7] And lastly, endeavour to inculcate submission on the part of the slaves, but whilst doing this be faithful in pleading the cause of the oppressed.

> Will *you* behold unheeding,
> Life's holiest feelings crushed,
> Where *woman's* heart is bleeding,
> Shall *woman's* voice be hushed?[8]

4. Act on this subject. Some of you *own* slaves yourselves. If you believe slavery is *sinful*, set them at liberty, "undo the heavy burdens and let the

---

[7] Anti-Catholic sentiments were common in abolitionist discourse. For example, it is important to Walker's politics in his *Appeal*.

[8] This verse seems to be original to Grimké.

oppressed go free." If they wish to remain with you, pay them wages, if not let them leave you. Should they remain teach them, and have them taught the common branches of an English education; they have minds and those minds, *ought to be improved*. So precious a talent as intellect, never was given to be wrapt in a napkin and buried in the earth. It is the *duty* of all, as far as they can, to improve their own mental faculties, because we are commanded to love God with *all our minds*, as well as with all our hearts, and we commit a great sin, if we *forbid or prevent* that cultivation of the mind in others, which would enable them to perform this duty. Teach your servants then to read &c, and encourage them to believe it is their *duty* to learn, if it were only that they might read the Bible.

But some of you will say, we can neither free our slaves nor teach them to read, for the laws of our state forbid it. Be not surprised when I say such wicked laws *ought to be no barrier* in the way of your duty, and I appeal to the Bible to prove this position.

[...]

But some of you may say, if we do free our slaves, they will be taken up and sold, therefore there will be no use in doing it. Peter and John might just as well have said, we will not preach the gospel, for if we do, we shall be taken up and put in prison, therefore there will be no use in our preaching. *Consequences*, my friends, belong no more to *you*, than they did to these apostles. Duty is ours and events are God's. If you think slavery is sinful, all you have to do is to set your slaves at liberty, do all you can to protect them, and in humble faith and fervent prayer, commend them to your common Father. He can take care of them; but if for wise purposes he sees fit to allow them to be sold, this will afford you an opportunity of testifying openly, wherever you go, against the crime of *manstealing*. Such an act will be *clear robbery*, and if exposed, might, under the Divine direction, do the cause of Emancipation more good, than any thing that could happen, for, "He makes even the wrath of man to praise him, and the remainder of wrath he will restrain."

I know that this doctrine of obeying *God*, rather than man, will be considered as dangerous, and heretical by many, but I am not afraid openly to avow it, because it is the doctrine of the Bible; but I would not be understood to advocate resistance to any law however oppressive, if, in obeying it, I was not obliged to commit *sin*. If for instance, there was a law, which imposed imprisonment or a fine upon me if I manumitted a slave, I would on no account resist that law, I would set the slave free, and then go to prison or pay the fine. If a law commands me to *sin* I will break it; if it calls me to *suffer*, I will let it take its course unresistingly. The doctrine of blind obedience and unqualified submission to *any human* power, whether civil or ecclesiastical, is the doctrine of despotism, and ought to have no place among Republicans and Christians.

[...]

Sisters in Christ, I have done. As a Southerner, I have felt it was my duty to address you. I have endeavoured to set before you the exceeding sinfulness of slavery, and to point you to the example of those noble women who have been raised up in the church to effect great revolutions, and to suffer for the truth's sake. I have appealed to your sympathies as women, to your sense of duty as *Christian women*. I have attempted to vindicate the Abolitionists, to prove the entire safety of immediate Emancipation, and to plead the cause of the poor and oppressed. I have done—I have sowed the seeds of truth, but I well know, that even if an Apollos were to follow in my steps to water them, "*God only* can give the increase." To Him then who is able to prosper the work of his servant's hand, I commend this Appeal in fervent prayer, that as he "hath *chosen the weak things of the world*, to confound the things which are mighty," so He may cause His blessing, to descend and carry conviction to the hearts of many Lydias through these speaking pages. Farewell—Count me not your "enemy because I have told you the truth," but believe me in unfeigned affection,

Your sympathizing Friend,
ANGELA E. GRIMKÉ

3

Louisa Piquet and Hiram Mattison, *Louisa Picquet, the Octoroon, or, Inside Views of Southern Domestic Life* (1861) (selections)

CHAPTER I. ILLUSTRIOUS BIRTH AND PARENTAGE.

LOUISA PICQUET, the subject of the following narrative, was born in Columbia, South Carolina, and is apparently about thirty-three years of age.[1] She is a little above the medium height, easy and graceful in her manners, of fair complexion and rosy cheeks, with dark eyes, a flowing head of hair with no perceptible inclination to curl, and every appearance, at first view, of an accomplished white lady.*[2] No one, not apprised of the fact, would suspect that she had a drop of African blood in her veins; indeed, few will believe it, at first, even when told of it.

But a few minutes' conversation with her will convince almost anyone that she has, at least, spent most of her life in the South. A certain menial-like diffidence, her plantation expression and pronunciation, her inability to read or write, together with her familiarity with and readiness in describing plantation scenes and sorrows, all attest the truthfulness of her declaration that she has been most of her life a slave. Besides, her artless simplicity and sincerity are sufficient to dissipate the last doubt. No candid person can talk with her without becoming fully convinced that she is a truthful, conscientious, and Christian woman. She is now, and has been for the last eight years, a member

---

[1] Piquet's coauthor Reverend Hiram Mattison (1811–1868) was a well-known minister and scientist whose writings on astronomy were for instructional use.

[2] The cut on the outside title-page is a tolerable representation of the features of Mrs. P., though by no means a flattering picture. [Mattison's original note]

of the Zion Baptist Church in Cincinnati, Ohio, of which Rev. Wallace Shelton is now (May, 1860) the pastor.

But, notwithstanding the fair complexion and lady-like bearing of Mrs. Picquet, she is of African descent on her mother's side[3]—an octoroon, or eighth blood—and, consequently, one of the four millions in this land of Bibles, and churches, and ministers, and "liberty," who "have *no rights that white men are bound to respect.*"[4]

The story of her wrongs and sorrows will be recited, to a large extent, in her own language, as taken from her lips by the writer, in Buffalo, N. Y., in May, 1860.

CHAPTER II. LOOKS TOO MUCH LIKE MADAME RANDOLPH'S CHILDREN, AND IS SOLD OUT OF THE FAMILY.

"I WAS born in Columbia, South Carolina. My mother's name was Elizabeth. She was a slave owned by John Randolph,*[5] and was a seamstress in his family. She was fifteen years old when I was born. Mother's mistress had a child only two weeks older than me. Mother's master, Mr. Randolph, was my father. So mother told me. She was forbid to tell who was my father, but I looked so much like Madame Randolph's baby that she got dissatisfied, and mother had to be sold. Then mother and me was sent to Georgia, and sold. I was a baby—don't remember at all, but suppose I was about two months old, maybe older."

---

[3] In the mid-seventeenth century, British colonies throughout the Americas began to follow the legal doctrine of *partus sequitur ventrem*—that is, children's status as free or enslaved would be that of their mother's.

[4] This infamous quote comes from Supreme Court Chief Justice Roger Taney's opinion in the 1857 *Dred Scott v. Sanford* case.

[5] "What 'John Randolph' this was, we know not; but suppose it was not the celebrated 'John Randolph of Roanoke,' though it may have been, and probably was, one of the same family. A gentleman in Xenia, Ohio, told Mrs. P. that if she could only make it out that her mother was one of John Randolph's slaves, there was money somewhere, now, of John Randolph's estate, to buy her mother and brother." [Mattison's original note]

CHAPTER III. THE SECOND MASTER FAILS, AND HIS SLAVES ARE SCATTERED.

"THEN I was sold to Georgia, Mr. Cook bought mother and me. When mother first went to Georgia she was a nurse, and suckled Madame Cook's child, with me. Afterward, she was a cook. I was a nurse. I always had plenty to do. Fast as one child would be walkin', then I would have another one to nurse."

Question (by the writer).—"Did your master ever whip you?"

Answer.—"Oh, very often; sometimes he would be drunk, and real funny, and would not whip me then. He had two or three kinds of drunks. Sometimes he would begin to fight at the front door, and fight everything he come to. At other times he would be real funny."

Q.—"He was a planter, was he?"

A.—"Yes; he had a large cotton plantation, and warehouse where he kept all the cotton in, and stores up the country, in a little town—Monticello—and then he had some in Georgia. He used to give such big parties, and everything, that he broke up. Then his creditors came, you know, and took all the property; and then he run off with my mother and me, and five other slaves, to Mobile, and hired us all out. He was goin' to have enough to wait on him, for he could not wait on his self. I was hired out to Mr. English. He was a real good man; I wouldn't care if I belonged to him, if I had to belong to any body. I'd like to swap Mr. Cook for him. Mr. English and his wife were very clever to me. They never whipped me. Mother had a little baby sister when we first went to Mobile—a little girl just running round. She died in Alabama. She had one before that, while she was in Georgia; but they all died but me and my brother, the oldest and the youngest."

Q.—"Had she any one she called her husband while she was in Georgia?"

A.—"No."

Q.—"Had she in Mobile?"

A.—"No."

Q.—"Had she any children while she lived in Mobile?"

A.—"None but my brother, the baby when we were all sold."

Q.—"Who was the father of your brother, the baby you speak of?"

A.—"I don't know, except Mr. Cook was. Mother had three children while Mr. Cook owned her."

Q.—"Was your mother white?"

A.—"Yes, she pretty white; not white enough for white people. She have long hair, but it was kind a wavy."

Q.—"Were you hired out in Mobile?"

A.—"Yes; with Mr. English."

CHAPTER VI. THE FAMILY SOLD AT AUCTION—LOUISA BOUGHT BY A "NEW ORLEANS GENTLEMAN," AND WHAT CAME OF IT.

Q.—"How did you say you come to be sold?"

A.—"Well, you see, Mr. Cook made great parties, and go off to watering-places, and get in debt, and had to break up [unclear], and then he took us to Mobile, and hired the most of us out, so the men he owe should not find us, and sell us for the debt. Then, after a while, the sheriff came from Georgia after Mr. Cook's debts, and found us all, and took us to auction, and sold us. My mother and brother was sold to Texas, and I was sold to New Orleans."

Q.—"How old were you, then?"

A.—"Well, I don't know exactly, but the auctioneer said I wasn't quite fourteen.[6] I didn't know myself."

Q.—"How old was your brother?"

A.—"I suppose he was about two months old. He was little bit of baby."

Q.—"Where were you sold?"

A.—"In the city of Mobile."

Q.—"In a yard? In the city?"

A.—"No. They put all the men in one room, and all the women in another; and then whoever want to buy come and examine, and ask you whole lot of questions. They began to take the clothes off of me, and a gentleman said they needn't do that, and told them to take me out. He said he knew I was a virtuous girl, and he'd buy me, anyhow.[7] He didn't strip me only just under my shoulders."

---

[6] Like other narratives by or about enslaved women, Picquet's emphasizes how early enslaved girls' "virtue" is at risk. As chapter five of *Louisa Picquet, The Octoroon* describes, Mr. Cook stripped and beat Picquet for avoiding his sexual violations. Later in the narrative Mattison laments the fact that offenders like Cook often retained their reputation as gentlemen.

[7] For abolitionists, stripping and exposing women and girls within public view epitomized the depravity of the slave trade. Describing inspections prior to sale shows that sexual exploitation was a frequent or primary reason for purchasing young female slaves. The decision to buy her "anyhow," despite her "virtue," suggests that her virginity was a problem rather than an asset.

Q.—"Were there any others there white like you?"

A.—"Oh yes, plenty of them. There was only Lucy of our lot, but others!"

Q.—"Were others stripped and examined?"

A.—"Well, not quite naked, but just same."

Q.—"You say the gentleman told them to 'take you out.' What did he mean by that?"

A.—"Why, take me out of the room where the women and girls were kept; where they examine them—out where the auctioneer sold us."

Q.—"Where was that? In the street, or in a yard?"

A.—"At the market, where the block is?"

Q.—"What block?"

A.—"My! don't you know? The stand, where we have to get up?"

Q.—"Did *you* get up on the stand?"

A.—"Why, of course; we all have to get up to be seen."

Q.—"What else do you remember about it?"

A.—"Well, they first begin at upward of six hundred for me, and then some bid fifty more, and some twenty-five more, and that way."

Q.—"Do you remember anything the auctioneer said about you when he sold you?"

A.—"Well, he said he could not recommend me for anything else only that I was a good-lookin' girl, and a good nurse, and kind and affectionate to children; but I was never used to any hard work. He told them they could see that. My hair was quite short, and the auctioneer spoke about it, but said, 'You see it good quality, and give it a little time, it will grew out again.' You see Mr. Cook had my hair cut off. My hair grew fast, and look so much better than Mr. Cook's daughter, and he fancy I had better hair than his daughter, and so he had it cut off to make a difference."

Q.—"Well, how did they sell you and your mother? that is, which was sold first?"

A.—"Mother was put up the first of our folks. She was sold for splendid cook, and Mr. Horton, from Texas, bought her and the baby, my brother. Then Henry, the carriage-driver, was put up, and Mr. Horton bought him, and then two field-hands, Jim and Mary. The women there tend mills and drive ox wagons, and plough, just like men. Then I was sold next. Mr. Horton run me up to fourteen hundred dollars. He wanted I should go with my mother. Then someone said 'fifty.' Then Mr. Williams allowed that he did not care what they bid, he was going to have me anyhow. Then he bid fifteen hundred. Mr. Horton said 'twas no use to bid any more, and I was sold to Mr. Williams. I went right to New Orleans then."

Q.—"Who was Mr. Williams?"

A.—"I didn't know then, only he lived in New Orleans. Him and his wife had parted, some way—he had three children boys. When I was going away I heard someone cryin', and prayin' the Lord to go with her only daughter, and protect me. I felt pretty bad then, but hadn't no time only to say good-bye. I wanted to go back and get the dress I bought with the half-dollars, I thought a good deal of that; but Mr. Williams would not let me go back and get it. He said he'd get me plenty of nice dresses. Then I thought mother could cut it up and make dresses for my brother, the baby. I knew she could not wear it; and I had a thought, too, that she'd have it to remember me."

Q.—"It seems like a dream, don't it?"

A.—"No; it seems fresh in my memory when I think of it—no longer than yesterday. Mother was right on her knees, with her hands up, prayin' to the Lord for me. She didn't care who saw her: the people all lookin' at her. I often thought her prayers followed me, for I never could forget her. Whenever I wanted anything real bad after that, my mother was always sure to appear to me in a dream that night, and have plenty to give me, always."

Q.—"Have you never seen her since?"

A.—"No, never since that time. I went to New Orleans, and she went to Texas. So I understood."

Q.—"Well, how was it with you after Mr. Williams bought you?"

A.—"Well, he took me right away to New Orleans."

Q.—"How did you go?"

A.—"In a boat, down the river. Mr. Williams told me what he bought me for, soon as we started for New Orleans. He said he was getting old, and when he saw me he thought he'd buy me, and end his days with me. He said if I behave myself he'd treat me well: but, if not, he'd whip me almost to death."

Q.—"How old was he?"

A.—"He was over forty; I guess pretty near fifty. He was gray headed. That's the reason he was always so jealous. He never let me go out anywhere."

Q.—"Did you never go to church?"

A.—"No, sir; I never darken a church door from the time he bought me till after he died. I used to ask him to let me go to church. He would accuse me of some object, and said there was more rascality done there than anywhere else. He'd sometimes say, 'Go on, I guess you've made your arrangements; go on, I'll catch up with you.' But I never dare go once."

Q.—"Had you any children while in New Orleans?"

A.—"Yes; I had four."

Q.—"Who was their father?"

A.—"Mr. Williams."

Q.—"Was it known that he was living with you?"

A.—"Everybody knew I was housekeeper, but he never let on that he was the father of my children. I did all the work in his house—nobody there but me and the children."

Q.—"What children?"

A.—"My children and his. You see he had three sons."

Q.—"How old were his children when you went there?"

A.—"I guess the youngest was nine years old. When he had company, gentlemen folks, he took them to the hotel. He never have no gentlemen company home. Sometimes he would come and knock, if he stay out later than usual time; and if I did not let him in in a minute, when I would be asleep, he'd come in and take the light, and look under the bed, and in the wardrobe, and all over, and then ask me why I did not let him in sooner. I did not know what it meant till I learnt his ways."

Q.—"Were your children mulattoes?"

A.—"No, sir! They were all white. They look just like him. The neighbors all see that. After a while he got so disagreeable that I told him, one day, I wished he would sell me, or 'put me in his pocket'—that's the way we say—because I had no peace at all. I rather die than live in that way. Then he got awful mad, and said nothin' but death should separate us; and, if I run off, he'd blow my brains out. Then I thought, if that be the way, all I could do was just to pray for him to die."

Q.—"Where did you learn to pray?"

A.—"I first begin to pray when I was in Georgia, about whippin'—that the Lord would make them forget it, and not whip me: and it seems if when I pray I did not get so hard whippin'."

CHAPTER XII. THE LONG-LOST MOTHER HEARD FROM.

Q.—"How came you to find out where your mother was?"

A.—"Well, I hear she was in Texas, and I keep writin' to Texas, and supposed it was one place, but never got no answer. But I kept prayin', and always believed that I should see her or hear from her, before I died."

Q.—"You kept up praying all this time, did you?"

A.—"Yes; but when I came to Cincinnati, I thought more about my mother—to think I was free, and so many others that I knew in Georgia, and she was still in slavery! It was a great weight on my mind; and I thought if I could get religion I should certainly meet her in heaven for I knew she was a Christian woman. I had thought of it very often, and thought how often I had told the Lord I would serve him and had not done so, till I was almost afraid to make another promise. Then I made up my mind to serve the Lord. I had often been to the Methodist meeting there, when there was great excitement; but I never went up to be prayed for. I thought it was a sin if I did not go up in the right way.

But I kept feelin' worse in my mind. Everything I had ever done all came up before me. I felt as if I could not look up; my eyes were fixed on the ground. In the evenin'—Sunday evenin'—I went to meetin' in the Zion Baptist Church. Mr. Shelton was preachin'. After he got through, they was singin'; I felt troubled all through it. Then I went up to the altar with others. I made up my mind that I would never hold up my head again on this earth till the Lord converted me. I prayed hard enough that night. My husband was so mortified to think I prayed so loud, and made so much noise; but I told him, Henry, I have to die for myself, and it did not set me back at all. But I did not get rid of the burden I felt till near daylight that night, or next mornin'. I was prayin' nearly all night, and near mornin' I felt worse, as if I would die; and I tried to wake Henry up, but I could not wake him at all. It seemed as if I had not time. All my long prayers had gone to just the one word, 'Lord, have mercy!' and I could not say anything but that. And the moment I believe that the Lord would relieve me, the burden went right off; and I felt as light as if I was right up in the air. And it seemed as if there was light in the room.[8] Then, the next Sunday, I joined the church, and the Sunday after was baptized. That was eight years ago, going on nine. I been in that church ever since."

Q.—"Is your husband a professor of religion?"

---

[8] Picquet's conversion adds an important generic dimension to *The Octoroon*. Narratives of Christian conversion often organized and occasioned early black political thought. Some of these narratives anchor full texts (e.g., John Marrant 1785; Jarena Lee 1836), while others constitute one among other major episodes (e.g., Equiano 1789, chapter ten).

A.—"Yes; he belongs to the same church. He experienced religion in Georgia."

Q.—"How about the two daughters?"

A.—"Elizabeth, my daughter, belongs to the same church. My husband's daughter, Harriet, does not belong to any church."

Q.—"Does your church commune with slaveholders?"

A.—"*No, sir; they will not.* The Union Baptist Church does. When white ministers come there from the South, they let them break the bread at the Communion; but in our church, if they come there, they don't do it, unless they come with a lie in their mouth. They ask them if they believe in slavery, or apologize for it, and if they do, then they don't preach there. No slaveholder, or apologist for slavery, can preach in that church; that was the foundation when they first started."

Q.—"Well, how did you find out where your mother was?"

A.— "Well, I have made it a business for about eleven years, to inquire of every one I saw, almost, about my mother. If any fugitives came through, I made it my business to get to see them, and inquire. A great many fugitives come through Cincinnati. I have had lots of them in my house.

One time a colored woman came there, real genteel, and ask to board. I thought she was a runaway slave, though she tried to make me believe she was free. Her name was Mary White. She was there two or three weeks, and I notice she never went out only on Sunday evenin's. One afternoon she went to our church, and heard it give out by the preacher, that if any of the friends knew of a woman by the name of Mary White, to tell her to be on the lookout, for the hell-hounds were after her up to one of the hotels. Then she spring up, and came to where I was and told me. That night we darken up the house, and a Quaker friend came there and had her fixed up; and next day she was on her way to Canada. After that I got a couple of letters from her, returning thanks to us all for helpin' her on her way. She was in a sheriff's family in Canada, and was doing well."

Q.—"Now tell me how you found your mother?"

A.—"I used to take in washin', and one day a gentleman, Mr. B., a good friend of ours in Cincinnati, sent some shirts there to be done up, and said he was goin' to Texas. Then my husband inquired, and found out that he knew Mr. Horton, in Texas, and told us what kind of a lookin' man he was. Then I remembered how he looked when he bought my mother in Mobile, and I knew it was the same man. Then he told us how to send a letter, and where to mail it. [There is a kink about mailing a letter, so as to have it reach a slave, that we never before dreamed of; but Mrs. P. does not wish it published, for fear it will hinder her from getting her letters.] Then I wrote a letter [got one written], and in three weeks I had a letter from my mother."[9]

Q.—"What became of the first letter you had from your mother, while you were in New Orleans?"

A.—"I never saw that. Mr. Williams only told me he got it, and what was in it. I only knew she was in Texas. I thought it was all Texas."

Q.—"Have you the first letter you received from your mother?"

A.—"Yes; up stairs. Shall I go and get it?"

Here the letter was brought. It is on a tough blue paper, well soiled and worn, but yet quite legible. The following chapter contains an exact copy.

CHAPTER XIII. LETTER FROM A SLAVE MOTHER.

WARTON, March 8, 1859
My Dear Daughter,

I a gane take my pen in hand to drop you a few lines.

I have written to you twice, but I hav not yet received an answer from you I can not imagin why you do not writ I feel very much troubel I fear you hav not recived my letters or you would hav written; I sent to my little grand children a ring also a button in my first letter I want you to writ to me on recept of this letter, whether you hav ever received the letters and presents or not I said in my letter to you that Col. Horton would let you have me for 1000 dol. or a woman that could fill my place; I think you could get one cheaper where you are*[10] that would fill my place than to pay him the money; I am anxios to hav you to make this trade. you hav no Idea what my feelings are. I hav not spent one happy moment since I received your kind letter. it is true I was more than rejoyest to hear from you my Dear child; but my feelings on this subject are in Expressible. no one but a mother can tell my feelings. in regard to your Brother John Col. Horton is willing for you to hav him for a boy a fifteen years old or fifteen hundred dol I think that 1000 dollars is too much for me you must writ very kind to Col Horton and try to Get me for less money; I think you can change his Price by writing Kindly to him aske him in a kind

---

[9] The brackets in this answer are from the original text.
[10] For particular reasons the letter was dated at St. Louis, where so many slaves are bought for Texas and Alabama; and this letter came first to St. Louis, and was forwarded by a friend to Cincinnati. Thus all letters come and go. [Mattison's original note]

manner to let you hav me for less I think you can soften his heart and he will let you hav me for less than he has offered me to you for.

You Brother John sends his love to you and 100 kisses to your little son; Kiss my Dear little children 100 times for me particuler Elizabeth say to her that she must writ to her grand mar ofton; I want you to hav your ambrotipe taken also your children and send them to me I would giv this world to see you and my sweet little children; may God bless you my Dear child and protect you is my prayer.

Your affectionate mother,
Elizabeth Ramsey.

direct your letter to Gov. A. C. Horton Wharton Wharton contey texas.

The reader will understand that the brother John, mentioned in this letter, was the "baby" sold with the mother some twenty years ago, in Mobile, whose slips were made of Louisa's pink dress bought with the half-dollars. Louisa's mother never would take the name of Randolph or Cook—the name of her owner—as other slaves do, so she still sticks to her first name of Ramsey, as when she lived in South Carolina thirty-five years ago.

This letter is dated at Wharton. Mrs. P. says it is "in the country, where they go in the winter, and live at Matagorda in the summer." By looking upon a map of Texas it may be seen that Matagorda is at the mouth of the Colorado River, on the Gulf of Mexico; and Wharton about forty miles northwest, on the same river, both in Southern Texas.

Another friend. Mrs. Ramsey now lives with Arthur, the coachman, who was sold at the same time with her in Mobile, as her husband. The letter is, of course, written by some white person, and is printed exactly as it is written.

There is a fact worth recording in regard to the first letter that reaches Mrs. Ramsey. It is thus described by Mrs. Picquet:

I had been tryin' hard to find out where my mother was twelve years, after I came to Cincinnati; and when I get that letter written, I just put my trust in the Lord to go with it. I had tried so long, and could not get no word at all. I prayed to the Lord to go with each seal. There was three envelopes: one to take the letter to my friend at St. Louis, to mail the letter that was in it to Matagorda for me. That letter was directed to the postmaster in Texas; and a letter to him in it, asking him, if Col. Horton was alive, to send it to him, and, if not, to send it to some of his children. And I prayed the Lord that he would work in the hearts of the man in St. Louis, and the postmaster at Matagorda, that my letter might reach my mother.

In that letter I ask Mr. Horton if he would please to read it to my mother, to let her know that I was yet alive; and, if he did not feel disposed to read it to her, would he be so kind as to drop me a few lines, just to let me know if she was alive; and, if she was dead, how long ago, and how she died; and, if she was livin', if she was well, and how she looked—just to ease my mind, for I had been weighed down with sorrow to see her for many years. I told him I had no silver nor gold to pay him; but I trust the Lord would reward him for his kindness, if he would do that much for me. I told him I had great faith in the Lord; and I would pray that his last days might be his best. I tell him if she was livin', and he would sell her, I would try to buy her. If I thought she would die the next week, it would be a great comfort for me to have her here to bury her.

Thus it seems that the Lord did go with the letter, and that Mrs. Horton read the letter to Louisa's mother. She then wrote two letters, but they did not reach Mrs. P. One of them, the one containing the button and the ring, was afterward found in the post-office in Matagorda, by Mrs. Ramsey. It was probably either not stamped, or not properly directed.

As soon as Mrs. P. got the first letter from her mother, she wrote two letters back, one to her mother, and the other to Mr. Horton, and both dated and mailed as before. In a short time she received another from her mother, written but a few days after the first received by Mrs. P.; and as it throws some additional light upon the question whether or not slaves have any proper affection for their offspring, we transcribe and print that also.[11]

SECOND LETTER FROM THE SLAVE MOTHER.

"WARTON, Warton County, March 13, '59."
"My Dear Daughter,"
"Your very kind and affectionate letters dated at St. Louis, One in January the other in Febuary has been received and contents partickularly notist, I had them read often creating in me both Sorrow and Joy. Joy that you were

---

[11] In offering the following letter, Mattison directly refutes claims that enslaved black persons lack familial feeling. Describing their feelings as "proper affection," he avoids Jeffersonian stereotypes of enslaved persons as improperly expressive and sentimentally defunct (see Stewart 12–13).

living & a doing wel so far as the comforts of this world are concerned and you seem to have a bright prospect in the World to come, this the brightest of all other prospects, If a Person should gain the whole world & lose there Soul they have lost all,[12] My Dear Daughter you say a great deal to me about instructing your Brother in his duty, I endeavor to set a good example before him it is all that I can do John is a good disposed Boy & a favorite with his Master, Arthur, Jim & Mary are all members of the Babtist Church, they are all well and a doing well, In your first letter you spoke of trying to purchase me & your Brother, the proposition was made to you to exchang Property of equal value, or to take One Thousand Dollars for me, & Fifteen Hundred for your Brother this may seem an extravagant price to you but it is not an average price for Servants, I know of nothing on this earth that would gratify me so much as to meet with My Dear & only daughter, I fear that I should not be able to retain my senses on account of the great Joy it would create in me, But time alone will develup whether this meeting will tak plase on earth or not Hope keeps the soul alive, but my Dear Daughter if this should not be our happy lot, I pray God that we may be able to hold fast to the end, & be the Happy recipients of the promise made to the faithful. There will be no parting there, but we shall live in the immediate presence and smiles of our God. It is not in our power to comply with your request in regard to the Degeurrotypes this tim, we shall move to Matagorda shortly, there I can comply with your request. Arthur, Jim, Mary and your brother desire to be very kindly remembered to you, Answer this at as early a date as convenient Direct your letter to Goven A. C. Horton, Matagorda, Texas.

May God guide and protect you through Life, & Finally save You in Heaven is the prayer of your affectionate mother,"

"Elizabeth Ramsey."

Before this second letter was received Mrs. P. writes to Mr. Horton, reminding him that her mother was growing old, and that it would be better for him to sell her cheaper, and buy a younger person. In answer to this letter the following was received from Mr. Horton himself.

---

[12] Though Picquet does not provide a conversion narrative for her mother, she does describe her mother as a "Christian woman" (Stewart 31). Here Ramsey paraphrases Jesus's call for his disciples to follow him despite the personal cost; this call appears in three of the four Gospels (Matthew 16:26, Mark 8:36, and Luke 9:25).

4

The Black Woman of the South

Her Neglects and Her Needs
By Rev. Alexander Crummell, D. D.,
[1883]
Rector of St. Luke's Church, Washington, D. C.

It is an age clamorous everywhere for the dignities, the grand prerogatives, and the glory of woman. There is not a country in Europe where she has not risen somewhat above the degradation of centuries, and pleaded successfully for a new position and a higher vocation. As the result of this new reformation we see her, in our day, seated in the lecture-rooms of ancient universities, rivaling her brothers in the fields of literature, the grand creators of ethereal art, the participants in noble civil franchises, the moving spirit in grand reformations, and the guide, agent, or assistant in all the noblest movements for the civilization and regeneration of man.

In these several lines of progress the American woman has run on in advance of her sisters in every other quarter of the globe. The advantage she has received, the rights and prerogatives she has secured for herself, are unequaled by any other class of women in the world. It will not be thought amiss, then, that I come here to-day to present to your consideration the one grand exception to this general superiority of women, viz., "THE BLACK WOMAN OF THE SOUTH."

In speaking to-day of the "black woman," I must needs make a very clear distinction. The African race in this country is divided into two classes, that is—the *colored people* and the *negro population*. In the census returns of the 1860 this whole population was set down at 4,500,000. Of these, the *colored* numbered 500,000; the *black* or *negro* population at 4,000,000. But notice these other broad lines of demarkation [sic] between them. The colored people, while indeed but *one-eighth* of the number of the blacks, counted more men and women who could read and write than the whole 4,000,000 of their brethren in bondage. A like disparity showed itself in regard to their *material* condition. The 500,000 colored people were absolutely richer in lands and houses than the many millions of their degraded kinsmen.

The causes of these differences are easily discovered. The colored population received, in numerous cases, the kindness and generosity of their white kindred—white fathers and relatives. Forbidden by law to marry the negro woman, very many slave-holders took her as the wife despite the law; and when children were begotten every possible recognition was given those children, and they were often cared for, educated, and made possessors of property. Sometimes they were sent to Northern schools, some-times to France or to England. Not unfrequently whole families, nay, at times, whole colonies, were settled in Western or Northern towns, and largely endowed with property. The colored population, moreover, was, as compared to the negro, the *urban* population. They were brought in large numbers to the cities, and thus largely partook of the civilization and refinement of the whites. They were generally the domestic servants of their masters, and thus, brought in contact with their superiors, they gained a sort of education which never came to the field hands, living in rude huts on the plantations. All this, however casual it may seem, was a merciful providence, by which some gleams of light and knowledge came, indirectly, to the race in this land.[1]

The rural or plantation population of the South was made up almost entirely of people of pure negro blood. And this brings out also the other disastrous fact, namely, that this large black population has been living from the time of their introduction into America, a period of more than two hundred years, in a state of unlettered rudeness. The Negro all this time has been an intellectual starveling. This has been more especially the condition of the black woman of the South. Now and then a black man has risen above the debased condition of his people. Various causes would contribute to the advantage of the *men*: the relation of servants to superior masters; attendance at courts with them; their presence at political meetings; listening to table-talk behind the chairs; traveling as valets; the privilege of books and reading in great houses, and with indulgent masters—all these served to lift up a black *man* here and there to something like superiority. But no such fortune fell

---

[1] Crummell's distinction between "colored" and "negro" hinges on one's ancestral, domestic, and geographic proximity to white benefactors, including but not limited to familial relations. "Colored" citizens, in his view, are also more likely to live in urban locales. Thus, Crummell's theory differs from discourses that not only distinguish between "colored" and "negroes" based on behavior and/or class but also that frame the city as the places of unavoidable moral turpitude and personal corruption. For him, rural isolation and propinquity to former slaveholders is the most detrimental scene, especially for black women.

to the lot of the plantation woman. The black woman of the South was left perpetually in a state of hereditary darkness and rudeness. Since the day of Phillis Wheatly no Negress in this land (that is, in the South) has been raised above the level of her sex. The lot of the black *man* on the plantation has been sad and desolate enough; but the fate of the black woman has been awful! Her entire existence from the day when she first landed, a naked victim of the slave-trade, has been degradation in its extremest forms.

In her girlhood al the delicate tenderness of her sex has been rudely outraged. In the field, in the rude cabin, in the press-room, in the factory, she was thrown into the companionship of coarse and ignorant men. No chance was given her for delicate reserve or tender modesty. From her childhood she was the doomed victim of the grossest passions. All the virtues of her sex were utterly ignored. If the instinct of chastity asserted itself then she had to fight like a tigress for the ownership and possession of her own person; and, oftentimes, had to suffer pains and lacerations for her virtuous self-assertion.[2] When she reached maturity all the tender instincts of her womanhood were ruthlessly violated. At the age of marriage—always prematurely anticipated under slavery—she was mated, as the stock of the plantation were mated, *not* to be the companion of a loved and chosen husband, but to be the breeder of human cattle, for the field or the auction-block. With that mate she went out, morning after morning to toil, as a common field hand. As it was *his*, so likewise was it her lot to wield the heavy hoe, or to follow the plow, or to gather in the crops. She was a "hewer of wood and a drawer of water."[3] She was a common field-hand. She had to keep her place in the gang from morn till eve, under the burden of a heavy task, or under the stimulus or the fear of a cruel lash. She was a picker of cotton. She labored at the sugar mill and in the tobacco factory. When, through weariness or sickness, she has fallen behind her allotted task then came, as punishment, the fearful stripes upon her shrinking, lacerated flesh.

Her home life was of the most degrading nature. She lived in the rudest huts, and partook of the coarsest food, and dressed in the scantiest garb, and slept, in multitudinous cabins, upon the hardest boards!

---

[2] Crummell asserts that virtues are intrinsic to womanly instinct; that is, women need not be taught to be virtuous but institutions such as chattel slavery actively sap their inherent morality.

[3] From Joshua 9:21–27, the phrase signifies menial labor. Antislavery writers and orators regularly used it, especially in reference to the toil of southern plantations. See Stewart "Lecture, Delivered at the Franklin Hall," 79.

Thus she continued a beast of burden down to the period of those maternal anxieties which, in ordinary civilized life, give, repose, quiet, and care to expectant mothers. But, under the slave system, few such relaxations were allowed. And so it came to pass that little children were ushered into the world under conditions which many cattle raisers would not suffer for their flocks and herds. Thus she became the mother of children. But even then there was for her no suretyship of motherhood, or training, or control. Her own offspring were not *her* own. She and husband and children were all the property of others. All these sacred ties were constantly snapped and cruelly sundered. *This* year she had one husband; and next year, through some auction sale, she might be separated from him and mated with another. There was no sanctity of family, no binding tie of marriage, none of the fine felicities and the endearing affections of home. None of these things were the lot of Southern black women. Instead thereof a gross barbarism which tended to blunt the tender sensibilities, to obliterate feminine delicacy and womanly shame, came down as her heritage from generation to generation; and it seems a miracle of providence and grace that, notwithstanding these terrible circumstances, so much struggling virtue lingered amid these rude cabins, that so much womanly worth and sweetness abided in their bosoms, as slaveholders themselves have borne witness to.

But some of you will ask: "Why bring up these sad memories of the past? Why distress us with these dead and departed cruelties?" Alas, my friends, these are not dead things. Remember that

"The evil that men do lives after them."[4]

The evil of gross and monstrous abominations, the evil of great organic institutions crop out long after the departure of the institutions themselves. If you go to Europe you will find not only the roots, but likewise many of the deadly fruits of the old Feudal system still surviving in several of its old states and kingdoms. So, too, with slavery. The eighteen years of freedom have not obliterated all its deadly marks from either the souls or bodies of the black woman. The conditions of life, indeed, have been modified since emancipation; but it still maintains that the black woman is the Pariah woman of this land! We have, indeed, degraded women, immigrants from foreign lands. In their own countries some of them were so low in the social scale that they were yoked with the cattle to plow the fields. They were rude, unlettered,

---

[4] From William Shakespeare's *Julius Caesar*, Act 3, scene ii.

coarse, and benighted. But when they reach *this* land there comes an end to the degraded condition.

"They touch our country and their shackles fall."[5]

As soon as they become grafted into the stock of American life they partake at once of all its large gifts and its noble resources.

Not so with the black woman of the South. Freed, legally, she has been; but the act of emancipation had no talismanic influence to reach to and alter and transform her degrading social life.

When that proclamation was issued she might have heard the whispered words in her every hut, "Open Sesame"; but, so far as her humble domicile and her degraded person was concerned, there was invisible but gracious Genii who, on the instant, could transmute the rudeness of her but into instant elegance, and change the crude surroundings of her home into neatness, taste, and beauty.

The truth is, "Emancipation Day" found her a prostrate and degraded being; and, although it has brought numerous advantages to her sons, it has produced but the simplest changes in her social and domestic condition. She is still the crude, rude, ignorant mother. Remote from cities, the dweller still in the old plantation hut, neighboring to the sulky, disaffected master class, who still think her freedom was a personal robbery of them-selves, none of the "fair humanities" have visited her humble home. The light of knowledge has not fallen upon her eyes. The fine domesticities which give the charm to family life, and which, by the refinement and delicacy of womanhood, preserve the civilization of nations, have not come to *her*. She has still the rude, coarse labor of men. With her rude husband she still shares the hard service of a field-hand. Her house, which shelters, perhaps, some six or eight children, embraces but two rooms. Her furniture is of the rudest kind. The clothing of the household is scant and of the coarsest material, has oft-times the garniture of rags; and for herself and offspring is marked, not seldom, by the absence of both hats and shoes. She has never been taught to sew, and the field labor of slavery times has kept her ignorant of the habitudes of neatness and the requirements of order. Indeed, coarse food, coarse clothes, coarse living, coarse manners, coarse companions, coarse surroundings, coarse neighbors, both white and black, yea, everything coarse, down to the coarse, ignorant, senseless religion, which excites her sensibilities and starts her passions, go

---

[5] From William Cowper's *The Task, A Poem, in Six Books* (1785). The stanza from which this line comes discusses the end of slavery in England.

to make up the life of the masses of black women in the hamlets and villages of the rural South.

This is the state of black womanhood. Take the girlhood of the same region, and it presents the same aspect, save that in large districts the white man has not forgotten the olden times of slavery, and, with indeed, the deepest sentimental abhorrence of "amalgamation," still thinks that the black girl is to be perpetually the victim of his lust! In the larger towns and in cities our girls, in common schools and academies, are receiving superior culture. Of the fifteen thousand colored school teachers in the South, more than half are colored young women, educated since emancipation. But even these girls, as well as their more ignorant sisters in rude huts, are followed and tempted and insulted by the ruffianly element of Southern society, who think that black *men* have no rights which white men should regard, and black *women* no virtue which white men should respect!

And now look at the *vastness* of this degradation. If I had been speaking of the population of a city, or a town, or even a village, the tale would be a sad and melancholy one. But I have brought before you the condition of millions of women. According to the census of 1880 there were, in the Southern States, 3,327,678 females of all ages of the African race. Of these there were 674,365 girls between twelve and twenty, 1,522,696 between twenty and eighty. "These figures," remarks an observant friend of mine, "are startling!" And when you think that the masses of these women live in the rural districts; that they grow up in rudeness and ignorance; that their former masters are using few means to break up their hereditary degradation, you can easily take in the pitiful condition of this population, and forecast the inevitable future to multitudes of females, unless a mighty special effort is made for the improvement of the black woman of the South.

I know the practical nature of the American mind, I know how the question of values intrudes itself into even the domain of philanthropy; and, hence I shall not be astonished if the query suggests itself, whether special interest in the black woman will bring any special advantage to the American nation.

Let me dwell for a few minutes upon this phase of the subject. Possibly the view I am about suggesting has never before been presented to the American mind. But, Negro as I am, I shall make no apology for venturing the claim that the Negress is one of the most interesting of all the classes of women on the globe. I am speaking of her, not as a perverted and degraded creature, but in her natural state, with her native instincts and peculiarities.

Let me repeat just here the words of a wise, observing, tender-hearted philanthropist, whose name and worth and words have attained celebrity. It is fully forty years ago since the celebrated Dr. Channing said: "We are holding in bondage of the best races of the human family. The Negro is among the mildest, gentlest of men. He is singularly susceptible of improvement from abroad. . . . His nature is affectionate, easily touched, and hence he is more open to religious improvement than the white man. . . . The African carries with him much more than *we* the genius of a meek, long-suffering, loving virtue."*[6]

I should feel ashamed to allow these words to fall from my lips if it were not necessary to the lustration of the character of my black sisters of the South. I do not stand here to-day to plead for the black *man*. He is a man; and if he is weak he must go to the wall. He is a man; he must fight his own way, and if he is strong in mind and body, he can take care of himself. But for the mothers, sisters, and daughters of my race I have a right to speak. And when I think of their sad condition down South, think, too, that since the day of emancipation hardly any ne has lifted up a voice in their behalf, I feel it a duty and a privilege to set forth their praises and to extol their excellencies. For, humble and benighted as she is, the black woman of the South is one of the queens of womanhood. If there is any other woman on this earth who is native aboriginal qualities is her superior, I know not where she is to be found; for, I do say, that in tenderness of feeling, in genuine native modesty, in large disinterestedness, in sweetness of disposition and deep humility, in unselfish devotedness, and in warm, motherly assiduities, the Negro woman is unsurpassed by any other woman on this earth.

The testimony to this effect is almost universal—our enemies themselves being witnesses. You know how widely and how continuously, for generations, the Negro has been traduced, ridiculed, derided. Some of you may remember the journals and the hostile criticisms of Coleridge and Trollope and Burton, West Indian and African travelers. Very many of you may remember the philosophical disquisitions of the ethnological school of 1847,

---

[6] William Ellery Channiing (1780–1842) was perhaps the most influential Unitarian minister in the nineteenth-century United States. His 1835 pamphlet *Slavery* offered abolitionism an astute rejection of slavery as a necessary evil on moral grounds because of its profitability. The quote here comes from Channing's analysis in *Emancipation* (1840) of recently emancipated slaves in the British West Indies, which was part of his call for global emancipation. Like Crummell, Channing regards the state of the home as the indicator of emancipation's success; he focuses on intact marriages, familial religiosity, relationships between mothers and their children, among other domestic concerns.

the contemptuous dissertations of Hunt and Gliddon.[7] But it is worthy of notice in all these cases that the sneer, the contempt, the bitter gibe, have been invariably leveled against the black *man*—never against the black woman! On the contrary, *she* has almost everywhere been extolled and eulogized. The black man was called a stupid, thick-lipped, flat-nosed, long-heeled, empty-headed animal; the link between the baboon and the human being, only fit to be a slave! But everywhere, even in the domains of slavery, how tenderly has the Negress been spoken of! She has been the nurse of childhood. To her all the cares and heart-griefs of youth have been intrusted [sic]. Thousands and tens of thousands in the West Indies and in our Southern States have risen up and told the tale of her tenderness, of her gentleness, patience, and affection. No other woman in the world has ever had such tributes to a high moral nature, sweet, gentle love, and unchanged devotedness. And by the memory of my own mother and dearest sisters I can declare to be true!

Hear the tribute of Michelet: "The Negress, of all others, is the most loving, the most generating; and this, not only because of her youthful blood, but we must also admit, for the rich-ness of her heart. She is loving among the loving, good among the good (ask the travelers whom she has so often saved). Goodness is creative, it is fruitfulness, it is the very benediction of a holy act. The fact that woman is so fruitful I attribute to her treasures of tenderness, to that ocean of goodness which permeates her heart. . . . Africa is a woman. Her races are feminine. . . . In many of the black tribes of Central Africa the women rule, and they are as intelligent as they are amiable and kind."*[8]

The references in Michelet to the generosity of the African woman to travelers brings to mind the incident in Mungo Park's travels, where the African woman fed, nourished, and saved him. The men had driven him away. They would not even allow him to feed with the cattle; and so, faint,

---

[7] James Hunt (1833–1869) and George R. Gliddon (1809–1857) were pioneers of nineteenth-century anthropology and race science whose theories of inherent intellectual and physical deficiencies in African populations bolstered proslavery, antiblack forces throughout the Atlantic world.

[8] Jules Michelet (1798–1874) was a French historian whose historiography of France and its culture remain cornerstone studies in European history. Crummell quotes carefully from his *La Femme* (1860), pulling passages that hail African women's innate goodness and virtue while avoiding Michelet's troubling antiblack racialism. Michelet distinguishes between types of African women: the unrefined "negress" and the "true black woman" who is in the process of becoming. The "true black woman" emerges as a result of being close to white men, their culture, and education. Although his theory of black womanhood evokes with Crummell's, they differ on the pedagogies and evaluative metrics of improvement: whereas Crummell favors bourgeois domesticity, Michelet turns to what he calls black women's "passions," namely, their adoration of white men, ability to anticipate others' desires, and desire to learn.

weary, and despairing, he went to a remote hut and lay down on the earth to die. One woman, touched with compassion, came to him, brought him food and milk, and at once he revived. Then he tells us of the solace and the assiduities of these gentle creatures for his comfort. I give you his own words: "The rites of hospitality thus per-formed towards a stranger in distress, my worthy benefactress, pointing to the mat, and telling me that I might sleep there without apprehension, called to the female part of her family which had stood gazing on me all the while in fixed astonishment, to resume the task of spinning cotton, in which they continued to employ themselves a great part of the night. They lightened their labors by songs, one of which was composed extempore, for I was myself the subject of it. It was sung by one of the young women, the rest joining in a sort of chime. The air was sweet and plaintive, and the words, literally translated, were these: 'The winds roared and the rains fell; the poor white man, faint and weary, came and sat under our tree. He has no mother to bring him milk, no wife to grind his corn. Let us pity the white man, no mother has he,'" etc., etc.[9]

Perhaps I may be pardoned the intrusion, just here, of my own personal experience. During a residence of nigh twenty years in West Africa, I saw the beauty and felt the charm of the native female character. I saw the native woman in her *heathen* state, and was delighted to see, in numerous tribes, that extraordinary sweetness, gentleness, docility, modesty, and especially those material solicitudes which make every African boy both gallant and defender of his mother.

I saw her in her *civilised* [sic] state, in Sierra Leone; saw precisely the same characteristics, but heightened, dignified, refined, and sanctified by the training of the schools, the refinements of civilization, and the graces of Christian sentiment and feeling. Of all the memories of foreign travel there are none more delightful than those of the families and the female friends of Freetown.

A French traveler speaks with great admiration of the black ladies of Hayti. "In the towns," he says, "I met all the charms of civilized life. The graces of the ladies of Port-au-Prince will never be effaced from my recollections."*

It was, without doubt, the instant discernment of these fine and tender qualities which prompted the touching Sonnet of Wordsworth, written in

---

[9] From Mungo Park's incredibly popular and influential *Travels in the Interior Districts of Africa* (1799).

1802, on the occasion of the cruel exile of Negroes from France by the French Government:

> Driven from the soil of France, a female came
>   From Calais with us, brilliant in array,
>   A Negro woman like a lady gay,
> Yet downcast as a woman fearing blame;
>   Meek, destitute, as seemed, of hope or aim
>   She sat, from notice turning not away,
> But on all proffered intercourse did lay
>   A weight of languid speech—or at the same
> Was silent, motionless in eyes and face.
>   Meanwhile those eyes retained their tropic fire,
>   Which burning independent of the mind,
>   Joined with the luster of her rich attire
> To mock the outcast—O ye heavens be kind!
> And feel thou earth for this afflicted race!*

But I must remember that I am to speak not only of the neglects of the black woman, but also of her needs. And the consideration of her needs suggests the remedy which should be used for the uplifting of this woman from a state of brutality and degradation.

I have two or three plans to offer which, I feel assured, if faithfully used, will introduce widespread and ameliorating influences amid this large population.

(a) The *first* of these is specially adapted to the adult female population of the South, and is designed form more immediate effect. I ask for the equipment and the mission of "sisterhoods" to the black women of the South. I wish to see large numbers of practical Christian women, women of intelligence and piety; women well trained in domestic economy; women who combine delicate sensibility and refinement with industrial acquaintance— scores of which women to go South; to enter every Southern State; to visit "Uncle Tom's Cabin"; to sit down with "Aunt Chloe" and her daughters[10]; to show and teach them the ways and habits of thrift, economy, neatness, and

---

[10] Aunt Chloe is Uncle Tom's wife in Harriet Beecher Stowe's *Uncle Tom's Cabin*. She became a model of black southern womanhood for several decades following the novel's publication. See Frances E. W. Harper's Aunt Chole poems in *Sketches of Southern Life* (1872).

order; to gather them into "Mothers' Meetings" and sewing schools; and by both lectures and "talks" guide these women and their daughters into the modes and habits of clean and orderly housekeeping.

There is no other way, it seems to me, to bring about this domestic revolution.—We cannot postpone this reformation to another generation. Postponement is the reproduction of the same evils in numberless daughters now coming up into life, imitators of the crude and untidy habits of their neglected mothers, and the perpetuation of plantation life to another generation. No, the effort must be made immediately, in *this* generation, with the rude, rough, neglected women of the times.

And it is to be done at their own homes, in their own huts. In this work all theories are useless. This is a practical need, and personal as practical. It is emphatically a personal work. It is to be done by example. The "Sister of Mercy," putting aside all fastidiousness, is to enter the humble and, perchance repulsive cabin of her black sister, and gaining her confidence, is to lead her out of the crude, disordered, and miserable ways of her plantation life into neatness, cleanliness, thrift, and self-respect. In every community women could be found who would gladly welcome such gracious visitations and instructors, and seize with eagerness their lessons and teachings. Soon their neighbors would seek the visitations which had lifted up friends and kinsfolk from inferiority and wretchedness. And then, erelong, whole communities would crave the benediction of these inspiring sisterhoods, and thousands and tens of thousands would hail the advent of these missionaries in their humble cabins. And then the seed of a new and orderly life planted in a few huts and localities, it would soon spread abroad, through the principle of imitation, and erelong, like the Banyan-tree, the beneficent work would spread far and wide through large populations. Doubtless they would be received, first of all, with surprise, for neither they nor their mothers, for two hundred years, have ever known the solicitudes of the great and cultivated for their domestic comfort. But surprise would soon give way to joy and exultation. Mrs. Fanny Kemble Butler, in her work, "Journal of a Residence on a Georgian Plantation in 1838–39," tells us of the amazement of the wretched slave women on her husband's plantation when she went among them, and tried to improve their quarters and to raise them above squalor; and then of their immediate joy and gratitude.[11]

---

[11] Frances Anne Kimble (Butler) (1809–1893) was an English actress and abolitionist whose *Journal of a Residence on a Georgian Plantation in 1838–1839* (1863) remains a vital resource for its observations of daily life on plantation, especially of enslaved black women.

There is nothing original in the suggestion I make for the "Sisters of Mercy." It is no idealistic and impractical scheme I am proposing, no new-fangled notion that I put before you. The Roman Catholic Church has, for centuries, been employing the agency of women in the propagation of her faith and has dispensers of charity. The Protestants of Germany are noted for the effective labors of holy women, not only in the Fatherland but in some of the most successful missions among the heathen in modern times. The Church of England, in that remarkable revival which has lifted her up as by a tidal wave, from the dead passivity of the last century, to an apostolic zeal and fervor never before known in her history, has shown, as one of her main characteristics, the wonderful power of "Sisterhoods," not only in the conversion of reprobates, but in the reformation of whole districts of abandoned men and women. This agency has been one of the most effective instrumentalities in the hands of that special school of devoted men called "Ritualists."[12] Women of every class in that Church, many of humble birth, and as many more from the ranks of the noble, have left home and friends and the choicest circles of society, and given up their lives to the lowliest service of the poor and miserable. They have gone down into the very slums of her great cities, among thieves and murderers and harlots; amid filth and disease and pestilence; and for Christ's sake served and washed and nursed the most repulsive wretches; and then have willingly laid down and died, either exhausted by their labors or poisoned by infectious disease. Anyone who will read the life of "Sister Dora"[13] and of Charles Lowder,[14] will see the glorious illustrations of my suggestion. Why can not this be done for the black women of the South?

(b) My *second* suggestion is as follows, and it reaches over to the future. I am anxious for a permanent and uplifting civilization to be engrafted on the Negro race in this land. And this can only be secured through the womanhood of a race. If you want the civilization of a people to reach the very best elements of their being, and then, having reached them, there to abide, as an indigenous principle, you must imbue the *womanhood* of that people with all its elements and qualities. Any movement which passes by the female sex is

---

[12] Ritualism was a major nineteenth-century movement in the Anglican Church for a revival of greater emphasis on ritual practice in worship.

[13] Dorothy Wyndlow Pattison (1832–1878) was an Anglican nurse and member of the Sister of the Good Samaritan Order.

[14] Charles Lowder (1820–1880) was a cofounder of The Society of the Holy Cross in 1855, a society for Anglo-Catholic priests.

an ephemeral thing. Without them, no true nationality, patriotism, religion, cultivation, family life, or true social status is a possibility. In *this* matter it takes *two* to make one—mankind is a duality. The *male* may bring, as an exotic, a foreign graft, say of a civilization, to a new people. But what then? Can a graft live or thrive of itself? By no manner of means. It must get vitality from the *stock* into which it is put; and it is the women who give the sap to every human organization which thrives and flourishes on earth. I plead, therefore, for the establishment of at least one large "INDUSTRIAL SCHOOL" in every Southern State for the black girls of the South. I ask for the establishment of schools which may serve especially the *home* life of the rising womanhood of my race. I am not soliciting for these girls scholastic institutions, seminaries for the cultivation of elegance, conservatories of music, and schools of classical and artistic training. I want such schools and seminaries for women of my race as much as any other race; and I am glad that there are such schools and colleges, and that scores of colored women are students within their walls.

But this higher style of culture is not what I am aiming after for *this* great need. I am seeking something humbler, more home-like and practical, in which the education of the hand and the use of the body shall be the specialties, and where the intellectual training will be the incident.

Let me state just here definitely what I want for the black girls of the South[15]:

1. I want boarding-schools for the *industrial training* of one hundred and fifty or two hundred of the poorest girls, of the ages of twelve to eighteen years.
2. I wish the *intellectual* training to be limited to reading, writing, arithmetic, and geography.
3. I would have these girls taught to do accurately all domestic work, such as sweeping floors, dusting rooms, scrubbing, bed making, washing and ironing, sewing, mending, and knitting.
4. I would have the trades of dressmaking, millinery, straw-platting, tailoring for men, and such like, taught them.

---

[15] The six objectives in Crummell's list align with the industrial-entrepreneurial aims Stewart outlines in her Franklin Hall address. Stewart, "Lecture, Delivered at the Franklin Hall," 79–84.

5. The art of cooking should be made a specialty, and every girl should be instructed in it.
6. In connection with these schools garden plats should be cultivated, and every girl should be required, daily, to spend at least an hour in learning the cultivation of small fruits, vegetables, and flowers.

I am satisfied that the expense of establishing such schools would be insignificant. As to their maintenance, there can be no doubt that, rightly managed, they would in a brief time be self-supporting. Each school would soon become a hive of industry, and a source of income. But the *good* they would do is the main consideration. Suppose that the time of a girl's schooling be limited to *three*, or perchance to *two* years. It is hardly possible to exaggerate either the personal family or society influence which would flow from these schools. Every class, yea, every girl in an outgoing class, would be a missionary of thrift, industry, common sense, and practicality. They would go forth, year by year, a leavening power into the houses, towns, and villages of the Southern black population; girls fit to be thrifty wives of the honest peasantry of the South, the worthy matrons of their numerous households.

I am looking after the domestic training of the MASSES; for the raising up women meet to be the helpers of *poor* men, the RANK AND FILE of black society, all through the rural districts of the South. The city people and the wealthy can seek more ambitious schools, and should pay for them.

Ladies and gentlemen, since the day of emancipation millions of dollars have been given by the generous Christian people of the North for the intellectual training of the black race in this land. Colleges and universities have been built in the South, and hundreds of youth have been gathered within their walls. The work of your own Church in this regard has been magnificent and unrivaled, and the results which have been attained have been grand and elevating to the entire Negro race in America. The complement to all this generous and ennobling effort is the elevation of the black woman. Up to this day and time your noble philanthropy has touched, for the most part, the male population of the South, given them superiority, and stimulated them to higher aspirations. But a true civilization can only then be attainted when the life of woman is reached, her whole being permeated by noble ideas, her fine taste enriched by culture, her tendencies to the beautiful gratified and developed, her singular and delicate nature lifted up to its full capacity, and then, when all these qualities are fully matured, cultivated, and sanctified; all their sacred influences shall circle around ten thousand firesides, and the cabins of the humblest freedmen shall become the homes of Christian refinement and of domestic elegance through the influence and the charm of the uplifted and cultivated black woman of the South!

5

Anna Julia Cooper, "Womanhood: A Vital Element in the Regeneration and Progress of a Race"

The two sources from which, perhaps, modern civilization has derived its noble and ennobling ideal of woman are Christianity and the feudal system.[1]

In Oriental countries woman has been uniformly devoted to a life of ignorance, infamy, and complete stagnation. The Chinese shoe of to-day does not more entirely dwarf, cramp, and destroy her physical powers, than have the customs, laws, and social instincts, which from remotest ages have governed our Sister of the East, enervated and blighted her mental and moral life.[2]

Mahomet makes no account of woman whatever in his polity. The Koran, which, unlike our Bible, was a product and not a growth, tried to address itself to the needs of Arabian civilization as Mahomet with his circumscribed powers saw them. The Arab was a nomad. Home to him meant his present camping place. That deity who, according to our western ideals, makes and sanctifies the home, was to him a transient bauble to be toyed with so long as it gave pleasure and then to be thrown aside for a new one. As a personality, an individual soul, capable of eternal growth and unlimited development, and destined to mould and shape the civilization of the future to an incalculable extent, Mahomet did not know woman. There was no hereafter, no paradise for her. The heaven of the Mussulman is peopled and made gladsome not by the departed wife, or sister, or mother, but by *houri*[3]—a figment

---

[1] Cooper does not frame the progress of civilizations by way of the philosophy and culture of classical antiquity, as had been dominant in antebellum discourse. Instead, she draws more on recent European civilizations and history, a rhetorical hallmark of fin-de-siècle (African) American thought.

[2] Cooper's criticism of "Oriental" societies is part of a broader rhetoric of exclusion and inclusion. Advocates for full citizenship and social integration of African Americans often juxtaposed the Americanness of African Americans with the perception of Chinese and other Asian immigrants as thoroughly foreign.

[3] "A nymph of the Muslim Paradise. Hence applied allusively to voluptuously beautiful women" (OED).

of Mahomet's brain, partaking of the ethereal qualities of angels, yet imbued with all the vices and inanity of oriental women. The harem here, and—"dust to dust" hereafter, this was the hope, the inspiration, the *summum bonum*[4] of the Eastern woman's life! With what result on the life of the nation, the "Unspeakable Turk,"[5] the "sick man"[6] of modern Europe can to-day exemplify.

Says a certain writer: "The private life the Turk is vilest of the vile, unprogressive, unambitious, and inconceivably low." And yet Turkey is not without her great men. She has produced most brilliant minds; men skilled in all the intricacies of diplomacy and statesmanship; men whose intellects could grapple with the deep problems of empire and manipulate the subtle agencies which check-mate kings. But these minds were not the normal outgrowth of a healthy trunk. They seemed rather ephemeral excrescencies which shoot far out with all the vigor and promise, apparently, of strong branches; but soon alas fall into decay and ugliness because there is no soundness in the root, no life-giving sap, permeating, strengthening and perpetuating the whole. There is a worm at the core! The homelife is impure! and when we look for fruit, like apples of Sodom, it crumbles within our grasp into dust and ashes.

It is pleasing to turn from this effete and immobile civilization to a society still fresh and vigorous, whose seed is in itself, and whose very name is synonymous with all that is progressive, elevating and inspiring, viz., the European bud and the American flower of modern civilization.

And here let me say parenthetically that our satisfaction in American institutions rests not on the fruition we now enjoy, but springs rather from the possibilities and promise that are inherent in the system, though as yet, perhaps, far in the future.

"Happiness," says Madame de Stael,[7] "consists not in perfections attained, but in a sense of progress, the result of our own endeavor under conspiring

---

[4] A Latin term denoting the "highest or supreme good, as the ultimate goal according to which values and priorities are established in an ethical system" (OED).

[5] Scholars attribute this phrase to Thomas Carlyle who, in 1876, wrote that "The unspeakable Turk should be immediately struck out of the question, and the country be left to honest European guidance" in a letter on the Balkan crisis of 1875–1878. The phrase was used in articles and cartoons to describe Turkish rulers.

[6] Scholars attribute this phrase to Czar Nicholas I, who described the declining Ottoman Empire as "a sick man" in 1853.

[7] Anne Louise Germaine de Staël-Holstein (1766–1817) was a political theorist and novelist who censured Napoleon and harbored his critics. Napoleon exiled her as a result.

circumstances *toward* a goal which continually advances and broadens and deepens till it is swallowed up in the Infinite." Such conditions in embryo are all that we claim for the land of the west. We have not yet reached our ideal in American civilization. The pessimists even declare that we are not marching in that direction. But there can be no doubt that here in America is the arena in which the next triumph of civilization is to be won; and here too we find promise abundant and possibilities infinite.

Now let us see on what basis this hope for our country primarily and fundamentally rests. Can any one doubt that it is chiefly on the homelife and on the influence of good women in those homes? Says Macaulay[8]: "You may judge a nation's rank in the scale of civilization from the way they treat their women." And Emerson, "I have thought that a sufficient measure of civilization is the influence of good women."[9] Now this high regard for woman, this germ of a prolific idea which in our own day is bearing such rich and varied fruit, was ingrafted into European civilization, we have said, from two sources, the Christian Church and the Feudal System. For although the Feudal System can in no sense be said to have originated the idea, yet there can be no doubt that the habits of life and modes of thought to which Feudalism gave rise, materially fostered and developed it; for they gave us chivalry, than which no institution has more sensibly magnified and elevated woman's position in society.

Tacitus dwells on the tender regard for woman entertained by these rugged barbarians before they left their northern homes to overrun Europe.[10] Old Norse legends too, and primitive poems, all breathe the same spirit of love of home and veneration for the pure and noble influence there presiding—the wife, the sister, the mother.

And when later on we see the settled life of the middle ages "oozing out," as M. Guizot[11] expresses it, from the plundering and pillaging life of barbarism

---

[8] Thomas Babington Macaulay (1800–1859) was an English historian and essayist.

[9] Ralph Waldo Emerson (1803–1882) was a US philosopher and leading figure of transcendentalism. The quote comes from a lecture he gave in the midst of US Civil War called "American Civilization" (1862).

[10] Nineteenth-century feminists and other social reformers frequently cited the Roman historian Tacitus whose historiography explained how and why women were consulted on matters of governance and politics at the time of the Roman Empire.

[11] Cooper is almost certainly referencing François Guizot's *Histoire de la Civilisation en Europe* (1830). Guizot (1787–1874) was help several posts in the French government, including prime minister, and wrote a number of European histories that were popular on the continent and in the United Kingdom.

and crystallizing into the feudal system, the tiger of the field is brought once more within the charmed circle of the goddesses of his castle, and his imagination weaves around them a halo whose reflection possibly has not yet altogether vanished.

It is true the spirit of Christianity had not yet put the seal of catholicity on this sentiment. Chivalry, according to Bascom, was but the toning down and softening of a rough and lawless period. It gave a roseate glow to a bitter winter's day. Those who looked out from castle windows revelled in its "amethyst tints."[12] But god's poor, the weak, the unlovely, the commonplace were still freezing and starving none the less, in unpitied, unrelieved loneliness.

Respect for woman, the much[-]lauded chivalry of the Middle Ages, meant what I fear it still means to some men in our own day—respect for the elect few among whom they expect to consort.

The idea of the radical amelioration of womankind, reverence for woman as woman regardless of rank, wealth, or culture, was to come from that rich and bounteous fountain from which flow all our liberal and universal ideas—the Gospel of Jesus Christ.

And yet the Christian Church at the time of which we have been speaking would seem to have been doing even less to protect and elevate woman than the little done by secular society. The Church as an organization committed a double offense against woman in the Middle Ages. Making of marriage a sacrament and at the same time insisting on the celibacy of the clergy and other religious orders, she gave an inferior if not an impure character to the marriage relation, especially fitted to reflect discredit on woman. Would this were all or the worst! but the Church by the licentiousness of its chosen servants invaded the household and established too often as vicious connections those relations which it forbade to assume openly and in good faith. "Thus," to use the words of our authority, "the religious corps became as numerous, as searching, and as unclean as the frogs of Egypt, which penetrated into all quarters, into the ovens and kneading troughs, leaving their filthy trail wherever they went."[13] Says Chaucer with characteristic satire, speaking of the friars:

---

[12] John Bascom (1827–1911) was an influential educator and president of the University of Wisconsin. Cooper quotes from his *Philosophy of English Literature* (1874), a series of lectures he gave at the Lowell Institute.

[13] This quote is also from Bascom's *Philosophy of English Literature* (1874).

> Women may now go safely up and doun,
> In every bush, and under every tree,
> Ther is non other incubus but he,
> And he ne will don hem no dishonour.[14]

Henry, Bishop of Liege, could unblushingly boast the birth of twenty-two children in fourteen years.*

It may help us under some of the perplexities which beset our way in "the one Catholic and Apostolic Church" to-day, to recall some of the corruptions and incongruities against which the Bride of Christ has had to struggle in her past history and in spite of which she has kept, through many vicissitudes, the faith once delivered to the saints. Individuals, organizations, whole sections of the church militant may outrage the Christ whom they profess, may ruthlessly trample under foot both the spirit and the letter of his precepts, yet not till we hear the voices audibly saying "Come let us depart hence," shall we cease to believe and cling to the promise, "*I am with you to the end of the world.*"

> Yet saints their watch are keeping,
> The cry goes up "How long!"
> And soon the night of weeping
> Shall be the morn of song.[15]

However much then the facts of any particular period of history may seem to deny it, I for one do not doubt that the source of the vitalizing principle of woman's development and amelioration is the Christian Church, so far as that church is coincident with Christianity.

Christ gave ideals not formulas. The Gospel is a germ requiring millennia for its growth and ripening. It needs and at the same time helps to form around itself a soil enriched in civilization, and perfected in culture and insight without which the embryo can neither be unfolded or comprehended. With all the strides our civilization has made from the first to the nineteenth century, we can boast not an idea, not a principle of action, not a progressive social force but was already mutely foreshadowed, or directly enjoined in

---

[14] From "The Wife of Bath's Tale" in *The Canterbury Tales*.
[15] From Samuel John Stone's hymn "The Church's One Foundation" (1866).

that simple tale of a meek and lowly life. The quiet face of the Nazarene is ever seen a little way ahead, never too far to come down to and touch the life of the lowest in days the darkest, yet ever leading onward, still onward, the tottering childish feet of our strangely boastful civilization.

By laying down for woman the same code of morality, the same standard of purity, as for man; by refusing to countenance the shameless and equally guilty monsters who were gloating over her fall,—graciously stooping in all the majesty of his own spotlessness to wipe away the filth and grime of her guilty past and bid her go in peace and sin no more; and again in the moments of his own careworn and footsore dejection, turning trustfully and lovingly, away from the heartless snubbing and sneers, away from the cruel malignity of mobs and prelates in the dusty marts of Jerusalem to the ready sympathy, loving appreciation and unfaltering friendship of that quiet home at Bethany; and even at the last, by his dying bequest to the disciple whom he loved, signifying the protection and tender regard to be extended to that sorrowing mother and ever afterward to the sex she represented;—throughout his life and in his death he has given to men a rule and guide for the estimation of woman as an equal, as a helper, as a friend, and as a sacred charge to be sheltered and cared for with a brother's love and sympathy, lessons which nineteen centuries' gigantic strides in knowledge, arts, and sciences, in social and ethical principles have not been able to probe to their depth or to exhaust in practice.

It seems not too much to say then of the vitalizing, regenerating, and progressive influence of womanhood on the civilization of today, that, while it was foreshadowed among Germanic nations in the far away dawn of their history as a narrow, sickly and stunted growth, it yet owes its catholicity and power, the deepening of its roots and broadening of its branches to Christianity.

The union of these two forces, the Barbaric and the Christian, was not long delayed after the Fall of the Empire. The church, which fell with Rome, finding herself in danger of being swallowed up by barbarism, with characteristic vigor and fertility of resources, addressed herself immediately to the task of conquering her conquer[o]rs. The means chosen does credit to her power of penetration and adaptability, as well as to her profound, un-erring, all-compassing diplomacy; and makes us even now wonder if aught human can successfully and ultimately withstand her far-seeing designs and brilliant policy, or gainsay her well-earned claim to the word *Catholic*.

She saw the barbarian, little more developed than a wild beast. She forbore to antagonize and mystify his warlike nature by a full blaze of the heartsearching and humanizing tenets of her great head. She said little of the rule "If thy brother smite thee on one cheek, turn to him the other also"; but thought it sufficient for the needs of those times, to establish the so-called "Truce of God" under which men were bound to abstain from butchering one another for three days of each week and on Church festivals. In other words, she respected their individuality: non-resistance pure and simple being for them an utter impossibility, she contented herself with less radical measures calculated to lead up finally to the full measure of the benevolence of Christ.

Next she took advantage of the barbarian's sensuous love of gaudy display and put all her magnificent garments on. She could not capture him by physical force, she would dazzle him by gorgeous spectacles. It is said that Romanism gained more in pomp and ritual during this trying period of the dark ages than throughout all her former history.

The result was she carried her point. Once more Rome laid her ambitions hand on the temporal power, and allied with Charlemagne, aspired to rule the world through a civilization dominated by Christianity and permeated by the traditions and instincts of those sturdy barbarians.

Here was the confluence of the two streams we have been tracing, which, united now, stretch before us as a broad majestic river. In regard to woman it was the meeting of two noble and ennobling forces, two kindred ideas the resultant of which, we doubt not, is destined to be a potent force in the betterment of the world.

Now after our appeal to history comparing nations destitute of this force and so destitute also of the principle of progress, with other nations among whom the influence of woman is prominent coupled with a brisk, progressive, satisfying civilization,—if in addition we find this strong presumptive evidence corroborated by reason and experience, we may conclude that these two equally varying concomitants are linked as cause and effect; in other words, that the position of woman in society determines the vital elements of its regeneration and progress.

Now that this is so on a priori grounds all must admit. And this not because woman is better or stronger or wiser than man, but from the nature of the case, because it is she who must first form the man by directing the earliest impulses of his character.

Byron and Wordsworth were both geniuses and would have stamped themselves on the thought of their age under any circumstances; and yet we find the one a savor of life unto life, the other of death unto death. "Byron, like a rocket, shot his way upward with scorn and repulsion, flamed out in wild, explosive, brilliant excesses and disappeared in darkness made all the more palpable."*16

Wordsworth lent of his gifts to reinforce that "power in the universe which makes for righteousness"[17] by taking the harp handed him from heaven and using it to swell the strains of angelic choirs. Two locomotives equally mighty stand facing opposite tracks; the one to rush headlong to destruction with all its precious freight, the other to toil grandly and gloriously up the steep embattlements to heaven and to God. Who—who can say what a world of consequences hung on the first placing and starting of these enormous forces!

Woman, Mother,—your responsibility is one that might make angels tremble and fear to take hold! To trifle with it, to ignore or misuse it, is to treat lightly the most sacred and solemn trust ever confided by God to human kind. The training of children is a task on which an infinity of weal or woe depends. Who does not covet it? Yet who does not stand awe-struck before its momentous issues! It is a matter of small moment, it seems to me, whether that lovely girl in whose accomplishments you take such pride and delight, can enter the gay and crowded salon with the ease and elegance of this or that French or English gentlewoman, compared with the decision as to whether her individuality is going to reinforce the good or the evil elements of the world. The lace and the diamonds, the dance and the theater, gain a new significance when scanned in their bearings on such issues. Their influence on the individual personality, and through her on the society and civilization which she vitalizes and inspires—all this and more must be weighed in the balance before the jury call return a just and intelligent verdict as to the innocence or banefulness of these apparently simple amusements.

Now the fact of woman's influence on society being granted, what are its practical bearings on the work which brought together this conference of colored clergy and laymen in Washington? "We come not here to talk." Life is too busy, too pregnant with meaning and far[-]reaching consequences to allow you to come this far for mere intellectual entertainment.

The vital agency of womanhood in the regeneration and progress of a race, as a general question, is conceded almost before it is fairly stated. I confess one of the difficulties for me in the subject assigned lay in its obviousness. The plea is taken away by the opposite attorney's granting the whole question.

---

[16] From Bascom's *Philosophy of English Literature*.

[17] A slightly altered quotation from cultural critic and poet Matthew Arnold's *Literature and Dogma* (1873).

"Woman's influence on social progress"—who in Christendom doubts or questions it? One may as well be called on to prove that, the sun is the source of light and heat and energy to this many-sided little world.

Nor, on the other hand, could it have been intended that I should apply the position when taken and proven, to the needs and responsibilities of the women of our race in the South. For is it not written, "Cursed is he that cometh after the king?" And has not the king already preceded me in "The Black Woman of the South"?*

They have had both Moses and the Prophets in Dr. Crummell and if they hear not him, neither would they be persuaded though one came up from the South.

I would beg, however, with the Doctor's permission, to add my plea for the *Colored Girls* of the South[18]:—that large, bright, promising fatally beautiful class that stand shivering like a delicate plantlet before the fury of tempestuous elements, so full of promise and possibilities, yet so sure of destruction; often without a father to whom they dare apply the loving term, often without a stronger brother to espouse their cause and defend their honor with his life's blood; in the midst of pitfalls and snares, waylaid by the lower classes of white men, with no shelter, no protection nearer than the great blue vault above, which half conceals and half reveals the one care-taker they know so little of. Oh, save them, help them, shield, train, develop, teach, inspire them! Snatch them, in God's name, as brands from the burning! There is material in them well worth your while, the hope in germ of a staunch, helpful, regenerating womanhood on which, primarily, rests the foundation stones of our future as a race.

It is absurd to quote statistics showing the Negro's bank account and rent rolls, to point to the hundreds of newspapers edited by colored men and lists of lawyers, doctors, professors, D. D's, LL D's, etc., etc., etc., while the source from which the life-blood of the race is to flow is subject to taint and corruption in the enemy's camp.

True progress is never made by spasms. Real progress is growth. It must begin in the seed. Then, "First the blade, then the ear, after that the full corn in the ear."[19] There is something to encourage and inspire us in the advancement

---

[18] Considering her direct reference to Crummell's essay, her use of "colored" here parallels Crummell's usage, which refers only to mixed women, not the general demographic of black women. Unlike the class of colored girls Crummell describes in "The Black Woman of the South" (Stewart, 44–45), those Cooper describes do not have elite or wealthy white relations to protect, educate, or empower them.

[19] From Mark 4:28, this image connotes a theory of gradual yet steady progress.

of individuals since their emancipation from slavery. It at least proves that there is nothing irretrievably wrong in the shape of the black man's skull, and that under given circumstances his development, downward or upward, will be similar to that of other average human beings.

But there is no time to be wasted in mere felicitation. That the Negro has his niche in the infinite purposes of the Eternal, no one who has studied the history of the last fifty years in America will deny. That much depends on his own right comprehension of his responsibility and rising to the demands of the hour, it will be good for him to see; and how best to use his present so that the structure of the future shall be stronger and higher and brighter and nobler and holier than that of the past, is a question to be decided each day by every one of us.

The race is just twenty-one years removed from the conception and experience of a chattel, just at the age of ruddy manhood. It is well enough to pause a moment for retrospection, introspection, and prospection. We look back, not to become inflated with conceit because of the depths from which we have arisen, but that we may learn wisdom from experience. We look within that we may gather together once more our forces, and, by improved and more practical methods, address ourselves to the tasks before us. We look forward with hope and trust that the same God whose guiding hand led our fathers through and out of the gall and bitterness of oppression, will still lead and direct their children, to the honor of his name, and for their ultimate salvation.

But this survey of the failures or achiev[e]ments of the past, the difficulties and embarrassments of the present, and the mingled hopes and fears for the future, must not degenerate into mere dreaming nor consume the time which belongs to the practical and effective handling of the crucial questions of the hour; and there can be no issue more vital and momentous than this of the womanhood of the race.

Here is the vulnerable point, not in the heel, but at the heart of the young Achilles; and here must the defenses be strengthened and the watch redoubled.

We are the heirs of a past which was not our fathers' moulding. "Every man the arbiter of his own destiny" was not true for the American Negro of the past: and it is no fault of his that he finds himself to-day the inheritor of a manhood and womanhood impoverished and debased by two centuries and more of compression and degradation.

But weaknesses and malformations, which to-day are attributable to a vicious schoolmaster and a pernicious system, will a century hence be rightly regarded as proofs of innate corruptness and radical incurability.

Now the fundamental agency under God in the regeneration, the retraining of the race, as well as the ground work and starting point of its progress upward, must be the *black woman*.

With all the wrongs and neglects of her past, with all the weakness, the debasement, the moral thralldom of her present, the black woman of to-day stands mute and wondering at the Herculean task devolving around her. But the cycles wait for her. No other hand can move the lever. She must be loosed from her bands and set to work.

Our meager and superficial results from past efforts prove their futility; and every attempt to elevate the Negro, whether undertaken by himself or through the philanthropy of others, cannot but prove abortive unless so directed as to utilize the indispensable agency of an elevated and trained womanhood.

A race cannot be purified from without. Preachers and teachers are helps, and stimulants and conditions as necessary as the gracious rain and sunshine are to plant growth. But what are rain and dew and sunshine and cloud if there be no life in the plant germ? We must go to the root and see that it is sound and healthy and vigorous; and not deceive ourselves with waxen flowers and painted leaves of mock chlorophyll.

We too often mistake individuals' honor for race development and so are ready to substitute pretty accomplishments for sound sense and earnest purpose.

A stream cannot rise higher than its source. The atmosphere of homes is no rarer and purer and sweeter than are the mothers in those homes. A race is but a total of families. The nation is the aggregate of its homes. As the whole is sum of all its parts, so the character of the parts will determine the characteristics of the whole. These are all axioms and so evident that it seems gratuitous to remark it; and yet, unless I am greatly mistaken, most of the unsatisfaction from our past results arises from just such a radical and palpable error, as much almost on our own part as on that of our benevolent white friends.

The Negro is constitutionally hopeful and proverbially irrepressible; and naturally stands in danger of being dazzled by the shimmer and tinsel of superficials. We often mistake foliage for fruit and overestimate or wrongly estimate brilliant results.

The late Martin R. Delany, who was an unadulterated black man, used to say when honors of state fell upon him, that when he entered the council of kings the black race entered with him; meaning, I suppose, that there was no discounting his race identity and attributing his achievements to some admixture of Saxon blood. But our present record of eminent men, when placed beside the actual status of the race in America to-day, proves that no man can represent the race. Whatever the attainments of the individual may be, unless his home has moved on *pari passu*, he can never be regarded as identical with or representative of the whole.

Not by pointing to sun-bathed mountain tops do we prove that Phoebus warms the valleys. We must point to homes, average homes, homes of the rank and file of horny handed toiling men and women of the South (where the masses are) lighted and cheered by the good, the beautiful, and the true,—then and not till then will the whole plateau be lifted into the sunlight.

Only the BLACK WOMAN can say "when and where I enter, in the quiet, undisputed dignity of my womanhood, without violence and without suing or special patronage, then and there the whole *Negro race enters with me*." Is it not evident then that as individual workers for this race we must address ourselves with no half-hearted zeal to this feature of our mission[?] The need is felt and must be recognized by all. There is a call for workers, for missionaries, for men and women with the double consecration of a fundamental love of humanity and a desire for its melioration through the Gospel; but superadded to this we demand an intelligent and sympathetic comprehension of the interests and special needs of the Negro.

I see not why there should not be an organized effort for the protection and elevation of our girls such as the White Cross League in England. English women are strengthened and protected by more than twelve centuries of Christian influences, freedom and civilization; English girls are dispirited and crushed down by no such all-levelling prejudice as that supercilious caste spirit in America which cynically assumes "A Negro woman cannot be a lady." English womanhood is beset by no such snares and traps as betray the unprotected, untrained colored girl of the south, whose only crime and dire destruction often is her unconscious and marvelous beauty. Surely then if English indignation is aroused and English manhood thrilled under the leadership of a Bishop of the English church to build up bulwarks around their wronged sisters, negro sentiment cannot remain callous and negro effort nerveless in view of the imminent peril of the mothers of the next generation. "*I am my sister's keeper!*" should be the hearty response of every man and woman of the race, and this conviction should purify and exalt the narrow, selfish and petty personal aims of life into a noble and sacred purpose.

We need men who can let their interest and gallantry extend outside the circle of their aesthetic appreciation; men who can be a father, a brother, a friend to every weak, struggling unshielded girl. We need women who are so sure of their own social footing that they need not fear leaning to lend a hand to a fallen or falling sister. We need men and women who do not exhaust their genius splitting hairs on aristocratic distinctions and thanking god they are not as others; but earnest, unselfish souls, who can go into the highways and byways, lifting up and leading, advising and encouraging with the truly catholic benevolence of the Gospel of Christ.

As Church workers we must confess our path of duty is less obvious; or rather our ability to adapt our machinery to our conception of the peculiar exigencies of this work as taught by experience and our own consciousness of the needs of the Negro, is as yet not demonstrable.[20] Flexibility and aggressiveness are not such strong characteristics of the Church to-day as in the Dark Ages.

As a Mission field for the Church the Southern negro is in some aspects most promising; in others, perplexing. Aliens neither in language and customs, nor in associations and sympathies, naturally of deeply rooted religious instincts and taking most readily and kindly to the worship and teachings of the church, surely the task of proselytizing the American Negro is infinitely less formidable than that which confronted the Church in the Barbarians of Europe. Besides, this people already look to the church as the hope of their race. Thinking colored men almost uniformly admit that the Protestant Episcopal Church with its quiet, chaste dignity and decorous solemnity, its instructive and elevating ritual, its bright chanting and joyous hymning, is eminently fitted to correct the peculiar faults of worship —the rank exuberance and often ludicrous demonstrativeness of their people. Yet, strange to say, the Church, claiming to be missionary and catholic, urging that schism is sin and denominationalism inexcusable, has made in all these years almost no inroads upon this semi-civilized religionism.

---

[20] Cooper's call for colored women to be church workers, which goes well beyond Crummell's educational program for girls, echoes Jarena Lee's desire for women to hold ecclesiastical and clerical offices.

Harvests from this over ripe field of home missions have been gathered in by Methodists, Baptists, and not least by Congregationalists, who were unknown to the freedmen before their emancipation.

Our clergy numbers less than two dozen* priests of Negro blood and we have hardly more than one self-supporting colored congregation in the entire Southland. While the organization known as the A. M. E. Church has 14,063 ministers, itinerant and local, 4,069 self-supporting churches, 4,275 Sunday-schools, with property valued at $7,772,284, raising yearly for church purposes $1,427, 000.

Stranger and more significant than all, the leading men of this race (I do not mean demagogues and politicians, but men of intellect, heart, and race devotion, men to whom the elevation of their people means more than personal ambition and sordid gain—and the men of that stamp have not all died yet) the Christian workers for the race, of younger and more cultured growth, are noticeably drifting into sectarian churches, many of them declaring all the time that they acknowledge the historic claims of the church, believe her apostolicity, and would experience greater personal comfort, spiritual and intellectual, in her revered communion. It is a fact which any one may verify for himself, that representative colored men, professing that in their heart of hearts they are Episcopalians, are actually working in Methodist and Baptist pulpits; while the ranks of the Episcopal clergy are left to be filled largely by men who certainly suggest the propriety of a "*perpetual* Diaconate" if they cannot be said to have created the necessity for it.

Now where is the trouble? Something must be wrong. What is it?

A certain Southern Bishop of our Church reviewing the situation, whether in Godly anxiety or in Gothic antipathy" I know not, deprecates the fact that the colored people do not seem *drawn* to the Episcopal Church, and comes to the sage conclusion that the Church is not adapted to the rude untutored minds of the Freedmen, and that they may be left to go to the Methodists and Baptists whither their racial proclivities undeniably tend. How the good Bishop can agree that all-foreseeing Wisdom, and Catholic love would have framed his Church as typified in his seamless garment and unbroken body, and yet not leave it broad enough and deep enough and loving enough to seek and save and hold seven millions of God's poor, I cannot see.

But the doctors while discussing their scientifically conclusive diagnosis of the disease, will perhaps not think it presumptuous in the patient if he dares to suggest where at least the pain is. If this be allowed, *Black Woman of the South* would beg to point out two possible oversights in this southern work which may indicate in part both a cause and a remedy for some failure. The first is *not calculating for the Black man's personality*; not having respect, if I may so express it, to his manhood or deferring at all to his conceptions of the needs of his people. When colored persons have been employed it was too often as machines or as manikins. There has been no disposition, generally, to get the black man's ideal or to let his individuality work by its own gravity, as it were. A conference of earnest Christian men have met at regular intervals for some years past to discuss the best methods of promoting the welfare and development of colored people in this country. Yet, strange as it may seem, they have never invited a colored man or even intimated that one would be welcome to take part in their deliberations. Their remedial contrivances are purely theoretical or empirical, therefore, and the whole machinery devoid of soul.

The second important oversight in my judgment is closely allied to this and probably grows out of it, and that is not developing Negro womanhood as an essential fundamental for the elevation of the race, and utilizing this agency in extending the work of the Church.

Of the first I have possibly already presumed to say too much since it does not strictly come within the province of my subject. However, Macaulay somewhere criticises the Church of England as not knowing how to use fanatics, and declares that had Ignatius Loyola been in the Anglican instead of the roman communion, the Jesuits would have been schismatics instead of Catholics; and if the religious awakenings of the Wesleys had been in Rome, she would have shaven their heads, tied ropes around their waists, and sent them out under her own banner and blessing. Whether this be true or not, there is certainly a vast amount of force potential for negro evangelization rendered latent, or worse, antagonistic by the halting, uncertain, I had almost said, *trimming* policy of the Church in the South. This may sound both presumptuous and ungrateful. It is mortifying, I know, to benevolent wisdom, after having spent itself in the execution of well conned theories for the ideal development of a particular work, to hear perhaps the weakest and humblest element of that work: asking "what doest thou?"

Yet so it will be in life. The "thus far and no farther" pattern cannot be fitted to any growth in God's kingdom. The universal law of development is "onward and upward." It is God-given and inviolable. From the unfolding of the germ in the acorn to reach the sturdy oak, to the growth of a human soul into the full knowledge and likeness of its Creator, the breadth and scope of the movement in each and all are too grand, too mysterious, too like God himself, to be encompassed and locked down in human molds.

After all the Southern slave owners were right: either the very alphabet of intellectual growth must be forbidden and the Negro dealt with absolutely as a chattel having neither rights nor sensibilities; or else the clamps and irons of mental and moral, as well as civil compression must be riven asunder and the truly enfranchised soul led to the entrance of that boundless vista through which it is to toil upwards to its beckoning God as the buried seed germ to meet the sun.

A perpetual colored diaconate, carefully and kindly superintended by the white clergy; congregations of shiny faced peasants with their clean white aprons and sunbonnets catechised at regular intervals and taught to recite the creed, the Lord's prayer and the ten commandments—duty towards God and duty towards neighbor, surely such well tended sheep ought to be grateful to their shepherds and content in that station of life to which it pleased God to call them. True, like the old professor lecturing to his solitary student, we make no provision here for irregularities. "Questions must be kept till after class," or dispensed with altogether. That some do ask questions and insist on answers, in class too, must be both impertinent and annoying. Let not our spiritual pastors and masters however be grieved at such self-assertion as merely signifies we have a destiny to fulfill and as men and women we must *be about our Father's business.*

It is a mistake to suppose that the Negro is prejudiced against a white ministry. Naturally there is not a more kindly and implicit follower of a white man's guidance than the average colored peasant. What would to others be an ordinary act of friendly or pastoral interest he would be more inclined to regard gratefully as a condescension. And he never forgets such kindness. Could the Negro be brought near to his white priest or bishop, he is not suspicious. He is not only willing but often longs to unburden his soul to this intelligent guide. There are no reservations when he is convinced that you are his friend. It is a saddening satire on American history and manners that it takes something to convince him.

That our people are not "drawn" to a church whose chief dignitaries they see only in the chancel, and whom they reverence as they would a painting or an angel, whose life never comes down to and touches theirs with the inspiration of an objective reality, may be "perplexing" truly (American caste and American Christianity both being facts) but it need not be surprising. There must be something of human nature in it, the same as that which brought about that "the Word was made flesh and dwelt among us" that He might "draw" us towards God.[21]

Men are not "drawn" by abstractions. Only sympathy and love can draw, and until our Church in America realizes this and provides a clergy that can come in touch with our life and have a fellow feeling for our woes, without being imbedded and frozen up in their "Gothic antipathies," the good bishops are likely to continue "perplexed" by the sparsity of colored Episcopalians.

A colored priest of my acquaintance recently related to me, with tears in his eyes, how his reverend Father in god, the Bishop who had ordained him, had met him on the cars on his way to the diocesan convention and warned him, not unkindly, not to take a seat in the body of the convention with the white clergy. To avoid disturbance of their godly placidity he would of cour[s]e please sit back and somewhat apart. I do not imagine that that clergyman had very much heart for the Christly (!) deliberations of that convention.

To return, however, it is not on this broader view of church work, which I mentioned as a primary cause of its halting progress with the colored people, that I am to speak. My proper theme is the second oversight of which in my judgment our Christian propagandists have been guilty: or, the necessity of church training, protecting and uplifting our colored womanhood as indispensable to the evangelization of the race.

Apelles did not disdain even that criticism of his lofty art which came from an uncouth cobbler; and may I not hope that the writer's oneness with her subject both in feeling and in being may palliate undue obtrusiveness of opinions here. That the race cannot be effectually lifted up till its women are truly elevated we take as proven. It is not for us to dwell on the needs, the neglects, and the ways of succor, pertaining to the black woman of the South. The ground has been ably discussed and an admirable and practical plan proposed by the oldest Negro priest in America, advising and urging that special organizations such as Church Sisterhoods and industrial schools be devised to meet her pressing needs in the southland. That some such movements are vital to the life of this people and the extension of the church among them, is not hard to see. Yet the pamphlet fell still-born from the press. So far as I am informed the Church has made no motion towards carrying out Dr. Crummell's suggestion.

---

[21] Cooper quotes John 1:14 to censure her own denomination's inability to attract black people, whereas the Congregationalists, Baptists, and Methodists have been because they are more "like Christ" in their proselytization approach.

The denomination which comes next our own in opposing the proverbial emotionalism of Negro worship in the South, and which in consequence like ours receives the cold shoulder from the old heads, resting as we do under the charge of not "having religion" and not believing in conversion—the Congregationalists—have quietly gone to work on the young, have established industrial and training schools, and now almost every community in the South is yearly enriched by a fresh infusion of vigorous young hearts, cultivated heads, and helpful hands that have been trained at Fisk, at Hampton, in Atlanta university, and in Tuskegee, Alabama.

These young people are missionaries actual or virtual both here and in Africa. They have learned to love the methods and doctrines of the church which trained and educated them; and so congregationalism surely and steadily progresses. Need I compare these well[-]known facts with results shown by the church in the same field and during the same or even a longer time.

The institution of the Church in the South to which she mainly looks for the training of her colored clergy and for the help of the "Black Woman" and "Colored Girl" of the South, has graduated since the year 1868, when the school was founded, *five young women*;* and while yearly numerous young men have been kept and trained for the ministry by the charities of the Church, the number of indigent females who have here been supported, sheltered and trained, is phenomenally small. Indeed, to my mind, the attitude of the Church toward this feature of her work is as if the solution of the problem of Negro missions depended solely on sending a quota of deacons and priests into the field, girls being a sort of *tertium quid* whose development may be promoted if they can pay their way and fall in with the plans mapped out for the training of the other sex. Now I would ask in all earnestness, does not this force potential deserve by education and stimulus to be made dynamic? Is it not a solemn duty incumbent on all colored churchmen to make it so? Will not the aid of the Church be given to prepare our girls in head, heart, and hand for the duties and responsibilities that await the intelligent wife, the Christian mother, the earnest, virtuous, helpful woman, at once both the lever and the fulcrum for uplifting the race.

As Negroes and churchmen we cannot be indifferent to these questions. They touch us most vitally on both sides. We believe in the Holy Catholic Church. We believe that however gigantic and apparently remote the consummation, the Church will go on conquering and to conquer till the kingdoms of this world, not excepting the black man and the black woman of the South, shall have become the kingdoms of the Lord and of his Christ.

That past work in this direction has been unsatisfactory we must admit. That without a change of policy results in the future will be as meagre, we greatly fear. Our life as a race is at stake. The dearest interests of our hearts are in the scales. We must either break away from dear old landmarks and plunge out in any line and every line that enables us to meet the pressing need of our people, or we must ask the church to allow and help us, untrammelled by the prejudices and theories of individuals, to work ag[g]ressively under her direction as we alone can, with god's help, for the salvation of our people.

The time is ripe for action. Self-seeking and ambition must be laid on the altar. The battle is one of sacrifice and hardship, but our duty is plain. We have been recipients of missionary bounty in some sort for twenty-one years. Not even the senseless vegetable is content to be a mere reservoir. Receiving without giving is an anomaly in nature. Nature's cells are all little workshops for manufacturing sunbeams, the product to be *given out* to earth's inhabitants in warmth, energy, thought, action. Inanimate creation always pays back an equivalent.

Now, *How much owest thou my lord?* Will his account be overdrawn if he call for singleness of purpose and self-sacrificing labor for your brethren? Having passed through your drill school, will you refuse a general's commission even if it entail responsibility, risk and anxiety, with possibly some adverse criticism? Is it too much to ask you to step forward and direct the work for your race along those lines which you know to be of first and vital importance?

Will you allow these words of Ralph Waldo Emerson? "In ordinary," says he, "we have a snappish criticism which watches and contradicts the opposite party. We want the will which advances and dictates [acts]. Nature has made up her mind that what cannot defend itself, shall not be defended. Complaining never so loud and with never so much reason, is of no use. What cannot stand must fall; *and the measure of our sincerity and therefore of the respect of men is the amount of health and wealth we will hazard in the defense of our right.*"[22]

*Bascom
*Bascom's Eng. Lit. p. 253.
*Pamphlet published by Dr. Alex. Crummell.

[22] From Emerson's "Courage" in *Society and Solitude* (1870).

*The published report of '91 shows 26 priests for the entire country, including one not engaged in work and one a professor in a non-sectarian school, since made Dean of an Episcopal Annex to Howard University known as King Hall.

*Five have been graduated since '86, two in '91, two in '92.

Stewart's Works

6

Lecture, Delivered at the Franklin Hall, Boston, Sept. 21, 1832.

[Maria W. Stewart, "Lecture Delivered at Franklin Hall" (1832)]

Why sit ye here and die?[1] If we say we will go to a foreign land, the famine and the pestilence are there, and there we shall die.[2] If we sit here, we shall die. Come let us plead our cause before the whites: if they save us alive, we shall live—and if they kill us, we shall but die.

Methinks I heard a spiritual interrogation—"Who shall go forward, and take off the reproach that is cast upon the people of color? Shall it be a woman?"[3] And my heart made this reply—"If it is thy will, be it even so, Lord Jesus!"

I have heard much respecting the horrors of slavery; but may Heaven forbid that the generality of my color throughout these United States should experience any more of its horrors than to be a servant of servants, or hewers of wood and drawers of water![4] Tell us no more of southern slavery; for with few exceptions, although I may be very erroneous in my opinion, yet I consider our condition but little better than that. Yet, after all, methinks there are no chains so galling as those that bind the soul, and exclude it from the vast field of useful and scientific knowledge. O, had I received the advantages of an early education, my ideas would, ere now, have expanded far and wide; but,

---

[1] The New England Antislavery Society frequently held meetings here.

[2] Stewart rejected the colonization movement and black resettlement in West Africa, Haiti, or elsewhere. The leading colonization organization, the American Colonization Society (ACS) founded in 1816, began sending freeborn and once-enslaved black people to what is now Liberia in the early 1820s. Boston abolitionists were among the most vehement opponents of the ACS, and Stewart regularly encountered anti-colonizationist thought in William Lloyd Garrison's *The Liberator*, including by writers like Zillah (Sarah Mapps Douglass) from women's intellectual societies.

[3] Stewart draws attention to the strangeness of her presence on stage as a woman before a promiscuous audience and then draws on histories of black women evangelists justifying their speaking out of place through the calling of God. See Jarena Lee, *Religious Experience and Journal* (Stewart, 195–206) for more of this construction of a religious ethos as justification of women's philosophical voices.

[4] A reference to Joshua 9:23, this idiom refers to menial laborers. After Joshua accuses the Gibeonites of deceiving him, he curses them to a life of drudgery and service to the Israelites.

alas! I possess nothing but moral capability—no teachings but the teachings of the Holy Spirit.

I have asked several individuals of my sex, who transact business for themselves, if providing our girls were to give them the most satisfactory references, they would not be willing to grant them an equal opportunity with others? Their reply has been—for their own part, they had no objection; but as it was not the custom, were they to take them into their employ, they would be in danger of losing the public patronage.

And such is the powerful force of prejudice. Let our girls possess whatever amiable qualities of soul they may; let their characters be fair and spotless as innocence itself; let their natural taste and ingenuity be what they may; it is impossible for scarce an individual of them to rise above the condition of servants. Ah! why is this cruel and unfeeling distinction? Is it merely because God has made our complexion to vary? If it be, O shame to soft, relenting humanity! "Tell it not in Gath! publish it not in the streets of Askelon!" Yet, after all, methinks were the American free people of color to turn their attention more assiduously to moral worth and intellectual improvement, this would be the result: prejudice would gradually diminish, and the whites would be compelled to say, unloose those fetters![5]

Though black their skins as shades of night
Their hearts are pure, their souls are white.[6]

Few white persons of either sex, who are calculated for anything else, are willing to spend their lives and bury their talents in performing mean, servile labor. And such is the horrible idea that I entertain respecting a life of servitude, that if I conceived of their [sic] being no possibility of my rising above the condition of servant, I would gladly hail death as a welcome messenger. O, horrible idea, indeed! to possess noble souls aspiring after high and honorable acquirements, yet confined by the chains of ignorance and poverty to lives of continual drudgery and toil. Neither do I know of any who have enriched themselves by spending their lives as house-domestics, washing windows, shaking carpets, brushing boots, or tending upon gentlemen's

---

[5] Here Stewart encapsulates the rhetorical project of moral suasion, one of the leading approaches to abolition and black citizenship in the period.

[6] This couplet appears in "Religion and the Pure Principles of Morality," but here Stewart uses third-person pronouns instead of second-person pronouns, as in her earlier essay. Stewart may have had in my mind William Blake's famous poem "The Little Black Boy" from his *Songs of Innocence* (1789). Blake opposed slavery, and abolitionists frequently appropriated his verse.

tables.[7] I can but die for expressing my sentiments: and I am as willing to die by the sword as the pestilence; for I am a true born American; your blood flows in my veins, and your spirit fires my breast.

I observed a piece in the Liberator [*sic*] a few months since, stating that the colonizationists had published a work respecting us, asserting that we were lazy and idle. I confute them on that point. Take us generally as a people, we are neither lazy nor idle; and considering how little we have to excite or stimulate us, I am almost astonished that there are so many industrious and ambitious ones to be found; although I acknowledge, with extreme sorrow, that there are some who never were and never will be serviceable to society. And have you not a similar class among yourselves?

Again. It was asserted that we were "a ragged set, crying for liberty."[8] I reply to it, the whites have so long and so loudly proclaimed the theme of equal rights and privileges, that our souls have caught the flame also, ragged as we are. As far as our merit deserves, we feel a common desire to rise above the condition of servants and drudges. I have learnt, by bitter experience, that continual hard labor deadens the energies of the soul, and benumbs the faculties of the mind; the ideas become confined, the mind barren, and, like the scorching sands of Arabia, produces nothing; or like the uncultivated soil, brings forth thorns and thistles.[9]

Again, continual and hard labor irritates our tempers and sours our dispositions; the whole system becomes worn out with toil and fatigue; nature herself becomes almost exhausted, and we care but little whether we live or die. It is true, that the free people of color throughout these United States are neither bought nor sold, nor under the lash of the cruel driver; many obtain a comfortable support; but few, if any, have an opportunity of becoming rich and independent; and the enjoyments we most pursue are as unprofitable to us as the spider's web or the floating bubbles that vanish into

---

[7] Stewart's call for the cultivation of women's full intellectual and spiritual selves here and throughout her writing anticipates Margaret Fuller's groundbreaking feminist philosophy, especially *Woman in the Nineteenth Century* (1845). Like Stewart, she paired the inherent right to intellectual development with liberation from patriarchal control for both women and black people: "If the negro be a soul, if the woman be a soul, apparelled in flesh, to one Master [God] only are they accountable" (26). For Fuller, the "soul" is the intellectual and spiritual self over whose development only God, and distinctly not men, should preside.

[8] This quotation comes from the *African Repository*, vol. 2 (1826), and then is reprinted and glossed extensively in William Lloyd Garrison's pamphlet *Thoughts on African Colonization* (1832). Gardner Jones's galvanizing anti-colonization letters were running on the front page of *The Liberator* at the time of the publication of *Thoughts*. Stewart likely conflated these sources.

[9] See Harriet E. Wilson's *Our Nig* (1859), the most thorough antebellum narrative exploration of the debilitating effects of "hard labor" on the black (female) mind, body, and soul.

air. As servants, we are respected; but let us presume to aspire any higher, our employer regards us no longer. And were it not that the King eternal has declared that Ethiopia shall stretch forth her hands unto God, I should indeed despair.[10]

I do not consider it derogatory, my friends, for persons to live out to service. There are many whose inclination leads them to aspire no higher; and I would highly commend the performance of almost anything for an honest livelihood; but where constitutional strength is wanting, labor of this kind, in its mildest form, is painful. And doubtless many are the prayers that have ascended to Heaven from Afric's daughters for strength to perform their work. Oh, many are the tears that have been shed for the want of that strength![11] Most of our color have dragged out a miserable existence of servitude from the cradle to the grave. And what literary acquirement can be made, or useful knowledge derived, from either maps, books, or charts, by those who continually drudge from Monday morning until Sunday noon? O, ye fairer sisters, whose hands are never soiled, whose nerves and muscles are never strained, go learn by experience! Had we had the opportunity that you have had, to improve our moral and mental faculties, what would have hindered our intellects from being as bright, and our manners from being as dignified as yours? Had it been our lot to have been nursed in the lap of affluence and ease, and to have basked beneath the smiles and sunshine of fortune, should we not have naturally supposed that we were never made to toil? And why are not our forms as delicate, and our constitutions as slender, as yours? Is not the workmanship as curious and complete? Have pity upon us, have pity upon us, O ye who have hearts to feel for other's woes; for the hand of God has touched us. Owing to the disadvantages under which we labor, there are many flowers among us that are

> ... born to bloom unseen
> And waste their fragrance on the desert air.[12]

---

[10] See note 2 in Stewart, "Cause for Encouragement" (175).

[11] In slavery and freedom, black women often worked the same jobs as black men. In the dominant American imagination, their blackness excluded them from the category of true womanhood according to white standards of femininity. Sojourner Truth regularly lectured on the differences between how men treated white women and black women, and in her famous "Aren't I A Woman?" (1851) address at the Women's Rights Convention in Akron, Ohio, she explained how she outworked men in onerous field labor, and her later career was marked by famous incidents in which her labor-strengthened body was read by whites as without gender, once leading her to expose her breasts as proof of her womanhood.

[12] Thomas Gray, "Elegy Written in a Country Churchyard" (1751). "Full many a flow'r is born to blush unseen, / And waste its sweetness on the desert air."

My beloved brethren, as Christ has died in vain for those who will not accept his offered mercy, so will it be vain for the advocates of freedom to spend their breath in our behalf, unless with united hearts and souls you make some mighty efforts to raise your sons and daughters from the horrible state of servitude and degradation in which they are placed. It is upon you that woman depends; she can do but little besides using her influence; and it is for her sake and yours that I have come forward and made myself a hissing and a reproach among the people[13]; for I am also one of the wretched and miserable daughters of the descendants of fallen Africa. Do you ask, why are you wretched and miserable? I reply, look at many of the most worthy and most interesting of us doomed to spend our lives in gentlemen's kitchens. Look at our young men, smart, active and energetic, with souls filled with ambitious fire; if they look forward, alas! What are their prospects? They can be nothing but the humblest laborers, on account of their dark complexions; hence many of them lose their ambition, and become worthless.[14] Look at our middle-aged men, clad in their rusty plaids and coats; in winter, every cent they earn goes to buy their wood and pay their rents; the poor wives also toil beyond their strength, to help support their families. Look at our aged sires, whose heads are whitened with the frosts of seventy winters, with their old wood-saws on their backs. Alas, what keeps us so? Prejudice, ignorance and poverty. But ah! methinks our oppression is soon to come to an end; yea, before the Majesty of heaven, our groans and cries have reached the ears of the Lord of Sabaoth. As the prayers and tears of Christians will avail the finally impenitent nothing; neither will the prayers and tears of the friends of humanity avail us anything, unless we possess a spirit of virtuous emulation within our breasts. Did the pilgrims, when they first landed on these shores, quietly compose themselves and say, "The Britons have all the money and all the power, and we must continue their servants forever?" Did they sluggishly sigh and say, "Our lot is hard, the Indians own the soil, and

---

[13] Jeremiah 29:18. The jeremiad was one of Stewart's favored rhetorical modes. See Stewart, 19–21 for more on the jeremiad.

[14] Stewart's emphasis on ambition, employment, and trade in this lecture evokes David Walker's denunciation of satisfaction with "low employments" among free black people in his *Appeal*. Walker writes, "Understand me, brethren, I do not mean to speak against the occupations by which we acquire enough and sometimes scarcely that, to render ourselves and families comfortable through life. I am subjected to the same inconvenience, as you all. —My objections are, to our *glorying* and being *happy* in such low employments; for if we are men, we ought to be thankful to the Lord for the past, and for the future. Be looking forward with thankful hearts to higher attainments than *wielding the razor* and *cleaning boots and shoes*. The man whose aspirations are not *above*, and even *below* these, is indeed, ignorant and wretched enough" (Stewart, 119).

we cannot cultivate it?" No; they first made powerful efforts to raise themselves, and then God raised up those illustrious patriots, WASHINGTON and LAFAYETTE, to assist and defend them.[15] And, my brethren, have you made a powerful effort? Have you prayed the legislature for mercy's sake to grant you all the rights and privileges of free citizens,[16] that your daughters may rise to that degree of respectability which true merit deserves, and your sons above the servile situations which most of them fill?

---

[15] Stewart frames African American achievement and uplift in terms of American nationalism. See Stewart, 176, n.4.

[16] One of only a few direct references to citizenship and black appeals to the US government in Stewart's oeuvre.

7

An Address Delivered Before the Afric-American Female Intelligence Society of Boston

[Maria W. Stewart, 1832]

The frowns of the world shall never discourage me, nor its smiles flatter me;[1] for with the help of God I am resolved to withstand the fiery darts of the devil, and the assaults of wicked men. The righteous are as bold as a lion, but the wicked flee when no man pursueth. I fear neither men nor devils; for the God in whom I trust is able to deliver me from the rage and malice of my enemies, and from them that rise up against me. The only motive that has prompted me to raise my voice in your behalf, my friends, is because I have discovered that religion is held in low repute among some of us; and purely to promote the cause of Christ and the good of souls, in the hope that others more experienced, more able and talented than myself, might go forward and do likewise. I expect to render a strict, a solemn, and an awful account to God for the motives that have prompted me to exertion, and for those with which I shall address you this evening.

What I have to say, concerns the whole of us as Christians and as a people; and if you will be so kind as to give me a hearing this once, you shall receive the incense of a grateful heart.

---

[1] The 1830s saw a blossoming of African American intellectual and literary societies. Very often offshoots of black churches, mutual aid societies, or Prince Hall Freemasonry, these societies were clustered in cities throughout the Northeast, although a few emerged in more rural areas and in the slave South. Membership consisted of all strata of the black population, including enslaved persons. For example, a young still-enslaved Frederick Douglass joined the East Baltimore Mental Improvement Society, where he met his future wife, Anna Murray. See McHenry (2002) for a fine history of black literary societies.

In February 1832, *The Liberator* published a notice on the formation of the Afric-American Intelligence Society along with its Constitution and bylaws. Dedicated to mutual aid, the Intelligence Society predicated itself on Christian virtue and fellow-feeling. Her jeremiad, then, may be more of an example for its listeners to emulate than a directed exhortation. This address was published in the Ladies Department of *The Liberator*, April 28, 1832.

The day is coming, my friends, and I rejoice in that day, when the secrets of all hearts shall be manifested before saints and angels, men and devils. It will be a great day of joy and rejoicing to the humble followers of Christ, but a day of terror and dismay to hypocrites and unbelievers. Of that day and hour knoweth no man, no, not even the angels in heaven, but the Father only. The dead that are in Christ shall be raised first. Blessed is he that shall have a part in the first resurrection. Ah, methinks I hear the finally impenitent crying, "Rocks and mountains! fall upon us, and hide us from the wrath of the Lamb, and from him that sitteth upon the throne"

> High on a cloud our God shall come
> Bright thrones prepare his way;
> Thunder and darkness, fire and storm,
> Lead on the dreadful day.

Christ shall descend in the clouds of heaven, surrounded by ten thousand of his saints and angels, and it shall be very tempestuous round about him, and before him shall be gathered all nations, and kindred, and tongues and people; and every knee shall bow, and every tongue confess—they also that pierced him shall look upon him, and mourn. Then shall the King separate the righteous from the wicked, as a shepherd divideth the sheep from the goats, and shall place the righteous on his right hand, and the wicked upon his left. Then, says Christ, shall be weeping, and wailing, and gnashing of teeth, when ye shall see Abraham and the prophets sitting in the kingdom of heaven, and ye yourselves thrust out. Then shall the righteous shine forth in the kingdom of their Father as the sun. He that hath ears to hear, let him hear. The poor despised followers of Christ will not then regret their sufferings here; they shall be carried by angels into Abraham's bosom, and shall be comforted; and the Lord God shall wipe away their tears. You will then be convinced before assembled multitudes, whether they strove to promote the cause of Christ, or whether they sought for gain or applause. "Strive to enter in at the strait gate; for many, I say unto you, shall seek to enter it, and shall not be able. For except your righteousness shall exceed the righteousness of the Scribes and Pharisees, ye shall in no wise enter into the kingdom of heaven."

Ah, methinks I see this people lying in wickedness; and as the Lord liveth, and as your souls live, were it not for the few righteous that are to be found among us, we should become as Sodom, and like unto Gomorrah. Christians have too long slumbered and slept; sinners stumbled into hell, and still are stumbling, for the want of Christian exertion; and the devil is going about like a roaring lion, seeking whom he may devour. And I make bold to say, that many who profess the name of Christ at the present day, live so widely different from what becometh the Gospel of our Lord Jesus Christ, that they cannot and they dare not reason to the world upon righteousness and judgment to come.

Be not offended because I tell you the truth; for I believe that God has fired my soul with a holy zeal for his cause. It was God alone who inspired my heart to publish the Meditations thereof[2]; and it was done with pure motives of love to your souls, in the hope that Christians might examine themselves, and sinners become pricked in their hearts. It is the word of God, though men and devils may oppose it. It is the word of God; and little did I think that any of the professed followers of Christ would have frowned upon me, and discouraged and hindered its progress.

Ah, my friends, I am speaking as one who expects to give account at the bar of God; I am speaking as a dying mortal to dying mortals. I fear there are many who have named the name of Jesus at the present day, that strain at a gnat and swallow a camel; they neither enter in to the kingdom of heaven themselves, nor suffer others to enter in. They would pull the motes out of their brother's eye, when they have a beam in their own eye. And were our blessed Lord and Saviour, Jesus Christ, upon the earth, I believe he would say of many that are called by his name, "O, ye hypocrites, ye generation of vipers, how can you escape the damnation of hell."

I have enlisted in the holy warfare, and Jesus is my captain; and the Lord's battle I mean to fight, until my voice expire in death. I expect to be hated of all men, and persecuted even unto death, for righteousness and the truth's sake.

A few remarks upon moral subjects, and I close. I am a strong advocate for the cause of God and for the cause of freedom. I am not your enemy, but a friend both to you and to your children. Suffer me, then, to express my sentiments but this once, however severe they may appear to be, and then hereafter let me sink into oblivion, and let my name die in forgetfulness.

Had the ministers of the gospel shunned the very appearance of evil; had they faithfully discharged their duty, whether we would have heard them or not; we should have been a very different people from what we now are; but

---

[2] Stewart published a series of Christian meditations and prayers in 1832. She presented them to the First African Baptist Church and Society in Boston; the publisher was Garrison and Knapp.

they have kept the truth as it were hid from our eyes, and have cried, "Peace! Peace" when there was no peace; they have plastered us with untempered mortar, and have been as it were blind leaders of the blind.

It appears to me that there are no people under the heavens so unkind and so unfeeling towards their own, as are the descendants of fallen Africa. I have been something of a traveller in my day; and the general cry among the people is, "Our own color are our greatest opposers"— and even the whites say that we are greater enemies towards each other, than they are towards us. Shall we be a hissing and a reproach amongst the nations of the earth any longer! Shall they laugh us to scorn forever? We might become a highly respectable people; respectable we now consider ourselves, but we might become a highly distinguished and intelligent people. And how? In convincing the world, by our own efforts, however feeble, that nothing is wanting on our part but opportunity.[3] Without these efforts, we shall never be a people, nor our descendants after us.[4]

But God has said that Ethiopia shall stretch forth her hands unto him. True, but God uses means to bring about His purposes; and unless the rising generation manifest a different temper and disposition towards each other from what we have manifested, the generation following will never be an enlightened people. We this day are considered as one of the most degraded races upon the face of the earth. It is useless for us any longer to sit with our hands folded, reproaching the whites; for that will never elevate us. All the nations of the earth have distinguished themselves, and have shown forth a noble and gallant spirit. Look at the suffering Greeks! Their proud souls revolted at the idea of serving a tyrannical nation, who were no better than themselves, and perhaps not so good. They made a mighty effort and arose; their souls were knit together in the holy bonds of love and union: they were united, and came off victorious. Look at the French in the late revolution! no traitors amongst them, to expose their plans to the crowned heads of Europe! "Liberty or Death!" was their cry. And the Haytians, though they have not been acknowledged as a nation,[5] yet their firmness of character, and

---

[3] Stewart intimates an early iteration of what we now call "the politics of respectability." Already respectable, the black community of Boston must exceed that standard by means of cross-class intraracial solidarity, she argues. See Rael (2002) on bourgeois and elite African Americans' expectations of representative activism. On the long life of respectability as a force that haunts Black women's activism and coincident efforts to overcome it, see Cooper (2017).

[4] Stewart hails the "descendants of Africa" as a coherent people. She is an important thinker who contributed to an early understanding of black nationalism in which common experience (e.g., black life in the United States) is an articulable communal identity.

[5] Stewart puts Haiti, the world's first black-led republic, in the context of other largely ethnic nations of oppressed but vindicated peoples. Like other African American thinkers and writers before

independence of spirit have been greatly admired, and high [sic] applauded. Look at the Poles, a feeble people! They rose against three hundred thousand mighty men of Russia; and though they did not gain the conquest, yet they obtained the name of gallant Poles. And even the wild Indians of the forest are more united than ourselves. Insult one of them, and you insult a thousand. They also have contended for their rights and privileges, and are held in higher repute than we are.

And why is it, my friends, that we are despised above all the nations upon the earth? Is it merely because our skins are tinged with a sable hue? No, nor will I ever believe that it is. What then is it? Oh, it is because that we and our fathers have dealt treacherously with one another, and because many of us now possess that envious and malicious disposition, that we had rather die than see each other rise an inch above a beggar. No gentle methods are used to promote love and friendship amongst us, but much is done to destroy it Shall we be a hissing and a reproach amongst the nations of the earth any longer? Shall they laugh us to scorn forever?

Ingratitude is one of the worst passions that reigns in the human breast: it is this that cuts the tender fibres of the soul; for it is impossible for us to love those who are ungrateful towards us. "Behold," says that wise man, Solomon, counting one by one, "a man have I found in a thousand, but a woman among all those have I not found."[6]

I have sometimes thought, that God had almost departed from among us. And why? Because Christ has said, if we say we love the Father, and hate our brother, we are liars, and the truth is not in us; and certainty if we were the true followers of Christ, I think we could not show such a disposition towards each other as we do—for God is all love.

A lady of high distinction among us, observed to me, that I might never expect your homage. God forbid! I ask it not. But I beseech you to deal with gentleness and godly sincerity towards me; and there is not one of you, my dear friends, who has given me a cup of cold water in the name of the Lord, or soothed the sorrows of my wounded heart, but God will bless, not only you,

---

the 1850s, she was wary of extolling Haiti too much in light of the macabre connotations the Haitian Revolution signified in the American imagination. The reason she raises Haiti here is to reemphasize the promise of black nationalism and its underlying ethos of racial solidarity.

[6] Ecclesiastes 7:27–28 (KJV). Stewart references the biblical claim that women are more sinful than men. The chapter goes on to say that all people are created inherently "upright" but many have since gone astray.

but your children for it. Cruel indeed, are those that indulge such an opinion respecting me as that.

Finally, I have exerted myself both for your temporal and eternal welfare, as far as I am able; and my soul has been so discouraged within me, that I have almost been induced to exclaim, "Would to God that my tongue hereafter might cleave to the roof of my mouth, and become silent forever!"[7] and then I have felt that the Christian has no time to be idle, and I must be active, knowing that the night of death cometh, in which no man can work—and my mind has become raised to such an extent, that I will willingly die for the cause that I have espoused—for I cannot die in a more glorious cause than in the defence of God and his laws.

O woman, woman! upon you I call; for upon your exertions almost entirely depends whether the rising generation shall be any thing more than we have been or not. O woman, woman! your example is powerful, your influence great; it extends over your husbands and your children, and throughout the circle of your acquaintance.[8] Then let me exhort you to cultivate among yourselves a spirit of christian love and unity, having charity one for another, without which all our goodness is as sounding brass, and as a tinkling cymbal. And, O, my God, I beseech thee to grant that the nations of the earth may hiss at us no longer! O suffer them not to laugh us to scorn forever!

---

[7] Psalm 137:6 (KJV). Nearly a third of this brief lecture is dedicated to Stewart's right to speak and the opposition she endured for doing so. Late the following year she departed from Boston and, for the next few decades, the public stage.

[8] In this address, Stewart holds several discourses of womanhood in tension. She moves from biblical associations of women with sin and a Victorian belief in the purifying influence of wives and mothers, to the dynamics of women's participation in public nondomestic spheres. Anchoring her argument in an understanding of "true womanhood," Stewart credits black women with the sole power to foster and ensure intraracial solidarity. Anna Julia Cooper (1892) would take up this idea in the 1890s and identify racial uplift work as an essential characteristic of true black womanhood.

8

Mrs. Stewart's Farewell Address to Her Friends in the City of Boston

Delivered September 21, 1833

> Is this vile world a friend to grace,
> To help me on to God?

Ah no! for it is with great tribulation that any shall enter through the gates into the holy city.

MY RESPECTED FRIENDS,[1]
You have heard me observe that the shortness of time, the certainty of death,[2] and the instability of all things here, induce me to turn my thoughts from earth to heaven. Borne down with a heavy load of sin and shame, my conscience filled with remorse; considering the throne of God forever guiltless, and my own eternal condemnation as just, I was at last brought to accept of salvation as a free gift, in and through the merits of a crucified Redeemer. Here I was brought to see,

> 'Tis not by works of righteousness
> That our own hands have done,
> But we are saved by grace alone,
> Abounding through the Son.

---

[1] This was Stewart's last public address in Boston. She would resume public speaking some thirty years later in Baltimore (see my Introduction to Stewart, xxix–xxxix). Stewart remained consistent in philosophical position and defiant in her rhetorical approach throughout her Boston years. The audacity of her claims and assumption of political leadership alienated the black Boston community, whose social pressure propelled her to leave the city for good.

[2] A likely allusion to the recent passing of both Stewart's husband James Stewart (1829) and close friend and mentor David Walker (1830). As a widow, Stewart was neither subject to the "protection" of her modesty in service of future marriage prospects nor tied to a husband's permission to act. Widowhood in the period was often the only status that allowed for a woman's financial independence and social mobility. That said, these deaths left her particularly isolated as a widow without children who was also an orphaned only child, excluded from most normative bonds that organized nineteenth-century women's lives.

After these convictions, in imagination I found myself sitting at the feet of Jesus, clothed in my right mind.[3] For I before had been like a ship tossed to and fro, in a storm at sea. Then was I glad when I realized the dangers I had escaped; and then I consecrated my soul and body, and all the powers of my mind to his service, from that time, henceforth; yea, even for evermore, amen.

I found that religion was full of benevolence; I found there was joy and peace in believing, and I felt as though I was commanded to come out from the world and be separate; to go forward and be baptized. Methought I heard a spiritual interrogation, are you able to drink of that cup that I have drank of? and to be baptized with the baptism that I have been baptized with? And my heart made this reply: Yea, Lord, I am able. Yet amid these bright hopes, I was filled with apprehensive fears, lest they were false. I found that sin still lurked within; it was hard for me to renounce all for Christ, when I saw my earthly prospects blasted. O, how bitter was that cup. Yet I drank it to its very dregs. It was hard for me to say, thy will be done; yet I was made to bend and kiss the rod. I was at last made willing to be any thing or nothing, for my Redeemer's sake. Like many, I was anxious to retain the world in one hand, and religion in the other. "Ye cannot serve God and mammon," sounded in my ear, and with giant-strength, I cut off my right hand, as it were, and plucked out my right eye, and cast them from me, thinking it better to enter life halt and maimed, rather than having two hands or eyes to be cast into hell. Thus ended these mighty conflicts, and I received this heart-cheering promise, "That neither death, nor life, nor principalities, nor powers, nor things present, nor things to come, should be able to separate me from the love of Christ Jesus, our Lord."

And truly, I can say with St. Paul, that at my conversion, I came to the people in the fulness of the gospel of grace. Having spent a few months in the city of—, previous, I saw the flourishing condition of their churches, and the progress they were making in their Sabbath Schools.[4] I visited their Bible

---

[3] The journey from sin to redemption through personal suffering and reflection is typical of "conversion narratives" of the eighteenth and early nineteenth centuries. The genre standardized during the First Great Awakening with the written and oral testimonies of white and black converts in Calvinist New England. See Johnathan Edwards's *Faithful Narrative* (1737) for a compendium from the era. See also John Marrant's *Narrative* (1785) and William Apess's *A Son of the Forest* for conversion narratives from black and Indigenous perspectives. Jarena Lee (1849), Sojourner Truth (1850), and Stewart herself (1879) offer sustained narrative explorations of the arc of conversion as black women.

[4] In the 1860s and 1870s, Stewart founded and ran schools for young black children in Washington, D.C., including Sunday schools. Here she returns to her contention that women are primary conduits for the piety and material well-being of black communities, especially in the home and in schools.

Classes, and heard of the union that existed in their Female Associations. On my arrival here, not finding scarce an individual who felt interested in these subjects, and but few of the whites, except Mr. Garrison, and his friend Mr. Knapp; and hearing that those gentlemen had observed that female influence was powerful, my soul became fired with a holy zeal for your cause; every nerve and muscle in me was engaged in your behalf. I felt that I had a great work to perform; and was in haste to make a profession of my faith in Christ, that I might be about my Father's business. Soon after I made this profession, the Spirit of God came before me, and I spoke before many. When going home, reflecting on what I had said, I felt ashamed, and knew not where I should hide myself. A something said within my breast, "press forward, I will be with thee."[5] And my heart made this reply, Lord, if thou wilt be with me, then will I speak for thee so long as I live. And thus far I have every reason to believe that it is the divine influence of the Holy Spirit operating upon my heart that could possibly induce me to make the feeble and unworthy efforts that I have.

But to begin my subject: "Ye have heard that it hath been said, whoso is angry with his brother without a cause, shall be in danger of the judgment; and whoso shall say to his brother, Raca, shall be in danger of the council. But whosoever shall say, thou fool, shall be in danger of hell-fire." For several years my heart was in continual sorrow. And I believe that the Almighty beheld from his holy habitation, the affliction wherewith I was afflicted, and heard the false misrepresentations wherewith I was misrepresented, and there was none to help. Then I cried unto the Lord in my troubles. And thus for wise and holy purposes, best known to himself, he has raised me in the midst of my enemies, to vindicate my wrongs before this people; and to reprove them for sin, as I have reasoned to them of righteousness and judgment to come. "For as the heavens are higher than the earth, so are his ways above our ways, and his thoughts above our thoughts." I believe, that for wise and holy purposes, best known to himself, he hath unloosed my tongue and put his word into my mouth, in order to confound and put all those to shame that have rose up against me. For he hath clothed my face with steel, and lined my

---

[5] Stewart draws on the figure of the reluctant prophet from the Hebrew Bible (e.g., Jeremiah; Jonah) to establish her rhetorical ethos. Even more, she draws attention to the weight of communal aversion for women's oratory, particularly their live performances before mixed-gender audiences, in this period. The failure of black solidarity she criticized in many of her lectures likely stems from experience as well as observation.

forehead with brass.[6] He hath put his testimony within me, and engraven his seal on my for[e]head. And with these weapons I have indeed set the fiends of earth and hell at defiance.

What if I am a woman; is not the God of ancient times the God of these modern days? Did he not raise up Deborah, to be a mother, and a judge in Israel? Did not queen Esther save the lives of the Jews? And Mary Magdalene first declare the resurrection of Christ from the dead? Come, said the woman of Samaria, and see a man that hath told me all things that ever I did, is not this the Christ? St. Paul declared that it was a shame for a woman to speak in public, yet our great High Priest and Advocate did not condemn the woman for a more notorious offence than this; neither will he condemn this worthless worm. The bruised reed he will not break, and the smoking flax he will not quench, till he send forth judgment unto victory. Did St. Paul but know of our wrongs and deprivations, I presume he would make no objections to our pleading in public for our rights.[7] Again; holy women ministered unto Christ and the apostles; and women of refinement in all ages, more or less, have had a voice in moral, religious and political subjects. Again; why the Almighty hath imparted unto me the power of speaking thus, I cannot tell. "And Jesus lifted up his voice and said, I thank thee, O Father, Lord of heaven and earth, that thou hast hid these things from the wise and prudent, and hast revealed them unto babes: even so, Father, for so it seemed good in thy sight."

But to convince you of the high opinion that was formed of the capacity and ability of woman, by the ancients, I would refer you to "Sketches of the Fair Sex."[8] Read to the 51st page, and you will find that several of the Northern nations imagined that women could look into futurity, and that they had about them, an inconceivable something, approaching to divinity. Perhaps that idea was only the effect of the sagacity common to the sex, and the advantages which their natural address gave them over rough and simple warriors. Perhaps, also, those barbarians, surprised at the influence which beauty has over force, were led to ascribe to the supernatural attraction, a charm which they could not comprehend. A belief, however, that the Deity

---

[6] The device of construing one's speech as a vehicle for the assertions of greater authority, including the supernatural, is a common rhetorical practice that was dominant in women's oratory at the time.

[7] This is a radical claim: black women speakers have a special dispensation for political advocacy via speech, one grounded in their unique experience of "wrongs and deprivations" as black women.

[8] First published in the late eighteenth century, this anonymously published set of sketches was circulated and reprinted on both sides of the Atlantic well into the nineteenth century. That Stewart adduces evidence from this text immediately doing so with the Bible is provocative because *Sketches of the Fair Sex* is a text that aims to titillate me and prod them toward marriage all the while criticizing women for purported transgressions and peccadillos.

more readily communicates himself to women, has at one time or other, prevailed in every quarter of the earth; not only among the Germans and the Britons, but all the people of Scandinavia were possessed of it. Among the Greeks, women delivered the Oracles; the respect the Romans paid to the Sybils, is well known. The Jews had their prophetesses. The prediction of the Egyptian women obtained much credit at Rome, even under the Emperors. And in the most barbarous nations, all things that have the appearance of being supernatural, the mysteries of religion, the secrets of physic, and the rites of magic, were in the possession of women.

If such women as are here described have once existed, be no longer astonished then, my brethren and friends, that God at this eventful period should raise up your own females to strive, by their example both in public and private, to assist those who are endeavoring to stop the strong current of prejudice that flows so profusely against us at present. No longer ridicule their efforts, it will be counted for sin. For God makes use of feeble means sometimes, to bring about his most exalted purposes.

In the 15th century, the general spirit of this period is worthy of observation. We might then have seen women preaching and mixing themselves in controversies. Women occupying the chairs of Philosophy and Justice; women haranguing in Latin before the Pope; women writing in Greek, and studying in Hebrew; Nuns were Poetesses, and women of quality Divines; and young girls who had studied Eloquence, would with the sweetest countenances, and the most plaintive voices, pathetically exhort the Pope and the Christian Princes, to declare war against the Turks. Women in those days devoted their leisure hours to contemplation and study. The religious spirit which has animated women in all ages, showed itself at this time. It has made them, by turns, martyrs, apostles, warriors, and concluded in making them divines and scholars.

Why cannot a religious spirit animate us now? Why cannot we become divines and scholars? Although learning is somewhat requisite, yet recollect that those great apostles, Peter and James, were ignorant and unlearned. They were taken from the fishing boat, and made fishers of men.

In the 13th century, a young lady of Bologne, devoted herself to the study of the Latin language, and of the Laws. At the age of twenty-three she pronounced a funeral oration in Latin, in the great church of Bologne. And to be admitted as an orator, she had neither need of indulgence on account of her youth or of her sex. At the age of twenty-six, she took the degree of Doctor of Laws, and began publicly to expound the Institutions of Justinian. At the age of thirty, her great reputation raised her to a chair, where she taught the law to a prodigious concourse of scholars from all nations. She joined the charms and accomplishments of a woman to all the knowledge of a man. And such was the power of her eloquence, that her beauty was only admired when her tongue was silent.

What if such women as are here described should rise among our sable race? And it is not impossible. For it is not the color of the skin that makes the man or the woman, but the principle formed in the soul. Brilliant wit will shine, come from whence it will; and genius and talent will not hide the brightness of its lustre.

But, to return to my subject; the mighty work of reformation has begun among this people. The dark clouds of ignorance are dispersing. The light of science is bursting forth. Knowledge is beginning to flow, nor will its moral influence be extinguished till its refulgent rays have spread over us from East to West, and from North to South. Thus far is this mighty work begun, but not as yet accomplished. Christians must awake from their slumbers. Religion must flourish among them before the church will be built up in its purity, or immorality be suppressed.

Yet, notwithstanding your prospects are thus fair and bright, I am about to leave you, perhaps, never more to return. For I find it is no use for me as an individual to try to make myself useful among my color in this city. It was contempt for my moral and religious opinions in private that drove me thus before a public. Had experience more plainly shown me that it was the nature of man to crush his fellow, I should not have thought it so hard. Wherefore, my respected friends, let us no longer talk of prejudice, till prejudice becomes extinct at home. Let us no longer talk of opposition, till we cease to oppose our own. For while these evils exist, to talk is like giving breath to the air, and labor to the wind. Though wealth is far more highly prized than humble merit, yet none of these things move me. Having God for my friend and portion, what have I to fear? Promotion cometh neither from the East or West, and as long as it is the will of God, I rejoice that I am as I am; for man in his best estate, is altogether vanity. Men of eminence have mostly risen from obscurity; nor will I, although a female of a darker hue, and far more obscure than they, bend my head or hang my harp upon willows; for though poor, I will virtuous prove. And if it is the will of my heavenly Father to reduce me to penury and want, I am ready to say, amen, even so be it. "The foxes have holes, and the birds of the air have nests, but the Son of man hath not where to lay his head."

During the short period of my Christian warfare, I have indeed had to contend against the fiery darts of the devil. And was it not that the righteous are kept by the mighty power of God through faith unto salvation, long before this I should have proved to be like the seed by the way-side. For it has actually appeared to me at different periods, as though the powers of earth and hell had combined against me, to prove my overthrow. Yet admist their dire attempts, I have found the Almighty to be "a friend that sticketh closer than a brother." He never will forsake the soul that leans on him; though he chastens and corrects, it is for the soul's best interest. "And as a Father pitieth his children, so the Lord pitieth them that fear him."

But some of you have said, "do not talk so much about religion, the people do not wish to hear you. We know these things, tell us something we do not know." If you know these things, my dear friends, and have performed them, far happier, and more prosperous would you now have been. "He that knoweth his Lord's will and obeyeth it not, shall be beaten with many stripes." Sensible of this, I have, regardless of the frowns and scoffs of a guilty world, plead up religion, and the pure principles of morality among you. Religion is the most glorious theme that mortals can converse upon. The older it grows the more new beauties it displays. Earth, with its brilliant attractions, appears mean and sordid when compared to it. It is that fountain that has no end, and those that drink thereof shall never thirst; for it is, indeed, a well of water springing up in the soul unto everlasting life.

Again, those ideas of greatness which are held forth to us, are vain delusions, are airy visions which we shall never realize. All that man can say or do can never elevate us, it is a work that must be effected between God and ourselves. And, how? by dropping all political discussions in our behalf, for these, in my opinion, sow the seed of discord, and strengthen the cord of prejudice. A spirit of animosity is already risen, and unless it is quenched, a fire will burst forth and devour us, and our young will be slain by the sword. It is the sovereign will of God that our condition should be thus and so. "For he hath formed one vessel for honor, and another for dishonor." And shall the clay say to him that formed it, why hast thou formed me thus? It is high time for us to drop political discussions, and when our day of deliverance comes, God will provide a for us to escape, and fight his own battles.

Finally, my brethren, let us follow after godliness, and the things which make for peace. Cultivate your own minds and morals; real merit will elevate you. Pure religion will burst your fetters. Turn your attention to industry. Strive to please your employers. Lay up what you earn. And remember, that in the grave distinction withers, and the high and how are alike renowned.

But I draw to a conclusion. Long will the kind sympathy of some much loved friend, be written on the tablet of my memory, especially those kind individuals who have stood by me like pitying angels, and befriended me when in the midst of difficulty; many blessings rest on them. Gratitude is all the tribute I can offer. A rich reward awaits them.

To my unconverted friends, one and all, I would say, shortly this frail tenement of mine will be dissolved and lie mouldering in ruins. O, solemn thought! Yet why should I revolt, for it is the glorious hope of a blessed immortality, beyond the grave, that has supported me thus far through this vale of tears. Who among you will strive to meet me at the right hand of Christ[?] For the great day of retribution is fast approaching, and who shall be able to abide his coming? You are forming characters for eternity. As you live so you will die; as death leaves you, so judgment will find you. Then shall we receive the glorious welcome, "Come, ye blessed of my Father, inherit the kingdom prepared for you from before the foundation of the world." Or, hear the heart-rending sentence, "Depart ye cursed into everlasting fire prepared for the devil and his angels." When thrice ten thousand years have rolled away, eternity will be but just begun. Your ideas will but just begin to expand. O, eternity, who can unfathom thine end, or comprehend thy beginning.

Dearly beloved: I have made myself contemptible in the eyes of many, that I might win some. But it has been like labor in vain. "Paul may plant, and Apollos water, but God alone giveth the increase."

To my brethren and sisters in the church, I would say, be ye clothed with the breast-plate of righteousness, having your loins girt about with truth, prepared to meet the Bridegroom[9] at his coming; for blessed are those servants that are found watching.

Farewell. In a few short years from now, we shall meet in those upper regions where parting will be no more. There we shall sing and shout, and shout and sing, and make heaven's high arches ring. There we shall range in rich pastures, and partake of those living streams that never dry. O, blissful thought! Hatred and contention shall cease, and we shall join with redeemed millions in ascribing glory and honor, and riches, and power and blessing

---

[9] This mixture of gendered metaphors, in which churchgoers are prepared for battle with pulled-up tunics (i.e., girded loins) and are simultaneously brides prepared for marriage, points to how Stewart views masculine and feminine forms of morality and spirituality as twin expressions of the same philosophy.

to the Lamb that was slain, and to Him that sitteth upon the throne. Nor eye hath seen, nor ear heard, neither hath it entered into the heart of man to conceive of the joys that are prepared for them that love God. Thus far has my life been almost a life of complete disappointment. God has tried me as by fire. Well was I aware that if I contended boldly for his cause, I must suffer. Yet, I chose rather to suffer affliction with his people, than to enjoy the pleasures of sin for a season. And I believe that the glorious declaration was about to be made applicable to me, that was made to God's ancient covenant people by the prophet, comfort ye, comfort ye, my people: say unto her that her warfare is accomplished, and that her iniquities are pardoned. I believe that a rich reward awaits me, if not in this world, in the world to come. O, blessed reflection. The bitterness of my soul has departed from those who endeavored to discourage and hinder me in my Christian progress; and I can now forgive my enemies, bless those who have hated me, and cheerfully pray for those who have despitefully used and persecuted me.[10]

Fare you well, farewell.
MARIA S. STEWART.
New York, April 14, 1834.

---

[10] Defiant to the end, Stewart reasserts that she cedes the Boston stage not because she has learned her place as a woman or feels her work is over, but because she does not see a way forward in a sinful and unfriendly Boston. Moving south, Stewart found arenas for writing, speaking, and teaching.

PART II
RACIAL ETHICS

Contextual Works

9

David Walker, *Walker's Appeal, in Four Articles: Together with a Preamble, to the Coloured Citizens of the World, but in Particular, and Very Expressly, to Those of the United States of America* (1829) (selections)

APPEAL, &c. PREAMBLE.

My dearly beloved Brethren and Fellow Citizens:

HAVING travelled over a considerable portion of these United States, and having in the course of my travels taken the most accurate observations of things as they exist—the result of my observations has warranted the full and unshaken conviction, that we, (coloured people of these United States) are the most degraded, wretched, and abject set of beings that ever lived since the world began; and I pray God, that none like us ever may live again until time shall be no more. They tell us of the Israelites in Egypt, the Helots in Sparta, and of the Roman Slaves, which last, were made up from almost every nation under heaven, whose sufferings under those ancient and heathen nations, were, in comparison with ours, under this enlightened and christian nation, no more than a cypher—or in other words, those heathen nations of antiquity, had but little more among them than the name and form of slavery; while wretchedness and endless miseries were reserved, apparently in a phial, to be poured out upon our fathers, ourselves and our children, by *christian* Americans![1]

---

[1] Walker refutes claims that slavery is a natural institution that was in great part responsible for the cultural and intellectual achievement of ancient civilization. Proslavery thinkers regularly compared chattel slavery in the Americas to slavery in classical antiquity to justify its perpetuation. Walker

These positions I shall endeavour, by the help of the Lord, to demonstrate in the course of this *appeal*, to the satisfaction of the most incredulous mind—and may God Almighty, who is the Father of our Lord Jesus Christ, open your hearts to understand and believe the truth.

The *causes*, my brethren, which produce our wretchedness and miseries, are so very numerous and aggravating, that I believe the pen only of a Josephus or a Plutarch, can well enumerate and explain them. Upon subjects, then, of such incomprehensible magnitude, so impenetrable, and so notorious, I shall be obliged to omit a large class of, and content myself with giving you an exposition of a few of those, which do indeed rage to such an alarming pitch, that they cannot but be a perpetual source of terror and dismay to every reflecting mind.

I am fully aware, in making this appeal to my much afflicted and suffering brethren, that I shall not only be assailed by those whose greatest earthly desires are, to keep us in abject ignorance and wretchedness, and who are of the firm conviction that Heaven has designed us and our children to be slaves and *beasts of burden* to them and their children.—I say, I do not only expect to be held up to the public as an ignorant, impudent and restless disturber of the public peace, by such avaricious creatures, as well as a mover of insubordination—and perhaps put in prison or to death, for giving a superficial exposition of our miseries, and exposing tyrants. But I am persuaded, that many of my brethren, particularly those who are ignorantly in league with slave-holders or tyrants, who acquire their daily bread by the blood and sweat of their more ignorant brethren—and not a few of those too, who are too ignorant to see an inch beyond their noses, will rise up and call me cursed—Yea, the jealous ones among us will perhaps use more abject subtlety, by affirming that this work is not worth perusing, that we are well situated, and there is no use in trying to better our condition, for we cannot. I will ask one question here.—Can our condition be any worse?—Can it be more mean and abject? If there are any changes, will they not be for the better, though they may appear for the worst at first? Can they get us any lower? Where can they get us? They are afraid to treat us worse, for they know well, the day they do it they are gone. But against all accusations which may or can be preferred against me, I appeal to Heaven for my motive in writing—who knows that my object is, if possible, to awaken in the breasts of my afflicted, degraded

---

rejects this argument on the grounds that those civilizations held a diverse (i.e., multiethnic) slave population and treated them well.

and slumbering brethren, a spirit of enquiry and investigation respecting our miseries and wretchedness in this *Republican Land of Liberty!!!!!!*

The sources from which our miseries are derived, and on which I shall comment, I shall not combine in one, but shall put them under distinct heads and expose them in their turn; in doing which, keeping truth on my side, and not departing from the strictest rules of morality, I shall endeavour to penetrate, search out, and lay them open for your inspection. If you cannot or will not profit by them, I shall have done *my* duty to you, my country and my God.

And as the inhuman system of *slavery*, is the *source* from which most of our miseries proceed, I shall begin with that *curse to nations*, which has spread terror and devastation through so many nations of antiquity, and which is raging to such a pitch at the present day in Spain and in Portugal.[2] It had one tug in England, in France, and in the United States of America; yet the inhabitants thereof, do not learn wisdom, and erase it entirely from their dwellings and from all with whom they have to do. The fact is, the labor of slaves comes so cheap to the avaricious usurpers, and is (as they think) of such great utility to the country where it exists, that those who are actuated by sordid avarice only, overlook the evils, which will as sure as the Lord lives, follow after the good. In fact, they are so happy to keep in ignorance and degradation, and to receive the homage and the labor of the slaves, they forget that God rules in the armies of heaven and among the inhabitants of the earth, having his ears continually open to the cries, tears and groans of his oppressed people; and being a just and holy Being will at one day appear fully in behalf of the oppressed, and arrest the progress of the avaricious oppressors; for although the destruction of the oppressors God may not effect by the oppressed, yet the Lord our God will bring other destructions upon them—for not unfrequently will he cause them to rise up one against another, to be split and divided, and to oppress each other, and sometimes to open hostilities with sword in hand. Some may ask, what is the matter with this united and happy people?—Some say it is the cause of political usurpers, tyrants, oppressors, &c. But has not the Lord an oppressed and suffering people among them? Does the Lord condescend to hear their cries and see their tears in consequence of oppression? Will he let the oppressors

---

[2] Spain and Portugal were engulfed in numerous wars during the nineteenth century. Walker's allusion here extends his broader prophecy that war would be the unavoidable consequence of maintaining slavery in the United States.

rest comfortably and happy always? Will he not cause the very children of the oppressors to rise up against them, and oftimes put them to death? "God works in many ways his wonders to perform."

I will not here speak of the destructions which the Lord brought upon Egypt, in consequence of the oppression and consequent groans of the oppressed—of the hundreds and thousands of Egyptians whom God hurled into the Red Sea for afflicting his people in their land—of the Lord's suffering people in Sparta or Lacedemon, the land of the truly famous Lycurgus—nor have I time to comment upon the cause which produced the fierceness with which Sylla usurped the title, and absolutely acted as dictator of the Roman people—the conspiracy of Cataline—the conspiracy against, and murder of Cæsar in the Senate house—the spirit with which Marc Antony made himself master of the commonwealth—his associating Octavius and Lipidus with himself in power—their dividing the provinces of Rome among themselves—their attack and defeat on the plains of Phillippi the last defenders of their liberty, (Brutus and Cassius)—the tyranny of Tiberius, and from him to the final overthrow of Constantinople by the Turkish Sultan, Mahomed II. A. D. 1453. I say, I shall not take up time to speak of the *causes* which produced so much wretchedness and massacre among those heathen nations, for I am aware that you know too well, that God is just, as well as merciful! I shall call your attention a few moments to that *christian* nation, the Spaniards—while I shall leave almost unnoticed, that avaricious and cruel people, the Portuguese, among whom all true hearted christians and lovers of Jesus Christ, must evidently see the judgments of God displayed. To sh[o]w the judgments of God upon the Spaniards, I shall occupy but a little time, leaving a plenty of room for the candid and unprejudiced to reflect.

All persons who are acquainted with history, and particularly the Bible, who are not blinded by the God of this world, and are not actuated solely by avarice—who are able to lay aside prejudice long enough to view candidly and impartially, things as they were, are, and probably will be—who are willing to admit that God made man to serve Him *alone,* and that man should have no other Lord or Lords but Himself—that God Almighty is the *sole proprietor* or *master* of the WHOLE human family, and will not on any consideration admit of a colleague, being unwilling to divide his glory with another.—And who can dispense with prejudice long enough to admit that we are *men,* notwithstanding our *improminent* [sic] *noses* and *woolly heads,* and believe that we feel for our fathers, mothers, wives and children, as well as the whites do for theirs.—I say, all who are permitted to see and believe these things, can easily recognize the judgments of God among the Spaniards. Though others may lay the cause of the fierceness with which they cut each other's throats, to some other circumstance, yet they who believe that God is a God of justice,[3] will believe that SLAVERY *is the principal cause.*

While the Spaniards are running about upon the field of battle cutting each other's throats, has not the Lord an afflicted and suffering people in the midst of them, whose cries and groans in consequence of oppression are continually pouring into the ears of the God of justice? Would they not cease to cut each other's throats if they could? But how can they? They very support which they draw from government to aid them in perpetrating such enormities, does it not arise in a great degree from the wretched victims of oppression among them? And yet they are calling for *Peace!—Peace!!* Will any peace be given unto them? Their destruction may indeed be procrastinated awhile, but can it continue long, while they are oppressing the Lord's people? Has He not the hearts of all men in His hand? Will he suffer one part of his creatures to go on oppressing another like brutes always, with impunity? And yet, those avaricious wretches are calling for *Peace!!!!* I declare, it does appear to me, as though some nations think God is asleep, or that he made the Africans for nothing else but to dig their mines and work their farms, or they cannot believe history, sacred or profane. I ask every man who has a heart, and is blessed with the privilege of believing—Is not God a God of justice to *all* his creatures? Do you say he is? Then if he gives peace and tranquility to tyrants, and permits them to keep our fathers, our mothers, ourselves and our children in eternal ignorance and wretchedness, to support them and their families, would he be to us a God of *justice?* I ask, O ye *christians!!!* who hold us and our children in the most abject ignorance and degradation, that ever a people were afflicted with since the world began—I say, if God gives you peace and tranquility, and suffers you thus to go on afflicting us, and our children, who have never given you the least provocation—would he be to us *a God of justice?* If you will allow that we are MEN, who feel for each other, does not the blood of our fathers and of us their children, cry aloud to the Lord of Sabaoth against you, for the cruelties and murders with which you have, and do continue to afflict us. But it is time for me to close my remarks

---

[3] Walker's emphasis on God's justice invokes Jefferson's fear of God's justice in Query XVIII *Notes on the State of Virginia*: "I tremble for my country when I reflect that God is just: that his justice cannot sleep forever."

on the suburbs, just to enter more fully into the interior of this system of cruelty and oppression.

ARTICLE II. OUR WRETCHEDNESS IN CONSEQUENCE OF IGNORANCE.

Ignorance, my brethren, is a mist, low down into the very dark and almost impenetrable abyss of which, our fathers for many centuries have been plunged. The christians, and enlightened of Europe, and some of Asia, seeing the ignorance and consequent degradation of our fathers, instead of trying to enlighten them, by teaching them that religion and light with which God had blessed them they have plunged them into wretchedness ten thousand times more intolerable, than if they had left them entirely to the Lord, and to add to their miseries, deep down into which they have plunged them, tell them, that they are an *inferior* and *distinct race* of beings, which they will be glad enough to recal[l] and swallow by and by. Fortune and misfortune, two inseparable companions, lay rolled up in the wheel of events, which have from the creation of the world, and will continue to take place among men until God shall dash worlds together.

When we take a retrospective view of the arts and sciences—the wise legislators—the Pyramids, and other magnificent buildings—the turning of the channel of the river Nile, by the sons of Africa or of Ham, among whom learning originated, and was carried thence into Greece, where it was improved upon and refined.[4] Thence among the Romans, and all over the then enlightened parts of the world, and it has been enlightening the dark and benighted minds of men from then, down to this day. I say, when I view retrospectively, the renown of that once mighty people, the children of our great progenitor I am indeed cheered. Yea further, when I view that mighty son of Africa, HANNIBAL, one of the greatest generals of antiquity, who defeated and cut off so many thousands of the white Romans or murderers, and who carried his victorious arms, to the very gate of Rome, and I give it as my candid opinion, that had Carthage been well united and had given him good support, he would have carried that cruel and barbarous city by storm. But they were disunited, as the coloured people are now, in the United States of

---

[4] Walker was among a host of abolitionist writers who argued Greek culture, so celebrated by the American public, originated in Africa. He makes sure to connect that claim to enslaved black persons by referencing the sons of Ham (Genesis 9:20–27).

America, the reason our natural enemies are enabled to keep their feet on our throats.

Beloved brethren—here let me tell you, and believe it, that the Lord our God, as true as he sits on his throne in heaven, and as true as our Saviour died to redeem the world, will give you a Hannibal, and when the Lord shall have raised him up, and given him to you for your possession, O my suffering brethren! remember the divisions and consequent sufferings of *Carthage* and of *Hayti*. Read the history particularly of Hayti, and see how they were butchered by the whites, and do you take warning. The person whom God shall give you, give him your support and let him go his length, and behold in him the salvation of your God. God will indeed, deliver you through him from your deplorable and wretched condition under the Christians of America. I charge you this day before my God to lay no obstacle in his way, but let him go.

The whites want slaves, and want us for their slaves, but some of them will curse the day they ever saw us. As true as the sun ever shone in its meridian splendor, my colour will root some of them out of the very face of the earth. They shall have enough of making slaves of, and butchering, and murdering us in the manner which they have. No doubt some may say that I write with a bad spirit, and that I being a black, wish these things to occur. Whether I write with a bad or a good spirit, I say if these things do not occur in their proper time, it is because the world in which we live does not exist, and we are deceived with regard to its existence.—It is immaterial however to me, who believe, or who refuse—though I should like to see the whites repent peradventure God may have mercy on them, some however, have gone so far that their cup must be filled.[5]

But what need have I to refer to antiquity, when Hayti, the glory of the blacks and terror of tyrants, is enough to convince the most avaricious and stupid of wretches—which is at this time, and I am sorry to say it, plagued with that scourge of nations, the Catholic religion[6]; but I hope and pray

---

[5] The image of the cup circulated throughout antislavery culture. Suffering Christians were said to be sharing their "Master's cup," an allusion to Jesus's appeal in the Garden of Gethsemane (Matthew 26:39). Walker's use here also draws on a biblical reference to Babylon in Revelations: "For her sins have reached unto heaven, and God hath remembered her iniquities. Reward her even as she rewarded you, and double unto her double according to her works: in the cup which she hath filled fill to her double" (Rev. 18:5–6).

[6] Anti-Catholicism was an integral part of British and American identities in the nineteenth century. As a newly liberated nation of former slaves, Haiti occupied prominent space in predominantly Protestant antislavery discourse. Thus, the image of Haiti as a free black republic complicated such narratives, prompting Walker to separate Haiti from Catholicism.

God that she may yet rid herself of it, and adopt in its stead the Protestant faith; also, I hope that she may keep peace within her borders and be united, keeping a strict look out for tyrants, for if they get the least chance to injure her, they will avail themselves of it, as true as the Lord lives in heaven. But one thing which gives me joy is, that they are men who would be cut off to a man, before they would yield to the combined forces of the whole world—in fact, if the whole world was combined against them, it could not do anything with them, unless the Lord delivers them up.

Ignorance and treachery one against the other—a servile and abject submission to the lash of tyrants, we see plainly, my brethren, are not the natural elements of the blacks, as the Americans try to make us believe; but these are misfortunes which God has suffered our fathers to be enveloped in for many ages, no doubt in consequence of their disobedience to their Maker, and which do, indeed, reign at this time among us, almost to the destruction of all other principles: for I must truly say, that ignorance, the mother of treachery and deceit, gnaws into our very vitals. Ignorance, as it now exits among us, produces a state of things, Oh my Lord! too horrible to present to the world. Any man who is curious to see the full force of ignorance developed among the coloured people of the United States of America, has only to go into the southern and western states of this confederacy, where, if he is not a tyrant, but has the feelings of a human being, who can feel for a fellow creature, he may see enough to make his very heart bleed! He may see there, a son take his mother, who bore almost the pains of death to give him birth, and by the command of a tyrant, strip her as naked as she came into the world, and apply the cow-hide to her, until she falls a victim to death in the road! He may see a husband take his dear wife, not unfrequently in a pregnant state, and perhaps far advanced, and beat her for an unmerciful wretch, until his infant falls a lifeless lump at her feet! Can the Americans escape God Almighty? If they do, can he be to us a God of Justice? God is just, and I know it—for he has convinced me to my satisfaction—I cannot doubt him. My observer may see fathers beating their sons, mothers their daughters, and children their parents, all to pacify the passions of unrelenting tyrants. He may also, see them telling news and lies, making mischief one upon another. These are some of the productions of ignorance, which he will see practised among my dear brethren, who are held in unjust slavery and wretchedness, by avaricious and unmerciful tyrants, to whom, and their hellish deeds, I would suffer my life to be taken before I would submit. And when my curious observer comes to take notice of those who are said to be free, (which assertion I deny) and who are making some frivolous pretentions to common sense, he will see that branch of ignorance among the slaves assuming a more cunning and deceitful course of procedure. He may see some of my brethren in league with tyrants, selling their own brethren into *hell upon earth*, not dissimilar to the exhibitions in Africa, but in a more secret, servile and abject manner. Oh Heaven! I am full!!! I can hardly move my pen!!!!! As I expect some will try to put me to death, to strike terror into others, and to obliterate from their minds the notion of freedom, so as to keep my brethren the more secure in wretchedness, where they will be permitted to stay but a short time (whether tyrants believe it or not)—I shall give the world a development of facts, which are already witnessed in the courts of heaven. My observer may see some of those ignorant and treacherous creatures (coloured people) sneaking about in the large cities, endeavouring to find out all strange coloured people, where they work and where they reside, asking them questions, and trying to ascertain whether they are runaways or not, telling them, at the same time, that they always have been, are, and always will be, friends to their brethren; and, perhaps, that they themselves are absconders, and a thousand such treacherous lies to get the better information of the more ignorant!!! There have been and are at this day in Boston, New-York, Philadelphia, and Baltimore, coloured men, who are in league with tyrants, and who receive a great portion of their daily bread, of the moneys which they acquire from the blood and tears of their more miserable brethren, whom they scandalously delivered into the hands of our *natural enemies!!!!!!*

To show the force of degraded ignorance and deceit among us some farther, I will give here an extract from a paragraph, which may be found in the Columbian Centinel of this city, for September 9, 1829, on the first page of which, the curious may find an article, headed

"AFFRAY AND MURDER."
"*Portsmouth, (Ohio) Aug.* 22, 1829.

"A most shocking outrage was committed in Kentucky, about eight miles from this place, on 14th inst. A negro driver, by the name of Gordon, who had purchased in Maryland about sixty negroes, was taking them, assisted by an associate named Allen, and the wagoner who conveyed the baggage, to the Mississippi. The men were hand-cuffed and chained together, in the usual manner for driving those poor wretches, while the women and children were suffered to proceed without incumbrance. It appears that, by means of a file the negroes, unobserved, had succeeded in separating the irons which bound their hands, in such a way as to be able to throw them off at any moment. About 8 o'clock in the morning, while proceeding on the state road leading from Greenup to Vanceburg, two of them dropped their shackles and commenced a fight, when the wagoner (Petit) rushed in with his whip to compel them to desist. At this moment, every negro was found to be perfectly at liberty; and one of them seizing a club, gave Petit a violent blow on the head, and laid him dead at his feet; and Allen, who came to his assistance, met a similar fate, from the contents of a pistol fired by another of the gang. Gordon was then attacked, seized and held by one of the negroes, whilst another fired twice at him with a pistol, the ball of which each time grazed his head, but not proving effectual, he was beaten with clubs, and left for dead. They then commenced pillaging the wagon, and with an axe split open the trunk of Gordon, and rifled it of the money, about $2,400. Sixteen of the negroes then took to the woods; Gordon, in the meantime, not being materially injured, was enabled, by the assistance of one of the women, to mount his horse and flee; pursued, however, by one of the gang on another horse, with a drawn pistol; fortunately he escaped with his life barely, arriving at a plantation, as the negro came in sight; who then turned about and retreated."

"The neighborhood was immediately rallied, and a hot pursuit given—which, we understand, has resulted in the capture of the whole gang and the recovery of the greatest part of the money.—Seven of the negro men and one woman, it is said were engaged in the murders, and will be brought to trial at the next court in Greenupsburg."

Here my brethren, I want you to notice particularly in the above article, the *ignorant* and *deceitful actions* of this coloured woman. I beg you to view it candidly, as for ETERNITY!!!! Here a *notorious wretch*, with two other confederates had SIXTY of them in a gang, driving them like *brutes*—the men all in chains and hand-cuffs, and by the help of God they got their chains and hand-cuffs thrown off, and caught two of the wretches and put them to death, and beat the other until they thought he was dead, and left him for dead; however, he deceived them, and rising from the ground, this *servile woman* helped him upon his horse, and he made his escape. Brethren, what do you think of this? Was it the natural *fine feelings* of this woman, to save such a wretch alive? I know that the blacks, take them half enlightened and ignorant, are more humane and merciful than the most enlightened and refined Europeans that can be found in all the earth. Let no one say that I assert this because I am prejudiced on the side of my colour, and against the whites or Europeans. For what I write, I do it candidly, for my God and the good of both parties: Natural observations have taught me these things; there is a solemn awe in the hearts of the blacks, as it respects *murdering* men:*[7] whereas the whites, (though they are great cowards) where they have the advantage, or think that there are any prospects of getting it, they murder all before them, in order to subject men to wretchedness and degradation under them. This is the natural result of pride and avarice.—But I declare, the actions of this black woman are really insupportable. For my own part, I cannot think it was anything but servile deceit, combined with the most gross ignorance: for we must remember that *humanity, kindness* and the *fear of the Lord*, does not consist in protecting *devils*. Here is a set of wretches, who had SIXTY of them in a gang, driving them around the country like *brutes*, to dig up gold and silver for them, (which they will get enough of yet.) Should the lives of such creatures be spared? Are GOD and Mammon in league?[8] What has the Lord to do with a gang of desperate wretches, who go *sneaking about the country like robbers*—light upon his people wherever they can get a chance, binding them with chains and hand-cuffs, beat and murder them as they would *rattle-snakes*? Are they not the Lord's enemies? Ought they not to be destroyed? Any person who will save such wretches from destruction, is fighting against the Lord, and will receive his just recompense. The black men acted like *blockheads*. Why did they not make sure of the wretch? He would have made sure of them, if he could. It is just the way with black men—eight white men can frighten fifty of them; whereas, if you can only get courage into the blacks, I do declare it, that one good black man can put to death six white men; and I give it as a fact, let twelve black men get well armed for battle, and they will kill and put to flight fifty whites. The reason is, the blacks, once you get them started, they glory in death. The whites have had us under them for more than three centuries, murdering, and treating us like brutes; and, as Mr. Jefferson wisely said, they have never *found us out*—they do not know, indeed, that there is an unconquerable disposition in the breasts of the blacks, which, when it is fully awakened and put in motion, will be subdued, only with the destruction of the animal existence.[9] Get the blacks started, and if you do not have a gang of tigers and lions to deal with, I am a deceiver of the blacks and of the whites. How sixty of them could let that wretch escape unkilled, I cannot conceive—they will have to suffer as much

---

[7] Which is the reason the whites take the advantage of us. (original note)

[8] Walker's rhetorical question would prompt an immediate "no" from any reader with biblical knowledge. The use of "mammon" calls to mind Luke 16:13 and Matthew 6:24, which specifically state "Ye cannot serve God and mammon." Walker depends on the absurdity of this alliance to reinforce his point that leaving the slaver driver to die is justifiable.

[9] Likely referencing Jefferson's claims in *Notes* about the rising spirit of enslaved persons.

for the two whom, they secured, as if they had put one hundred to death: if you commence, make sure work—do not trifle, for they will not trifle with you—they want us for their slaves, and think nothing of murdering us in order to subject us to that wretched condition--therefore, if there is an *attempt* made by us, kill or be killed. Now, I ask you, had you not rather be killed than to be a slave to a tyrant, who takes the life of your mother, wife, and dear little children? Look upon your mother, wife and children, and answer God Almighty; and believe this, that it is no more harm for you to kill a man, who is trying to kill you, than it is for you to take a drink of water when thirsty; in fact, the man who will stand still and let another murder him, is worse than an infidel, and, if he has common sense, ought not to be pitied.— The actions of this deceitful and ignorant coloured woman, in saving the life of a desperate wretch, whose avaricious and cruel object was to drive her, and her companions in miseries, through the country like cattle, to make his fortune on their carcasses, are but too much like that of thousands of our brethren in these states: if anything is whispered by one, which has any allusion to the melioration of their dreadful condition, they run and tell tyrants, that they may be enabled to keep them the longer in wretchedness and miseries. Oh! coloured people of these United States, I ask you, in the name of that God who made us, have we, in consequence of oppression, nearly lost the spirit of man, and, in no very trifling degree, adopted that of brutes? Do you answer, No?—I ask you, then, what set of men can you point me to, in all the world, who are so abjectly employed by their oppressors, as we are by our *natural enemies*? How can, Oh! how can those enemies but say that we and our children are not of the HUMAN FAMILY, but were made by our Creator to be an inheritance to them and theirs forever? How can the slaveholders but say that they can bribe the best coloured person in the country, to sell his brethren for a trifling sum of money, and take that atrocity to confirm them in their avaricious opinion, that we were made to be slaves to them and their children? How could Mr. Jefferson but say,[10]: "I advance it therefore as a suspicion only, that the blacks, whether originally a distinct race, or made distinct by time and circumstances, are *inferior* to the whites in the endowments both of body and mind?"[11] "It," says he, "is not against experience to suppose, that different species of the same genus, or varieties of the same species, may possess different qualifications."[12] [Here, my brethren, listen to him.]

[10] See his *Notes on Virginia*, p. 213 (Walker's note).
[11] See Stewart, 17.
[12] See Stewart, 17.

☛ "Will not a lover of natural history, then one who views the gradations in all the races of *animals* with the eye of philosophy, excuse an effort to keep those in the department of MAN as *distinct* as nature has formed them?"[13]— I hope you will try to find out the meaning of this verse—its widest sense and all its bearings: whether you do or not, remember the whites do. This very verse, brethren, having emanated from Mr. Jefferson, a much greater philosopher the world never afforded, has in truth injured us more, and has been as great a barrier to our emancipation as anything that has ever been advanced against us. I hope you will not let it pass unnoticed. He goes on further, and says: "This *unfortunate* difference of colour, and *perhaps* of *faculty*, is a powerful obstacle to the emancipation of these people. Many of their advocates, while they wish to vindicate the liberty of human nature are anxious also to preserve its *dignity* and *beauty*. Some of these, embarrassed by the question, 'What further is to be done with them?' join themselves in opposition with those who are actuated by sordid avarice only."[14] Now I ask you candidly, my suffering brethren in time, who are candidates for the eternal worlds, how could Mr. Jefferson but have given the world these remarks respecting us, when we are so submissive to them, and so much servile deceit prevail among ourselves—when we so *meanly* submit to their murderous lashes, to which neither the Indians nor any other people under Heaven would submit? No, they would die to a man, before they would suffer such things from men who are no better than themselves, and *perhaps not so good*. Yes, how can our friends but be embarrassed, as Mr. Jefferson says, by the question, "What further is to be done with these people?" for while they are working for our emancipation, we are, by our treachery, wickedness and deceit, working against ourselves and our children—helping ours, and the enemies of God, to keep us and our dear little children in their infernal chains of slavery!!! Indeed, our friends cannot but relapse and join themselves "with those who are actuated by *sordid avarice* only!!!!" For my own part, I am glad Mr. Jefferson has advanced his positions for your sake; for you will either have to contradict or confirm him by your own actions, and not by what our friends have said or done for us; for those things are other men's labors, and do not satisfy the Americans, who are waiting for us to prove to them ourselves, that we are MEN, before they will be willing to admit the fact; for I pledge you my sacred word of honor, that Mr. Jefferson's remarks respecting us, have sunk

---

[13] See Stewart, 18.
[14] See Stewart, 18.

deep into the hearts of millions of the whites and never will be removed this side of eternity. For how can they, when we are confirming him every day, by our *groveling submissions* and *treachery?* I aver, that when I look over these United States, and see the ignorant deceptions and consequent wretchedness of my brethren, I am brought ofttimes solemnly to a stand, and in the midst of my reflections I exclaim to my God, 'Lord didst thou make us to be slaves to our brethren, the whites?' But when I reflect that God is just, and that millions of my wretched brethren would meet death with glory—yea, more, would plunge into the very mouths of cannons and be torn into particles as minute as the atoms which compose the elements of the earth, in preference to a mean submission to the lash of tyrants, I am with streaming eyes, compelled to shrink back into nothingness before my Maker, and exclaim again, thy will be done, O Lord God Almighty.

Men of color, who are also of sense, for you particularly is my APPEAL designed. Our more ignorant brethren are not able to penetrate its value. I call upon you therefore to cast your eyes upon the wretchedness of your brethren, and to do your utmost to enlighten them—*go to work and enlighten your brethren!*—let the Lord see you doing what you can to rescue them and yourselves from degradation. Do any of you say that you and your family are free and happy, and what have you to do with the wretched slaves and other people? So can I say, for I enjoy as much freedom as any of you, if I am not quite as well off as the best of you. Look into our freedom and happiness, and see of what kind they are composed!! They are of the very lowest kind—they are the very *dregs!*—they are the most servile and abject kind, that ever a people was in possession of! If any of you wish to know how FREE you are, let one of you start and go through the southern and western States of this country, and unless you travel as a slave to a white man (a servant is a *slave* to the man whom he serves) or have your free papers, (which if you are not careful they will get from you) if they do not take you up and put you in jail, and if you cannot give good evidence of your freedom, sell you into eternal slavery, I am not a living man: or any man of color, immaterial who he is, or where he came from, if he is not *the fourth from the negro race!!* (as we are called) the white Christians of America will serve him the same they will sink him into wretchedness and degradation for ever while he lives. And yet some of you have the hardihood to say that you are free & happy! May God have mercy on your freedom and happiness!! I met a coloured man in the street a short time since, with a string of boots on his shoulders; we fell into conversation, and in course of which, I said to him, what a miserable set of people we are! He asked, why?—Said

I, we are so subjected under the whites, that we cannot obtain the comforts of life, but by cleaning their boots and shoes, old clothes, waiting on them, shaving them, &c. Said he, (with the boots on his shoulders) "I am completely happy!!! I never want to live any better or happier than when I can get a plenty of boots and shoes to clean!!!" Oh! how can those who are actuated by avarice only, but think, that our creator made us to be an inheritance to them forever, when they see that our greatest glory is centered in such mean and low objects? Understand me, brethren, I do not mean to speak against the occupations by which we acquire enough and sometimes scarcely that, to render ourselves and families comfortable through life. I am subjected to the same inconvenience, as you all. My objections are, to our *glorying* and being *happy* in such low employments; for if we are men, we ought to be thankful to the Lord for the past, and for the future. Be looking forward with thankful hearts to higher attainments than *wielding the razor* and *cleaning boots and shoes*. The man whose aspirations are not *above*, and even *below* these, is indeed, ignorant and wretched enough. I advance it therefore to you, not as a *problematical*, but as an unshaken and forever immoveable *fact*, that your full glory and happiness, as well as all other coloured people under heaven, shall never be fully consummated, but with the *entire emancipation of your enslaved brethren all over the world*. You may therefore, go to work and do what you can to rescue, or join in with tyrants to oppress them and yourselves, until the Lord shall come upon you all like a thief in the night. For I believe it is the will of the Lord that our greatest happiness shall consist in working for the salvation of our whole body. When this is accomplished a burst of glory will shine upon you, which will indeed astonish you and the world. Do any of you say this never will be done? I assure you that God will accomplish it—if nothing else will answer, he will hurl tyrants and devils into *atoms* and make way for his people. But O my brethren! I say unto you again, you must go to work and *prepare the way* of the Lord.

There is a great work for you to do, as trifling as some of you may think of it. You have to prove to the Americans and the world, that we are MEN, and not *brutes*, as we have been represented, and by millions treated. Remember, to let the aim of your labours among your brethren, and particularly the youths, be the dissemination of education and religion. It is lamentable, that many of our children go to school, from four until they are eight or ten, and sometimes fifteen years of age, and leave school knowing but a little more about the grammar of their language than a horse does about handling a musket—and not a few of them are really so ignorant, that they are unable to answer a person correctly, general questions in geography, and to hear them read, would only be to disgust a man who has a taste for reading; which, to do well, as trifling as it may appear to some, (to the ignorant in particular) is a great part of learning. Some few of them, may make out to scribble tolerably well, over a half sheet of paper, which I believe has hitherto been a powerful obstacle in our way, to keep us from acquiring knowledge. An ignorant father, who knows no more than what nature has taught him, together with what little he acquires by the senses of hearing and seeing, finding his son able to write a neat hand, sets it down for granted that he has as good learning as anybody; the young, ignorant gump, hearing his father or mother, who perhaps may be ten times more ignorant, in point of literature, than himself, extolling his learning, struts about, in the full assurance, that his attainments in literature are sufficient to take him through the world, when, in fact, he has scarcely any learning at all!!!!

I promiscuously fell in conversation once, with an elderly coloured man on the topics of education, and of the great prevalency of ignorance among us: Said he, "I know that our people are very ignorant but my son has a good education: I spent a great deal of money on his education: he can write as well as any white man, and I assure you that no one can fool him," &c. Said I, what else can your son do, besides writing a good hand? Can he post a set of books in a mercantile manner? Can he write a neat piece of composition in prose or in verse? To these interrogations he answered in the negative. Said I, Did your son learn, while he was at school, the width and depth of English Grammar? to which he also replied in the negative, telling me his son did not learn those things. Your son, said I, then, has hardly any learning at all—he is almost as ignorant, and more so, than many of those who never went to school one day in all their lives. My friend got a little put out, and so walking off, said that his son could write as well as any white man.—Most of the coloured people, when they speak of the education of one among us who can write a neat hand, and who perhaps knows nothing but to scribble and puff pretty fair on a small scrap of paper, immaterial whether his words are grammatical, or spelt correctly, or not; if it only looks beautiful, they say he has as good an education as any white man—he can write as well as any white man, &c. The poor, ignorant creature, hearing, this, he is ashamed, forever after, to let any person see him humbling himself to another for knowledge but going about trying to deceive those who are more ignorant than himself, he at last falls an ignorant victim to death in wretchedness. I pray that the

Lord may undeceive my ignorant brethren, and permit them to throw away pretensions, and seek after the substance of learning. I would crawl on my hands and knees through mud and mire, to the feet of a learned man, where I would sit and humbly supplicate him to instil[l] into me, that which neither devils nor tyrants could remove, only with my life—for colored people to acquire learning in this country, makes tyrants quake and tremble on their sandy foundation. Why, what is the matter? Why, they know that their infernal deeds of cruelty will be made known to the world. Do you suppose one man of good sense and learning would submit himself, his father, mother, wife and children, to be slaves to a wretched man like himself, who, instead of compensating him for his labours, chains, handcuffs and beats him and family almost to death, leaving life enough in them, however, to work for, and call him master? No! no! he would cut his devilish throat from ear to ear, and well do slave-holders know it. The bare name of educating the coloured people, scares our cruel oppressors almost to death. But if they do not have enough to be frightened for yet, it will be, because they can always keep us ignorant, and because God approbates their cruelties, with which they have been for centuries murdering us. The whites shall have enough of the blacks, yet, as true as God sits on his throne in Heaven.

Some of our brethren are so very full of learning, that you cannot mention any thing to them which they do not know better than yourself!!—nothing is strange to them!!—they knew every thing years ago!—if anything should be mentioned in company where they are, immaterial how important it is respecting us or the world, if they had not divulged it; they make light of it, and affect to have known it long before it was mentioned and try to make all in the room, or wherever you may be, believe that your conversation is nothing!!—not worth hearing! All this is the result of ignorance and ill-breeding; for a man of good-breeding, sense and penetration, if he had heard a subject told twenty times over, and should happen to be in company where one should commence telling it again, he would wait with patience on its narrator, and see if he would tell it as it was told in his presence before—paying the most strict attention to what is said, to see if any more light will be thrown on the subject: for all men are not gifted alike in telling, or even hearing the most simple narration. These ignorant, vicious, and wretched men, contribute almost as much injury to our body as tyrants themselves, by doing so much for the promotion of ignorance amongst us; for they, making such pretensions to knowledge, such of our youth as are seeking after knowledge, and can get access to them, take them as criterions to go by, who will lead them into a channel, where, unless the Lord blesses them with the privilege of seeing their folly, they will be irretrievably lost forever, while in time!!!

I must close this article by relating the very heart-rending fact, that I have examined school-boys and young men of colour in different parts of the country, in the most simple parts of Murray's English Grammar, and not more than one in thirty was able to give a correct answer to my interrogations. If anyone contradicts me, let him step out of his door into the streets of Boston, New-York, Philadelphia, or Baltimore, (no use to mention any other, for the Christians are too charitable further south or west!)—I say, let him who disputes me, step out of his door into the streets of either of those four cities, and promiscuously collect one hundred school-boys, or young men of colour, *who have been to school*, and who are considered by the coloured people to have received an excellent education, because, perhaps, some of them can write a good hand, but who, notwithstanding their neat writing, may be almost as ignorant, in comparison, as a horse.—And, I say it, he will hardly find (in this enlightened day, and in the midst of this *charitable* people) five in one hundred, who, are able to correct the false grammar of their language.—The cause of this almost universal ignorance among us, I appeal to our school-masters to declare. Here is a fact, which I this very minute take from the mouth of a young coloured man, who has been to school in this state (Massachusetts) nearly nine years, and who knows grammar this day, *nearly* as well as he did the day he first entered the school-house, under a white master. This young man says: "My master would never allow me to study grammar." I asked him, why? "The school committee," said he "forbid the coloured children learning grammar"—they would not allow any but the white children "to study grammar." It is a notorious fact, that the major part of the white Americans, have, ever since we have been among them, tried to keep us ignorant, and make us believe that God made us and our children to be slaves to them and theirs. *Oh! my God, have mercy on Christian Americans!!!*

10

"Zillah" (Sarah Mapps Douglass) Writings

Published in *The Liberator* (1831–1832)

MORAL.

[By a young lady of color.]

For the Liberator.

MOONLIGHT.

I look back on the days that are past.

—Ossian.[1]

I have a melancholy pleasure in looking upon the moon in a cloudless night, when she hangs like a lamp of silver in the sky, and throws her pure light abroad on spire and cottage, hill and dale. Oh! it is in such a night as this that memory brings before me all the friends I have ever loved, all I have lost. It is then I seem again to stand by the dying couch of the dearest friend of my childhood. I witness the calm composure of her countenance, and hear her voice faultering in death say, "Weep not for me; the sting of death is taken away, for Christ has died."[2] It is then I think of my beloved instructress, and her mild and gracious countenance; her dignified and queen-like person passes in review before me. Amiable and excellent woman! though the damp clods of the valley hide thee from my sight, yet thy memory lives, and is as grateful to the heart of thy sorrowing pupil as the flowers is spring. It is then I think of my happy school days,—my school companions,—to many of whom

---

[1] The epigraph comes from *The Works of Ossian* (1765), James Macpherson's (1736–1796) collection of purportedly ancient Scottish epics and folklore. Zillah's reference is both to pseudonymity and the value of the history of colonized and objected cultures. At the same time, the address in the referenced poem is to the night and the moon as it is in Zillah's work.

[2] Zillah repeats these lines in the August 18th entry in the Juvenile Department of *The Liberator* (1831), and she may be referencing the same person and circumstance. "The sting of death" trope comes from Corinthians 15:56.

I was tenderly attached. Some of these were feelingly alive to the beauties of moonlight. O, my heart! where are they now? Two or three have left their native city for a foreign land; others have passed away to that bourne from which no traveller ever returns; and the few that remain, alas! alas!

> They meet me in the glittering throng,
> With cold averted eyes.[3]

Then, too, Hope whispers,—"The time is not far distant, when the wronged and enslaved children of America shall cease to be a 'by-word and a reproach'[4] among their brethren." ZILLAH
Philadelphia.

FEMALE LITERARY ASSOCIATION.

During his recent sojourn in Philadelphia, (rendered inexpressibly delightful by the kindness of friends,) the Editor of the Liberator had the privilege of visiting and addressing a society of colored ladies called the "FEMALE LITERARY ASSOCIATION."[5] It was one of the most interesting spectacles he had ever witnessed. If the traducers of the colored race could be acquainted with the moral worth, just refinement, and large intelligence of this association, their mouths would hereafter be dumb. The members assemble together every Tuesday evening, for the purpose of mutual improvement in moral and literary pursuits. Nearly all of them write, almost weekly, original pieces, which are put anonymously into a box, and afterwards criticised by a committee. Having been permitted to bring with him several of these pieces, he ventures to commence their publication, not only for their merit, but in order to induce the colored ladies of other places to go and do likewise. This society is at present composed of about twenty members, but is increasing, and full of intellectual promise.

---

[3] This verse comes from a popularly reprinted poem which negatively compares the coldness of lost friends to the respected absence of deceased religious friends. The poem echoes Stewart's frequent concern with the betrayal of insufficiently pious friends. *Graham's Illustrated Magazine* attributed to the poem to popular hymn writer James Montgomery (1771–1854), but the veracity of their attribution is difficult to determine.

[4] From Ezekiel 36:3. The enslavement of the Israelites and the destruction of their homelands became a common point of derision for the Israelites.

[5] See Elizabeth McHenry's *Forgotten Readers* for an extended examination of nineteenth-century Black women's literary associations.

TO A FRIEND.

You ask me if I do not despair on account of the Bill now before Legislature?*6 I am cast down, but not in despair. I am aware that it will be our lot to suffer much persecution, and I have endeavored, for the last year, to fortify my mind against approaching trials, by reading what others have suffered. In perusing Sewell's History of the people called the Quakers,[7] I was particularly struck with the account of Barbara Blaugdon, a young and timid woman, who, by the help of the Almighty, was enabled to endure cruel persecution, not only with patience but with joy. On one occasion, being severely whipped, even until the blood streamed down her back, she sang the praises of her God aloud, rejoicing that she was counted worthy to suffer for his name; which increased the anger of the executioner, and made him say, "Do ye sing? I'll make you cry by and by." But Barbara was strengthened by an invisible power, and afterwards declared if she had been whipped to death, she should not have dismayed. Earnestly have I prayed, my friend, that a double portion of her humility and fortitude may be ours. In despair! no, no—God is on our side. With the eye of faith, I pierce the veil of futurity, and I see our advocate, after having honorably borne the burden and heat of the day, sitting down peaceably by his "ain fire-side."[8] Time has scattered a few blossoms on his head, but left his manly brow without a wrinkle. Hundreds of liberated slaves are pressing round him, eager to testify their gratitude.

See yonder mother, with her infant! She approaches him, and kneels at his feet, aises her eyes to heaven, and would speak her gratitude; but tears and sobs impede her utterance. O, her tears are far more eloquent than words.

I see black and white mingle together in social intercourse, without a shadow of disgust appearing on the countenance of either no wailing is heard, no clanking chains; but the voice of peace and love and joy is wafted to my car by every breeze.

And what has wrought this mighty change? Religion, my sister; the religion of the meek and lowly Jesus; and such are its effects wherever it appears. Could I not thus look forward, I should indeed despair. ZILLAH.

---

[6] "This Bill is 'to prohibit the migration of negroes and mulattoes into the Commonwealth.' It has been postponed to the next Legislature—we trust, for the honor of Pennsylvania, postponed forever.—*Ed.*" (original note). The bill never became law.

[7] Willem Sewell's *History* was published in Dutch in 1717 and in English in 1722. Quakers were a major force in early American abolitionism. Douglass was born into a Quaker family, though her Zillah seems to be less familiar with the religion.

[8] Another Scottish reference, probably a song, that was of wide use in Romantic culture from and about Gaelic cultures.

Philadelphia, April 1st, 1832.

☛ By a young lady of color.

For the Liberator.

A TRUE TAKE FOR CHILDREN.

I hope the children who may read this tale, are very gentle and obedient to their teachers, because a teacher has many difficulties to encounter, and the good or bad conduct of children greatly increases or lessens difficulties.

It is my lot to be a teacher, and there have been times when my spirit has been bowed as it were to the earth by the unkind behavior of children, and I have been ready to say, "I will not, I cannot be a teacher." But notwithstanding the path which I have been called to walk in is rugged, it has its sunny spots: the following incident is one of them.

One morning early in the spring, a little orphan boy, one of my scholars, brought into the schoolroom a few violets, and laying them on the desk before me, he said, with a countenance beaming with affection, "I have brought thee flowers, teacher, and I have some pretty verses to repeat about them." I requested to hear them, and he replied,

> First violets of early spring,
> To my teacher I will bring.[9]

I was inexpressibly touched with the delivery of the offering—they were the first violets I had seen that season. Flowers have ever been dear to me, and peculiarly so when presented to me by children.

> They are a language—and they tell
> Of thoughts unspoken, words unwrit;
> They weave around the heart a spell,
> And few there are would banish it.[10]

Perhaps some children may think there was nothing great in this child's presenting his teacher with a few flowers. Trifling as the circumstance may appear to you, my little readers, it repaid me, yes, more than repaid me for months of anxiety which I had suffered on his account; for though this little

---

[9] Part of Zillah's delight may be that the couplet is original to the student.
[10] The origin of this verse is unclear; it may be original to Zillah or traditional.

boy was affectionate, he was mischievous, and sometimes disobedient; but I am happy to say, that is he now much improved, and that his conduct is in the highest degree satisfactory to my mind. He is industrious, and his kind mistress has furnished him with a box of paints, and he employs his leisure in painting ships and steamboats; and he has presented me with a ship in full sail, which he delights in calling after my name. I could mention many other winnings proofs of his regard, which are more dear to me than silver or gold; but I fear making my story too long.

I have sometimes wished that the enemies of my wronged people could look into this child's heart: if they could, I think they would learn that gratitude is not confined to a fair complexion. I hope none of my little readers are so wicked as to despise children whose complexions God has cause to differ from theirs. If there are any so cruel, I hope they will, after reading this, retire to their chambers, and there kneel down and say, "O Lord, teach me to love my neighbor as myself. Let me not despise any whom thou has created." And then they will receive strength to do what is right; for the Lord loves, and ever lends an attentive ear to the prayers of children.

I think, dear children, from what I have written, that you will understand that you have it in your power always to make the situation of your teachers pleasant. Will you not do so?

The flowers presented to me by my young scholar are faded and dead, but the memory of his gratitude and affections lives in the heart of his teacher and friend.

Philadelphia. ZILLAH.

☛ By a young lady of color.

For the Liberator.

Extract from a letter written to a friend, Feb. 23d, 1832.

You do not agree with me, in regard to emigration.[11] Would that I had eloquence enough to convince you that I am right! You say, "if we better our situation by removing, why oppose [it?]" Believe me, my friend, there is no spot in [the] known world where people are happier than America. And bethink thee, dearest; it is home! Think of this for one moment, and every memory will call up so many fond and soothing reflections as will make the loth to leave it.

---

[11] Voluntary, self-directed emigration and forced deportation of free and formerly enslaved black persons to places like Haiti, Liberia, Canada, and Mexico were hotly debated proposed solutions to the US race problems. These solutions were largely promoted by majority-white associations, particularly those that opposed enslavement but also denied racial equality and feared "miscegenation," although they too had African American advocates like Zillah's friend as well. See Stewart, 81 for Stewart's position on colonization, which paralleled Zillah's.

[If] we should bend our steps to Hayti, there is [no] security for life and property; too many of [its] people are desperately wicked. If we go to Mexico, it is the same there. Why through ourselves upon the protection of Great Britain, when thousands of her own children are starving? Do [you] suppose she can feel more love for us than she does for her own? For my part, I can truly [say],

> All those nameless ties,
> In which the charm of country lies,
> Have round my heart been hourly spun,
> Till Columbia's cause and mine are one;[12]

[And] though she unkindly strives to throw me from [her] bosom,[13] I will but embrace her the closer, determining never to part with her whilst I have [unclear].

ZILLAH.

☞ By a young lady of color.

For the Liberator.

A MOTHER'S LOVE

> All our passions change
> With changing circumstances; rise or fall,
> Dependent on their object; claim returns;
> Live on reciprocation and expire
> Unfed by hope. A mother's fondness reigns
> Without a rival, and without an end.[14]

And dost though, poor slave, feel this holy passion? Does thy heart swell with anguish, when thy helpless infant is torn from thine arms, and carried then [unclear] whither? when thou hast no hope left that thou shalt ever see his innocent face again? Yes, I know thou dost feel all this.

I well remember conversing with a liberator slave, who told me of the many hardships she had to encounter while in a state of captivity. At one time, after having been reaping all the morning, she returned at noon to a spring near her master's house to carry water in some hired laborers. At this spring her

---

[12] An adaptation of a stanza from Thomas Moore's *Lalla Rookh* (1817), a book of orientalist narrative poems that center on the conflicts that emerge from tensions between national loyalties and personal relationships. Moore (1779–1852) was a Catholic Irish nationalist.

[13] Compare to Zillah on Stewart, 129 and the importance of the bosom as a symbol of racialized womanhood. Zillah frames herself as an unwanted but fiercely loyal child of the United States.

[14] From Hannah More's "Moses in the Bulrushes" in *Sacred Dramas* (1782).

babe was tied; she had not been allowed to some [unclear], the time at which it was placed there; her heart yearned with pity and affection for her boy, and while she kneeled at the spring and dipped the water with one hand, she drew her babe to her aching bosom with the other. She would have fed it from the fountain,[15] troubled and almost dried with grief; but, alas! the [unclear] was denied her. Her cruel mistress observed her from the window where she was sitting, and immediately ran to her, and seizing a large stick beat her cruelly upon her neck and bosom, bidding her begone to work. Poor creature! rage against her mistress almost emboldened her to return the blow; she cared not for herself, but when she reflected that her child would probably be the sufferer, her maternal tenderness triumphed over ever other feeling, and she again tied her child, and returned to the labors of the field.

American Mothers! can you doubt that the slave feels as tenderly for her offspring as you do for yours? Do your hearts feel no throb of pity for her [unclear]? Will you not raise your voices, and plead for her emancipation—her immediate emancipation!

At another time, when assisting her mistress to get dinner, she dropped the skin of a potato in what she was preparing. The angry woman snatched the knife from her hand, and struck her with it upon her bosom! My countenance expressed so much horror at the account, that I believe this poor woman thought I doubted her veracity. Baring her aged bosom, "Look," said she, "my child, here is the scar"[16]—and I looked and wept that women should have so far forgot her gentle nature. Soon after this, she was sold to another person, and at his death freed. She then went to reside in a neighboring city. Her old mistress, after a series of misfortune, was reduced almost to beggary, and [unclear] her weary footsteps to the same city; and would you believe, reader? She sent for the woman she had so cruelly wronged, to come and assist her. Her friends persuaded her not to go; but she, able creature! Womanlike, weeping that a lady should be so reduced, obeyed the call, and waited upon her as faithfully as if she had been her dearest friend.

Calumniators of my despised race, read this and blush.   ZILLAH.
Philadelphia, July 8th, 1832.

☛ By a lady of color.

---

[15] Her breast.
[16] This revelation anticipates Sojourner Truth's reported baring of her own breast during an antislavery lecture to prove her womanhood. Both evoke challenges of authenticity and the racialization of embodied sex the formerly enslaved faced.

For the Liberator.

TO ZILLAH.

MY DEAREST FRIEND—On reviewing the sentiments expressed in your reply to "A Colored Female of Philadelphia," read at our last meeting, I was struck with the difference between the thoughts that I had upon it; and it occurred so forcibly to my mind that you have mistaken or overlooked the design of the colored female, that I shall endeavor to explain her meaning, confident that my friend would not willingly misconstrue it.

Our friend's subject was so excellent, the facts were so clear, that I am almost afraid to handle it; but according to my opinion, her meaning was this: that in case there should be a day when we might be obliged to remove, there should be a place refuge which we might adopt, if driven by oppression from our native country and the endearments of our youth. For if the people of these United States should make such compulsory laws,[17] we could not, as a people, step forward and bid it to be otherwise; no—none but that God who rule over the universe, and who is mysterious in all his ways. Our friend is opposed to colonizing anywhere; nor would I, for any sum be obliged to leave this place—for I never knew any other; but I merely want to show you how you have mistaken her meaning. "There are wicked people everywhere": very true, but we may remember that God has said, if there be but three righteous, he is willing to save. Dear friend, read it again and again, and do not suffer feeling to overpower reflection.

Philadelphia. WOODBY.[18]
[By a young lady of color.]

REPLY TO WOODBY.

My friend Woodby has entirely mistaken the design of the communication placed in the box last week. It was not intended as a reply to "A Colored Female of Philadelphia," but is simply what its title proclaims it to be, "An extract from a letter written to a friend many miles distant."

---

[17] Woodby does not include herself and Zillah as "people of the United States" because they cannot take part, via representative democracy, of creating the laws to which they may be subject. Black women's disenfranchisement, in Woodby's formulation, is exclusion from not only from citizenship but also national identity.

[18] There is no clear referent for this pseudonym, and it may be the writer's real surname. Alice Woodby McKane, born in 1865 in Philadelphia and educated at the Institute for Colored Youth, became a prominent doctor and activist in the latter half of the nineteenth century. The writer of this article, also an educated black woman from Philadelphia and active a generation before McKane, may have been related to or associated with McKane's family. McKane, it bears noting, worked for a period in Liberia.

I will, however, endeavor to answer you. You say "that God promised to save a city of old, if three righteous persons were found in it."[19] And shall he not for his own great name's sake, preserve us, in the land of our nativity, from the machinations of our enemies? Will you not trust him? I firmly believe it is his will that we remain. I would not give up this belief for a thousand worlds.

I wish you would read what is said on emigration in the Address of our fearless advocate G—;[20] ay, fearless, because he knows the cause in which he is engaged is holy, and that it has the approval is Heaven. Is not your heart, my sister, exceedingly joyful with the thought that we have one so willing to plead our cause? and shall we not imitate his example, by throwing off all fear of man, and placing our dependance on the Rock of Ages?[21] Surely, you will answer, yes! Cease, then, to think of any other city of refuge. Listen to the voice of our dear Redeemer! It says: "Fear not, little flock; it is your Father's good pleasure to give you the kingdom."

You have advised me to read the piece referred to, again and again. Believe me, my friend, were I to read it a thousand times, it could not alter feelings and opinions which have entwined themselves round every fibre of my hear, from my childhood: even at that early period, when I heard encomiums lavished upon this favored country, my heart exulted, and I said, "This is my own, my native land."[22]

Philadelphia.   ZILLAH.

☛ By a young lady of color.

For the Liberator.

FOR THE CHILDREN WHO READ THE LIBERATOR.

Elizabeth was the eldest of a family of six children. She was a child of many sorrows, having been afflicted from the age of eighteen months till the time of her death, a period of fourteen years, with a disorder called a Diseased Hip Joint. During that time not a passed in which she could say, I have no pain. When about ten year old, her parents sent her to a school in the neighborhood of her home, where by diligence and attention to her studies she

---

[19] From Genesis 18, in which Abraham pleads to God to spare Sodom for the sake of even a few righteous inhabitants. Zillah points out that Woodby's argument that the righteousness of black communities could save the places to where they emigrate could just as well apply to the United States.
[20] William Lloyd Garrison.
[21] Common biblical term for God.
[22] From Walter Scott's *Lay of the Last Minstrel* (1805). Like the Ossian epigraph to her "Moral" (Stewart, 123), this line references romantic reconstructions of Gaelic identity as an analogue to African American subjectivity.

secured the approbation oof her instructress. It is very probable she would have remained some time at the school, if it had not been for the unkind behaviour of her school-mates; where by superior industry she gained the head of the class. These silly children would pout, and call her "negro"; and the complained so frequently to their parents, that a negro stood above them, that her teacher, much as she loved her, was obliged to part with her.

Methinks I see the blush of conscious shame mantling the cheek of some of my little readers, who have been guilty of the like sin. O, children, did you know the bitterness of having the finger of score pointed at you where you appear, at school, in the streets, and even in the Lord's house; could you feel for one moment the anguish of being despised, merely for your complexion, surely you would throw this unholy prejudice from you with disdain.

After this time, Elizabeth had no opportunity of going to school; but her kind mother supplied the place of her teacher, and she learned to read and sew extremely well. She was never better pleased than when employed for her parents. Whatever she undertook to do was well done. She would pull out her work twenty times rather than have long stitches in it. Obedience, gentleness, patience and perseverance, shone with peculiar lustre in her character. The holy Bible was her delight; she knew many of the longest Psalms and chapter in Proverbs by heart; and it was her practice to repeat them daily. Pleasant and consoling it was to her mother's heart, to see her afflicted child thus early directing her thoughts to heavenly things. By her conciliating temper, she gained such an influence over the family, that her mother could entrust her with the management of the little household in her absence. Four little brothers and one sister were frequently left in her charge: the youngest of these children, a boy of three years, was self-willed and obstinate, and his mother had much difficulty in controlling him; yet he was generally submissive to Elizabeth. She would coax him to be good, and laying her hand on his head, would softly say, "Willie, mother says you must not do so; come and sit down by me"—and he would sit down by her, and be quiet as a little mouse.

Children, love one another. E. governed her brothers and sister by the law of love; and though long years have passed away since she was laid in the cold grave, she is still fondly remembered in the domestic circle, and her sister who is now grown to woman's estate, ofttimes weeps, when she thinks of her love, her gentleness, and her lamb-like patience during her protracted illness.

I shall now finish my story by relating the circumstance of E's death. She was seized with a bleeding at the nose. The kind physician who attended the family was called. When he saw her he looked sorrowful, and said, "Poor little thing! I can do nothing for her—life is ebbing."[23] When she was told what the Doctor said, she seemed alarmed, and desired not to be left alone. She passed that night inn deep exercise of mind, frequently groaning, which caused her mother to ask if she was in much pain. "No," said she, "I have not more pain that usual." In the morning she called her mother to her and said, "Now I know I shall die, and I quite willing to go if you can spare me—the sting of death is taken away, for Christ has died." Her mother replied, she would pray for strength to give her up. In the afternoon she desired her brothers and sister might be brought to her: when they came to the bedside, she bade them an affectionate farewell, and with a countenance, in which love and resignation were beautifully blended, asked to have a hymn sung; again expressed her willingness to depart—laid her dear head upon the pillow, and said to her weeping parents, 'I cannot talk any more to you—now you must talk to me." She spoke no more after this, but lay for two days like a person asleep, the peacefully departed.

I would now ask my little readers, if the character of Elizabeth appears the less lovely to them, because her complexion differed from theirs? I am sure every good child will answer, "No!"

ZILLAH.

Philadelphia, Aug. 8, 1832.

---

[23] Such appeals to sympathy, particularly through the death or suffering of a young woman or child, is typical of women's literature of the time. Little Eva from Harriet Beecher Stow's *Uncle Tom's Cabin* (1852) is the famous example from the era.

11

Hosea Easton, *A Treatise on the Intellectual Character, and Civil and Political Condition of the Colored People of the U. States; And the Prejudice Exercised Towards Them; With a Sermon on the Duty of the Church to Them* (1837) (selections)

CHAPTER I. ON THE INTELLECTUAL CHARACTER OF THE COLORED PEOPLE OF THESE UNITED STATES OF AMERICA.

In this country we behold the remnant of a once noble, but now heathenish people. In calling the attention of my readers to the subject which I here present them, I would have them lose sight of the African character, about which I have made some remarks in my introduction.[1] For at this time, circumstances have established as much difference between them and their ancestry, as exists between them and any other race or nation. In the first place the colored people who are born in this country, are Americans in every sense of the word. Americans by birth, genius, habits, language, &tc. It is supposed, and I think not without foundation, that the slave population labor under an intellectual and physical disability or inferiority.[2] The

---

[1] In the introduction to the *Treatise*, Easton considers the ancestral histories of African peoples from the story Ham in Genesis. He repositions Africans as the source of nobility and civilization. What he calls the "uninterrupted chain" of civilization moves from Egypt to Greece, Rome, and then Europe. Egyptian, Ethiopian, and Carthaginian civilizations represented the height of African nobility, he argues, and the denigration of what would become the black race resulted from European pillaging and violence.

[2] Prominent scholars across fields claimed Africans were naturally inferior (e.g., Thomas Jefferson in *Notes on the State of Virginia* in Stewart, 5–22). Phrenologists supported this notion with

justness of these conclusions, however, will apply only to such as have been subject to slavery some considerable length of time. I have already made some remarks with regard to the cause of apparent differences between nations.[3] I shall have cause to remark again, that as the intellectual as well as the physical properties of mankind, are subject to cultivation, I have observed that the growth or culture depends materially on the means employed to that end.[4] In those countries in which the maxims and laws are such as are calculated to employ the physical properties mostly, such as racing, hunting, &c, there is uniformly a full development of physical properties. We will take the American Indian for example. A habit of indolence produces a contrary effect. History, as well as experience, will justify me in saying that a proper degree of exercise is essential to the growth of the corporeal system; and that the form and size depends on the extent and amount of exercise. On comparing one who is brought up from his youth a tradesman, with one who is brought up a farmer, the difference is manifestly apparent according to the difference of their exercise. Change of public sentiment indirectly affects the form and size of whole nations, inasmuch as public sentiment dictates the mode and kind of exercise. The muscular yeomanry who once formed a majority of our country's population, are now but seldom found; those who fill their places in society, in no way compare with them in that respect. Compare our farmer's daughters, who have been brought up under the influence of country habits, with those brought up under city habits, and a difference is most manifest.

But there is another consideration worthy of notice. Education, says D. D. Hunter,*[5] on the part of the mother, commences from the moment she has the prospect of being a mother. And her own health thenceforth is the first duty she owes to her child. The instructions given to the wife of Manoah, and mother of Sampson, the Nazarite, (Jud. 13,4:) "Now, therefore, beware, I pray thee, drink not wine nor strong drink, and eat not any unclean thing" are not

pseudo-data about head shape, size, and volume, arguing that these measurements proved the intellectual and moral inferiority of enslaved black persons.

[3] Easton's reference to "apparent differences between nations" likely alludes to phenotypic distinctions between races. In the introduction to the *Treatise*, he explains these differences as the result "the same laws which variegate the whole creation."

[4] Easton emphasizes the role of cultivation (e.g., education; exposure to the world) rather than nature in the mental and moral inferiority of African Americans. Unlike *natural* physical variation, intellectual differences result from the influence of sin and the Fall, he argues.

[5] Henry Hunter (1741-1802) was a Scottish minister who wrote popular histories and sermons. The rest of this paragraph comes directly from Hunter's *Sacred Biography* (1794), a series of lectures he delivered between 1783 and 1792. Easton's original note directs readers to Hunter's *Sacred Biography* (1794), vol. 7, p. 10.

merely arbitrarily adapted only to a particular branch of political economy, and intended to serve local and temporary purposes; no, the constitutions of nature, reason, and experience, which unite in recommending to those who have the prospect of being mothers, a strict attention to diet, to exercise, to temper, to everything, which affecting the frame of their own body or mind, may communicate an important, a lasting, perhaps indelible impression, to the mind or body of their offspring. A proper regimen for themselves, is therefore the first stage of education for their children. The neglect of it is frequently found productive of effects which no future culture is able to alter or rectify.

These most just remarks confirm me in the opinion, that the laws of nature may be crossed by the misconduct or misfortune of her who has the prospect of being a mother. Apply these remarks to the condition of slave mothers, as such, and what are the plain and natural inferences to be drawn. Certainly, if they are entitled to any weight at all, the intellectual and physical inferiority of the slave population can be accounted for without imputing it to an original hereditary cause. Contemplate the exposed condition of slave mothers—their continual subjection to despotism and barbarity; their minds proscribed to the narrow bounds of servile obedience, subject to irritation from every quarter; great disappointment, and physical suffering themselves, and continual eye-witnesses to maiming and flagellation; shrieks of wo borne to their ears on every wind. Indeed, language is lame in the attempt to describe the condition of those poor daughters of affliction. Indeed, I have no disposition to dwell on the subject; to be obliged to think of it at all, is sufficiently harrowing to my feelings. But I would inquire how it can be possible for nature, under such circumstances, to act up to her perfect laws?

The opprobrious terms used in common by most all classes, to describe the deformities of the offspring of these parents, is true in part, though employed with rather bad grace by those in whom the cause of their deformity originates. I will introduce those terms, not for the sake of embellishing my treatise with their modest style, but to show the lineal effects of slavery on its victims. Contracted and sloped foreheads; prominent eye-balls; projecting underjaw; certain distended muscles about the mouth, or lower parts of the face; thick lips and flat nose; hips and rump projecting; crooked shins; flat feet, with large projecting heels. This, in part, is the language used by moderns to philosophize, upon the negro character. With regard to their mind, it is said that their intellectual brain is not fully developed; malicious disposition;

no taste for high and honorable attainments; implacable enemies one to another; and that they sustain the same relation to the ourangoutang, that the whites do to them. Now, as it respects myself, I am perfectly willing to admit the truth of these remarks, as they apply to the character of a slave population; for I am aware that no language capable of being employed by mortal tongue, is sufficiently descriptive to set forth in its true character the effect of that cursed thing, slavery. I shall here be under the necessity of calling up those considerations connected with the subject, which I but a little time since entertained a hope that I should be able to pass by unnoticed; I have reference to a mother who is a slave, bringing into the world beings whose limbs and minds were lineally fashioned for the yoke and fetter, long before her own immortal mind was clothed in materiality.

I would ask my readers to think of woman as the greatest natural gift to man—think of her in delicate health, when the poor delicate fabric is taxed to the utmost to answer the demands of nature's laws—when friends and sympathies, nutricious aliments, and every other collateral aid is needed. O think of poor woman, a prospective mother; and when you think, feel; as a heart of flesh can feel; see her weeping eyes fixed alternately upon the object of her affections and him who accounts her a brute—think how she feels on beholding the gore streaming from the back, the naked back, of the former, while the latter wields the accursed lash, until the back of a husband, indeed the whole frame, has become like a loathsome heap of mangled flesh. How often has she witnessed the wielding club lay him prostrate, while the purple current followed the damning blow. How the rattling of the chain, the lock of which has worn his ancles and his wrists to the bone, falls upon her ear. O, has man fallen so far below the dignity of his original character, as not to be susceptible of feeling. But does the story stop here. I would that it were even so. But alas! this, the ornamental production of nature's God, is not exempt, even in this state, from the task of a slave. And, as though cursed by all the gods, her own delicate frame is destined to feel the cruel scourge. When faint and weary she lags her step, the overseer, as though decreed to be a tormenting devil, throws the coiling lash upon her naked back; and in turn, the master makes it his pleasure to despoil the works of God, by subjecting her to the rank of goods and chattels, to be sold in the shambles. Woman, you who possess a woman's nature, can feel for her who was destined by the Creator of you both, to fill the same sphere with yourself. You know by experience the claims of nature's laws—you know too well the irritability of your natures when taxed to the utmost to fulfil the decree of nature's God.

I have in part given a description of a mother that is a slave. And can it be believed to be possible for such a one to bring perfect children into the world. If we are permitted to decide that natural causes produce natural effects, then it must be equally true that unnatural causes produce unnatural effects. The slave system is an unnatural cause, and has produced its unnatural effects, as displayed in the deformity of two and a half millions of beings, who have been under its soul-and-body-destroying influence, lineally, for near three hundred years; together with all those who have died their progenitors since that period. But again, I believe it to be an axiom generally admitted, that mind acts on matter, then again, that mind acts on mind; this being the case, is it a matter of surprise that those mothers who are slaves, should, on witnessing the distended muscles on the face of whipped slaves, produce the same or similar distensions on the face of her offspring, by her own mind being affected by the sight; and so with all other deformities. Like causes produce like effects. If by Jacob's placing ring-streaked elder in the trough where Laban's flocks drank, caused their young to be ring-streaked and speckled, why should not the offspring of slave mothers, who are continually witnessing exciting objects, be affected by the same law; and why should they not be more affected, as the mother is capable of being more excited.[6]

From the foregoing I draw the following conclusions, with regard to the different degrees of effect produced by slavery. Compare slaves that are African born, with those who are born in slavery, and the latter will in no wise compare with the former in point of form of person or strength of mind. The first and second generation born in this country are generally far before the fourth and fifth, in this respect. Compare such as have been house servants, as they are called, for several generations with such as have been confined to plantations the same term of time, and there will be a manifest inferiority in the latter. Observe among the nominally free, their form of person, features, strength of mind, and bent of genius, fidelity, &c., and it will evidently appear that they who sustain a relation of no further than the third generation from African birth, are in general far before those who sustain a more distant relation. The former generally acquire small possessions, and conform their habits of life and modes of operation with those common where they live, while those who have been enslaved for several generations or whose progenitors in direct line were thus enslaved, cannot be induced to conform to any regular rule of life or operation. I intend this last statement as general

---

[6] As a precedent for his argument, Easton references the story of Laban's flock in Genesis 30:30–43.

fact, of which, however, there are exceptions; where there is a mixture of blood, as it is sometimes called, perhaps these remarks may not apply. I suppose, however, that in case of a union between a degraded American slave of the last order spoken of, and a highly intelligent free American, whether white or colored, that the offspring of such parents are as likely to partake of the influence of slavery through the lineal medium of the slave parent, as to receive natural intelligence through the medium of the other. So far as I understand, nature's law seems not to be scrupulously rigid in this particular: there appears to be no rule, therefore, by which to determine the effect or lineal influence of slavery on a mixed race. I am satisfied with regard to one fact, however, that caste has no influence whatever: for a union between a highly cultivated black and a degraded one, produces an exact similar effect. Whatever complexion or nation parents thus connected, may be of, the effect produced would be the same, but it would not be certain that their children would occupy a midway region between the intelligent and degraded parent, as in other cases part of a family may be below mediocrity, and part above, in point of form and intellect. One thing is certain, which may have some bearing in the case; that when nature has been robbed, give her a fair chance and she will repair her loss by her own operations, one of which is to produce variety. But to proceed further with any remarks on this point, I feel myself not at liberty. In view of what I have said on this subject, I am aware of having fallen short of giving a full description of the lineal influence and effects slavery has upon the colored population of this country. Such is the nature of the subject, that it is almost impossible to arrange our thoughts so as to follow it by any correct rule of investigation. Slavery, in its effects, is like that of a complicated disease, typifying evil in all its variety—in its operations, omnipotent to destroy—in effect, fatal as death and hell. Language is lame in its most successful attempt, to describe its enormity; and with all the excitement which this country has undergone, in consequence of the discussion of the subject, yet the story is not half told, neither can it be. We, who are subject to its fatal effects, cannot fully realize the disease under which we labor. Think of a colored community, whose genius and temperament of minds all differ in proportion as they are lineally or personally made to feel the damning influence of slavery, and, as though it had the gift of creating tormenting pangs at pleasure, it comes up, in the character of an accuser, and charges our half destroyed, discordant minds, with hatred one towards the other, as though a body composed of parts, and systematized by the laws of nature, were capable of continuing its regular configurative movements after it has been decomposed. When I think of nature's laws, that with scrupulous exactness they are to be obeyed by all things over which they are intended to bear rule, in order that she may be able to declare, in all her variety, that the hand that made her is divine, and when, in this case, I see and feel how she has been robbed of her means to perform her delightful task—her law r s trampled under feet with all their divine authority, despoiling her works even in her most sacred temples—1 wonder that I am a man; for though of the third generation from slave parents, yet in body and mind nature has never been permitted to half finish her work. Let all judge who is in the fault, God, or slavery, or its sustniners?

CHAPTER II. ON THE POLITICAL CONDITION AND CHARACTER OF THE COLORED PEOPLE.

A government like this is at any time liable to be revolutionized by the people, at any and every time there is a change of public sentiment. This, perhaps, is as it should be. But when the subjects of a republican government become morally and politically corrupt, there is but little chance remaining for republicanism. A correct standard may be set up, under which parties may pretend to aim at a defence of the original principles upon which the government was based; but if the whole country has become corrupt, what executive power is there remaining to call those parties in question, and to decide whether their pretensions and acts correspond with the standard under which they profess to act. Suppose the Constitution and articles of confederation, be the admitted correct standard by all parties, still the case is no better, when there is not honesty enough in either, to admit a fair construction of their letter and spirit. Good laws, and a good form of government, are of but very little use to a wicked people, further than they are able to restrain them from wickedness.

Were a fallen angel permitted to live under the government of heaven, his disposition would first incline him to explain away the nature of its laws; this done, their spirit becomes perverted, which places him back in hell from whence he came; for, though he could not alter the laws of heaven, yet he could pervert their use, in himself, and act them out in this perverted state, which would make him act just like a devil. The perversion of infinite good, is infinite evil—and if the spiritual use of the laws of an infinitely perfect government is productive of a perfect heaven, in like manner their spiritual perversion is productive of perfect or infinite hell. Hence it is said to be a bottomless pit—ay, deep as the principle is high? from which the distortion is made. I have taken this course to illustrate the state of a people with a good government and laws, and with a disposition to explain away all their meaning. My conclusions are, that such republicans are capable, like the angel about which I have spoken, to carry out their republicanism into the most fatal despotism. A republican form of government, therefore, can be a blessing to no people, further than they make honest virtue the rule of life. Indeed, honesty is essential to the existence of a republican form of government, for it originates in a contract or agreement of its subjects, relative to the disposal of their mutual interests. If conspiracy is got up by any of the contracters, against the fundamental principles of the honest contract, (which, if republican, embraced those interests which are unalienable, and no more,) and if, by an influence gained by them, so as to make its intent null and void, the foundation of the government is thereby destroyed; leaving its whole fabric a mere wreck, inefficient in all its executive power. Or if the contract had the form of honesty only, when there was a secret design of fraud in the minds of the parties contracting, then of course, it is a body without a soul—a fabric without a foundation; and, like a dead carcass entombed, will tumble to pieces as soon as brought to the light of truth, and into the pure air of honesty.

With regard to the claims of the colored subjects of this government to equal political rights, I maintain that their claims are founded in an original agreement of the contracting parties, and that there is nothing to show that color was a consideration in the agreement. It is well known that when the country belonged to Great Britain, the colored people were slaves. But when America revolted from Britain, they were held no longer by any legal power. There was no efficient law in the land except marshal law, and that regarded no one as a slave. The inhabitants were governed by no other law, except by resolutions adopted from time to time by meetings convoked in the different colonies. Upon the face of the warrants by which these district and town meetings were called, there is not a word said about the color of the attendants. In convoking the continental Congress of the 4th of September, 1776, there was not a word said about color. In November of the same year, Congress met again, to get in readiness twelve thousand men to act in any emergency; at the same time, a request was forwarded to Connecticut, New Hampshire, and Rhode Island, to increase this army to twenty thousand men. Now it is well known that hundreds of the men of which this army was composed, were colored men, and recognized by Congress as Americans.

An extract from the speech of Richard Henry Lee, delivered in Congress, assembled June 8, 1776, in support of a motion, which he offered, to declare America free and independent, will give some view of the nature of the agreement upon which this government is based. "The eyes of all Europe are fixed upon us; she demands of us a living example of freedom, that may contrast, by the felicity of her citizens, (I suppose black as well as white,) with the ever increasing tyranny which desolates her polluted shores. She invites us to prepare an asylum where the unhappy may find solace, and the persecuted, repose. She entreats us to cultivate a propitious soil, where that generous plant which first sprang up and grew in England, but is now withered by the poisonous blasts of Scottish tyranny, may revive and flourish, sheltering under its salubrious and interminable shade all the unfortunate of the human race."[7]

The principles which this speech contains, are manifestly those which were then acted upon. To remove all doubt on this point, I will make a short extract from the Declaration of Independence, in Congress assembled, fourth of July, 1776. "We, the representatives of these United States of America, in general Congress assembled, appealing to the Supreme Judge of the world for the rectitude of our intentions, and by the authority of the good people of these Colonies, solemnly publish and declare, that these united colonies are, and of right ought to be, free and independent States. (And now for the pledge.) We mutually pledge to each other our lives, our fortunes, and our sacred honor." The representatives who composed that Congress were fifty-five in number, and all signed the declaration and pledge in behalf of the good people of the thirteen States. Now I would ask, can it be said, from any fair construction of the foregoing extracts, that the colored people are not recognized as citizens. Congress drew up articles of confederation also, among which are found the following reserved state privileges. "Each state has the exclusive right of regulating its internal government, and of framing its own laws, in all matters not included in the articles of confederation, and which are not repugnant to it." Another article reads as follows: "There shall be a public treasury for the service of the confederation, to be replenished by the particular contributions of each state, the same to be proportioned according to the number of inhabitants of every age, sex, or condition, with

---

[7] Richard Henry Lee (1732–1794) was a Virginian representative to the Second Continental Congress. He proposed the resolution for the thirteen colonies to break from British Empire, and he delivered this speech the following day amid calls to delay or abandon Lee's resolution. Though the full passage is placed in quotations, the parentheticals are Easton's commentary.

the exception of Indians."[8] These extracts are sufficient to show the civil and political recognition of the colored people. In addition to which, however, we have an official acknowledgment of their equal, civil, and political relation to the government, in the following proclamation of Major General Andrew Jackson, to the colored people of Louisiana, Sept. 21, 1814; also of Thomas Butler, Aid de Camp:

"*Head Quarters, Seventh Military District, Mobile, September 21, 1814. To the Free Colored Inhabitants of Louisiana.*[9]

"Through a mistaken policy you have heretofore been deprived of a participation in the glorious struggle for national rights, in which our country is engaged. This no longer shall exist.

"As sons of Freedom, you are now called upon to defend our most inestimable blessing. As Americans, your country looks with confidence to her adopted children, for a valorous support, as a faithful return for the advantages enjoyed under her mild and equitable government. As fathers, husbands, and brothers, you are summoned to rally round the standard of the Eagle, to defend all which is dear in existence.

"Your country, although calling for your exertions, does not wish you to engage in her cause, without remunerating you for the services rendered. Your intelligent minds are not to be led away by false representations—your love of honor would cause you to despise the man who should attempt to deceive you. In the sincerity of a soldier, and the language of truth, 1 address you.

"To every noble hearted free man of color, volunteering to serve during the present contest with Great Britain and no longer, there will be paid the same bounty in money and lands, now received by the white soldiers of the United States, viz., one hundred and twenty-four dollars in money, and one hundred and sixty acres of land. The non-commissioned officers and privates will also be entitled to the same monthly pay and daily rations and clothes, furnished to any American soldier.

"On enrolling yourselves in companies, the Major General commanding, will select officers for your government, from your white fellow citizens. Your non-commissioned officers will be appointed from among yourselves.

---

[8] Easton seems to be quoting a draft of the Articles of Confederation published before the version adopted on November 15, 1777. This quotation most closely resembles Articles 3 and 11.

[9] Published in the *Niles Weekly Register* on December 3, 1814.

"Due regard will be paid to the feelings of freemen and soldiers. You will not, by being associated with white men in the same corps, be exposed to improper comparisons or unjust sarcasm. As a distinct, independent battalion or regiment, pursuing the path of glory, you will, undivided, receive the applause and gratitude of your countrymen.

"To assure you of the sincerity of my intentions, and my anxiety to engage your invaluable services to our country, I have communicated my wishes to the Governor of Louisiana, who is fully informed as to the manner of enrolments, and will give you every necessary information on the subject of this address."

"ANDREW JACKSON, *Major General Commmanding* [sic].
"*Proclamation to the Free People of Color.*[10]

"Soldiers!—When on the banks of the Mobile, I called you to take arms, inviting you to partake the perils and glory of your white fellow citizens, *I expected much from you*; for I was not ignorant that you possessed qualities most formidable to an invading enemy. I knew with what fortitude you could endure hunger and thirst, and all the fatigues of a campaign. *I knew well how you loved your native country*, and that you had, as well as ourselves, to defend what man holds most dear— his parents, relations, wife; children and property: *You have done more than I expected*. In addition to the previous qualities I before knew you to possess, I found moreover, among you, a noble enthusiasm which leads to the performance of great things.

"Soldiers!—The President of the United States shall hear how praiseworthy was your conduct in the hour of danger, and the representatives of the American people will, I doubt not, give you the praise your exploits entitle you to. Your General anticipates them in applauding your noble ardor.

"The enemy approaches, his vessels cover our lakes; our brave citizens are united, and all contention has ceased among them. Their only dispute is, who shall win the prize of valor, or who the most glory, its noblest reward."

"By Order, THOMAS BUTLER, Aid de Camp."

All the civil and political disabilities of the colored people, are the effect of usurpation. It is true, slavery is recognized by the articles of confederation; but there is not a public document of the government, which recognizes a colored man as a slave, not even in the provision for Southern representation.

---

[10] Published in the *Liberator* on March 24, 1832.

When fugitive slaves are demanded by Southern slaveholders, they are recovered by virtue of a provision made to recover prisoners held to labor, in the state from whence they have absconded; but how that provision can be construed in such a manner, as to give them that advantage, I cannot conceive. I am satisfied, that it only serves as a pretext to justify a base perversion of the law, for the sake of pleasing evil doers. In the first place, a slave is not held to labor legally in slave states, because, according to the extract I have made, viz., that each state has a right to frame laws which are not *prejudicial* to the articles of confederation; there is a limitation to which every other article of the document is subject. Now, what says another article of confederation? Why, that a person held to labor, shall be recovered. But in what way held? Upon this the articles of confederation, are silent; in fact, they may as well be silent; for had they pointed out the manner of persons being held to labor, they would have assumed the province of common law; this, the framers of the constitution and documents of confederation, knew full well; and the administrators of justice now know, that no person under heaven can be held to labor, other than by virtue of a contract, recognizable by common law. Neither do the administrators of justice, found their decisions on anything found in the articles of confederation; for a proof of which, 1 will call the attention of my readers to the following considerations.

If a white person is arraigned before a justice, as a fugitive slave, it would not be all the evidence that could be collected to prove him a slave, however true, that would induce a justice at the North to give him up, if he were able to prove that he was of white parentage. It would be the same, in case that an Indian was arraigned [sic]. There have been such claims made, I believe, and the defendants acquitted, even where there was proof positive, on the part of the claimant. This is proof positive, that decisions in such cases are not founded on a sentence contained in the articles of confederation, for there is nothing said, in that instrument, about nation or complexion; but persons held to labor. Now, if it is by virtue of that instrument, that the black man is held to labor, why not hold the white person, and the Indian, by the same power? And if they cannot be held by that instrument, how can any person be held, when no particular person is described? It is evident that decisions in favor of claimants are founded in the fact of the defendants being a black person, or descendants of blacks or Africans. Now, for all this mode of administering justice, there cannot be found a single sentence of justification, in any public document in the country, except such as have been framed by individual states; and these are prejudicial to the articles of confederation.

If there is any thing in the articles of confederation, which justifies such a course of procedure, I have never found it. Only think, if one is claimed who is black, or who is a descendant of a black, (though he be whiter than a white man,) he must be given up to hopeless bondage, by virtue of the articles of confederation, when there is not a word about black contained in the instrument; whereas, if a white person be claimed, if he is half negro, if he can prove himself legally white, or of white parentage, he is acquitted. This course of conduct would be scouted by heathens, as a gross libel upon humanity and justice. It is so; and a violation of the Constitution, and of the Bill of Rights—the rights of the people; and every State which connives at such robbing in high places, clothed with a legal form, without a vestige of legal authority; and that too, after having taken the tremendous oath, as recorded in the Declaration of Independence, ought to have perjury written upon their statute books, and upon the ceiling of their legislative halls, in letters as large as their crime, and as black as the complexion of the injured.

Excuses have been employed in vain to cover up the hypocrisy of this nation. The most corrupt policy which ever disgraced its barbarous ancestry, has been adopted by both church and state, for the avowed purpose of withholding the inalienable rights of one part of the subjects of the government. Pretexts of the lowest order, which are neither witty or decent, and which rank among that order of subterfuges, under which the lowest of ruffians attempt to hide, when exposed to detection, are made available. Indeed, I may say in candor, that a highwayman or assassin acts upon principles far superior, in some respects, in comparison with those under which the administrators of the laws of church and state act, especially in their attempts to hide themselves and their designs from the just censure of the world, and from the burning rays of truth. I have no language to express what I see, and hear, and feel, on this subject. Were I capable of dipping my pen in the deepest dye of crime, and of understanding the science of the bottomless pit, I should then fail in presenting to the intelligence of mortals on earth, the true nature of American deception. There can be no appeals made in the name of the laws of the country, of philanthropy, or humanity, or religion, that is capable of drawing forth any thing but the retort,— *you are a negro!* If we call to our aid the thunder tones of the cannon and the arguments of fire arms, (vigorously managed by black and white men, side by side,) as displayed upon Dorchester Heights, arid at Lexington, and at White Plains, and at Kingston, and at Long Island, and elsewhere, the retort is, *you are a negro*—if we present to the nation a Bunker's Hill, our nation's altar, (upon which she offered her choicest sacrifice,) with our fathers, and brothers, and sons, prostrate thereon, wrapped in fire and smoke—the incense of blood borne upward upon the wings of sulphurous vapor, to the throne of national honor, with a halo of national glory echoing back, and spreading and astonishing the civilized world[11];—and if we present the thousands of widows and orphans, whose only earthly protectors were thus sacrificed, weeping over the fate of the departed; and anon, tears of blood are extorted, on learning that the government for which their lovers and sires had died, refuses to be their protector;—if we tell that angels weep in pity, and that God, the eternal Judge, "will hear the desire of the humble, judge the fatherless and the oppressed, that the man of the earth may no more oppress,"[12]—the retort is, YOU ARE A NEGRO! If there is a spark of honesty, patriotism, or religion, in the heart or the source from whence such refuting arguments emanate, the devil incarnate is the brightest seraph in paradise.

---

[11] Dorchester Heights, Lexington, White Plains, Kingston, Long Island, and Bunker's Hill were all important battles in the American War for Independence. Easton mentions them to establish a pattern of African American service and sacrifice.

[12] Easton modifies Psalm 10:17-18: "Lord, thou has heard the desire of the humble: thou wilt prepare their heart, thou wilt cause thine ear to hear: To judge the fatherless and the oppressed, that the man of the earth may no more oppress."

12

Selections from Mary Ann Shadd Cary: Open Letter to Frederick Douglass

WILMINGTON, Jan. 25, 1849[1]

FREDERICK DOUGLASS: Though native of a different State, still in anything relating to our people, I am insensible of boundaries. The statement of Rev. H. H. Garnet[2] which appeared in the North Star of the 19th inst.[3], relative to the very wretched condition of thirty thousand of our people in your State, and your willingness to listen to suggestions from any one interested, has induced me to send you these lines, which I beg you to insert if you think worthy.

The picture he drew, sir, of thirty thousand, is a fair representation of many more thousands in this country. The moral and intellectual debasement portrayed, is true to the life. How, in view of everything, can it be otherwise? We bring a heavy charge against the church and people of this country, which they themselves can hardly deny; but have we not been, and are we not still, "adding fuel to the flame;" or do our efforts, to the contrary, succeed as we have reason to expect? We are not satisfied with the result in every way—maybe we have reason for not being. With others, I have for some time doubted the efficiency of the means for the end. Do you not think, sir, that we should direct our attention more to the farming interest than hitherto? I suggest this, as concerning the entire people. The estimation in which we would

---

[1] This letter appeared in Frederick Douglass's *North Star* on March 23, 1849. The *North Star* was Douglass's first newspaper published out of Rochester, New York (1847–1851). His subsequent antebellum periodicals were *Frederick Douglass' Paper* (1851–1859) and *Douglass' Monthly* (1859–1863).

[2] Henry Highland Garnet (1815–1882) was an abolitionist orator and minister known for his "Address to the Slaves of the United States" delivered at the 1843 National Colored Convention. His address marked a clear contrast between his militant abolitionism and Douglass's abolitionism at the time, which was still largely nonviolent.

[3] Shadd references Garnet's article "Self-Help—The Wants of Western New York" published on January 19, 1849, in the *North Star*. In his article, Garnet laments the "young people rushing on to ruin" because "their religious institutions are very limited." Like Shadd, Garnet blames the church for the degradation of African American communities.

be held by those in power, would be quite different, were we producers, and not merely, as now, consumers. He, sir, proposed a Convention without distinction of caste—proposition which no doubt will be acceptable, because by exchanging views with those who have every advantage, we are materially benefitted.[4] Persons likely to associate with our people, and possessed of depth of sentiment. Their influence on us should not be lightly considered. We have been holding conventions for years—have been assembling together and whining over our difficulties and afflictions; passing resolutions on resolutions to any extent; but it does really seem that we have made but little progress, considering our resolves. We have put forth few practical efforts to an end. I, as one of the people, see no need for our distinctive meetings, if we do not do something. We should do more, and talk less. What intellectually we most need, and the absence of which we most feel, is the knowledge of the white man, a great amount of which, by intercourse in public meetings, &c., we could glean, and no possible opportunity to seize upon which should be allowed to escape. Should not the importance of his literature upon us, and everything tending to add to his influence, be forcibly impressed, and we be directed to that course? The great fault of our people, is in imitating his follies; individual enterprise and self-reliance are not sufficiently insisted upon. The influence of a corrupt clergy among us, sapping our every means, and, as a compensation, inculcating ignorance as a duty, superstition as true religion—in short, hanging like millstones about our necks,[5] should be faithfully proclaimed. I am willing to be convinced to the contrary, if possible; but it does really seem to me that our distinctive churches and the frightfully wretched instruction of our ministers—their gross ignorance and insolent bearing, together with the sanctimonious garb, and by virtue of their calling, a character for mystery they assume, is attributable more of the downright degradation of the free colored people of the North, than from the effect of corrupt public opinion; for, sir, notwithstanding the cry of prejudice against

---

[4] Shadd is referencing Garnet's plan for a "Christian Convention of the colored people and their friends to be called at some central place. Let there be no caste or sectarianism encouraged in that meeting; but let us come together in good earnest to do something for our afflicted fellow-men."

[5] Although the image of the millstone about one's neck represents the sociocultural shortcomings Shadd censures, the religious tenor of her argument suggests the biblical source of that image is deeply significant. In the Gospels, Jesus says of a person who would "offend one of these little ones which believe in me" that "it were better for him that a millstone were hanged about his neck, and that he were drowned in the depth of the sea" (Matthew 5:6; see also in Mark 9:42 and Luke 17:2). Thus, the invocation of this scripture is also an indictment on the clergy, who in her estimation have offended and exploited vulnerable black populations. Her language thus carries the threat of divine judgment.

color, some think it will vanish by a change of condition, and that we can, despite this prejudice, change that condition. The ministers assume to be instructors in every matter, a thing we would not object to, provided they taught, even in accordance with the age; but in our literature, they hang tenaciously to exploded customs, (as if we were not creatures of progress as well as others,) as they do in everything else. The course of some of our high priests, makes your humble servant, and many others, think money, and not the good of the people, is at the bottom.—The great aim of these gentlemen now, is secrecy in all affairs where our spiritual welfare is being considered. Our conferences, they say, are too public. The open-stated people and laymen learn, as they should not, the transactions in conference and sessions, of these men of God. Depend upon it, sir, "men love darkness rather than light, because their deeds are evil." One thing is clear: this hiding the light under a bushel, is not, to those who dare think, very satisfactory; their teaching tends to inculcate submission to them in all things. "Pay no attention to your perishing bodies, children, but get your souls converted; prepare for heaven. The elective franchise would not profit you; a desire for such things indicates worldly mindedness."—Thus any effort to a change of condition by our people is replied to, and a shrinking, priest-rid people, are prevented from seeing clearly. The possibility of final success, when using proper means, the means to be used, the possibility of bringing about the desired end ourselves, and not waiting for the whites of the country to do so, should be impressed on the people by those teachers, as they assume to be the only true ones; or at least there should be no hindrance to their seeing for themselves.

Yours for a better condition,
M.A. SHADD.

ADIEU.[6]

With this number of the paper we consign to other hands the literary department of the same, and in the course of a few weeks, shall pass over the keys of the business department also, and content ourself with active numbers to get subscribers for. In taking leave of our readers, at this time, we do so for the best interests of the enterprise, and with the hope that our absence be their

---

[6] This farewell notice appeared on June 30, 1855 in the *Provincial Freeman* (1854–1857), which Mary Ann Shadd founded and operated in what is now Ontario, Canada.

gain. We want the *Freeman* to prosper, and shall labour to that end. When it was *not*, but was said to be needed, we travelled to arouse a sentiment in favor of it, and from then until now, have worked for it, how well others must say, but, through difficulties, and opposed to obstacles such as we feel confident few, if any, females have had to contend against in the same business, except the sister who shared our labors for awhile; and now after such a familiar acquaintanceship with difficulties, oof many shapes, in trying with a few others to keep it alive for one year, as at first promised, we present it in its second year, afresh to the patronage of friends to truth and justice, and its Editor, the Rev. WM. P. NEWMAN,[7] to their kind consideration. To its enemies, we would say, be less captious to him than to us; be more considerate, if you will; it is fit that you should deport your ugliest to a woman. To colored women, we have a word—we have "broken the Editorial ice," whether willingly or not, for your class in America; so go to Editing, as many of you as are willing, and able, and as soon as you may, if you think you are ready; and to those who will not, we say, help us when we visit you, to make brother Newman's burdens lighter, by subscribing to the paper, paying for it, and getting your neighbors to the same.

[Speech, to Judiciary Committee re: The Right of Women to Vote, January 1872][8]

Mr. Chairman, and gentlemen of the Judiciary Committee:

In respectfully appearing before you, to solicit in concert with these ladies, your good offices, in securing to the women of the United States, and particularly, to the women of the District of Columbia, the right to vote, a right exerc[ized] by a portion of American women,[9] at one period, in the hi[story] of this country, I am not vain enough to suppose, for [a] moment, that words of mine could add one iota of weight to the arguments from these learned and earnest women, nor that I could bring out material facts not

---

[7] William Newman (181?–1866) was an enslaved fugitive, minister, and orator who lived in the United States, Canada, and the Caribbean.

[8] Several rips and tears appear in Shadd Cary's handwritten manuscript. Her text also includes a number of underlined words that it seems she wanted to place specifical emphasis on in her delivery to the committee. For clarity and consistency's sake I have removed those markings.

[9] Across the early United States, qualified women could vote in some states until those state governments limited the franchise to qualified men only. For example, some women could vote in New Jersey in 1797 but lost that right in 1807. Territories such as Wyoming and Utah allowed women to vote (beginning in 1869 and 1870, respectively) and maintained that privilege when they became states (1890 and 1896, respectively). Congress repealed women's suffrage in Utah in 1887 to curb Mormon influence in the territory, but women regained the right to vote when Utah became a state in 1896.

heretofore used by them in one stage or another of this advocacy. But, as a colored woman, a resident of this District, a tax-payer of the same; as one of a class equal in point of numbers to the male colored voters herein; claiming affilliation [sic] with two and a half millions of the same sex, in the country at large, included in the provisions of recent constitutional amendments, and not least, by virtue of a decision of the Supreme Court of this District a citizen, my presence, at this time, and on an errand so important, may not I trust be without slight significance.

The crowning glory of American citizenship is that it may be shared equally by people of every nationality, complexion and sex, should they of foreign birth so desire; and that in the inscrutable rulings of an All-wise providence, millions of citizens of every complexion, and embracing both sexes, are born upon the soil and claim the honor. I would be particularly clear upon this point. By the provisions of the 14th & 15th amendments to the Constitution of the United States, a logical sequence of which is the representation by colored men of time-honored commonwealths in both houses of Congress, millions of colored women, to-day, share with colored men the responsibilities of freedom from chattel slavery. From the introduction of African slavery to its extinction, a period of more than two hundred years, they shared equally with fathers, brothers, denied the right to vote. This fact of their investiture with the privileges of free women of the same time and by the same amendments which disenthralled their kinsmen and conferred upon the latter the right of franchise, without so endowing themselves is one of the anomalies of a measure of legislation otherwise grand in conception and consequences beyond comparison. The colored women of this country though heretofore silent, in great measure upon this question of the right to vote by the women of the, so long and ardently the cry of the noblest of the land, have neither been indifferent to their own just claims under the amendments, in common with colored men, nor to the demand for political recognition so justly made by the women suffragists of the country for women every where within its borders throughout the land. The strength and glory of a free nation, is not so much in the size and equipments of its armies, as in the loyal hearts and willing hands of its men and women; And this fact has been illustrated in an eminent degree by well-known events in the history of the United States. To the women of the nation conjointly with the men, is it indebted for arduous and dangerous personal service, and generous expenditure of time, wealth and counsel, so indispensable to success in its hour of danger. The colored women though humble in sphere, and unendowed with worldly goods, yet, led as by inspiration, not only fed, and sheltered, and guided in safety the prisoner soldiers of the Union when escaping from the enemy, or the soldier who was compelled to risk life itself in the struggle to break the back-bone of rebellion, but gave their sons and brothers to the armies of the nation and their prayers to high Heaven for the success of the Right.

The surges of fratricidal war have passed we hope never to return; the premonitions of the future, are peace and good will; these blessings, so greatly to be desired, can only be made permanent, in responsible governments, based as you affirm upon the consent of the governed, by giving to both sexes practically the equal powers conferred in the provisions of the Constitution as amended. In the District of Columbia the women in common with the women of the states and territories, feel keenly the discrimination against them in the retention of the word *male* in the organic act for the same, and as by reason of its retention, all the evils incident to partial legislation are endured by them, they sincerely hope that the word *male* may be stricken out by Congress on your recommendation without delay. Taxed, and governed in other respects, without their consent, they respectfully demand, that the principles of the founders of the government may not be disregarded in their case; but, as there are laws by which they are tried, with penalties attached thereto, that they may be invested with the right to vote as do men, that thus as in all Republics *indeed*, they may in future, be governed by their own consent.[10]

[ON THE BACK OF TWO PAGES, THE FOLLOWING APPEARS WITHOUT USUAL PUNCTUATION]

The Women's Convention for the extension of the franchise was as the press of the District have been gallantly constrained to say the most harmonious and the most practical in every way of any of the many gatherings ever held here. And In this connection it is but just to give credit where it is due, or rather to divide the honors among those who by their work at the time are clearly entitled to them.

Mrs. Cady Stanton Miss Anthony Mrs Blake and Miss Cozzens did effective work as every one readily admits and Mrs. Gage too a very John Hancock in radicalism all said words of wisdom which though new to many of the

---

[10] What follows from here appeared on the back of two pages of the manuscript. The punctuation is erratic and often missing,

many hundreds gathered there were listened to with positive delight by the entire grand assembly and voted their own sentiments.

It is a question so unexpectedly pleasant was every thing connected with the convention, if Mrs. Stanton & Miss Anthony were not as much surprised as any body not thoroughly posted upon the resources of the District when work of the kind is to be done. No city in the country possesses workers in the cause of woman suffrage or any other positive moral need of human society who can bring talent of a higher order or executive ability than Washington. To Mrs. Spencer Dr Susan B Edson Mrs. Lockwood Dr Winslow Mrs. Archibald, the bone and sinew of the working talent of that convention were the hundreds of delighted listeners indebted largely for the preparatory work and co-operation with the distinguished stranger(?) ladies which in this case redowned to the credit of all concerned.

It is due to the indefatigable zeal and splendid accomplishments of the District ladies that the people at large should become better informed of their unselfish efforts in every noble cause and especially of their struggle for just and equal political recognition in this District.

Letters to the People—No. 1.

Trades for our Boys:
To the Editor of the New National Era[11]:

I wish to call your attention to the importance of some movement whereby trades, &c., may be secured to our boys. There are hundreds of boys in this city alone who, after having exhausted every effort to secure employment, from the fact that paper-peddling, boot-blacking, driving, waiting and choosing, have more than their quota of employ[ee]s, resort, to petty crimes; thence, through successive stages, to bolder schemes against the peace and security of society, and thus swell the number of criminals and vagrants, and prey upon the community, because an unrighteous public sentiment excludes them from the workshops, and religion, philanthropy, patriotism, have not a word to say in condemnation of the anti-American policy.

---

[11] The *National Era* (1847–1860) was an abolitionist magazine published in Washington, D.C. Frederick Douglass assumed control as editor in 1870 and renamed it the *New National Era* (1870–1874), dedicated to the social and economic conditions of African Americans during Reconstruction. Shadd Cary published this article on March 21, 1872.

To the son, of the German, the Irishman, the Canadian, Scotchman, the far off Pagan Japanese, the doors of your manufactories open wide, the next day after arrival; yes, before one word of the language has been mastered, while against the native-born colored youth, with the same aspirations as a white American, to appropriate and apply mechanical knowledge, and to improve upon it by application and invention, the doors are not only closed by individual bosses, but society combinations supplement the injustice by voting exclusion.

We have in this city colored mechanics whose work upon inspection equals the very best done by the fairest American or foreigner; these men take colored boys to be taught, but the hand of God is upon them in that He gave them a color which suited Him, so that the large number are so poorly patronized that but a limited number are now instructed.

The condition of colored youth in this city and District is true of them throughout the country. But the opposition by Americans is not the only cause of this sorry state of things, though mainly so; indifference on the part of leading colored men, and the death like silence of colored women, contribute to it. A people whose leaders seek to learn the tortuous ways of speculation, and whose women are awed into silence upon vital questions, must for the time take back seats among the people. The white men of this and other countries deal vigorously now with every issue for the good of their youth, and white women are to the front with them in the work as having a common mission; they even unite in our exclusion and mutual congratulations, the result, are neither few nor whispered. Our women must speak out; the boys must have trades. What the crowned heads of Europe, and the poorest of white Americans do for their sons, we cannot afford to neglect.

I have a boy who must and shall have a trade, (D. V.,) and yet where may he learn it, or where exercise it when learned?

To begin at headquarters, not under Government patronage surely, for there, should a colored lad upon examination distance competitors, let but a persistent Southern rebel, a clamorous foreigner, or a Canadian rebel, seek the position also, and even after given, the well-known out-cry, "reduction of force" is made, which, by interpretation, means change of base, and down comes the headsman's axe upon apprentice, mechanic, clerk, and into his place goes the anti-Government aspirant.

Where then exercise it? The people exclude him. Clannish they worship their kind. As much as may be said about race ostracism by whites, and how much may not be, too much cannot be said against indifference among ourselves. I want our poor tongue-tied, hoppled and "scart" [i.e., scared] colored women—"black ladies" as Faith Lichen had the bravery to call them, in her Mary-Clemmer-Ames-i-ades—to let the nation know how they stand.[12] White women are getting to be a power in the land, and colored women cannot any longer afford to be neutrals. Never fear the ward-meetings; get the boys started properly in life, and the ward-meetings will come right.

I want to see the colored preacher canonized, who looking after the great interests of the Master's flock, will, Beecher-like,[13] cry out on Sunday against this sin of keeping our boys from trades, to the fostering of iniquity and the ruin of their souls.

Four millions of "laborers" in the midst of thirty millions of active, energetic people with arts, science, and commerce in their hands, and the love of domination a cardinal point in their creed—four millions that chain to this dank and hoary labor carcass—are as certain of subjugation, ultimately, as were the Helots;[14] and this should arouse to action the entire force among the people. I know we have resolutions of conference and of conventions, and have had for a generation; and that each convention is the greatest ever held; but the people know comparatively little about them or their resolutions. We want then, an arousing of the people, and the pulpit must help in the work.

We have no theatres, beer-gardens, opera, nor grand lecture amp[h]itheatres, wherein such questions may, be discussed, reshapen, dramatized, made vital issues; the church—the pulpit stands to us in this stead; our preachers, as they should be, are politicians, and do use their churches often as places in which blessed white [C]hristians help them to adjust, arrange, and work party laws. No greater party work than this for our boys can they do.

I have not forgotten that we have a few live members of Congress, though I believe no one has as yet got around to trades; and although we must have Civil Rights, I look upon trades exclusion as meanly and wickedly beyond

---

[12] A Faith Lichen, which was likely pseudonym, wrote "That Woman's Letter from Washington" for the *New National Era* (February 22, 1872) as a condemnatory response to the racist characterizations of black women in Mary Clemmer Ames's January 25 edition of her highly popular column "A Woman's Letter from Washington," which she published in the *Independent* (New York).

[13] Refers to Henry Ward Beecher (1813–1887), abolitionist minister and orator famed for his fiery dedication to social reform, including temperance, Chinese immigration, and women's suffrage.

[14] The Helots were an oppressed population in ancient Sparta. Historians from the period and since disagree on whether they were enslaved or occupied a position somewhere between free persons and the enslaved.

even the reach of that. In parenthesis, another of the many weak places in "your armor," so be it.

I know that we have members of State Legislatures and from whom more may be expected than from even Congress; also, attach[é]s of the learned professions, and aspirants in the field of letters, all of which is enjoyably rose-tinted and gilded as compared with the past; but we, no more than others, can afford to build at the top of the house only. Ill-timed and unseemly as it may appear, the craftsman, the architect, the civil engineer, the manufacturer, the thoroughly equipped citizen, must all come, though silently, surely through the door opened to us by the mechanic. So agitate for the boys!

· MARY A. SHADD CARY.

Stewart's Works

13

Religion and the Pure Principles of Morality, the Sure Foundation on Which We Must Build

INTRODUCTION

[1831]

Feeling a deep solemnity of soul, in view of our wretched and degraded situation, and sensible of the gross ignorance that prevails among us, I have thought proper thus publicly to express my sentiments before you. I hope my friends will not scrutinize these pages with too severe an eye, as I have not calculated to display either elegance or taste in their composition, but have merely written the meditations of my heart as far as my imagination led; and have presented them before you, in order to arouse you to exertion, and to enforce upon your minds the great necessity of turning your attention to knowledge and improvement.

I was born in Hartford, Connecticut, in 1803; was left an orphan at five years of age; was bound out in a clergyman's family; had the seeds of piety and virtue early sown in my mind; but was deprived of the advantages of education, though my soul thirsted for knowledge. Left them at 15 years of age; attended Sabbath schools until I was 20; in 1826, was married to James W. Steward [sic]; was left a widow in 1829; was, as I humbly hope and trust, brought to the knowledge of the truth, as it is in Jesus, in 1830; in 1831, made a public profession of my faith in Christ.

From the moment I experienced the change, I felt a strong desire, with the help and assistance of God, to devote the remainder of my days to piety and virtue, and now possess that spirit of independence, that, were I called upon, I would willingly sacrifice my life for the cause of God and my brethren.

All the nations of the earth are crying out for Liberty and Equality. Away, away with tyranny and oppression! And shall Afric's sons be silent any longer? Far be it from me to recommend to you, either to kill, burn, or destroy. But I would strongly recommend to you, to improve your talents; let not one lie buried in the earth. Show forth your powers of mind. Prove to the world, that

> Though black your skins as shades of night,
> Your hearts are pure, your souls are white.[1]

This is the land of freedom. The press is at liberty.[2] Every man has a right to express his opinion. Many think, because your skins are tinged with a sable hue, that you are an inferior race of beings; but God does not consider you as such. He hath formed and fashioned you in his own glorious image, and hath bestowed upon you reason and strong powers of intellect. He hath made you to have dominion over the beasts of the field, the fowls of the air, and the fish of the sea. He hath crowned you with glory and honor; hath made you but a little lower than the angels; and, according to the Constitution of these United States, he hath made all men free and equal. Then why should one worm say to another, "Keep you down there, while I sit up yonder; for I am better than thou?" It is not the color of the skin that makes the man, but it is the principles formed within the soul.

Many will suffer for pleading the cause of oppressed Africa, and I shall glory in being one of her martyrs; for I am firmly persuaded, that the God in whom I trust is able to protect me from the rage and malice of mine enemies, and from them that will rise up against me; and if there is no other way for me to escape, he is able to take me to himself, as he did the most noble, fearless, and undaunted David Walker.

***

NEVER WILL VIRTUE, KNOWLEDGE, AND TRUE POLITENESS BEGIN TO FLOW, TILL THE PURE PRINCIPLES OF RELIGION AND MORALITY ARE PUT INTO FORCE.

---

[1] This verse is Stewart's.

[2] This assertion was more of a normative claim than a factual one, especially as it related to abolitionism. The 1830s and early 1840s saw a proliferation of individual and mob attacks on antislavery editors, publishers, and writers, including the sensational murder of Ohio-based journalist Elijah Lovejoy in 1837. Stewart emphasizes normativity in this essay as an effort to align the professed ideals of the United States with her religious ethics.

MY RESPECTED FRIENDS,

I feel almost unable to address you; almost incompetent to perform the task; and, at times, I have felt ready to exclaim, O that my head were waters, and mine eyes a fountain of tears, that I might weep day and night, for the transgressions of the daughters of my people. Truly, my heart's desire and prayer is, that Ethiopia might stretch forth her hands unto God.[3] But we have a great work to do. Never, no, never will the chains of slavery and ignorance burst, till we become united as one, and cultivate among ourselves the pure principles of piety, morality and virtue. I am sensible of my ignorance; but such knowledge as God has given to me, I impart to you. I am sensible of former prejudices; but it is high time for prejudice and animosities to cease from among us. I am sensible of exposing myself to calumny and reproach; but shall I, for fear of feeble man who shall die, hold my peace? shall I for fear of scoffs and frowns, refrain my tongue? Ah, no! I speak as one that must give an account at the awful bar of God; I speak as a dying mortal, to dying mortals. O, ye daughters of Africa, awake! awake! arise! no longer sleep nor slumber, but distinguish yourselves. Show forth to the world that ye are endowed with noble and exalted faculties. O, ye daughters of Africa![4] what have ye done to immortalize your names beyond the grave? what examples have ye set before the rising generation? what foundation have ye laid for generations yet unborn?[5] where are our union and love? and where is our sympathy, that weeps at another's wo, and hides the faults we see? And our daughters, where are they? blushing in innocence and virtue? And our sons, do they bid fair to become crowns of glory to our hoary heads? Where is the parent who is conscious of having faithfully discharged his duty, and at the last awful day of account, shall be able to say, here, Lord, is thy poor, unworthy servant, and the children thou hast given me? And where are the children that will arise, and call them blessed? Alas, O God! forgive me if I speak amiss; the minds of our tender babes are tainted as soon as they are born; they go astray, as it were, from the womb. Where is the maiden who will blush at vulgarity and where is the youth who has written upon his manly brow a

---

[3] Psalm 68:31. It is almost certainly the most cited biblical verse in African American politics and literary culture of the long nineteenth century, prophesying black deliverance from bondage and dominion.

[4] Such moments of apostrophe or direct address suggest Stewart regards women as the primary audience and agents of the racial ethics she propounds.

[5] Stewart's emphases on motherhood, children, and education do not reflect a dedication to dominant forms of domestic femininity subsumed under the category of "True Womanhood." Rather, Stewart conceives of (American) blackness as a generationally produced subjectivity which black women have a singular ability to sustain.

thirst for knowledge;[6] whose ambition mind soars above trifles, and longs for the time to come, when he shall redress the wrongs of his father, and plead the cause of his brethren? Did the daughters of our land possess a delicacy of manners, combined with gentleness and dignity; did their pure minds hold vice in abhorrence and contempt, did they frown when their ears were polluted with its vile accents, would not their influence become powerful? Would not our brethren fall in love with their virtues? Their souls would become fired with a holy zeal for freedom's cause. They would become ambitious to distinguish themselves. They would become proud to display their talents. Able advocates would arise in our defence. Knowledge would begin to flow, and the chains of slavery and ignorance would melt like wax before the flames. I am but a feeble instrument. I am but as one particle of the small dust of the earth. You may frown or smile. After I am dead, perhaps before, God will surely raise up those who will more powerfully and eloquently plead the cause of virtue and the pure principles of morality than I am able to do. O virtue! How sacred is thy name! how pure are thy principles! Who can find a virtuous woman? for her price is far above rubies. Blessed is the man who shall call her his wife; yea, happy is the child who shall call her mother. O, woman, woman, would thou only strive to excel in merit and virtue; would thou only store thy mind with useful knowledge, great would be thine influence.[7] Do you say, you are too far advanced in life now to begin? You are not too far advanced to instill these principles into the minds of your tender infants. Let then by no means be neglected. Discharge your duty faithfully, in every point of view: leave the event with God. So shall your skirts become clear of their blood.

When I consider how little improvement has been made the last eight years; the apparent cold and indifferent state of the children of God; how few have been hopefully brought to the knowledge of the truth as it is in Jesus; that our young men and maidens are fainting and drooping, as it were, by the way-side, for the want of knowledge; when I see how few care to distinguish themselves either in religious or moral improvement, and when I see the greater part of our community following the vain bubbles of life with so much eagerness, which will only prove to them like the serpent's sting upon

---

[6] Stewart evokes David Walker's criticism of young black men who approach education as a marker of freedom rather than as a mechanism for the development of intellectual achievement and, thus, leaders for racial uplift. See Article II of Walker's *Appeal* in Stewart, 110–122.

[7] Stewart refigures the "Great Man" model of racial uplift leadership—that is, masculinist, bourgeois, and top-down rather than grassroots—in order to hail women's roles in fostering black accomplishment, morality, and politics.

the bed of death, I really think we are in as wretched and miserable a state as was the house of Israel in the days of Jeremiah.

I suppose many of my friends will say, "Religion is all your theme," I hope my conduct will ever prove me to be what I profess, a true follower of Christ; and it is the religion of Jesus alone, that will constitute your happiness here, and support you in a dying hour. O, then, do not trifle with God and your own souls any longer. Do not presume to offer him the very dregs of your lives; but now, whilst you are blooming in health and vigor, consecrate the remnant of your days to him. Do you wish to become useful in your day and generation? Do you wish to promote the welfare and happiness of your friends, as far as your circle extends? Have you one desire to become truly great? O, then, become truly pious, and God will endow you with wisdom and knowledge from on high.

> Come, turn to God, Who did thee make,
> And at his presence fear and quake;
> Remember him now in thy youth,
> And let thy soul take told of truth.
>
> The devil and his ways defy,
> Believe him not, he doth but lie;
> His ways seem sweet: but youth, beware!
> He for thy soul hath laid a snare.[8]

Religion is pure; it is ever new; it is beautiful; it is all that is worth living for; it is worth dying for. O, could I but see the church built up in the most holy faith; could I but see men spiritually minded, walking in the fear of God, nor given to filthy lucre, not holding religion in one hand and the world in the other, but diligent in business, fervent inspirit, serving the Lord, standing upon the walls of Zion, crying to passers by, "He, every one that thirsteth, come ye to the waters, and he that hath no money; yea, come and buy wine and milk without money and without price; Turn ye, turn ye, for why will ye die?" Could I but see mothers in Israel, chaste, keepers at home, not busy bodies, meddlers in other men's matters, whose adorning is of the inward man, possessing a meek and quiet spirit, whose sons were like olive-plants,

---

[8] This verse comes from a "A DIALOGUE between CHRIST, YOUTH, and the Devil" in *The New England Primer* (1777). The separation of stanzas seems to be Stewart's doing. She could have encountered one of the many editions of the *Primer* in Boston homes or Sabbath schools.

and whose daughters were as polished corner-stones; could I but see young men and maidens turning their feet from impious ways, rather choosing to suffer affliction with the people of God than to enjoy the pleasures of sin for a season; could I but see the rising youth blushing in artless innocence, then could I say, now, Lord, let thine unworthy handmaiden depart in peace, for I have seen the desire of mine eyes, and am satisfied.

PRAYER.

O, Lord God, the watchmen of Zion have cried peace, peace, when there was no peace; they have been, as it were, blind leaders of the blind. Wherefore hast thou so long withheld from us the divine influences of thy Holy Spirit? Wherefore hast thou hardened our hearts and blinded our eyes? It is because we have honored thee with our lips, when our hearts were far from thee. We have polluted thy Sabbaths, and even our most holy things have been solemn mockery to thee. We have regarded iniquity in our hearts, therefore thou will not hear. Return again unto us. O Lord God, we beseech thee, and pardon this the iniquity of thy servants. Cause thy face to shine upon us, and we shall be saved. O visit us with thy salvation. Raise up sons and daughters unto Abraham, and grant that there might come a mighty shaking of dry bones among us, and a great ingathering of souls. Quicken thy professing children. Grant that the young may be constrained to believe that there is a reality in religion and a beauty in the fear of the Lord. Have mercy on the blighted sons and daughters of Africa. Grant that we may soon become so distinguished for our moral and religious improvements, that the nations of the earth may take knowledge of us; and grant that our cries may come up before thy throne like holy incense. Grant that every daughter of Africa may consecrate her sons to thee from the birth. And do thou, Lord, bestow upon them wise and understanding her hearts. Clothe us with humility of souls, and give us a becoming dignity of manners: may we imitate the character of the meek and lowly Jesus; and do thou grant the Ethiopia may soon stretch forth her hands unto thee. And now, Lord, be pleased to grant that Satan's kingdom may be destroyed; that the kingdom of our Lord Jesus Christ may be built up; that all nations, and kindreds, and tongues, and people might be brought to the knowledge of the truth, as it is in Jesus, and we at last meet around thy throne, and join in celebrating thy praises.

I have been taking a survey of the American people in my own mind, and I see them thriving in arts, and sciences, and in polite literature. Their highest aim is to excel in political, moral and religious improvement. They early consecrate their children to God, and their youth indeed are blushing in artless innocence; they wipe the tears from the orphan's eyes, and they cause the widow's heart to sing for joy! and their poorest ones, who have the least wish to excel, they promote! And those that have but one talent, they encourage. But how very few are there among them that bestow one thought upon the benighted sons and daughters of Africa, who have enriched the soils of America with their tears and blood: few to promote their cause, none to encourage their talents. Under these circumstances, do not let our hearts be any longer discouraged; it is no use to murmur nor to repine; but let us promote ourselves and improve our own talents.[9] And I am rejoiced to reflect that there are many able and talented ones among us, whose names might be recorded on the bright annals of fame. But, "*I can't*," is a great barrier in the way. I hope it will soon be removed, and "*I will*," resume its place.

Righteousness exalteth a nation, but sin is a reproach to any people. Why is it, my friends, that our minds have been blinded by ignorance, to the present moment? 'Tis on account of sin. Why is it that our church is involved in so much difficulty?[10] It is on account of sin. Why is it that God has cut down, upon our right hand and upon our left, the most learned and intelligent of our men? O, shall I say, is it on account of sin! Why is it that thick darkness is mantled upon every brow, and we, as it were, look sadly upon one another? It is on account of sin. O, then, let us bow before the Lord our God, with all our hearts, and humble our very souls in the dust before him; sprinkling, as it were, ashes upon our heads, and awake to righteousness and sin not. The arm of the Lord is not shortened, that it cannot save; neither is his ear heavy, that it cannot hear; but it is your iniquities that have separated you from me, saith the Lord. Return, O ye backsliding children, and I will return unto you, and ye shall be my people, and I will be your God.

---

[9] Stewart distinguishes African Americans ("the benighted sons and daughters of Africa") from their white counterparts ("the American people") not only to frame her censure of the lack of full citizenship and social inclusion for black people in the United States but also to reinforce the ethic of black nationalism that runs throughout her early writings.

[10] The African Baptist Church in Boston went through a number of leadership changes after the resignation of Rev. Thomas Paul as pastor in 1829. See Levesque (1994) for discussion of how the tumult at the church wracked the black community.

O, ye mothers, what a responsibility rests on you! You have souls committed to your charge, and God will require a strict account of you. It is you that must create in the minds of your little girls and boys a thirst for knowledge, the love of virtue, the abhorrence of vice, and the cultivation of a pure heart. The seeds thus sown will grow with their growing years; and the love of virtue thus early formed in the soul will protect their inexperienced feet from many dangers. O, do not say, you cannot make any thing of your children; but say, with the help and assistance of God, we will try. Do not indulge them in their little stubborn ways; for a child left to himself, bringeth his mother to shame. Spare not, for their crying; thou shalt beat them with a rod, and they shall not die; and thou shalt save their souls from hell. When you correct them, do it in the fear of God, and for their own good. They will not thank you for your false and foolish indulgence; they will rise up, as it were, and curse you in this world, and, in the world to come, condemn you. It is no use to say, you can't do this, or, you can't do that; you will not tell your Maker so, when you meet him at the great day of account. And you must be careful that you that set an example worthy of following, for you they will imitate. There are many instances, even among us now, where parents have discharged their duty faithfully, and their children now reflect honor upon their gray hairs.

Perhaps you will say, that many parents have set pure examples at home, and they have not followed them. True, our expectations are often blasted; but let not this dishearten you. If they have faithfully discharged their duty; even after they are dead, their works may live; their prodigal children may then return to God, and become heirs of salvation; if not, their children cannot rise and condemn them at the awful bar of God.

Perhaps you will say, that you cannot send them to high schools and academies. You can have them taught in the first rudiments of useful knowledge, and then you can have private teachers, who will instruct them in the higher branches; and their intelligence will become greater than ours, and their children will attain to higher advantages and *their* children still higher; and then though we are dead, our works shall live: though we are mouldering, our names shall not be forgotten.

Finally, my heart's desire and prayer to God is, that there might come a thorough reformation among us. Our minds have too long grovelled in ignorance and sin. Come, let us incline our ears to wisdom, and apply our hearts to understanding; promote her, and she shall exalt thee; she shall bring thee to honor when thou dost embrace her. An ornament of grace shall she be thy head, and a crown of glory shall she deliver to thee. Take fast hold of instruction; let her not go; keep her, for she is thy life. Come, let us turn unto the Lord our God, with all our heart and soul, and put away every unclean and unholy thing from among us, and walk before the Lord our God, with a perfect heart, all the days of our lives: then we shall be a people with whom God shall delight to dwell; yea, we shall be that happy people whose God is the Lord.

I am of a strong opinion, that the day on which we unite, heart and soul, and turn our attention to knowledge and improvement, that day the hissing and reproach among the nations of the earth against us will cease. And even those who now point at us with the finger of scorn, will aid and befriend us. It is of no use for us to sit with our hands folded, hanging our heads like bulrushes, lamenting our wretched condition; but let us make a mighty effort, and arise; and if no one will promote or respect us, let us promote and respect ourselves.

The American ladies have the honor conferred on them, that by prudence and economy in their domestic concerns, and their unwearied attention in forming the minds and manners of their children, they laid the foundation of their becoming what they now are. The good women of Wethersfield, Conn. toiled in the blazing sun, year after year, weeding onions, then sold the seed and procured money enough to erect them a house of worship; and shall we not imitate their examples, as far as they are worthy of imitation?[11] Why cannot we do something to distinguish ourselves, and contribute some of our hard earnings that would reflect honor upon our memories, and cause our children to arise and call us blessed? Shall it any longer be said of the daughters of Africa, they have no ambition, they have no force? By no means. Let every female heart become united, and let us raise a fund ourselves; and at the end of one year and a half, we might be able to lay the corner-stone for the building of a High School, that the higher branches of knowledge might be enjoyed by us; and God would raise us up, and enough to aid us in our laudable designs. Let each one strive to excel in good housewifery, knowing that prudence and economy and the road to wealth. Let us not say, we know this, or we know that, and practise nothing; but let us practise what we do know.

---

[11] Known as the "onion maidens," the women of Wethersfield began harvesting the red onion indigenous to the area in the mid-seventeenth century. Proceeds from their efforts helped pay for the building (1761) and taxes of the local Congregational Church.

How long shall the fair daughters of Africa be compelled to bury their minds and talents beneath a load of iron pots and kettles? Until union, knowledge and love begin to flow among us. How long shall a mean set of men flatter us with their smiles, and enrich themselves with our hard earnings; their wives' finger's sparkling with rings, and they themselves laughing at our folly? Until we begin to promote and patronize each other.[12] Shall we be a by-word among the nations any longer? Shall they laugh us to scorn forever? Do you ask, what can we do? Unite and build a store of your own, if you cannot procure a license. Fill one side with dry goods, and the other with groceries. Do you ask, where is the money? We have spent more than enough for nonsense, to do what building we should want. We have never had an opportunity of displaying our talents; therefore the world thinks we know nothing. And we have been possessed of by far too mean and cowardly a disposition, though I highly disapprove of an insolent or impertinent one. Do you ask the disposition I would have you possess? Possess the spirit of independence. The Americans do, and why should not you? Possess the spirit of men, bold and enterprising, fearless and undaunted.[13] Sue for your rights and privileges. Know the reason that you can attain them. Weary them with your importunities. You can but die, if you make the attempt; and we shall certainly die if you do not. The Americans have practiced nothing but head-work these 200 years, and we have done their drudgery. And is it not high time for us to imitate their examples, and practise head-work too, and keep what we have got, and get what we can? We need never to think that any body is going to feel interested for us, if we do not feel interested for ourselves. That day we, as a people, hearken unto the voice of the Lord our God, and walk in his ways and ordinances, and become distinguished for our ease, elegance and grace, combined with other virtues, that day the Lord will raise us up, and enough to aid ago befriend us, and we shall begin to flourish.

Did every gentleman in America realize, as one, that they had got to become bondmen, and their wives, their sons, and their daughters, servants forever, to Great Britain, their very joints would become loosened, and tremblingly would smite one against another; their countenance would be filled

---

[12] For Stewart, black girls' intellectual excellence and femininity both require hard work. She argues that only a righteous racial solidarity among black women can raise up black girls in the right way. Economic solidarity among black businesses, for instance, is key to that vision.

[13] It is unclear whom Stewart is calling on to take on the "spirit of men," because her gendered address vacillates throughout this essay. This rich ambiguity might be intentional.

with horror, every nerve and muscle would be forced into action, their souls would recoil at the very thought, their hearts would die within them, and death would be far more preferable. Then why have not Afric's sons a right to feel the same? Are not their wives, their sons, and their daughters, as dear to them as those of the white man's? Certainly, God has not deprived them of the divine influences of his Holy Spirit, which is the greatest of all blessings, if they ask him. Then why should man any longer deprive his fellow-man of equal rights and privileges? Oh, America, America, foul and indelible is thy stain! Dark and dismal is the cloud that hangs over thee, for thy cruel wrongs and injuries to the fallen sons of Africa. The blood of her murdered ones cries to heaven for vengeance against thee. Thou art almost become drunken with the blood of her slain; thou hast enriched thyself through her toils and labors; and now thou refuseth to make even a small return. And thou hast caused the daughters of Africa to commit whordoms and fornications; but upon thee be their curse.

O, ye great and mighty men of America, you much and powerful ones, many of you will call for the rocks and mountains to fall upon you, and to hide you from the wrath of the Lamb, and from him that sitteth upon the throne; whilst many of the sable-skinned Africans you now despise, will shine in the kingdom of heaven as the stars forever and ever. Charity begins at home, and those that provide not for their own, are worse than infidels. We know that you are raising contributions to aid the gallant Poles; we know that you have befriended Greece and Ireland; and you have rejoiced with France, for her heroic deeds of valor.[14] You have acknowledged all the nations of the earth, except Hayti; and you may publish, as far as the East is from the West, that you have two millions of negroes, who aspire no higher than to bow at your feet, and to court your smiles. You may kill, tyrannize, and oppress as much as you choose, until our cry shall come up before the throne of God; for I am firmly persuaded, that he will not suffer you to quell the proud, fearless and undaunted spirits of the African forever; for in his own time, he is able to plead our cause against you, and to pour out upon you the ten plagues of Egypt. We will not come out against you with swords and staves, as against a

---

[14] Such comparisons between white populations in Europe who resisted oppression and the treatment of African Americans is a familiar theme in nineteenth-century black writing, running from David Walker to Anna Julia Cooper. The point was to call attention to the racialized hypocrisy that regulated the distribution of white American sympathy and politicized sentiment.

thief; but we will tell you that our souls are fired with the same love of liberty and independence with which your souls are fired. We will tell you that too much of your blood flows in our veins, and too much of your color in our skins, for us not to possess your spirits.[15] We will tell you, that it is our gold that clothes you in fine linen and purple, and causes you to fare sumptuously every day; and it is the blood of our fathers, and the tears of our brethren that have enriched your soils. AND WE CLAIM OUR RIGHTS. We will tell, you that we are not afraid of them that kill the body, and after that can do no more; but we will tell you whom we do fear. We fear Him who is able, after he hath killed, to destroy both souls and body in hell forever. Then, my brethren, sheath your swords, and calm your angry passions. Stand still, and know that the Lord he is God. Vengeance is his, and he will repay. It is a long lane that has no turn. America has risen to her meridian. When you begin to thrive, she will begin to fall. God hath raised you up a Walker and a Garrison. Though Walker sleeps, yet he lives, and his name shall be had in everlasting remembrance. I even I, who am but a child, inexperienced to many of you, am a living witness to testify unto you this day, that I have seen the wicked in great power, spreading himself like a green bay tree, and lo, he passed away; yea, I diligently sought him, but he could not be found; and it is God alone that has inspired my heart to feel for Afric's woes. Then fret not yourselves because of evil doers. Fret not yourselves because the men who bring wicked devices to pass; for they shall be cut down as the grass, and wither as the green herb. Trust in the Lord, and do good; so shalt thou dwell in the land, and verily thou shalt be fed. Encourage the noble-hearted Garrison. Prove to the world that you are neither ourang-outangs, nor a species of mere animals, but that you possess the same powers of intellect as those of the proud-boasting American.

I am sensible, my brethren and friends, that many of you have been deprived of advantages, kept in utter ignorance, and that your minds are now darkened; and if any of you have attempted to aspire after high and noble enterprises, you have met with so much opposition that your souls have become discouraged. For this very cause, a few of us have ventured to expose our lives in your behalf, to plead your cause against the great; and it will be

---

[15] Stewart inverts what we now call the "one-drop rule" by homing in on white blood coursing through black bodies. The construction of mixed-race persons as definitively black was a staple of antebellum literature and social criticism in order to highlight the brutal inconsistencies that shaped raced-based chattel slavery. Dion Boucicault's *The Octoroon* (1859) is the quintessential text of the genre.

of no use, unless you feel for yourselves and your little ones, and exhibit the spirits of men. Oh, then, turn your attention to knowledge and improvement; for knowledge is power. And God is able to fill you with wisdom and understanding, and to dispel your fears. Arm yourselves with the weapons of prayer. Put your trust in the living God. Persevere strictly in the paths of virtue. Let nothing be lacking on your part; and, in God's own time, and his time is certainly the best, he will surely deliver you with a mighty hand and with an outstretched arm.

I have never taken one step, my friends, with a design to raise myself in your esteem, or to gain applause. But what I have done, has been done with an eye single to the glory of God, and to promote the good of souls. I have neither kindred nor friends. I stand alone in your midst, exposed to the fiery darts of the devil, and to the assaults of wicked men. But though all the powers of earth and hell were to combine against me, though all nature should sink into decay, still would I trust in the Lord, and joy in the God of my salvation. For I am fully persuaded, that he will bring me off conqueror, yea, more than conqueror, through him who hath loved me and given himself for me.

Boston, October, 1831.

HYMN

God is a spirit, just and wise,
    He knows our inmost minds;
In vain to heaven we raise our cries,
    And leave our souls behind.

Nothing but truth before his throne,
    With honor can appear;
The painted hypocrites are known
    By the disguise they wear.

Their lifted eyes salute the skies,
    Their blended knees the ground;
But God abhors the sacrifice,
    Where not the heart is found.

> Lord, search my heart, and try my reins,
> And make my souls sincere;
> So shall I stand before thy throne,
> And find acceptance there.
>
> Watts.

14

Cause for Encouragement

☞ By a lady of color.
[1832]

For the *Liberator*.
Composed upon hearing the Editor's account of the late Convention in Philadelphia.[1]

O, who can be discouraged from persevering in the paths of virtue, and in the ways of well-doing? Where is the soul amongst us that is not fired with a holy ambition? Has not every one [sic] a wish to excel, in order to encourage those benevolent hearts who are making every exertion in our behalf—whose prayers are ascending up before the majesty on high, like holy incense—whose tears are beginning to flow at Afric's woes? Many have desired to hear those things which we hear, and have not heard them; and to see those things that we see, and have not seen them.

The day-star from on high is beginning to dawn upon us, and Ethiopia will soon stretch forth her hands unto God.[2] These Anti-slavery societies, in my

---

[1] Stewart wrote this letter in response to William Lloyd Garrison's report in *The Liberator* (June 30, 1832) of the Second Annual Convention for the Improvement of Free People of Color in These United States. The National Colored Conventions, as they came to be called, began in 1830 and brought free, enslaved, and formerly enslaved black people together to develop strategies toward issues including abolition, economic justice, full black citizenship, and the education of black children. State and regional conventions began in the early 1840s, though they were more sporadic than the national meetings. The convention movement halted in the mid-1850s and then resumed from the mid-1860s through the 1890s.
Garrison delivered an address at the Second Annual Convention, which was actually the third meeting notwithstanding the moniker, and published the entirety of his text in the *Liberator*. In addition to Garrison's speech and account of the convention, this issue included articles and notices about Liberian colonization, slavery in the then-Southwest (e.g., Mississippi) and West Indies, and proposed restrictions on black and mixed-raced persons' rights in states, among other concerns. Stewart may have been especially drawn in the issue by the appearance of other black women intellectuals in *The Liberator*, including a letter from Sarah Mapps Douglass aka "Zillah" (in Stewart 123–133) that highlights black women's Christian duty to America in contrast to colonization schemes as well as a description of a Philadelphia "society of colored ladies" called the Female Literary Association whom Garrison visited while in the city for the convention.

[2] Psalm 68:31—"Princes shall come out of Egypt; Ethiopia shall soon stretch out her hands unto God" (KJV)—was a favored reference among African American thinkers and writers before Emancipation. They used Ethiopia to connote black conversion to Christianity, racial particularity, African history, and black sociopolitical striving.

opinion, will soon cause many grateful tears to flow, and many desponding hearts to bound and leap for joy.

And is it the applause of men that has prompted these benevolent ones to take their lives in their hands, as it were, to plead our cause before the great and powerful? Ah, no! It is that holy religion (which is held in derision and contempt by many[3]) whose precepts will raise and elevate us above our present condition, and cause our aspirations to ascend up in unison with theirs, and become the final means of bursting the bands of oppression.

Who have been the greatest and most powerful men since the first foundations of the earth were laid? Those who have been the most eminent for their piety and virtue. Upon what was America founded? Upon religion and pure principles. O, America, America! thou land of my birth! I love and admire thy virtues as much as I abhor and detest thy vices; and I am in hopes that thy stains will soon be wiped away, and thy cruelties forgotten.[4] O, ye southern slaveholders! we will no longer curse you for your wrongs; but we will implore the Almighty to soften your hard hearts towards our brethren, and to send them a speedy deliverance.

What has caused the downfall of nations, kings and empires? Sin, that abominable thing which God hates. Why has the Almighty commissioned the destroying angels to execute the fierceness of his anger upon the inhabitants of the earth? Because they have made light of the name of the Lord, and forgotten the rock of their salvation.[5] Why is it that churches and societies are not more flourishing among us? Because so much self-will and prejudice exists. Shall we, for a moment, persist in a course that will dampen the zeal of our benefactors? On the other hand, shall we not convince them

---

[3] Fervent black Christians like Stewart were often unsparing in their rebukes of mainstream Christianity for its slaveholding practices and proslavery theology. Although he was not the religionist Stewart was, Frederick Douglass offered one of the most memorable censures on American Christianity to close out his *Narrative* (1845): "I love the pure, peaceable, and impartial Christianity of Christ: I therefore hate the corrupt, slaveholding, women-whipping, cradle-plundering, partial and hypocritical Christianity of this land."

[4] This qualified paean to America reflects the inclusionary aims of early black nationalism. The more well-known black nationalism based in racial separatism only began to prevail in African American political philosophy in the early 1850s. Stewart's concession to the possible softening of southern slaveholders' hearts frames early black nationalism in moral sentimentalism, which is ubiquitous in antebellum didactic women's writing.

[5] Stewart's reference to the "downfall of nations, kings, and empires" resonated in two interrelated directions: (1) Old Testament prophecies of God's retribution against haughty, depraved societies, especially Jeremiah's; and (2) a general concern among American intellectuals and reformers that materialism, decadence, and industrialization will trigger the downfall of the United States as they did the Roman Empire. *Rock of their salvation*: 2 Samuel 22:47.

that our souls respond with theirs? Do you say, how can we? In a thousand ways, I reply. 1st. In prompting, encouraging and holding each other up by the hand; and secondly, in preserving our lips from slander and our tongues from deceit. It is high time for us to promote ourselves by some meritorious acts. And would to God that the advocates of freedom might perceive a trait in each one of us, that would encourage their hearts and strengthen their hands.[6]

Many bright and intelligent ones are in the midst of us; but because they are not calculated to display a classical education, they hide their talents behind a napkin.[7] I should rejoice to behold my friends or foes far exceed my feeble efforts. I should be happy to discern among them patterns worthy of imitation, and become proud to acknowledge them as my superiors. O, how I long for the time to come when I shall behold our young men anxious to inform their minds on moral and political subjects—ambitious to become distinguished men of talents—view them standing pillars in the church, qualifying themselves to preach the everlasting gospel of Our Lord Jesus Christ—becoming useful and active members in society, and the future hopes of our declining years.

Finally, it appears to me, as though eternity would be too short for me to admire and adore that Being who first directed my inexperienced footsteps to the abode of piety and virtue, where I was early taught to look upon vice with abhorrence and disgust. And could I now receive my choice, I would prefer moral worth and excellence of character to the wealth of the Indies, or the gold of Peru.

M.W.S.

---

[6] Throughout her early writings, Stewart commends white abolitionists and social reformers to set up her rhetorical move to censure African Americans' behavioral and ethical shortcomings vis-à-vis black uplift. As the Introduction to this volume explains, Stewart's political philosophy emphasized personal rectitude, self-directed community building, and racial solidarism above all.

[7] Luke 19:20: "And another came, saying, Lord, behold, here is thy pound, which I have kept laid up in a napkin" (KJV). This synoptic version of the "Parable of the Talents" about a servant who fails to invest his master's money wisely criticizes those who have gifts (money, salvation, and in this case, intelligence) but do not use them for the betterment of God or other Christians. By framing young black men who do not turn their education or energy toward liberatory work as cowardly and wasteful, Stewart justifies both her own right as a "feeble" woman to speak in the absence of "superior" men and her pious critique of frivolous young men. This same criticism of wasted youthful energy is taken up against the spendthrift black men of New York by William J. Wilson aka Ethiop in 1852 (see Stewart, 207–210).

15

An Address

Delivered at the African Masonic Hall, Boston, Feb. 27, 1833

BY MRS MARIA W. STEWART.

African rights and liberty is a subject that ought to fire the breast of every free man of color in these United States, and excite in his bosom a lively, deep, decided and heart-felt interest.[1] When I cast my eyes on the long list of illustrious names that are enrolled on the bright annals of fame amongst the whites, I turn my eyes within, and ask my thoughts, "Where are the names of *our* illustrious ones?" It must certainly have been for the want of energy on the part of the free people of color, that they have been long willing to bear the yoke of oppression. It must have been the want of ambition and force that has given the whites occasion to say, that our natural abilities are not as good, and our capacities by nature inferior to theirs. They boldly assert, that, did we possess a natural independence of soul, and feel a love for liberty within our breasts, some one of our sable race, long before this, would have testified it, notwithstanding the disadvantages under which we labor. We have made ourselves appear altogether unqualified to speak in our own defence, and are therefore looked upon as objects of pity and commiseration. We have been imposed upon, insulted and derided on every side; and now, if we complain, it is considered as the height of impertinence. We have suffered ourselves to be considered as dastards, cowards, mean, faint-hearted wretches; and on this account, (not because of our complexion,) many despise us, and would gladly spurn us from their presence.[2]

---

[1] Early black masonic societies across the Atlantic were crucial sites of activism and leadership training; they were also vital for the development of a racial consciousness across the African diaspora. The founder of black freemasonry, Prince Hall, gave an address in 1797 at the Boston African Masonic Hall advocating similar themes of education, racial solidarity, and (masculinist) uplift through moral purity. Stewart may have spoken in the same building, and this address was likely one of her unusual "promiscuous" (i.e., mixed-sex) audiences.

[2] Stewart regularly ascribed antiblack animus to what she perceived as the lack of moral virtue and courage among African Americans, often downplaying or, as in this case, rejecting racism.

These things have fired my soul with a holy indignation, and compelled me thus to come forward, and endeavor to turn their attention to knowledge and improvement; for knowledge is power. I would ask, is it blindness of mind, or stupidity of soul, or the want of education, that has caused our men who are 60 to 70 years of age, never to let their voices be heard, nor their hands be raised in behalf of their color? Or has it been for the fear of offending the whites? If it has, O ye fearful ones, throw off your fearfulness, and come forth in the name of the Lord, and in the strength of the God of Justice, and make yourselves useful and active members in society; for they admire a noble and patriotic spirit in others—and should they not admire it in us? If you are men, convince them that you possess the spirit of men; and as your day, so shall your strength be. Have the sons of Africa no souls? feel they no ambitious desires? shall the chains of ignorance forever confine them? shall the insipid appellation of "clever negroes," or "good creatures," any longer content them? Where can we find amongst ourselves the man of science, or a philosopher, or an able statesman, or a counsellor at law? Show me our fearless and brave, our noble and gallant ones. Where are our lecturers on natural history, and our critics in useful knowledge? There may be a few such men amongst us, but they are rare. It is true, our fathers bled and died in the revolutionary war, and others fought bravely under the command of Jackson, in defence of liberty.[3] But where is the man that has distinguished himself in these modern days by acting wholly in the defence of African rights and liberty? There was one—although he sleeps, his memory lives.[4]

I am sensible that there are many highly intelligent gentlemen of color in these United States, in the force of whose arguments, doubtless, I should discover my inferiority; but if they are blest with wit and talent, friends and fortune, why have they not made themselves men of eminence, by striving to take all the reproach that is cast upon the people of color, and in endeavoring to alleviate the woes of their brethren in bondage? Talk, without effort, is nothing; you are abundantly capable, gentlemen, of making yourselves men of distinction; and this gross neglect, on your part, causes my blood to boil within me. Here is the grand cause which hinders the rise and progress of the people of color. It is their want of laudable ambition and requisite courage.

---

[3] The War of 1812, led by then-General Andrew Jackson. Jackson was president at the time of this address.
[4] Almost certainly an allusion to David Walker, whom would have been immediately recognizable to a black Boston audience.

Individuals have been distinguished according to their genius and talents, ever since the first formation of man, and will continue to be whilst the world stands. The different grades rise to honor and respectability as their merits may deserve. History informs us that we sprung from one of the most learned nations of the whole earth—from the seat, if not the parent of science; yes, poor, despised Africa was once the resort of sages and legislators of other nations, was esteemed the school for learning, and the most illustrious men in Greece flocked thither for instruction.[5] But it was our gross sins and abominations that provoked the Almighty to frown thus heavily upon us, and give our glory unto others. Sin and prodigality have caused the downfall of nations, kings and emperors; and were it not that God in wrath remembers mercy, we might indeed despair; but a promise is left us; "Ethiopia shall again stretch forth her hands unto God."

But it is of no use for us to boast that we sprung from this learned and enlightened nation, for this day a thick mist of moral gloom hangs over millions of our race. Our condition as a people has been low for hundreds of years, and it will continue to be so, unless, by true piety and virtue, we strive to regain that which we have lost. White Americans, by their prudence, economy and exertions, have sprung up and become one of the most flourishing nations in the world, distinguished for their knowledge of the arts and sciences, for their polite literature. Whilst our minds are vacant and starving for want of knowledge, theirs are filled to overflowing. Most of our color have been taught to stand in fear of the white man from their earliest infancy, to work as soon as they could walk, and call "master" before they scarce could lisp the name of *mother*. Continual fear and laborious servitude have in some degree lessened in us that natural force and energy which belong to man; or else, in defiance of opposition, our men, before this, would have nobly and boldly contended for their rights. But give the man of color an equal opportunity with the white, from the cradle to manhood, and from manhood to the grave, and you would discover the dignified statesman, the man of science, and the philosopher. But there is no such opportunity for the sons of Africa, and I fear that our powerful ones are fully determined that there never shall be. Forbid, ye Powers on High, that it should any longer be said that our men possess no force. O ye sons of Africa, when will your voices be heard in our

---

[5] Such references to Alexandria in Hellenistic Egypt as an origin site of black culture and intellectual achievement recur throughout African American writings of the long nineteenth century, culminating in the imagery and rhetoric of Harlem Renaissance arts and letters.

legislative halls, in defiance of your enemies, contending for equal rights and liberty? How can you, when you reflect from what you have fallen, refrain from crying mightily unto God, to turn away from us the fierceness of his anger, and remember our transgressions against us no more forever. But a God of infinite purity will not regard the prayers of those who hold religion in one hand, and prejudice, sin and pollution in the other; he will not regard the prayers of self-righteousness and hypocrisy. Is it possible, I exclaim, that for the want of knowledge, we have labored for hundreds of years to support others, and been content to receive what they chose to give us in return? Cast your eyes about—look as far as you can see—all, all is owned by the lordly white, except here and there a lowly dwelling which the man of color, midst deprivations, fraud and opposition, has been scarce able to procure. Like king Solomon, who put neither nail nor hammer to the temple, yet received the praise; so also have the white Americans gained themselves a name, like the names of the great men that are in the earth, whilst in reality we have been their principal foundation and support. We have pursued the shadow, they have obtained the substance; we have performed the labor, they have received the profits; we have planted the vines, they have eaten the fruits of them.

(To be concluded.)

AN ADDRESS
Delivered at the African Masonic Hall, Boston, Feb. 27, 1833
BY MRS MARIA W. STEWART.
(Concluded)

I would implore our men, and especially our rising youth, to flee from the gambling board and the dance hall; for we are poor, and have no money to throw away. I do not consider dancing as criminal in itself, but it is astonishing to me that our young men are so blind to their own interest and the future welfare of their children, as to spend their hard earnings for this frivolous amusement; for it has been carried on among us to such an unbecoming extent, that it has become absolutely disgusting. "Faithful are the wounds of a friend, but the kisses of an enemy are deceitful."[6] Had those men amongst us,

---

[6] Proverbs 27:6. Stewart frames her criticism and throughout her corpus as "faithful" and loving in that they originate from within black communities and are aimed for their benefit, however harsh they may be.

who have had an opportunity, turned their attention as assiduously to mental and moral improvement as they have to gambling and dancing, I might have remained quietly at home, and they stood contending in my place.[7] These polite accomplishments will never enrol [sic] your names on the bright annals of fame, who admire the belle void of intellectual knowledge, or applaud the dandy that talks largely on politics, without striving to assist his fellow in the revolution, when the nerves and muscles of every other man forced him into the field of action. You have a right to rejoice, and to let your hearts cheer you in the days of your youth; yet remember that for all these things, God will bring you into judgment. Then, O ye sons of Africa, turn your mind from these perishable objects, and contend for the cause of God and the rights of man. Form yourselves into temperance societies. There are temperate men amongst you; then why will you any longer neglect to strive, by your example, to suppress vice in all its abhorrent forms? You have been told repeatedly of the glorious results arising from temperance, and can you bear to see the whites arising in honor and respectability, without endeavoring to grasp after that honor and respectability also?

But I forbear. Let our money, instead of being thrown away as heretofore, be appropriated for schools and seminaries of learning for our children and youth. We ought to follow the example of the whites in this respect. Nothing would raise our respectability, add to our peace and happiness, and reflect so much honor upon us, as to be ourselves the promoters of temperance, and the supporters, as far as we are able, of useful and scientific knowledge. The rays of light and knowledge have been hid from our view; we have been taught to consider ourselves as scarce superior to the brute creation; and have performed the most laborious part of American drudgery. Had we as a people received one half the early advantages the whites have received, I would defy the government of these United States to deprive us any longer of our rights.

I am informed that the agent of the Colonization Society has recently formed an association of young men, for the purpose of influencing those of us to go to Liberia who may feel disposed. The colonizationists are blind to their own interest, for should the nations of the earth make war with America, they would find their forces much weakened by our absence; or

---

[7] Stewart frames her public speech as discordant to proper "place," which is "quietly at home." Drawing on the language of nineteenth-century True Womanhood domesticity, Stewart justifies her ostensible violation of gendered spheres by adjudging the men in her community as feeble and inadequate political actors.

should we remain here, can our "brave soldiers," and "fellow-citizens," as they were termed in time of calamity, condescend to defend the rights of the whites, and be again deprived of their own, or sent to Liberia in return? Or, if the colonizationists are real friends to Africa, let them expend the money which they collect in erecting a college to educate her injured sons in this land of gospel light and liberty; for it would be most thankfully received on our part, and convince us of the truth of their professions, and save time, expense and anxiety. Let them place before us noble objects, worthy of pursuit, and see if we prove ourselves to be those unambitious negroes they term us. But ah! methinks their hearts are so frozen towards us, they had rather their money should be sunk in the ocean than to administer it to our relief; and I fear, if they dared, like Pharaoh, king of Egypt, they would order every male child among us to be drowned.[8] But the most high God is still as able to subdue the lofty pride of these white Americans, as He was the heart of that ancient rebel. They say, though we are looked upon as *things*, yet we sprang from a scientific people. Had our men the requisite force and energy, they would soon convince them by their efforts both in public and private, that they were men, or things in the shape of men. Well may the colonizationists laugh us to scorn for our negligence; well may they cry, "Shame to the sons of Africa." As the burden of the Israelites was too great for Moses to bear, so also is our burden too great for our noble advocate to bear. You must feel interested, my brethren, in what he undertakes, and hold up his hands by your good works, or in spite of himself his soul will become discouraged, and his heart will die within him; for he has, as it were, the strong bulls of Bashan to contend with.

It is of no use for us to wait any longer for a generation of well educated men to arise. We have slumbered and slept too long already; the day is far spent; the night of death approaches; and you have sound sense and good judgement sufficient to begin with, if you feel disposed to make a right use of it. Let every man of color throughout the United States, who possesses the spirit and principles of a man, sign a petition to Congress, to abolish slavery in the District of Columbia, and grant you the rights and privileges

---

[8] Antebellum black writers regularly toggled between Egypt as black homeland of cultural and intellectual excellence to Egypt as land of slave (i.e., Israelite) oppression. The move between classical and biblical references targeted both highly educated and less-educated readers and audience members. Here Stewart aligns African Americans with enslaved Israelites suffering under Egyptian rule; earlier in the address she aligned upper-class black Bostonians with the scholarly elite of Hellenistic Egypt.

of common free citizens; for if you had had faith as a grain of mustard seed, long before this the mountains of prejudice might have been removed. We are all sensible that the Anti-Slavery Society has taken hold of the arm of our whole population, in order to raise them out of the mire. Now all we have to do is, by a spirit of virtuous ambition to strive to raise ourselves; and I am happy to have it in my power thus publicly to say that the colored inhabitants of this city, in some respects, are beginning to improve. Had the free people of color in these United States nobly and boldly contended for their rights, and showed a natural genius and talent, although not so brilliant as some; had they held up, encouraged and patronized each other, nothing could have hindered us from being a thriving and flourishing people. There has been a fault among us. The reason why our distinguished men have not made themselves more influential is, because they fear that the strong current of opposition through which they must pass, would cause their downfall and prove their overthrew. And what gives rise to this opposition? Envy. And what has it amounted to? Nothing. And who are the cause of it? Our whited sepulchers,[9] who want to be great, and don't know how; who love to be called of men "Rabbi, Rabbi," who put on false sanctity, and humble themselves to their brethren, for the sake of acquiring the highest place in the synagogue, and the uppermost seats at the feast. You, dearly beloved, who are the genuine followers of our Lord Jesus Christ, the salt of the earth and the light of the world, are not so culpable. As I told you, in the very first of my writing, I tell you again, I am but as a drop in the bucket—as one particle of the small dust of the earth. God will surely raise up those amongst us who will plead the cause of virtue, and the pure principles of morality, more eloquently than I am able to do.

It appears to me that America has become like the great city of Babylon, for she has boasted in her heart,—"I sit a queen, and am no widow, and shall see no sorrow." She is indeed a seller of slaves and the souls of men; she has made the Africans drunk with the wine of her fornication; she has put them completely beneath her feet, and she means to keep them there; her right hand supports the reins of government, and her left hand the wheel of power, and she is determined not to let go her grasp. But many powerful sons and daughters of Africa will shortly arise, who will put down vice and immorality amongst us, and declare by Him that sitteth upon the throne, that they will

---

[9] Idiomatic for hypocrites, derived from Matthew 23:27.

have their rights; and if refused, I am afraid they will spread horror and devastation around.[10] I believe that the oppression of injured Africa has come up before the majesty of Heaven; and when our cries shall have reached the ears of the Most High, it will be a tremendous day for the people of this land; for strong is the arm of the Lord God Almighty.

Life has almost lost its charms for me; death has lost its sting and the grave its terrors; and at times I have a strong desire to depart and dwell with Christ, which is far better. Let me entreat my white brethren to awake and save our sons from dissipation, and our daughters from ruin. Lend the hand of assistance to feeble merit, and plead the cause of virtue amongst our sable race; so shall our curses upon you be turned into blessings; and though you should endeavor to drive us from these shores, still we will cling to you the more firmly; nor will we attempt to rise above you; we will presume to be called your equals only.

The unfriendly whites first drove the native American from his much loved home. Then they stole our fathers from their peaceful and quiet dwellings, and brought them hither, and made bond men and bond women of them and their little ones: they have obliged our brethren to labor, kept them in utter ignorance, nourished them in vice, and raised them in degradation; and now that we have enriched their soil, and filled their coffers, they say that we are not capable of becoming like white men, and that we never can rise to respectability in this country. They would drive us to a strange land. But before I go, the bayonet shall pierce me through. African rights and liberty is a subject that ought to fire the breast of every free man of color in these United States, and excite in his bosom a lively, deep, decided and heartfelt interest.[11]

---

[10] This reference to insurrection is one of the few Stewart made in her corpus. She delivered this address in the aftermath of Nat Turner's rebellion in Southampton, Virginia (1831), as its ramifications continued to impact free and enslaved black persons across the United States. Even before Turner's rebellion, African American writers were reticent about the prospects of insurrection against slavery and white supremacy, with the notable exception of David Walker in his *Appeal*.

[11] The article in *The Liberator* that follows Stewart's address is called "Gaming." It is a reprint of an account from the *Boston Atlas* that tells the tale of man whose "passion for gaming ... operated like a slow poison," leading him to robbery and suicide. Garrison's inclusion of "Gaming" suggests that social reformers believed gambling was a vice that devastated young men across racial difference.

16

The Proper Training of Children

BY MRS. MARIA W. STEWART.

Delivered Nov. 21, 1860, at The Ladies' Litera[r]y Festival, in St. James' Protestant Episcopal Church, Baltimore.

LADIES AND GENTLEMEN,—The proper training of the young is a subject that ought to excite the religious attention of the community at large. But the force of precept and example at home has a more powerful influence over the mind of children and youth than all the instruction that teachers can impart to them in christendom.

Again, the parental duty of teaching children the first lessons of piety and obedience at home, in some cases appear to be little thought of, if not altogether neglected. And when the children of such parents are sent abroad for instruction, they appear ignorant of God, the reading of his Holy Word is irksome to them, and they pay little or no attention to the prayers that may be offered up in their hearing. And unless reproved for their irreverent behavior, they by their actions say, "Who is the Lord that I should obey him? I know not the Lord, neither will I obey his voice."[1] Hence arises want of respect and reverence for their Spiritual pastors, ministers and teachers, and those whom God has placed in authority over them. They are not taught to order themselves lowly and reverently to all their betters. They are not taught to rise up before the hoary head and honor grey hairs. Thus the poor, the decrepit, and the old, are ofttimes treated with scarce common respect by the giddy young, and are cast aside as things of naught.

We are not always to bloom in youth and beauty, and God has wisely arranged that the old and the middle-aged, by their wisdom and discretion, should counsel and guide the young. And there is as much need of pious missionary labor in different parts of this city as there is among the Hottentots

---

[1] Exodus 5:2, spoken by Pharaoh to Moses. Stewart analogizes disrespectful children to little Pharaohs, condemning disorderly hierarchies as much as a lack of piety.

or the wild Hindoo.[2] There, were wicked and insolent children, in the days of the prophet Elisha, and there are wicked and insolent children now, and though God may not perform a miracle by sending the bears out of the wood to destroy them, yet their punishment is certain and sure, for the sins of youth follow them to old age.[3]

Again, lying is one of the grand characteristics of children; and if all liars are to have their part in the lake that burns with fire and brimstone, what a fearful doom awaits the many; and those children that are distinguished for always telling the truth, like the illustrious General George Washington, may be considered gems of rare value.[4] And this fact and observation gives rise to the thought, that there must have been some first great cause. Why? We as the citizens of the State of Maryland are denied our oath.[5]

Again, the unruly tempers and passions of some children when let loose, are like the ragings of a *bear*; and unless children are taught self-government of temper at home, their tempers will govern them and become fastened upon them as iron bands. Thus, many for want of being early taught the fear of God, and self-government of temper at home, in after-life become the authors of their own misery and the misery of those around them. And such children, with such tempers, could never enter the kingdom of heaven were they to die, according to God's Holy word, and if permitted so to do, they would deprive its inmates of their happiness. Oh, horrible! to allow children to possess ungovernable tempers and unbridled tongue to have the last word, to call ill-names, to wrangle quarrel, and fight.

As you pass along the streets, look at the votaries of vice and shudder. Says the poet:

---

[2] Hottentot is an archaic, now offensive term for the Khoekhoe peoples indigenous to southern African. Europeans often used the term to name African and African-descended persons, usually as a pejorative. *Hindoo*: archaic spelling of Hindu. Both Hindu and Hottentot connoted pagan and uncivilized groups bereft of Christian salvation.

[3] This a reference to a story from 2 Kings 2:23–24 in which bears maul youths who mock the prophet Elisha's baldness. Stewart argues that poorly raised children cannot escape God's punishment, though they may receive it much later in life.

[4] American educators, historians, and cultural producers crafted mythologies of George Washington in the decades following his death. Part of their project was to turn him into a shining example of personal integrity and civic virtue for children. Stewart draws on that effort here, almost certainly alluding to the famed cherry tree anecdote that Mason Locke Weems included in the fifth edition of his incredibly popular and often fabricated in *The Life of Washington* (1809). The story holds that a young Washington disobeyed his father's commands and purposefully hacked a cherry tree in his family's garden. When confronted, he confessed: "I can't tell a lie, Pa; you know I can't tell a lie. I did cut it with my hatchet" (14). Versions of Weems's fable appeared in all realms of American culture, including primers and other forms of children's literature.

[5] Possibly an allusion to African Americans' limited status in Maryland courts, particularly their inability to serve as witnesses against white persons, which had been a long-standing preclusion since the eighteenth century.

> Soon as we draw our infant breath,
> The seeds of sin grow up for death.[6]

And well might the Psalmist exclaim. "Deliver me from the strife of tongues. Deliver me from blood-guiltiness. O God, thou that art the God of my salvation, and my tongue shall sing aloud of Thy righteousness."

God overthrew the house of Eli, because he restrained not his sons; and what has happened to others should prove a warning to us. And Saul lost his kingdom by his disobedience to the commands of the prophet Samuel, and, Oh, wretched man was he, for the Lord departed from him. And unless those whom God has placed in authority over our children take this matter into a more serious consideration than heretofore, there will a generation spring up, among whom the Lord will not delight to dwell. And God has put a rod in the hand of this great American nation, to scourge those of us who are living in the neglect of this one great and important duty, and He alone prevents them from doing it. But if we make up our minds from this time henceforth, to train up our children in the way they should go, so that when they are old they will not depart from it, He will fight our every battle and defend us from every foe.

Again, as God punishes nations and individuals for their disobedience to His commands, Lo, He abundantly rewards those that are obedient. He established the throne of David His servant, forever, because He knew that David would teach his children the fear of the Lord. And as the Lord declared there should not fail Him a man to sit upon the throne of David, who knows but the nobility of England, her kings and her queens, her princes and her princesses, her dukes and her duchies, her lords and ladies, may have descended from David's royal line? And who knows but what the royal sovereignty of England shall stand until the end of time. For righteousness exalteth a nation, but sin is a reproach to any people.

Mrs. President and Gentlemen,—Look at this great American continent. It is supposed to have been inhabited twelve hundred years by native Indians, before its discovery by Columbus. And what did they do for God? Their delight was to hunt the buffalo and wild deer; and being ignorant of God's Holy will and commandments, they and their children gave vent to their unholy tempers until some of their altars became literally drenched with the blood

---

[6] From Isaac Watts's "Lord, I am Vile, Conceived in Sin" in his *The Psalms of David* (1719).

of human victims.[7] Therefore, God in his wise and holy providence, saw fit to take this goodly land from them, and to give it to a nation wiser and better than themselves, and suffered that nation to exterminate millions of their race, and to drive their posterity on our far Western borders.[8]

Behold! yonder, that feeble band of Pilgrim fathers, landing in this dreary wilderness, on Plymouth Rock, at an inclement season of the year, amid sufferings indescribable. But their first effort was to rear an altar to the living God, and lay the foundation of piety, obedience, and intelligence, for their children to walk upon. They had made themselves acquainted with the God of Abraham, of Isaac, and of Jacob, and the Bible was the chart by which they steered their course. And however much the present race may have degenerated from the religious principles of their forefathers, yet see by their union and by their strength, by their industry, and energy of character, by their self-determination, to equal, if not to excel, other nations. From the Northern Arctic to the South Antarctic, from the Atlantic on the East, to the Pacific on the West, what mighty achievements they have accomplished in three hundred and sixty-eight years! They have leveled forests, reared cities, their fields wave with the finest of the wheat; and this vast continent is besprinkled from one end to the other with towns and villages. Look at their churches, their colleges, their schools, and their academies of giant intellect,

>Their men,
>Their mighty men,[9]

Their valiant men, their men of renown, their House of Congress, their Senate, their House of Representatives, and their Legislature, their State Department, their War Department, and their military, their Naval Department by sea and by land, their their [sic] commerce, second to none but Europe; their Agricultural Department, and their manufactures, their Arts, their Sciences, their Steam inventions, their Railroad construction, their Geographical plans, their Astronomical discoveries, and their Telegraphic wire, and their large lakes and rivers, and mighty oceans, bedecked with ships of the largest

---

[7] Charges of human sacrifice and cannibalism were often levied against indigenous American, African, and Pacific populations, generally without evidence.

[8] Echoes of the doctrine of Manifest Destiny ring here and over the next section of this address.

[9] "Mighty men" could be an allusion to the warriors who fought alongside King David (2 Samuel 23:8–38), especially because the sentence names "valiant men" and "men of renown." It does not seem as if this is Stewart's or someone else's verse.

magnitude to those of the smallest dimensions, and their Star-spangled Banner floating in the breeze.

Oh, can we curse whom God has blessed? Happy is that nation whose God is the Lord. And who knows what miracle of wonder He may perform for us if we only make up our mind to serve the Lord our God with all our heart, soul, sought, mind, and strength, and lay the platform of piety and intelligence for our children to walk upon. For we also are His people and the sheep of His pasture. He formed and fashioned us, and we are the workmanship of his hands. He knows our griefs and our sorrows, our fearful apprehension of the future, and like a father pitieth his children, so the Lord pitieth them that fear Him.

Dear Fathers and Mothers,—It rests with you whether your sons and daughters shall become as polished corner-stones, after the similitude of a palace in the house of our God. And though you may not hope to see them reach the Presidential chair, from circumstances under which we are placed, yet who knows what great shaggy lion may rouse from his lair, and roar terribly, from among them! What man of gigantic intellect rise up, to confute and confound the mighty hosts of arguments that are leveled against us by the haughty oppressor! What David, ruddy, and withal a beautiful countenance, run from the sheepfold with sling and pebble to strike Goliah in the forehead and kill him with his own sword! If we only lay the foundation of piety and intelligence for our children to walk upon, God has raised up one wonder in this nineteenth century and who knows what wonder He may raise up in the twentieth!

Sin is such a hideous monster, that were I to live my life over again, I would shun it as the most deadly poison. For there is an inconceivable beauty in the fear and service of God, a beauty past expression.

PART III
LITERARY PRODUCTIONS

Contextual Works

17

Jarena Lee, *The Life and Religious Experience of Jarena Lee* (1849) (selections)

Religious Experience and Journal of Mrs. Jarena Lee, Giving an Account of Her Call to Preach the Gospel

"And it shall come to pass . . . that I will pour out my Spirit upon all flesh; and your sons and your *daughters* shall prophesy"—*Joel* ii.28.[1]

I was born February 11th, 1783, at Cape May, State of New Jersey. At the age of seven years I was parted from my parents, and went to live as a servant maid, with a Mr. Sharp, at the distance of about sixty miles from the place of my birth.

My parents being wholly ignorant of the knowledge of God, had not therefore instructed me in any degree in this great matter. Not long after the commencement of my attendance on this lady, she had bid me do something respecting my work, which in a little while after she asked me if I had done, when I replied, Yes—but this was not true.

At this awful point, in my early history, the Spirit of God moved in power through my conscience, and told me I was a wretched sinner. On this account so great was the impression, and so strong were the feelings of guilt, that I promised in my heart that I would not tell another lie.

But notwithstanding this promise my heart grew harder, after a while, yet the Spirit of the Lord never entirely forsook me, but continued mercifully striving with me, until his gracious power converted my soul.

---

[1] This verse is one of the most common pieces of texts that advocates for women's equality in ecclesiastical ranks and throughout the church used to press their case. They also frequently adduced women leaders and prophets in the Bible (e.g., Esther and Deborah) and scriptures that detail divine inspiration visited upon women.

The manner of this great accomplishment was as follows: In the year 1804, it so happened that I went with others to hear a missionary of the Presbyterian order preach. It was an afternoon meeting, but few were there, the place was a school room; but the preacher was solemn, and in his countenance the earnestness of his master's business appeared equally strong, as though he were about to speak to a multitude.

At the reading of the Psalms, a ray of renewed conviction darted into my soul. These were the words, composing the first verse of the Psalms for the service:

> Lord, I am vile, conceived in sin,
> Born unholy and unclean.
> Sprung from man, whose guilty fall
> Corrupts the race, and taints us all.[2]

This description of my condition struck me to the heart, and made me to feel in some measure, the weight of my sins, and sinful nature. But not knowing how to run immediately to the Lord for help, I was driven of Satan, in the course of a few days, and tempted to destroy myself.

There was a brook about a quarter of a mile from the house, in which there was a deep hole, where the water whirled about among the rocks; to this place, it was suggested, I must go and drown myself.

At the time I had a book in my hand; it was a Sabbath morning, about ten o'clock; to this place I resorted, where on coming to the water I sat down on the bank, and on my looking into it, it was suggested that drowning would be an easy death. It seemed as if someone was speaking to me, saying put your head under, it will not distress you. But by some means, of which I can give no account, my thoughts were taken entirely from this purpose, when I went from the place to the house again. It was the unseen arm of God which saved me from self-murder.

But notwithstanding this escape from, my mind was not at rest—but so great was the labor of my spirit and the fearful oppression of a judgement to come, that I was reduced as one extremely ill, on which account a physician was called to attend me, from which illness I recovered in about three months.

---

[2] These lines are the first stanza of Isaac Watts's "Original and Actual Sin Confessed," published in his *The Psalms of David* (1719). Watts linked the hymn to Psalm 51.

But as yet I had not found Him of whom Moses and the prophets did write, being extremely ignorant: there being no one to instruct me in the way of life and salvation as yet. After my recovery, I left the lady, who, during my sickness, was exceedingly kind, and went to Philadelphia. From this place I soon went a few miles into the country, where I resided in the family of a Roman Catholic. But my anxiety still continued respecting my poor soul, on which account I used to watch my opportunity to read in the Bible; and this lady observing this, took the Bible from me and hid it, giving me a novel in its stead—which when I perceived, I refused to read.

Soon after this I again went to the city of Philadelphia, and commenced going to the English Church, the pastor of which was an Englishman, by the name of Pilmore[3], one of the number who at first preached Methodism in America, in the city of New York.

But while sitting under the ministration of this man, which was about three months, and at the last time, it appeared that there was a wall between me and a communion with that people, which was higher than I could possibly see over, and seemed to make this impression upon my mind, *this is not the people for you.*

But on returning home at noon I inquired of the head cook of the house respecting the rules of the Methodists, as I knew she belonged to that society, who told me what they were; on which account I replied, that I should not be able to abide by such strict rules not even one year—however, I told her that I would go with her and hear what they had to say.

The man who was to speak in the afternoon of that day, was the Rev. Richard Allen,[4] since bishop of the African Episcopal Methodists in America. During the labors of this man that afternoon, I had come to the conclusion, that this is the people to which my heart unites, and it so happened, that as soon as the service closed he invited such as felt a desire to flee the wrath to come, to unite on trial with them—I embraced the opportunity. Three weeks from that day, my soul was gloriously converted to God, under preaching, at the very outset of the sermon. The text was barely pronounced, which was "I perceive thy heart is not right in the sight of God," when there appeared to *my*

---

[3] Almost certainly a reference to Joseph Pilmore (1739–1825), who as a young man converted to Methodism and worked alongside John Wesley. In 1769 he left England to evangelize in several British North American colonies.

[4] Richard Allen (1760–1831) was founding bishop of the African Methodist Episcopal Church. Poet, psalmist, and author of one of the earliest African American autobiographies, Allen was also a pioneer of early black institutional culture. He was a cofounder of the Free African Society of Philadelphia and helped establish what we now call the National Colored Convention movement.

view, in the centre of the heart, *one* sin; and this was *malice* against one particular individual, who had strove deeply to injure me, which I resented. At this discovery I said, *Lord* I forgive *every* creature. That instant, it appeared to me as if a garment, which had entirely enveloped my whole person, even to my fingers' ends, split at the crown of my head, and was stripped away from me, passing like a shadow from my sight—when the glory of God seemed to cover me in its stead.

That moment, though hundreds were present, I did leap to my feet and declare that God, for Christ's sake, had pardoned the sins of my soul. Great was the ecsta[s]y of my mind, for I felt that not only the sin of *malice* was pardoned, but all other sins were swept away together. That day was the first when my heart had believed, and my tongue had made confession unto salvation—the first words uttered, a part of that song, which shall fill eternity with its sound, was *glory to God*. For a few moments I had power to exhort sinners, and to tell of the wonders and of the goodness of Him who had clothed me with *His* salvation. During this the minister was silent, until my soul felt its duty had been performed, when he declared another witness of the power of Christ, to forgive sins on earth, was manifest in my conversion.

From the day on which I first went to the Methodist Church, until the hour of my deliverance, I was strangely buffetted by that enemy of all righteousness—the devil.

I was naturally of a lively turn of disposition; and during the space of time from my first awakening until I knew my peace was made with God, I rejoiced in the vanities of this life, and then again sunk back into sorrow.

For four years I had continued in this way, frequently laboring under the awful apprehension, that I could never be happy in this life. This persuasion was greatly strengthened during the three weeks, which was the last of Satan's power over me, in this peculiar manner, on which account I had come to the conclusion that I had better be dead than alive. Here I was again tempted to destroy my life by drowning; but suddenly this mode was changed—and while in the dusk of the evening as I was walking to and for in the yard of the house, I was beset to hang myself with a cord suspended from the wall enclosing the secluded spot.

But no sooner was the intention resolved on in my mind, than an awful dread came over me, when I ran into the house; still the tempter pursued me. There was standing a vessel of water—into this I was strangely impressed to plunge my head, so as to extinguish the life which God had given me. Had I done this, I have been always of the opinion, that I should have been unable to release myself; although the vessel was scarcely large enough to hold a gallon of water. Of me may it not be said, as written by Isaiah (chap 65, verses 1, 2.) "I am sought of them that asked not for me; I am found of them that sought me not." Glory be to God for his redeeming power, which saved me from the violence of my own hands, from the malice of Satan, and from eternal death; for had I have killed myself, a great ransom could not have delivered me; for it is written—"No murder hath eternal life abiding in him." How appropriately can I sing—

> Jesus sought me when a stranger,
> Wandering from the fold of God;
> He to rescue me from danger,
> Interposed his precious blood[5]

But notwithstanding the terror which seized upon me, when about to end my life, I had not view of the precipice on the edge of which I was tottering, until it was over, and my eyes were opened. Then the awful gulf of hell seemed to be open beneath me, covered only, as it were, by a spider's web, on which I stood. I seemed to hear the howling of the damned, to see the smoke of the bottomless pit, and to hear the rattling of those chains, which hold the impenitent under clouds of darkness to the judgment of the great day.

I trembled like Belshazzar, and cried out in the horror of my spirit, "God be merciful to me a sinner."[6] That night I found a resolution to pray; which, when resolved upon, there appeared, sitting in one corner of the room, Satan, in the form of a monstrous dog, and in a rage, as if in pursuit, his tongue protruding from his mouth to a great length, and his eyes looked like two balls of fire; it soon, however, vanished out of my sight. From this state of terror and dismay, I was happily delivered under the preaching of the Gospel as before related.

This view which I was permitted to have of Satan, in the form of a dog, is evidence, which corroborates in my estimation, the Bible account of a hell of fire, which burneth with brimstone, called in Scripture the bottomless pit;

---

[5] From the second verse of Robert Robinson's "Come Thou Fount of Every Blessing" (1758).

[6] Lee conflates different responses to sin to describe her own. Belshazzar, king of Babylon, was warned of the punishment that will come of his sin, but, notwithstanding "trembling," he dismissed the "writing on the wall," to borrow the phrase that comes Belshazzar's story (Daniel 5–8). In Jesus's parable of the Pharisee and the Publican, the Publican humbles himself before God, admits he is a sinner, and asks for mercy. The moral of the parable, Jesus says, is that "for every one that exalteth himself shall be abased; and he that humbleth himself shall be exalted" (Luke 18:9–14).

the place where all liars, who repent not, shall have their portion; as also the Sabbath breaker, the adulterer, the fornicator, with the fearful, the abominable, and the unbelieving, this shall be the portion of their cup.

This language is too strong and expressive to be applied to any state of suffering in *time*. Were it to be thus applied, the reality could no where be found in human life; the consequence would be, that *this* scripture would be found a false testimony. But when made to apply to an endless state of perdition, in eternity, beyond the bounds of human life, then this language is found not to exceed our views of a state of eternal damnation.

During the latter part of my state of conviction, I can now apply to my case, as it then was, the beautiful words of the poet:

> The more I strove against its power,
> I felt its weight and guilt the more;
> Till late I heard my Saviour say,
> Come hither soul, I am the way.[7]

This I found to be true, to the joy of my disconsolate and despairing heart, in the hour of my conversion to God.

During this state of mind, while sitting near the fire one evening, after I had heard Rev. Richard Allen, as before related, a view of my distressed conditions so affected my heart, that I could not refrain from weeping and crying aloud; which caused the lady with whom I then lived, to inquire, with surprise, what ailed me; and to which I answered, that I knew not what ailed me. She replied that I ought to pray. I arose from where I was sitting, being in an agony, and weeping convulsively, requested her to pray for me; but at the very moment when she would have done so, some person wrapped heavily at the door for admittance; it was but a person of the house, but this occurrence was sufficient to interrupt us in our intentions; and I believe to this day, I should then have found salvation to my soul. This interruption was, doubtless, the work of Satan.

Although at this time, when my conviction was so great, yet I knew not that Jesus Christ was the Son of God, the second person in the adorable

---

[7] This is the seventh stanza of John Cennik's "Hymn LXIV: Following Christ, the Sinners Way to God," published in his *Sacred Hymns for the Use of Religious Societies* (1743). Cennik (1718–1755) worked with John Wesley and George Whitefield until the two split; then he followed Whitefield for several years until joining the Moravians.

Trinity. I knew him not in the pardon of my sins, yet I felt a consciousness that if I died without pardon, that my lot must inevitably be damnation. If I would pray—I knew not how. I could form no connexion of ideas into words; but I knew the Lord's prayer; this I uttered with a loud voice, and with all my might and strength. I was the most ignorant creature in the world; I did not even know that Christ had died for the sins of the world, and to save sinners. Every circumstance, however, was so directed as still to continue and increase the sorrows of my heart, which I now know to have been a Godly sorrow which wrought repentance, which is not to repented of. Even the falling of the dead leaves from the forests, and the dried spires of the mown grass, showed me that I too must die in like manner. But my case was awfully different from that of the grass of the field, or the wide spread decay of a thousand forests, as I felt within me a living principle, an immortal spirit, which cannot die, and must forever either enjoy the smiles of the Creator, or feel the pangs of ceaseless damnation.

But the Lord led me on; being gracious, he took pity on my ignorance; he heard my wailings, which had entered into the ear of the Lord of Saboath.[8] Circumstances so transpired that I soon came to a knowledge of the being and character of the Son of God, of whom I knew nothing.

My strength had left me. I had become feverish and sickly through the violence of my feelings, on which account I left my place of service to spend a week with a colored physician, who was a member of the Methodist society, and also to spend this week in going to places where prayer and supplication was statedly made for such as me.

Through this means I had learned much, so as to be able in some degree to comprehend the spiritual meaning of the text, which the minister took on the Sabbath morning, as before related, which was "I perceive thy heart is not right in the sight of God."— Acts, chap. 8, verse 21.

This text, as already related, became the power of God unto salvation to me, because I believed. I was baptized according to the direction of our Lord, who said, as he was about to ascend from the mount, to his disciples, "Go ye into all the world and preach my gospel to every creature, he that believeth and is baptized shall be saved."

I have now passed through the account of my conviction, and also of my conversion to God; and shall next speak of the blessings of sanctification.

---

[8] Translated as the "Lord of hosts [i.e., sun, moon, and stars]" or "Lord of armies," this reference to God only appears twice in the Bible, Romans 9:29 and James 5:4. In both instances, these scriptures describe God to whom one who prays to be spared from divine wrath.

A time, after I had received forgiveness, flowed sweetly on; day and night my joy was full, no temptation was permitted to molest me. I could say continually with the psalmist, that "God had separated my sins from me as far as the east is from the west." I was ready continually to cry,

> Come all the word, come sinner thou,
> All things in Christ are ready now.[9]

I continued in this happy state of mind for almost three months, when a certain coloured man, by name William Scott, came to pay me a religious visit. He had been for many years the faithful follower of the Lamb; and he had also taken much time in visiting the sick and distressed of our color, and understood well the great things belonging to a man of full stature in Christ Jesus.

In the course of our conversation, he inquired if the Lord had justified my soul. I answered yes. He then asked me if he had sanctified me. I answered no; and that I did not know what that was. He then undertook to instruct me further in the knowledge of the Lord respecting this blessing.

He told me the progress of the soul from a state of darkness, or of nature, was three-fold; or consisted in three degrees, as follows: First, conviction for sin. Second, justification from sin. Third, the entire sanctification of the soul to God.[10] I thought this description was beautiful, and immediately believed in it. He then inquired if I would promise to pray for this in my secret devotions. I told him yes. Very soon I began to call upon the Lord to show me all that was in my heart, which was not according to his will. Now there appeared to be a new struggle commencing in my soul, not accompanied with fear, guilt, and bitter distress, as while under my first conviction for sin, but a laboring of the mind to know more of the right way of the Lord. I began now to feel that my heart was not clean in his sight; that there yet remained the roots of bitterness, which if not destroyed, would ere long sprout up from these roots, and overwhelm me in a new growth of the brambles and brushwood of sin.

---

[9] The second verse of Charles Wesley's "Hymn L: The Great Supper," published in his Hymns for Those That Seek and Those That Have Redemption in the Blood of Jesus Christ (1747). Wesley (1707–1788) was a leader of the early Methodist movement.

[10] John Wesley (1703–1791), founder of Methodism, established this "three-fold" doctrine in his sermon "The Scripture-Way of Salvation" (1765).

By the increasing light of the Spirit, I had found there yet remained the root of pride, anger, self-will, with many evils, the result of fallen nature. I now became alarmed at this discovery, and began to fear that I have been deceived in my experience. I was now greatly alarmed, lest I should fall away from what I knew I had enjoyed; and to guard against this I prayed almost incessantly, without setting faith on the power and promises of God to keep me from falling. I had not yet learned how to war against temptation of this kind. Satan well knew that if he could succeed in making me disbelieve my conversion, that he would catch me either on the ground of complete despair, or on the ground of infidelity. For if all I had passed through was to go for nothing, and was but a fiction, the mere ravings of a disordered mind, that I would naturally be led to believe that there is nothing in religion at all.

From this snare I was mercifully preserved, and led to believe that there was yet a greater work than that of pardon to be wrought in me. I retired to a secret place, (after having sought this blessing, as well as I could, for nearly three months, from the time brother Scott had instructed me respecting it,) for prayer, about four o'clock in the afternoon. I had struggled long and hard, but found not the desire of my heart. When I rose from my knees, there seemed a voice speaking to me, as I yet stood in a leaning posture—"Ask for sanctification." When to my surprise, I recollected that I had not even thought of it in my whole prayer. It would seem Satan had hidden the very object from my mind, for which I had purposely kneeled to pray. But when this voice whispered in my heart, saying, "Pray for sanctification," I again bowed in the same place, at the same time, and said, "Lord *sanctify* my soul for Christ's sake." That very instant, as if lightning had darted through me, I sprang to my feet, and cried, "The Lord has sanctified my soul!" There was none to hear this but the angels who stood around to witness my joy—and Satan, whose malice raged the more. That Satan was there, I knew; for no sooner had I cried out "The Lord has sanctified my soul," than there seemed another voice behind me, saying, "No, it is too great a work to be done." But another spirit said, "Bow down for the witness—I received it—*thou art sanctified!*" The first I knew of myself after that, I was standing in the yard with my hands spread out, and looking with my face toward heaven.

I now ran into the house and told them what had happened to me, when, as it were a new rush of the same ecsta[s]y came upon me, and caused me to feel as if I were in an ocean of light and bliss.

During this, I stood perfectly still, the tears rolling in a flood from my eyes. So great was the joy, that it is past description. There is no language that can describe it, except that which was heard by St Paul, when he was caught up to third heaven, and heard words which it was not lawful to utter.

MY CALL TO PREACH THE GOSPEL.

Between four and five years after my sanctification, on a certain time, an impressive silence fell upon me, and I stood as if someone was about to speak to me, yet I had no such thought in my heart—But to my utter surprise there seemed to sound a voice which I thought I distinctly heard, and most certainly understand, which said to me, "Go preach the Gospel!" I immediately replied aloud, "No one will believe me." Again I listened, and again the same voice seemed to say—"Preach the Gospel; I will put words in your mouth, and you will turn your enemies to become your friends."[11]

At first I supposed that Satan had spoken to me, for I had read that he could transform himself into an angel of light for the purpose of deception. Immediately I went into a secret place, and called upon the Lord to know if he had called me to preach, and whether I was deceived or not; when there appeared to my view the form and figure of a pulpit, with a Bible lying thereon, the back of which was presented to me as plainly as if it had been a literal fact.

In consequence of this, my mind became so exercised, that during the night following, I took a text and preached in my sleep. I thought there stood before me a great multitude, while I expounded to them the things of religion. So violent were my exertions and so loud were my exclamations, that I awoke from the sound of my own voice, which also awoke the family of the house where I resided. Two days after I went to see the preacher in charge of the African Society, who was the Rev. Richard Allen, the same before named in these pages, to tell him that I felt it my duty to preach the gospel. But as I drew near the street in which his house was, which was in the city of Philadelphia, my courage began to fail me; so terrible did the cross appear, it seemed that I should not be able to bear it. Previous to my setting out to go to see him, so agitated was my mind, that my appetite for my daily food failed me entirely. Several times on my way there, I turned back again; but as often I felt my strength again renewed, and I soon found that the nearer

---

[11] Lee invokes Moses's response when God instructed him to return to Egypt as His spokesman. Like Lee, Moses expressed concern that he would not be believed—a common worry among religious and secular prophets alike (Exodus 4:1–12).

I approached to the house of the minister, the less was my fear. Accordingly, as soon as I came to the door, my fears subsided, the cross was removed, all things appeared pleasant—I was tranquil.

I now told him, that the Lord had revealed it to me, that [I] must preach the gospel. He replied, by asking, in what sphere I wished to move in? I said, among the Methodists. He then replied, that a Mrs. Cook, a Methodist lady, had also some time before requested the same privilege; who, it was believed, had done much good in the way of exhortation, and holding prayer meetings; and who had been permitted to do so by the verbal license of the preacher in charge at the time. But as to women preaching, he said that our Discipline knew nothing at all about it—that it did not call for women preachers. This I was glad to hear, because it removed the fear of the cross—but no sooner did this feeling cross my mind, than I found that a love of souls had in a measure departed from me; that holy energy which burned within me, as a fire, began to be smothered. This I soon perceived.

O how careful ought we to be, lest through our by-laws of church government and discipline, we bring into disrepute even the word of life. For as unseemly as it may appear now-a-days for a woman to preach, it should be remembered that nothing is impossible with God. And why should it be thought impossible, heterodox, or improper for a woman to preach? seeing the Saviour died for the woman as well as for the man.

If the man may preach, because the Saviour died for him, why not the woman? seeing he died for her also. Is he not a whole Saviour, instead of a half one? as those who hold it wrong for a woman to preach, would seem to make it appear.

Did not Mary *first* preach the risen Saviour, and is not the doctrine of the resurrection the very climax of Christianity—hangs not all our hope on this, as argued by St Paul? Then did not Mary, a woman, preach the gospel? for she preached the resurrection of the crucified son of God.

But some will say that Mary did not expound the Scripture, therefore, she did not preach, in the proper sense of the term. To this I reply, it may be that the term preach in those primitive times, do not mean exactly what it is now made to mean; perhaps it was a great deal more simple then, than it is now—if it were not, the unlearned fishermen could not have preached the gospel at all, as they had no learning.

To this it may be replied, by those who are determined not to believe that it is right for a woman to preach, that the disciples, though they were fishermen and ignorant of letters too, were inspired so to do. To which

I would reply, that though they were inspired, yet that inspiration did not save them from showing their ignorance of letters and of man's wisdom; this the multitude soon found out, by listening to the remarks of the envious Jewish priests. If then, to preach the gospel, by the gift of heaven, comes by inspiration solely, is God straitened: must he take the man exclusively? May he not, did he not, and can he not inspire a female to preach the simple story of the birth, life, death, and resurrection of our Lord, and accompany it too with power to the sinner's heart. As for me, I am fully persuaded that the Lord called me to labor according to what I have received, in his vineyard. If he has not, how could he consistently hear testimony in favor of my poor labors, in awakening and converting sinners?

In my wanderings up and down among men, preaching according to my ability, I have frequently found families who told me that they had not for several years been to a meeting, and yet, while listening to hear what God would say to his poor female instrument, have believed with trembling—tears rolling down their cheeks, the signs of contrition and repentance towards God. I firmly believe that I have sown seed, in the name of the Lord, which shall appear with its increase at the great day of accounts, when Christ shall come to make up his jewels.

At a certain time, I was beset with the idea, that soon or late I should fall from grace and lose my soul at last. I was frequently called to the throne of grace about this matter, but found no relief; the temptation pursued me still. Being more and more afflicted with it, till at a certain time, when the spirit strongly impressed it on my mind to enter into my closet and carry my case once more to the Lord; the Lord enabled me to draw nigh to him, and to his mercy seat, at this time, in an extraordinary manner; for while I wrestled with him for the victory over this disposition to doubt whether I should persevere, there appeared a form of fire, about the size of a man's hand, as I was on my knees; at the same moment there appeared to the eye of faith a man robed in a white garment, from the shoulders down to the feet; from him a voice proceeded, saying: "Thou shalt never return from the cross." Since that time I have never doubted, but believe that God will keep me until the day of redemption. Now I could adopt the very language of St Paul, and say, that nothing could have separated me from the love of God, which is in Christ Jesus. Since that time, 1807, until the present, 1833, I have not even doubted the power and goodness of God to keep me from falling, through the sanctification of the spirit and belief of the truth.

18

[William J. Wilson, aka "Ethiop" (1855)]

FROM OUR BROOKLYN CORRESPONDENT.——

MY DEAR DOUGLASS:—Feeling in rather a genial, or as the boy said in the potential mood, one fine afternoon last week, I brushed up my hair, put on my best collar, and made myself look as smart as possible, for one of my cut: and pulling on my gloves, sallied forth from my lodgings, jumped upon the boat, and passed over into Gotham,[1] and took a stroll about that mysterious city— I say mysterious, because half of its doings have never yet been revealed. The dark veil of mystery hangs o'er more than half its darker deeds.—It is a Sahara, with but here and there a fertile spot; a cavern, in which are hung up a few lighted but dimly burning lanterns.—Thus thinking, and sauntering up Fulton St., gazing at the wondrous sights in the shop-windows, and out of them, I was suddenly brought to a dead halt—Broadway was before me. It has been, my dear Douglass, I believe, your good fortune to cross and recross the *Atlantic*, amidst peril and danger; and yet I doubt, if at any time, you were surrounded by half as much of either as I was in my attempts to gain what is called the "FASHIONABLE SIDE" of this great thoroughfare of *all Gotham*. On either side of this noisy, rattling, clattering, bustling ocean, (for I can call it by no better name,) were congregated persons of all sexes, sizes, and conditions, anxious to cross, or making attempts to do so. Now launching off in the turbulent whirlpool, now twirling about, now beating a retreat, now under full sail before the hurricane, now landing in safety, or sticking fast in the mud. Finally, I plunged off; and after being tossed, and pitched, and thumped, and bumped about for a time, in this perilous *sea*, landed on the

---

[1] According to Edwin G. Burrows and Mike Wallace's *Gotham: A History of New York to 1898* (1998), Washington Irving coined "Gotham" as a term for Manhattan in the *Salmagundi* (1807). The Anglo-Saxon etymology of Gotham (i.e., "Goats' Town") suggests "a place of fable, its inhabitants proverbial for their folly," they write, which allowed Irving to use the "well-known name of Gotham . . . to underscore [the] depiction of Manhattan as a city of self-important and foolish people" (xii). Using the nickname in this correspondence, Wilson shows his familiarity with Irving's writings; he, too, uses Gotham to point out the egoistic pomposity of New York City.

fashionable *side*; and throwing myself in a more congenial current, suffered myself to be borne, almost imperceptibly, up the great thoroughfare.

If, my dear sir, Gotham was one vast show, you, the looker on, you would readily perceive that the *whites* exhibited the two features, wealth and poverty; while the *blacks* exhibited an intermediate one. You would see, as I saw in this human tide, wealth, fat, proud, pompous, arrogant, overbearing, rioting in purple and fine linen, regardless of the wants around it, and as deaf to the cries of misery, as the idle flies of a midsummer's day. You would see, as I saw, shrunken-framed, thin-visaged, sunken-eyed, tattered *poverty*, with tottering step, reeling in uncertainty, and shaking its bony fingers, and cowering before this pomp of wealth and pride. But in all, the same white, ghost-like, motionless face, the same hawk-line nose, and thin, livid lip, and restless, wolf-like countenance, indicative of keen scent after what is another's, presents itself to you at every step. Cold, stern, rigid, without a redeeming feature.—The propensity for *grasping* and *appropriating*, are as indelibly stamped in every face, as the mark of Cain;[2] and though *players*, all, 'tis all the same, whether *priest*, *prince*, or *beggar*. These are the extremes. But look, the scene is changed!!! We have now a medium. Life, vivacity, merriment, mark the faces that now present themselves. There is a seeming indifference to all around. No straining after effect, no bringing things from afar. Content is as much the predominant feature now, as discontent was in the former view. Cares, such as engross men's attention, often to distraction, have never yet troubled their heads to any considerable extent, if I may judge from the light step and free and easy gait. They play an easy part. They hold up, as it were, the veil of the *plot*, and perform certain other easy services. They have passion for comedy, not tragedy, though will not play even in the *afterpiece*. But if nothing else, the six groups of almost less than human *whit*[e] *beggars*, ranging from five to eight in a group on a single block of this fashionable promenade, are sufficient to induce me from my reverie. If anything else was wanted, the half dozen gaily-dressed young colored men, leisurely sauntering up before me, would supply the deficiency. They turn down Leonard Street, to Church Street, alias (black) Broadway.[3]

---

[2] In Genesis 4:15, God marks Cain "lest any finding him should kill him." Throughout the eighteenth and nineteenth centuries, proponents of chattel slavery interpreted this "mark" as Africans' dark skin, using it as justification for the institution. Here, Wilson reverses the association between Cain's mark and African Americans: he associates the mark with white "fashionable" Broadway.

[3] Black life along Church Street dates to the mid-seventeenth century. It became a temporary haven for black fugitives, the Negro Barracks was located on Broadway and Church Street, and a number of free black families settled there after receiving plots of land after their manumissions. By the turn of

St. Charles, St. Dennis, and *Eldorado*[4] are here. Talk not of your *Astor*, and your *Irving House*.[5] In one respect, they are but the mere shadows; the substance is here. Pleasure here is neither mockery, nor is she mocked. Enter one of these resorts, and behold, for yourself, my dear sir. Rosewood and marble tables, spring sofas, and wilton covers, are scattered around in confused order; fashionable books, periodicals, and papers of the day, *theatre bills* and *opera cards*, are strewed about like autumn leaves. Easy chairs that yield to your touch, ere you are fairly seated in them; *Billiard-tables*, *Pianos*, *Sporting-Rings*, and *Debating-Galleries*; in fine, all the requisites for fancy gentlemen are here. Wealth may be found at your Astor, and your Irving, but easy negligence, careless abandonment and refined freedom may be studied here. Here you will find young men of every taste, and some of the finest looking and finest-appearing in the country, in form, unsurpassed; in dress, without a rival. If you would know the height of fashion, you can as well learn it there, as in *upper tendom*.[6] Patent leather boots and claret coats, tight pants and pointed collars French wrappers, and Scotch shawls, diamond rings and studded breast-pins, gold watches and California chains, are all exhibited here, from finer forms, and with more taste, than above Bleecker Street. Better *Wines* and *Claret*, better *Champaign*, and *Havannas* are to be had here too. No smuggling in of second quality; all are good judges. Most of the *whites* of your Astor, Irving, Howard, and like resorts, are fresh from the country. Money they may have, but good judges of these luxuries, never. Oh, sir, if the inclination of these young men could be changed, it the congregated motive power could be made available, what might not be done in a very short space of time, for the improvement of our people!—Here are all the requisites for a mighty people. Here are bone and muscle and intellect; and above all, life and vivacity; great power of endurance, notwithstanding this pernicious *hot-house* and *pot-house* culture.

I now wound my way up to *St. Philip's Row*. Notwithstanding all that may be said of Church Street, it is but the counterpart of *St. Philip's Row*. When compared with what may be seen here, Church Street is but the rough marble, the last strokes of the chisel are here. In the comparison, it is but the

---

the nineteenth century, Church Street became a center of black culture; churches, societies, and employment blossomed along the street.

[4] These were hotels along Church Street.
[5] Wilson refers to two of the city's most prominent hotels owned by wealthy New York families.
[6] Colloquial phrase for the American aristocracy.

mere *Crayon sketch*, of which the finer original is here. Here are the crowning touches of the pencil:

> Here Dame Fashion is enthroned,
> And with unbridled sway she reigns;
> Though not in wealth, with grace,
> And ease, and eloquence of mein.

What a pity it is that so much toil and substance is thus wanted, for what is, and ever must be, under the circumstances, the mere bauble of the day "Thy people have money enough," said the *old Quaker* to Dr. Pennington,[7] one evening, as they were riding in the *cars* together, "*Thy people get money enough but they do not thrive.*" Think of that, Mr. editor, think of *that*, gentle reader, and see to it that you not only get, and have money like the whites, but thrive also.

Communipaw[8] shall have due attention in due time.

Yours truly,
ETHIOP.

---

[7] Reverend James W. C. Pennington (1808–1870), formerly James Pembroke, was a fugitive slave who, in 1851, served as the Pastor of Shiloh Presbyterian Church in New York. In several addresses and his autobiography, *The Fugitive Blacksmith; or, Events in the History of James W.C. Pennington, Pastor of a Presbyterian Church, New York, Formerly a Slave in the State of Maryland* (1849), he references a Quaker family with which he stayed during his escape. The "old Quaker" Wilson refers to here could be a member of that family; it also could be one of the many other Quakers that worked with Pennington after his escape.

[8] James McCune Smith used this pseudonym as a correspondent for *Frederick Douglass's Paper*. His repartee with Wilson was one of the most defining features of the newspaper.

19

Frances Ellen Watkins (Harper)

"Two Offers" and "Aunt Chloe's Politics" (1859)

The Two Offers

BY FRANCES ELLEN WATKINS.

"What is the matter with you, Laura, this morning?[1] I have been watching you this hour, and in that time you have commenced a half dozen letters and torn them all up. What matter of such grave moment is puzzling your dear little head, that you do not know how to decide?"

"Well, it is an important matter: I have two offers for marriage, and I do not know which to choose."

"I should accept neither, or to say the least, not at present."

"Why not?"

"Because I think a woman who is undecided between two offers, has not love enough for either to make a choice; and in that very hesitation, indecision, she has a reason to pause and seriously reflect, lest her marriage, instead of being an affinity of souls or a union of hearts, should only be a mere matter of bargain and sale, or an affair of convenience and selfish interest."

"But I consider them both very good offers, just such as many a girl would gladly receive. But to tell you the truth, I do not think that I regard either as a woman should the man she chooses for her husband. But then if I refuse, there is the risk of being an old maid, and that is not to be thought of."

"Well, suppose there is, is that the most dreadful fate that can befall a woman? Is there not more intense wretchedness in an ill-assorted marriage—more utter loneliness in a loveless home, than in the lot of the old maid who accepts her earthly mission as a gift from God, and strives to walk the path of life with earnest and unfaltering steps?"

---

[1] One of the first short stories in African American letters, "The Two Offers" appeared in two parts in *The Anglo-African Magazine*. The first was Vol. 1, no. 9 (September 1859), and the second was Vol. 1, no. 10 (October 1859).

"Oh! what a little preacher you are. I really believe that you were cut out for an old maid; that when nature formed you, she put in a double portion of intellect to make up for a deficiency of love; and yet you are kind and affectionate. But I do not think that you know anything of the grand, overmastering passion, or the deep necessity of woman's heart for loving."

"Do you think so?" resumed the first speaker; and bending over her work she quietly applied herself to the knitting that had lain neglected by her side, during this brief conversation; but as she did so, a shadow flitted over her pale and intellectual brow, a mist gathered in her eyes, and a slight quivering of the lips, revealed a depth of feeling to which her companion was a stranger.

But before I proceed with my story, let me give you a slight history of the speakers. They were cousins, who had met life under different auspices. Laura Lagrange, was the only daughter of rich and indulgent parents, who had spared no pains to make her an accomplished lady. Her cousin, Janette Alston, was the child of parents, rich only in goodness and affection. Her father had been unfortunate in business, and dying before he could retrieve his fortunes, left his business in an embarrassed state. His widow was unacquainted with his business affairs, and when the estate was settled, hungry creditors had brought their claims and the lawyers had received their fees, she found herself homeless and almost penniless, and she who had been sheltered in the warm clasp of loving arms, found them too powerless to shield her from the pitiless pelting storms of adversity. Year after year she struggled with poverty and wrestled with want, till her foil-worn hands became too feeble to hold the shattered chords of existence, and her tear-dimmed eyes grew heavy with the slumber of death. Her daughter had watched over her with untiring devotion, had closed her eyes in death, and gone out into the busy, restless world, missing a precious tone from the voices of earth, a beloved step from the paths of life. Too self [-] reliant to depend on the charity of relations, she endeavored to support herself by her own exertions, and she had succeeded. Her path for a while was marked with struggle and trial, but instead of uselessly repining, she met them bravely, and her life became not a thing of ease and indulgence, but of conquest, victory, and accomplishments. At the time when this conversation took place, the deep trials of her life had passed away. The achievements of her genius had won her a position in the literary world, where she shone as one of its bright particular stars. And with her fame came a competence of worldly means, which gave her leisure for improvement, and the riper development of her rare talents. And she, that pale intellectual woman, whose genius gave life and vivacity to the social circle, and whose presence throw a halo of beauty and grace around the charmed atmosphere in which she moved, had at one period of her life, known the mystic and solemn strength of an all-absorbing love. Years faded into the misty past, had seen the kindling of her eye, the quick flushing of her cheek, and the wild throbbing of her heart, at tones of a voice long since hushed to the stillness of death. Deeply, wildly, passionately, she had loved. Her whole life seemed like the pouring out of rich, warm and gushing affections. This love quickened her talents, inspired her genius, and threw over her life a tender and spiritual earnestness. And then came a fearful shock, a mournful waking from that "dream of beauty and delight." A shadow fell around her path; it came between her and the object of her heart's worship; first a few cold words, estrangement, and then a painful separation; the old story of woman's pride—digging the sepulcher of her happiness, and then a new-made grave, and her path over it to the spirit world; and thus faded out from that young heart her bright, brief and saddened dream of life. Faint and spirit-broken, she turned from the scenes associated with the memory of the loved and lost. She tried to break the chain of sad associations that bound her to the mournful past; and so, pressing back the bitter sobs from her almost breaking heart, like the dying dolphin, whose beauty is born of its death anguish, her genius gathered strength from suffering and wonderous power and brilliancy from the agony she hid within the desolate chambers of her soul. Men hailed her as one of earth's strangely gifted children, and wreathed the garlands of fame for her brow, when it was throbbing with a wild and fearful unrest. They breathed her name with applause, when through the lonely halls of her stricken spirit, was an earnest cry for peace, a deep yearning for sympathy and heart-support.

But life, with its stern realities, met her; its solemn responsibilities confronted her, and turning, with an earnest and shattered spirit, to life's duties and trials, she found a calmness and strength that she had only imagined in her dreams of poetry and song. We will now pass over a period of ten years, and the cousins have met again. In that calm and lovely woman, in whose eyes is a depth of tenderness, tempering the flashes of her genius, whose looks and tones are full of sympathy and love, we recognize the once smitten and stricken Janette Alston. The bloom of her girlhood had given way to a higher type of spiritual beauty, as if some unseen hand had been polishing and refining the temple in which her lovely spirit found its habitation; and this had been the fact. Her inner life had grown beautiful, and it was this that was constantly developing the outer. Never, in the early flush of womanhood, when an absorbing love had lit up her eyes and glowed in her life, had she appeared so interesting as when, with a countenance which seemed overshadowed with a spiritual light, she bent over the death-bed of a young woman, just lingering at the shadowy gates of the unseen land.

"Has he come?" faintly but eagerly exclaimed the dying woman. "Oh! how I have longed for his coming, and even in death he forgets me."

"Oh, do not say so, dear Laura, some accident may have detained him," said Janette to her cousin; for on that bed, from whence she will never rise, lies the once beautiful and light-hearted Laura Lagrange, the brightness of whose eyes has long since been dimmed with tears, and whose voice had become like a harp whose every chord is tuned to sadness—whose faintest thrill and loudest vibrations are but the variations of agony. A heavy band was laid upon her once warm and bounding heart, and a voice came whispering through her soul, that she must die. But, to her, the tidings was a message of deliverance—a voice, hushing her wild sorrows, to the calmness of resignation and hope. Life had grown so weary upon her head—the future looked so hopeless—she had no wish to tread again the track where thorns had pierced her feet, and clouds overcast her sky; and she hailed the coming of death's angel as the footsteps of a welcome friend. And yet, earth had one object so very dear to her weary heart. It was her absent and recreant husband; for, since that conversation, she had accepted one of her offers, and become a wife. But, before she married, she learned that great lesson of human experience and woman's life, to love the man who bowed at her shrine, a willing worshipper. He had a pleasing address, raven hair, flashing eyes, a voice of thrilling sweetness, and lips of persuasive eloquence; and being well versed in the ways of the world, he won his way to her heart, and she became his bride, and he was proud of his prize. Vain and superficial in his character, he looked upon marriage not as a divine sacrament for the soul's development and human progression, but as the title-deed that gave him possession of the woman he thought he loved. But alas for her, the laxity of his principles had rendered him unworthy of the deep and undying devotion of a pure-hearted woman; but, for awhile, he hid from her his true character, and she blindly loved him, and for a short period was happy in the consciousness of being beloved; though sometimes a vague unrest would fill her soul, when, overflowing with a sense of the good, the beautiful, and the true, she would turn to him, but find no response to the deep yearnings of her soul— no appreciation of life's highest realities—its solemn grandeur and significant importance. Their souls never met, and soon she found a void in her bosom, that his earth-born love could not fill. He did not satisfy the wants of her mental and moral nature—between him and her there was no affinity of minds, no intercommunion of souls.

Talk as you will of woman's deep capacity for loving, of the strength of her affectional nature. I do not deny it; but will the mere possession of any human love, fully satisfy all the demands of her whole being? You may paint her in poetry or fiction, as a frail vine, clinging to her brother man for support, and dying when deprived of it; and all this may sound well enough to please the imaginations of school-girls, or love-lorn maidens. But woman— the true woman—if you would render her happy, it needs more than the mere development of her affectional nature. Her conscience should be enlightened, her faith in the true and right established, and scope given to her Heaven-endowed and God-given faculties. The true aim of female education should be, not a development of one or two, but all the faculties of the human soul, because no perfect womanhood is developed by imperfect culture.[2] Intense love is often akin to intense suffering, and to trust the whole wealth of a woman's nature on the frail bark of human love, may often be like trusting a cargo of gold and precious gems, to a bark that has never battled with the storm, or buffetted the waves. Is it any wonder, then, that so many life-barks go down, paving the ocean of time with precious hearts and wasted hopes? that so many float around us, shattered and dismasted wrecks? that so many are stranded on the shoals of existence, mournful beacons and solemn warnings for the thoughtless, to whom marriage is a careless and hasty rushing together of the affections? Alas that an institution so fraught with good for humanity should be so perverted, and that state of life, which should be filled with happiness, become so replete with misery. And this was the fate of Laura Lagrange. For a brief period after her marriage her life seemed like a bright and beautiful dream, full of hope and radiant with joy. And then there came a change—he found other attractions that lay beyond the pale of home influences. The gambling saloon had power to win him from her side, he had lived in an element of unhealthy and unhallowed excitements, and the society of a loving wife, the pleasures of a well-regulated home, were enjoyments too tame for one who had vitiated his tastes by the pleasures of sin. There were charmed houses of vice, built upon dead men's loves, where,

---

[2] Watkins emphasizes the need for women's education. Like Stewart, she urges for an education that develops "all the faculties of the human soul" and links this education to the state of a wider culture. This is a much more expansive understanding of women's education than the education Crummell outlines in "The Black Woman of the South: Her Neglects and Her Needs" (1883). See Crummell in Stewart 44–57.

amid a flow of song, laughter, wine, and careless mirth, he would spend hour after hour, forgetting the cheek that was paling through his neglect, heedless of the tear-dimmed eyes, peering anxiously into the darkness, waiting, or watching his return.

TO BE CONTINUED.
The Two Offers
Frances Ellen Watkins
Concluded.

The influence of old associations was upon him. In early life, home had been to him a place of ceilings and walls, not a true home, built upon goodness, love and truth. It was a place where velvet carpets hushed his tread, where images of loveliness and beauty invoked into being by painter's art and sculptor's skill, pleased the eye and gratified the taste, where magnificence surrounded his way and costly clothing adorned his person; but it was not the place for the true culture and right development of his soul. His father had been too much engrossed in making money, and his mother in spending it, in striving to maintain a fashionable position in society, and shining in the eyes of the world, to give the proper direction to the character of their wayward and impulsive son. His mother put beautiful robes upon his body, but left ugly scars upon his soul; she pampered his appetite, but starved his spirit. Every mother should be a true artist, who knows how to weave into her child's life images of grace and beauty, the true poet capable of writing on the soul of childhood the harmony of love and truth, and teaching it how to produce the grandest of all poems—the poetry of a true and noble life.[3] But in his home, a love for the good, the true and right, had been sacrificed at the shrine of frivolity and fashion. That parental authority which should have been preserved as a string of precious pearls, unbroken and unscattered, was simply the administration of chance. At one time obedience was enforced by authority, at another time by flattery and promises, and just as often it was not enforced all. His early associations were formed as chance directed, and from his want of home-training, his character received a bias, his life a shade, which ran through every avenue of his existence, and darkened all his future hours. Oh, if we would trace the history

---

[3] An extension of her claims about education in part one, Watkins's opening of part two of "The Two Offers" considers the consequences of an inadequate education. Laura Legrange's husband was a product of a home where improper education ruined his adult family. See Stewart's "The Proper Training of Children" (Stewart, 186–190) for a similar, albeit far more strident, perspective.

of all the crimes that have o'ershadowed this sin-shrouded and sorrow-darkened world of ours, how many might be seen arising from the wrong home influences, or the weakening of the home ties. Home should always be the best school for the affections, the birth-place of high resolves, and the altar upon which lofty aspirations are kindled, from whence the soul may go forth strengthened, to act its part aright in the great drama of life, with conscience enlightened, affections cultivated, and reason and judgment dominant. But alas for the young wife. Her husband had not been blessed with such a home. When he entered the arena of life, the voices from home did not linger around his path as angels of guidance about his steps; they were not like so many messages to invite him to deeds of high and holy worth. The memory of no sainted mother arose between him and deeds of darkness; the earnest prayers of no father arrested him in his downward course: and before a year of his married life had waned, his young wife had learned to wait and mourn his frequent and uncalled-for absence. More than once had she seen him come home from his midnight haunts, the bright intelligence of his eye displaced by the drunkard's stare, and his manly gait changed to the inebriate's stagger; and she was beginning to know the bitter agony that is compressed in the mournful words, a drunkard's wife. And then there came a bright but brief episode in her experience; the angel of life gave to her existence a deeper meaning and loftier significance: she sheltered in the warm clasp of her loving arms, a dear babe, a precious child, whose love filled every chamber of her heart, and felt the fount of maternal love gushing so new within her soul. That child washers. How overshadowing was the love with which she bent over its helplessness, how much it helped to fill the void and chasms in her soul. How many lonely hours were beguiled by its winsome ways, its answering smiles and fond caresses. How exquisite and solemn was the feeling that thrilled her heart when she clasped the tiny hands together and taught her dear child to call God "Our Father."

What a blessing was that child. The father paused in his headlong career, awed by the strange beauty and precocious intellect of his child; and the mother's life had a better expression through her ministrations of love. And then there came hours of bitter anguish, shading the sunlight of her home and hushing the music of her heart. The angel of death bent over the couch of her child and beaconed it away. Closer and closer the mother strained her child to her wildly heaving breast, and struggled with the heavy hand that lay upon its heart. Love and agony contended with death, and the language of the mother's heart was,

> Oh, Death, away! that innocent is mine;
> I cannot spare him from my arms
> To lay him, Death, in mine.
> I am a mother, Death; I gave that darling birth
> I could not bear his lifeless limbs
> Should moulder in the earth.

But death was stronger than love and mightier than agony and won the child for the land of crystal founts and deathless flowers, and the poor, stricken mother sat down beneath the shadow of her mighty grief, feeling as if a great light had gone out from her soul, and that the sunshine had suddenly faded around her path. She turned in her deep anguish to the father of her child, the loved and cherished dead. For awhile his words wore kind and tender, his heart seemed subdued, and his tenderness fell upon her worn and weary heart like rain on perishing flowers, or cooling waters to lips all parched with thirst and scorched with fever; but the change was evanescent, the influence of unhallowed associations and evil habits had vitiated and poisoned the springs of his existence. They had bound him in their meshes, and he lacked the moral strength to break his fetters, and stand erect in all the strength and dignity of a true manhood, making life's highest excellence his ideal, and striving to gain it.

And yet moments of deep contrition would sweep over him, when he would resolve to abandon the wine-cup forever, when he was ready to forswear the handling of another card, and he would try to break away from the associations that he felt were working his ruin; but when the hour of temptation came his strength was weakness, his earnest purposes were cob-webs, his well-meant resolutions ropes of sand, and thus passed year after year of the married life of Laura Lagrange. She tried to hide her agony from the public gaze, to smile when her heart was almost breaking. But year after year her voice grew fainter and sadder, her once light and bounding step grew slower and faltering Year after year she wrestled with agony, and strove with despair, till the quick eyes of her brother read, in the paling of her cheek and the dimming eye, the secret anguish of her worn and weary spirit. On that wan, sad face, he saw the death-tokens, and he knew the dark wing of the mystic angel swept coldly around her path. "Laura," said her brother to her one day, "you are not well, and I think you need our mother's tender care and nursing. You are daily losing strength, and if you will go I will accompany you." At first, she hesitated, she shrank almost instinctively from presenting that pale sad face to the loved ones at home. That face was such a telltale;

it told of heart-sickness, of hope deferred, and the mournful story of unrequited love. But then a deep yearning for home sympathy woke within her a passionate longing for love's kind words, for tenderness and heart-support, and she resolved to seek the home of her childhood, and lay her weary head upon her mother's bosom, to be folded again in her loving arms, to lay that poor, bruised and aching heart where it might beat and throb closely to the loved ones at home. A kind welcome awaited her. All that love and tenderness could devise was done to bring the bloom to her cheek and the light to her eye; but it was all in vain; hers was a disease that no medicine could cure, no earthly balm would heal. It was a slow wasting of the vital forces, the sickness of the soul. The unkindness and neglect of her husband, lay like a leaden weight upon her heart, and slowly oozed away its life-drops. And where was he that had won her love, and then cast it aside as a useless thing, who rifled her heart of its wealth and spread bitter ashes upon its broken altars? He was lingering away from her when the death-damps were gathering on her brow, when his name was trembling on her lips! lingering away! when she was watching his coming, though the death films were gathering before her eyes, and earthly things were fading from her vision. "I think I hear him now," said the dying woman, "surely that is his step;" but the sound died away in the distance. Again she started from an uneasy slumber, "that is his voice! I am so glad he has come." Tears gathered in the eyes of the sad watchers by that dying bed, for they know that she was deceived. He had not returned. For her sake they wished his coming. Slowly the hours waned away, and then came the sad, soul-sickening thought that she was forgotten, forgotten in the last hour of human need, forgotten when the spirit, about to be dissolved, paused for the last time on the threshold of existence, a weary watcher at the gates of death. "He has forgotten me," again she faintly murmured, and the last tears she would ever shed on earth sprung to her mournful eyes, and clasping her hands together in silent anguish, a few broken sentences issued from her pale and quivering lips. They were prayers for strength and earnest pleading for him who had desolated her young life, by turning its sunshine to shadows, its smiles to tears. He has forgotten me, she murmured again, but I can bear it, the bitterness of death is passed, and soon I hope to exchange the shadows of death for the brightness of eternity, the rugged paths of life for the golden streets of glory, and the care and turmoils of earth for the peace and rest of heaven. Her voice grew fainter and fainter, they saw the shadows that never deceive flit over her pale and faded face, and knew that the death angel waited to soothe their weary one to rest, to calm the throbbing of her bosom and cool the fever of her brain. And amid the silent hush of their grief the freed spirit, refined through suffering, and brought into divine harmony through the spirit of the living Christ, passed over the dark waters of death as on a bridge of light, over whose radiant arches hovering angels bent. They parted the dark locks from her marble brow, closed the waxen lids over the once bright and laughing eye, and left her to the dreamless slumber of the grave. Her cousin turned from that death-bed a sadder and wiser woman. She resolved more earnestly than ever to make the world better by her example, gladder by her presence, and to kindle the fires of her genius on the altars of universal love and truth. She had a higher and better object in all her writings than the mere acquisition of gold, or acquirement of fame. She felt that she had a high and holy mission on the battle-field of existence, that life was not given her to be frittered away in nonsense, or wasted away in trifling pursuits. She would willingly espouse an unpopular cause but not an unrighteous one. In her the down-trodden slave found an earnest advocate; the flying fugitive remembered her kindness as he stepped cautiously through our Republic, to gain his freedom in a monarchial land, having broken the chains on which the rust of centuries had gathered. Little children learned to name her with affection, the poor called her blessed, as she broke her bread to the pale lips of hunger. Her life was like a beautiful story, only it was clothed with the dignity of reality and invested with the sublimity of truth. True, she was an old maid, no husband brightened her life with his love, or shaded it with his neglect. No children nestling lovingly in her arms called her mother. No one appended Mrs. to her name; she was indeed an old maid, not vainly striving to keep up an appearance of girlishness, when departed was written on her youth.[4] Not vainly pining at her loneliness and isolation: the world was full of warm, loving hearts, and her own beat in unison with them. Neither was she always sentimentally sighing for something to love, objects of affection were all around her, and the world was not so wealthy in love that it had no use for hers; in blessing others she made a life and benediction, and as old age descended peacefully and gently upon her, she had learned one of life's most precious lessons, that true happiness consists not so much in the fruition of our wishes as in the regulation of desires and the full development and right culture of our whole natures.

---

[4] Watkins broadens the value of black women beyond their status as wives and mothers. Though Watkins repeatedly describes Janette Alston as an "old maid," the story values Alston's contributions to the production of "right" culture.

Aunt Chloe's Politics.

Of course, I don't know very much
    About these politics,
But I think that some who run 'em
    Do mighty ugly tricks.[5]

I've seen 'em honey-fugle round,
    And talk so awful sweet,
That you'd think them full of kindness,
    As an egg is full of meat.

Now I don't believe in looking
    Honest people in the face,
And saying when you're doing wrong,
    That "I haven't sold my race."

When we want to school our children,
    If the money isn't there,
Whether black or white have took it,
    The loss we all must share.[6]

And this buying up each other
    Is something worse than mean,
Though I thinks a heap of voting,
    I go for voting clean.

---

[5] This is the third of six poems Harper writes in the voice of Aunt Chloe Fleet. The others are "Aunt Chloe," "The Deliverance," "Aunt Chloe's Politics," "Learning to Read," "Church Building," and "The Reunion." The character alludes to Aunt Chloe from Harriet Beecher Stowe's *Uncle Tom's Cabin* (1852). Harper also drew on Stowe's novel for poem "Eliza Harris" (1854), which reimagines Eliza's escape in Stowe's novel.

[6] Of all the issues she could have raised here, Harper focuses on education. As in "The Two Offers" and elsewhere throughout her oeuvre, Harper claims widespread education is essential to a thriving culture.

20

[Charlotte Forten, "Life on the Sea Islands" (1864)]

Life on the Sea Islands.

[To THE EDITOR OF THE "ATLANTIC MONTHLY."—The following graceful and picturesque description of the new condition of things on the Sea Islands of South Carolina, originally written for private perusal, seems to me worthy of a place in the "Atlantic." Its young author—herself akin to the long-suffering race whose Exodus she so pleasantly describes—is still engaged in her labor of love on St. Helena Island.—J. G. W.[1]]

PART I.

IT was on the afternoon of a warm, murky day late in October that our steamer, the United States, touched the landing at Hilton Head. A motley assemblage had collected on the wharf,—officers, soldiers, and contrabands of every size and hue: black was, however, the prevailing color. The first view of Hilton Head is desolate enough,—a long, low, sandy point, stretching out into the sea, with no visible dwellings upon it, except the rows of small white-roofed houses which have lately been built for the freed people.

After signing a paper wherein we declared ourselves loyal to the Government, and wherein, also, were set forth fearful penalties, should we ever be found guilty of treason, we were allowed to land, and immediately took General Saxton's boat,[2] the Flora, for Beaufort. The General was on

---

[1] "J.G.W." is John Greenleaf Whittier (1807–1892). Whittier was a leading American poet, statesman, and abolitionist. He was also a founder of *The Atlantic Monthly*. When Forten's essays appeared in the magazine, James T. Fields (1817–1881) was the editor.

[2] General Rufus Saxton (1824–1908), abolitionist and Brigadier General, earned the Medal of Honor in 1862 service for protecting Harper's Ferry against Confederate forces. That same year he took command of the islands off the coast of South Carolina. One of his principal tasks was the recruitment of black southern soldiers. His brief report (October 26, 1862) on Confederate attempts to regain Saint Helena Island, the setting of Forten's story, highlighted the role of "negro pickets"

board, and we were presented to him. He is handsome, courteous, and affable, and looks—as he is—the gentleman and the soldier.

From Hilton Head to Beaufort the same long, low line of sandy coast, bordered by trees; formidable gunboats in the distance, and the gray ruins of an old fort, said to have been built by the Huguenots more than two hundred years ago. Arrived at Beaufort, we found that we had not yet reached our journey's end. While waiting for the boat which was to take us to our island of St. Helena, we had a little time to observe the ancient town. The houses in the main street, which fronts the "Bay," are large and handsome, built of wood, in the usual Southern style, with spacious piazzas, and surrounded by fine trees. We noticed in one yard a magnolia, as high as some of our largest shade-maples, with rich, dark, shining foliage. A large building which was once the Public Library is now a shelter for freed people from Fernandina. Did the Rebels know it, they would doubtless upturn their aristocratic noses, and exclaim in disgust, "To what base uses," etc. We confess that it was highly satisfactory to us to see how the tables are turned, now "that the whirligig of time has brought about its revenges."[3] We saw the market-place, in which slaves were sometimes sold; but we were told that the buying and selling at auction were usually done in Charleston. The arsenal, a large stone structure, was guarded by cannon and sentinels. The houses in the smaller streets had, mostly, a dismantled, desolate look. We saw no one in the streets but soldiers and freed people. There were indications that already Northern improvements had reached this Southern town. Among them was a wharf, a convenience that one wonders how the Southerners could so long have existed without. The more we know of their mode of life, the more are we inclined to marvel at its utter shiftlessness.

Little colored children of every hue were playing about the streets, looking as merry and happy as children ought to look,—now that the evil shadow of Slavery no longer hangs over them. Some of the officers we met did not impress us favorably. They talked flippantly, and sneeringly of the negroes, whom they found we had come down to teach, using an epithet more offensive than gentlemanly. They assured us that there was great danger of Rebel attacks, that the yellow fever prevailed to an alarming extent, and that,

---

in defending the island. Shortly after this report, he delivered Proclamation, for a Day of Public Thanksgiving and Praise," which Forten recounts later in her essay.

[3] Mocking the Southern aristocracy, Forten imagines their reversal of fortunes via Shakespeare's *Twelfth Night* 5.1.399–400.

indeed, the manufacture of coffins was the only business that was at all flourishing at present. Although by no means daunted by these alarming stories, we were glad when the announcement of our boat relieved us from their edifying conversation.

We rowed across to Ladies Island, which adjoins St. Helena, through the splendors of a grand Southern sunset. The gorgeous clouds of crimson and gold were reflected as in a mirror in the smooth, clear waters below. As we glided along, the rich tones of the negro boatmen broke upon the evening stillness, o—sweet, strange, and solemn:—

> Jesus make de blind to see,
> Jesus make de cripple walk,
> Jesus make de deaf to hear.
> Walk in, kind Jesus!
> No man can hender me.[4]

It was nearly dark when we reached the island, and then we had a three-miles' drive through the lonely roads to the house of the superintendent. We thought how easy it would be for a band of guerrillas, had they chanced that way, to seize and hang us; but we were in that excited, jubilant state of mind which makes fear impossible, and sang "John Brown"[5] with a will, as we drove through the pines and palmettos. Oh, it was good to sing that song in the very heart of Rebeldom! Harry, our driver, amused us much. He was surprised to find that we had not heard of him before. "Why, I thought ebery body at de Nort had heard o' me!" he said, very innocently. We learned afterward that Mrs. F., who made the tour of the islands last summer, had publicly mentioned Harry. Some one had told him of it, and he of course imagined that he had become quite famous. Notwithstanding this little touch of vanity, Harry is one of the best and smartest men on the island.

Gates occurred, it seemed to us, at every few yards' distance, made in the oddest fashion,—opening in the middle, like folding-doors for the accommodation of horsemen. The little boy who accompanied us as gate-opener

---

[4] According to William Francis Allen's 1867 *Slave Songs of the United States* (1867), this song is "No Man Can Hinder Me" (59–60).

[5] "John Brown's Body." Set to the tune of "The Battle Hymn of the Republic," the song reimagined John Brown's execution in 1859 as an essential symbol of the Civil War. For Union soldiers and their supporters, John Brown's soul lived on in their campaigns. Confederate soldiers and their supporters emphasized the image of Brown's hanging body. In 1861, Julia Ward Howe recorded the version Union soldiers sang, which the Library of Congress holds.

answered to the name of Cupid. Arrived at the headquarters of the general superintendent, Mr. S., we were kindly received by him and the ladies, and shown into a large parlor, where a cheerful wood-fire glowed in the grate. It had a home-like look; but still there was a sense of unreality about everything, and I felt that nothing less than a vigorous "shaking-up," such as Grandfather Smallweed[6] daily experienced, would arouse me thoroughly to the fact that I was in South Carolina.

The next morning L. and I were awakened by the cheerful voices of men and women, children and chickens, in the yard below. We ran to the window, and looked out. Women in bright colored handkerchiefs, some carrying pails on their heads, were crossing the yard, busy with their morning work; children were playing and tumbling around them. On every face there was a look of serenity and cheerfulness. My heart gave a great throb of happiness as I looked at them, and thought, "They are free! so long down trodden, so long crushed to the earth, but now in their old homes, forever free!" And I thanked God that I had lived to see this day.

After breakfast Miss T. drove us to Oaklands, our future home. The road leading to the house was nearly choked with weeds. The house itself was in a dilapidated condition, and the yard and garden had a sadly neglected look. But there were roses in bloom; we plucked handfuls of feathery, fragrant acacia-blossoms; ivy crept along the ground and under the house. The freed people on the place seemed glad to see us. After talking with them, and giving some directions for cleaning the house, we drove to the school, in which I was to teach. It is kept in the Baptist Church,—a brick building, beautifully situated in a grove of live oaks. These trees are the first objects that attract one's attention here: not that they are finer than our Northern oaks, but because of the singular gray moss with which every branch is heavily draped. This hanging moss grows on nearly all the trees, but on none so luxuriantly as on the live-oak. The pendants are often four or five feet long, very graceful and beautiful, but giving the trees a solemn, almost funereal look. The school was opened in September. Many of the children had, however, received instruction during the summer. It was evident that they had made very rapid improvement, and we noticed with pleasure how bright and eager to learn many of them seemed. They sang in rich, sweet tones, and with a peculiar swaying motion of the body, which made their singing the more effective.

---

[6] This is a reference to Charles Dickens's character in *Bleak House* (1853).

They sang "Marching Along," with great spirit, and then one of their own hymns, the air of which is beautiful and touching:—

> My sister, you want to git religion,
> Go down in de Lonesome Valley;
> My brudder, yon want to git religion,
> Go down in de Lonesome Valley.

CHORUS.

> Go down in de Lonesome Valley,
> Go down in de Lonesome Valley, my Lord,
> Go down in de Lonesome Valley,
> To meet my Jesus dere!
>
> Oh, feed on milk and honey,
> Oh, feed on milk and honey, my Lord,
> Oh, feed on milk and honey,
> Meet my Jesus dere!
> Oh, John he brought a letter,
> Oh, John he brought a letter, my Lord,
> Oh, Mary and Maria read 'em,
> Meet my Jesus dere!

CHORUS.

"Go down in de Lonesome Valley," etc.

They repeat their hymns several times, and while singing keep perfect time with their hands and feet.

On our way homeward we noticed that a few of the trees were beginning to turn, but we looked in vain for the glowing autumnal hues of our Northern forests. Some brilliant scarlet berries—the cassena—were growing along the roadside, and on every hand we saw the live-oak with its moss-drapery.[7] The palmettos disappointed me; stiff and ungraceful, they

---

[7] Forten is referring to the falling appearance of the so-called Spanish moss, a flowering plant, that is ubiquitous in the region.

have a bristling, defiant look, suggestive of Rebels starting up and defying everybody. The land is low and level,—not the slightest approach to a hill, not a rock, nor even a stone to be seen. It would have a desolate look, were it not for the trees, and the hanging moss and numberless vines which festoon them. These vines overrun the hedges, form graceful arches between the trees, encircle their trunks, and sometimes climb to the topmost branches. In February they begin to bloom, and then throughout the spring and summer we have a succession of beautiful flowers. First comes the yellow jessamine, with its perfect, gold-colored, and deliciously fragrant blossoms. It lights up the hedges, and completely canopies some of the trees. Of all the wild-flowers this seems to me the most beautiful and fragrant. Then we have the snow-white, but scentless Cherokee rose, with its lovely, shining leaves. Later in the season come the brilliant trumpet-flower, the passion-flower, and innumerable others.

The Sunday after our arrival we attended service at the Baptist Church. The people came in slowly; for they have no way of knowing the hour, except by the sun. By eleven they had all assembled, and the church was well filled. They were neatly dressed in their Sunday attire, the women mostly wearing clean, dark frocks, with white aprons and bright-colored head-handkerchiefs. Some had attained to the dignity of straw hats with gay feathers, but these were not nearly as becoming nor as picturesque as the handkerchiefs. The day was warm, and the windows were thrown open as if it were summer, although it was the second day of November. It was very pleasant to listen to the beautiful hymns, and look from the crowd of dark, earnest faces within, upon the grove of noble oaks without. The people sang, "Roll, Jordan, roll," the grandest of all their hymns. There is a great, rolling wave of sound through it all.

> Mr. Fuller settin' on de Tree ob Life,
> Fur to hear de ven Jordan roll.
> Oh, roll, Jordan! roll, Jordan! roll, Jordan
>   roll!
>   CHORUS.
>
> Oh, roll, Jordan, roll! oh, roll, Jordan, roll!
> My soul arise in heab'n, Lord,
> Fur to hear de ven Jordan roll!

Little chil'en, learn to fear de Lord,
And let your days be long.
Oh, roll, Jordan! roll, Jordan! roll, Jordan,
roll!

CHORUS.

Oh, march, de angel, march! oh, march, de angel, march!
My soul arise in heab'n, Lord,
Fur to hear de ven Jordan roll!

The "Mr. Fuller" referred to was their former minister, to whom they seem to have been much attached. He is a Southerner, but loyal, and is now, I believe, living in Baltimore. After the sermon the minister called upon one of the elders, a gray-headed old man, to pray. His manner was very fervent and impressive, but his language was so broken that to our unaccustomed ears it was quite unintelligible. After the services the people gathered in groups outside, talking among themselves, and exchanging kindly greetings with the superintendents and teachers. In their bright handkerchiefs and white aprons they made a striking picture under the gray-mossed trees. We drove afterward a mile farther, to the Episcopal Church, in which the aristocracy of the island used to worship. It is a small white building, situated in a fine grove of live-oaks, at the junction of several roads. On one of the tombstones in the yard is the touching inscription in memory of two children,—"Blessed little lambs, and *art thou* gathered into the fold of the only tree shepherd? Sweet *lillies* of the valley, and *art thou* removed to a more congenial soil?" The floor of the church is of stone, the pews of polished oak. It has an organ, which is not so entirely out of tune as are the pianos on the island. One of the ladies played, while the gentlemen sang,—old-fashioned New-England church-music, which it was pleasant to hear, but it did not thrill us as the singing of the people had done.

During the week we moved to Oaklands, our future home. The house was of one story, with a low-roofed piazza running the whole length. The interior had been thoroughly scrubbed and whitewashed; the exterior was guiltless of white-wash or paint. There were five rooms, all quite small, and several dark little entries, in one of which we found shelves lined with old medicine-bottles. These were a part of the possessions of the former owner, a Rebel physician, Dr. Sams by name. Some of them were still filled with his nostrums. Our furniture consisted of a bedstead, two bureaus, three small pine tables, and two chairs, one of which had a broken back. These were lent to us by the people. The masters, in their hasty flight from the islands, left nearly all their furniture; but much of it was destroyed or taken by the soldiers who came first, and what they left was removed by the people to their own houses. Certainly, they have the best right to it. We had made up our minds to dispense with all luxuries and even many conveniences; but it was rather distressing to have no fire, and nothing to eat. Mr. H. had already appropriated a room for the store which he was going to open for the benefit of the freed people, and was superintending the removal of his goods. So L. and I were left to our own resources. But Cupid the elder came to the rescue,—Cupid, who, we were told, was to be our right-hand man, and who very graciously informed us that he would take care of us; which he at once proceeded to do by bringing in some wood, and busying himself in making a fire in the open fire-place. While he is thus engaged, I will try to describe him. A small, wiry figure, stockingless, shoeless, out at the knees and elbows, and wearing the remnant of an old straw hat, which looked as if it might have done good service in scaring the crows from a cornfield. The face nearly black, very ugly, but with the shrewdest expression I ever saw, and the brightest, most humorous twinkle in the eyes. One glance at Cupid's face showed that he was not a person to be imposed upon, and that he was abundantly able to take care of himself, as well as of us. The chimney obstinately refused to draw, in spite of the original and very uncomplimentary epithets which Cupid heaped upon it,—while we stood by, listening to him in amusement, although nearly suffocated by the smoke. At last, perseverance conquered, and the fire began to burn cheerily. Then Amaretta, our cook,—a neat-looking black woman, adorned with the gayest of head-handkerchiefs,—made her appearance with some eggs and hominy, after partaking of which we proceeded to arrange our scanty furniture, which was soon done. In a few days we began to look civilized, having made a table-cover of some red and yellow handkerchiefs which we found among the store-goods,—a carpet of red and black woollen plaid, originally intended for frocks and shirts,—a cushion, stuffed with corn-busks and covered with calico, for a lounge, which Ben, the carpenter, had made for us of pine boards,—and lastly some corn-husk beds, which were an unspeakable luxury, after having endured agonies for several nights, sleeping on the slats of a bedstead. It is true, the said slats were covered with blankets, but these might as well have been sheets of paper for all the good they did us. What a resting-place it was! Compared to it, the gridiron of St. Lawrence—fire excepted—was as a bed of roses.

The first day at school was rather trying. Most of my children were very small, and consequently restless. Some were too young to learn the alphabet. These little ones were brought to school because the older children—in whoso care their parents leave them while at work—could not come without them. We were therefore willing to have them come, although they seemed to have discovered the secret of perpetual motion, and tried one's patience sadly. But after some days of positive, though not severe treatment, order was brought out of chaos, and I found but little difficulty in managing and quieting the tiniest and most restless spirits. I never before saw children so eager to learn, although I had had several years' experience in New-England schools. Coming to school is a constant delight and recreation to them. They come here as other children go to play. The older ones, during the summer, work in the fields from early morning until eleven or twelve o'clock, and then come into school, after their hard toil in the hot sun, as bright and as anxious to learn as ever.

Of course there are some stupid ones, but these are the minority. The majority learn with wonderful rapidity. Many of the grown people are desirous of learning to read. It is wonderful how a people who have been so long crushed to the earth, so imbruted as these have been,—and they are said to be among the most degraded negroes of the South,—can have so great a desire for knowledge, and such a capability for attaining it. One cannot believe that the haughty Anglo-Saxon race, after centuries of such an experience as these people have had, would be very much superior to them. And one's indignation increases against those who, North as well as South, taunt the colored race with inferiority while they themselves use every means in their power to crush and degrade them, denying them every right and privilege, closing against them every avenue of elevation and improvement. Were they, under such circumstances, intellectual and refined, they would certainly be vastly superior to any other race that ever existed.

After the lessons, we used to talk freely to the children, often giving them slight sketches of some of the great and good men. Before teaching them the "John Brown" song, which they learned to sing with great spirit, Miss T. told them the story of the brave old man who had died for them. I told them about Toussaint, thinking it well they should know what one of their own color had done for his race. They listened attentively, and seemed to understand. We found it rather hard to keep their attention in school. It is not strange, as they have been so entirely unused to intellectual concentration. It is necessary to interest them every moment, in order to keep their thoughts from wandering. Teaching here is consequently far more fatiguing than at the North. In the church, we had of course but one room in which to hear all the children; and to make one's self heard, when there were often as many as a hundred and forty reciting at once, it was necessary to tax the lungs very severely.

My walk to school, of about a mile, was part of the way through a road lined with trees,—on one side stately pines, on the other noble live-oaks, hung with moss and canopied with vines. The ground was carpeted with brown, fragrant pine-leaves; and as I passed through in the morning, the woods were enlivened by the delicious songs of mocking-birds, which abound here, making one realize the truthful felicity of the description in "Evangeline,"—

> The mocking-bird, wildest of singers,
> Shook from his little throat such floods of delirious music
> That the whole air and the woods and the waves seemed silent to listen.[8]

The hedges were all aglow with the brilliant scarlet berries of the cassena, and on some of the oaks we observed the mistletoe, laden with its pure white, pearl-like berries. Out of the woods the roads are generally bad, and we found it hard work plodding through the deep sand.

Mr. H.'s store was usually crowded, and Cupid was his most valuable assistant. Gay handkerchiefs for turbans, pots and kettles, and molasses, were principally in demand, especially the last. It was necessary to keep the molasses-barrel in the yard, where Cupid presided over it, and harangued and scolded the eager, noisy crowd, collected around, to his heart's content; while up the road leading to the house came constantly processions of men, women, and children, carrying on their heads cans, jugs, pitchers, and even bottles,—anything, indeed, that was capable of containing molasses. It is wonderful with what ease they carry all sorts of things on their head,—heavy bundles of wood, hoes and rakes, everything, heavy or light, that can be carried in the hands; and I have seen a woman, with a bucketful of water on her head, stoop down and take up another in her hand, without spilling a drop from either.

---

[8] From Henry Wadsworth Longfellow's *Evangeline* (1847). From the stanza Forten omits the line: "Swinging aloft on a willow spray that hung o'er the water."

We noticed that the people had much better taste in selecting materials for dresses than we had supposed. They do not generally like gaudy colors, but prefer neat, quiet patterns. They are, however, very fond of all kinds of jewelry. I once asked the children in school what their ears were for. "To put ring in," promptly replied one of the little girls.

These people are exceedingly polite in their manner towards each other, each new arrival bowing, scraping his feet, and shaking hands with the others, while there are constant greetings, such as, "Huddy? How's yer lady?" ("How d' ye do? How's your wife?) The hand-shaking is performed with the greatest possible solemnity. There is never the faintest shadow of a smile on anybody's face during this performance. The children, too, are taught to be very polite to their elders, and it is the rarest thing to hear a disrespectful word from a child to his parent, or to any grown person. They have really what the New-Englanders call "beautiful manners."

We made daily visits to the quarters, which were a few rods from the house. The negro-houses, on this as on most of the other plantations, were miserable little huts, with nothing comfortable or home-like about them, consisting generally of but two very small rooms,—the only way of lighting them, no matter what the state of the weather, being to leave the doors and windows open. The windows, of course, have no glass in them. In such a place, a father and mother with a large family of children are often obliged to live. It is almost impossible to teach them habits of neatness and order, when they are so crowded. We look forward anxiously to the day when better houses shall increase their comfort and pride of appearance.

Oaklands is a very small plantation. There were not more than eight or nine families living on it. Some of the people interested us much. Celia, one of the best, is a cripple. Her master, she told us, was too mean to give his slaves clothes enough to protect them, and her feet and legs were so badly frozen that they required amputation. She has a lovely face,—well-featured and singularly gentle. In every household where there was illness or trouble, Celia's kind, sympathizing face was the first to be seen, and her services were always the most acceptable.

Harry, the foreman on the plantation, a man of a good deal of natural intelligence, was most desirous of learning to read. He came in at night to be taught, and learned very rapidly. I never saw any one more determined to learn. We enjoyed hearing him talk about the "gunshoot,"—so the people call the capture of Bay Point and Hilton Head. They never weary of telling you "how Massa run when he hear de fust gun."

"Why didn't you go with him, Harry?" I asked.

"Oh, Miss, 't was n't 'cause Massa did n't try to 'suade me. He tell we dat de Yankees would shoot we, or would sell we to Cuba, an' do all de wast tings to we, when dey come. 'Bery well, Sar,' says I. 'If I go wid you, I be good as dead. If I stay here, I can't be no wust; so if I got to dead, I might's well dead here as anywhere. So I'll stay here an' wait for de 'dam Yankees.' Lor', Miss, I knowed he wasn't tellin' de truth all do time."

"But why did n't you believe him, Harry?"

"Dunno, Miss; somehow we hear de Yankees was our friends, an' dat we 'd be free when dey come, an' 'pears like we believe *dat*."

I found this to be true of nearly all the people I talked with, and I thought it strange they should have had so much faith in the Northerners. Truly, for years past, they had had but little cause to think them very friendly. Cupid told us that his master was so daring as to come back, after he had fled from the island, at the risk of being taken prisoner by our soldiers; and that he ordered the people to get all the furniture together and take it to a plantation on the opposite side of the creek, and to stay on that side themselves. "So," said Cupid, "dey could jus' sweep us all up in a heap, an' put us in de boat. An' he telled me to take Patience—dat 's my wifel—an' de chil'en down to a certain pint, an' den I could come back, if I choose. Jus' as if I was gwine to be sich a goat!" added he, with a look and gesture of ineffable contempt. He and the rest of the people, instead of obeying their master, left the place and hid themselves in the woods; and when he came to look for them, not one of all his faithful servants was to be found. A few, principally house servants, had previously been carried away.

In the evenings, the children frequently came in to sing and shout for us. These "shouts" are very strange,—in truth, almost indescribable. It is necessary to hear and see in order to have any clear idea of them. The children form a ring, and move around in a kind of shuffling dance, singing all the time. Four or five stand apart, and sing very energetically, clapping their hands, stamping their feet, and rocking their bodies to and fro. These are the musicians, to whose performance the shouters keep perfect time. The grown people on this plantation did not shout, but they do on some of the other plantations. It is very comical to see little children, not more than three or four years old, entering into the performance with all their might. But the shouting of the grown people is rather solemn and impressive than otherwise We cannot determine whether it has a religious character or not. Some of the people tell us that it has, others that it has not. But as the shouts of the grown people are always in connection with their religious meetings, it is probable that they are the barbarous expression of religion, handed down to them from their African ancestors, and destined to pass away under the influence of Christian teachings. The people on this island have no songs. They sing only hymns, and most of these are sad. Prince, a large black boy from a neighboring plantation, was the principal shouter among the children. It seemed impossible for him to keep still for a moment. His performances were most amusing specimens of Ethiopian gymnastics. Amaretta the younger, a cunning, kittenish little creature of only six years old, had a remarkably sweet voice. Her favorite hymn, which we used to hear her singing to herself as she walked through the yard, is one of the oddest we have heard:—

>What makes ole Satan follow me so?
>Satan got nuttin' 't all fur to do wid me.

>CHORUS.

>Tiddy Rose, hold your light!
>Brudder Tony, hold your light!
>All de member, hold bright light
>On Canaan's shorts!

This is one of the most spirited shouting-tunes. "Tiddy" is their word for sister.

    A very queer looking old man came into the store one day. He was dressed in a complete suit of brilliant Brussels carpeting. Probably it had been taken from his master's house after the "gun-shoot"; but he looked so very dignified that we did not like to question him about it. The people called him Doctor Crotts,—which was, I believe, his master's name, his own being Scipio. He was very jubilant over the new state of things, and said to Mr. H.,—"Don't hab me feelins hurt now. Used to hab me feelins hurt all de time. But don't hab 'em hurt now no more." Poor old soul! We rejoiced with him that he and his brethren no longer have their "feelins" hurt, as in the old time.

    On the Sunday before Thanksgiving, General Saxton's noble Proclamation was read at church. We could not listen to it without emotion. The people listened with the deepest attention, and seemed to understand and appreciate it. Whittier has said of it and its writer,—"It is the most beautiful and touching official document I ever read. God bless him! 'The bravest are the tenderest.'"

General Saxton is truly worthy of the gratitude and admiration with which the people regard him. His unfailing kindness and consideration for them—so different from the treatment they have sometimes received at the hands of other officers—have caused them to have unbounded confidence in General "*Sazby*," as they call him.

After the service, there were six couples married. Some of the dresses were unique. One was particularly fine,—doubtless a cast-off dress of the bride's former mistress. The silk and lace, ribbons, feathers and flowers, were in a rather faded and decayed condition. But, comical as the costumes were, we were not disposed to laugh at them. We were too glad to see the poor creatures trying to lead right and virtuous lives. The legal ceremony, which was formerly scarcely known among them, is now everywhere consecrated. The constant and earnest advice of the minister and teachers has not been given in vain; nearly every Sunday there are several couples married in church. Some of them are people who have grown old together.

Thanksgiving-Day was observed as a general holiday. According to General Saxton's orders, an ox had been killed on each plantation, that the people might that day have fresh meat, which was a great luxury to them, and, indeed, to all of us. In the morning, a large number—superintendents, teachers, and freed people—assembled in the Baptist Church. It was a sight not soon to be forgotten,—that crowd of eager, happy black faces, from which the shadow of Slavery had forever passed. "Forever free! forever free!" those magical words of the Proclamation were constantly singing themselves in my soul. After an appropriate prayer and sermon, by Mr. P., and singing by the people, General Saxton made a short, but spirited speech, urging the young men to enlist in the regiment then forming under Colonel Higginson.[9] Mrs. Gage told the people how the slaves in Santa Cruz had secured their liberty. It was something entirely new and strange to them to hear a woman speak in public; but they listened with great attention, and seemed much interested. Before dispersing, they sang "Marching Along," which is an especial favorite with them. It was a very happy Thanksgiving-Day for all of us. The weather was delightful; oranges and figs were banging on the trees; roses, oleanders,

---

[9] Thomas Wentworth Higginson (1823–1911) became an important chronichler of the Civil War and black culture. Like several other white leaders of all-black regiments, he had very limited military experience before the war. especially after the war. Before the war he was an abolitionist who supported John Brown.

and japonicas were blooming out-of-doors; the sun was warm and bright; and over all shone gloriously the blessed light of Freedom,—Freedom forevermore!

One night, L. and I were roused from our slumbers by what seemed to us loud and most distressing shrieks, proceeding from the direction of the negro-houses. Having heard of one or two attempts which the Rebels had recently made to land on the island, our first thought was, naturally, that they had forced a landing, and were trying to carry off some of the people. Every moment we expected to hear them at our doors; and knowing that they had sworn vengeance against all the superintendents and teachers, we prepared ourselves for the worst. After a little reflection, we persuaded ourselves that it could not be the Rebels; for the people had always assured us, that, in case of a Rebel attack, they would come to us at once,—evidently thinking that we should be able to protect them. But what could the shrieks mean? They ceased; then, a few moments afterwards, began again, louder, more fearful than before; then again they ceased, and all was silent. I am ashamed to confess that we had not the courage to go out and inquire into the cause of the alarm. Mr. H.'s room was in another part of the house, too far for him to give us any aid. We hailed the dawn of day gladly enough, and eagerly sought Cupid,—who was sure to know everything,—to obtain from him a solution of the mystery, "Why, you was n't scared at *dat?*" he exclaimed, in great amusement; "'t was n't nuttin' but do black sogers dat comed up to see der folks on t' oder side ob de creek. Dar was n't no boat fur 'em on dis side, so dey jus' blowed de whistle dey hab, so do folks might bring one ober fur 'em. Dat was all 't was." And Cupid laughed so heartily that we felt not a little ashamed of our fears. Nevertheless, we both maintained that *we* had never seen a whistle from which could be produced sounds so startling, so distressing, so perfectly like the shrieks of a human being.

Another night, while staying at a house some miles distant from ours, I was awakened by hearing, as I thought, some one trying to open the door from without. The door was locked; I lay perfectly still, and listened intently. A few moments elapsed, and the sound was repeated; whereupon I rose, and woke Miss W., who slept in the adjoining room. We lighted a candle, took our revolvers, and seated ourselves on the bed, keeping our weapons, so formidable in practised male hands, steadily pointed towards the door, and uttering dire threats against the intruders,—presumed to be Rebels, of course. Having maintained this tragical position for some time, and hearing no further noise, we began to grow sleepy, and extinguished our candle, returned to bed, and slept soundly till morning. But that mystery remained unexplained. I was sure that the door had been tried,—there could be no mistaking it. There was not the least probability that any of the people had entered the house, burglars are unknown on these islands, and there is nobody to be feared but the Rebels.

The last and greatest alarm we had was after we had removed from Oaklands to another plantation. I woke about two o'clock in the morning, bearing the tramp of many feet in the yard below,—the steady tramp of soldiers' feet. "The Rebels! they have come at last! all is over with us now!" I thought at once, with a desperate kind of resignation. And I lay still, waiting and listening. Soon I heard footsteps on the piazza; then the hall-door was opened, and steps were heard distinctly in the hall beneath; finally, I heard some one coming up the stairs. Then I grasped my revolver, rose, and woke the other ladies.

"There are soldiers in the yard! Somebody has opened the hall-door, and is coming up-stairs!"

Poor L., but half awakened, stared at me in speechless terror. The same thought filled our minds. But Mrs. B., after listening for a moment, exclaimed,—

"Why, that is my husband! I know his footsteps. He is coming up-stairs to call me."

And so it proved. Her husband, who was a lieutenant in Colonel Montgomery's regiment, had come up from camp with some of his men to look after deserters. The door had been unfastened by a servant who on that night happened to sleep in the house. I shall never forget the delightful sensation of relief that came over me when the whole matter was explained. It was almost overpowering; for, although I had made up my mind to bear the worst, and bear it bravely, the thought of falling into the hands of the Rebels was horrible in the extreme. A year of intense mental suffering seemed to have been compressed into those few moments.

Life on the Sea Islands.

Part II.

A FEW days before Christmas, we were delighted at receiving a beautiful Christmas Hymn from Whittier, written by request, especially for our children. They learned it very easily, and enjoyed singing it. We showed them the writer's picture, and told them he was a very good friend of theirs, who felt the deepest interest in them, and had written this hymn expressly for them to sing,—which made them very proud and happy. Early Christmas morning, we were wakened by the people knocking at the doors and windows, and shouting, "Merry Christmas!" After distributing some little presents among them, we went to the church, which had been decorated with holly, pine, cassena, mistletoe, and the hanging moss, and had a very Christmas-like look. The children of our school assembled there, and we gave them the nice, comfortable clothing,[10] and the picture-books, which had been kindly sent by some Philadelphia ladies. There were at least a hundred and fifty children present. It was very pleasant to see their happy, expectant little faces. To them, it was a wonderful Christmas-Day,—such as they had never dreamed of before. There was cheerful sunshine without, lighting up the beautiful moss-drapery of the oaks, and looking in joyously through the open windows; and there were bright faces and glad hearts within. The long, dark night of the Past, with all its sorrows and its fears, was forgotten; and for the Future,—the eyes of these freed children see no clouds in it. It is full of sunlight, they think, and they trust in it, perfectly.

After the distribution of the gifts, the children were addressed by some of the gentlemen present. They then sang Whittier's Hymn, the "John Brown" song, and several of their own hymns, among them a very singular one, commencing,—

> I wonder where my mudder gone;
> Sing, O graveyard!
> Graveyard ought to know me;
> Ring, Jerusalem!
> Grass grow in de graveyard;
> Sing, O graveyard!
> Graveyard ought to know me;
> Ring, Jerusalem!

They improvise many more words as they sing. It is one of the strangest, most mournful things I ever heard. It is impossible to give any idea of the deep pathos of the refrain,—

---

[10] Under US chattel slavery, Christmas time was commonly when new clothing and other provisions for the upcoming year were given to enslaved persons These gifts might reflect efforts to accommodate existing patterns of clothing use and related measures in the years immediately after Emancipation.

"Sing, O graveyard!"

In this, and many other hymns, the words seem to have but little meaning; but the tones,—a whole lifetime of despairing sadness is concentrated in them. They sing, also, "Jehovyah, Hallelujah," which we like particularly:—

> De foxes hab holes,
> An de birdies hab nes'
> But de Son ob Man he hab not where
> To lay de weary head.

> CHORUS.

> Jehovyah, Hallelujah! De Lord He will purvide!
> Jehovyah, Hallelujah! De Lord He will purvide!

They repeat the words many times.

"De foxes hab holes," and the succeeding lines, are sung in the most touching, mournful tones; and then the chorus—"Jehovyah, Hallelujah"—swells forth triumphantly, in glad contrast.

Christmas night, the children came in and had several grand shouts. They were too happy to keep still.

"Oh, Miss, all I want to do is to sing and shout!" said our little pet, Amaretta. And sing and shout she did, to her heart's content.

She read nicely, and was very fond of books. The tiniest children are delighted to get a book in their hands. Many of them already know their letters. The parents are eager to have them learn. They sometimes said to me,—

"Do, Miss, let de chil'en learn eberyting dey can. *We* nebber hab no chance to learn nuttin', but we wants de chil'en to learn."

They are willing to make many sacrifices that their children may attend school. One old woman, who had a large family of children and grandchildren, came regularly to school in the winter, and took her seat among the little ones. She was at least sixty years old. Another woman—who had one of the best faces I over saw—came daily, and brought her baby in her arms. It happened to be one of the best babies in the world, a perfect little model of deportment, and allowed its mother to pursue her studies without interruption.

While taking charge of the store, one day, one of the men who came in told me a story which interested me much. He was a carpenter, living on this island, and just before the capture of Port Royal had been taken by his master to the mainland,—"the Main," as the people call it,—to assist in building some houses which were to shelter the families of the Rebels in case the "Yankees" should come. The master afterward sent him back to the island, providing him with a pass, to bring away a boat and some of the people. On his arrival he found that the Union troops were in possession, and determined to remain here with his family instead of returning to his master. Some of his fellow servants, who had been left on "the Main," hearing that the Federal troops had come, resolved to make their escape to the islands. They found a boat of their master's, out of which a piece six feet square had been cut. In the night they went to the boat, which had been sunk in a creek near the house, measured the hole, and, after several nights' work in the woods, made a piece large enough to fit in. They then mended and sank it again, as they had found it. The next night five of them embarked. They had a perilous journey, often passing quite near the enemy's boats. They travelled at night, and in the day ran close up to the shore out of sight. Sometimes they could hear the hounds, which had been sent in pursuit of them, baying in the woods. Their provisions gave out, and they were nearly exhausted. At last they succeeded in passing all the enemy's boats, and reached one of our gun-boats in safety. They were taken on board and kindly cared for, and then sent to this island, where their families, who had no hope of ever seeing them again, welcomed them with great rejoicing.

We were also told the story of two girls, one about ten, the other fifteen, who, having been taken by their master up into the country, on the mainland, at the time of the capture of the islands, determined to try to escape to their parents, who had been left on this island. They stole away at night, and travelled through woods and swamps for two days, without eating. Sometimes their strength gave out, and they would sink down, thinking they could go no farther; but they had brave little hearts, and got up again and struggled on, till at last they reached Port-Royal Ferry, in a state of utter exhaustion. They were seen there by a boat-load of people who were also making their escape. The boat was too full to take them in; but the people, on reaching this island, told the children's father of their whereabouts, and he immediately took a boat, and hastened to the ferry. The poor little creatures were almost wild with joy when they saw him. When they were brought to their mother, she fell down "jes' as if she was dead,"—so our informant expressed it,—overpowered with joy on beholding the "lost who were found."

New-Year's-Day—Emancipation-Day—was a glorious one to us. The morning was quite cold, the coldest we had experienced; but we were determined to go to the celebration at Camp Saxton,—the camp of the First Regiment South-Carolina Volunteers,[11]—whither the General and Colonel Higginson had bidden us, on this, "the greatest day in the nation's history." We enjoyed perfectly the exciting scene on board the Flora. There was an eager, wondering crowd of the freed people in their holiday-attire, with the gayest of head-handkerchiefs, the whitest of aprons, and the happiest of faces. The band was playing, the flags streaming, everybody talking merrily and feeling strangely happy. The sun shone brightly, the very waves seemed to partake of the universal gayety, and danced and sparkled more joyously than ever before. Long before we reached Camp Saxton we could see the beautiful grove, and the ruins of the old Huguenot fort near it. Some companies of the First Regiment were drawn up in line under the trees, near the landing, to receive us. A fine, soldierly-looking set of men: their brilliant dress against the trees (they were then wearing red pantaloons) invested them with a semi-barbaric splendor. It was my good fortune to find among the officers an old friend,—and what it was to meet a friend from the North, in our isolated Southern life, no one can imagine who has not experienced the pleasure, Letters were an unspeakable luxury,—we hungered for them, we could never get enough; but to meet old friends,—that was too much, too much, as the people here say, when they are very much in earnest. Our friend took us over the camp, and showed us all the arrangements. Everything looked clean and comfortable, much neater, we were told, than in most of the white camps. An officer told us that he had never seen a regiment in which the men were so honest. "In many other camps," said he, "the colonel and the rest of us would find it necessary to place a guard before our tents. We never do it here. They are left entirely unguarded. Yet nothing has ever been touched." We were glad to know that. It is a remarkable fact, when we consider that these men have all their lives been *slaves;* and we know what the teachings of Slavery are.

The celebration took place in the beautiful grove of live-oaks adjoining the camp. It was the largest grove we had seen. I wish it were possible to describe fitly the scene which met our eyes as we sat upon the stand, and looked down on the crowd before us. There were the black soldiers in their blue coats and scarlet pantaloons, the officers of this and other regiments in their handsome uniforms, and crowds of lookers-on,—men, women, and children, of every complexion, grouped in various attitudes under the moss-hung trees. The

---

[11] This was an all-black regiment.

faces of all wore a happy, interested look. The exercises commenced with a prayer by the chaplain of the regiment. An ode, written for the occasion by Professor Zachos,[12] was read by him, and then sung. Colonel Higginson then introduced Dr. Brisbane, who read the President's Proclamation, which was enthusiastically cheered. Rev. Mr. French presented to the Colonel two very elegant flags, a gift to the regiment from the Church of the Puritans, accompanying them by an appropriate and enthusiastic speech. At its conclusion, before Colonel Higginson could reply, and while he still stood holding the flags in his hand, some of the colored people, of their own accord, commenced singing, "My Country, 't is of thee." It was a touching and beautiful incident, and sent a thrill through all our hearts. The Colonel was deeply moved by it. He said that that reply was far more effective than any speech he could make. But he did make one of those stirring speeches which are "half battles." All hearts swelled with emotion as we listened to his glorious words,—"stirring the soul like the sound of a trumpet."

His soldiers are warmly attached to him, and he evidently feels towards them all as if they were his children. The people speak of him as the officer who never leaves his regiment for pleasure, but devotes himself, with all his rich gifts of mind and heart, to their interests. It is not strange that his judicious kindness, ready sympathy, and rare fascination of manner should attach them to him strongly. He is one's ideal of an officer. There is in him much of the grand, knightly spirit of the olden time,—scorn of all that is mean and ignoble, pity for the weak, chivalrous devotion to the cause of the oppressed.

General Saxton spoke also, and was received with great enthusiasm. Throughout the morning, repeated cheers were given for him by the regiment, and joined in heartily by all the people. They know him to be one of the best and noblest men in the world. His Proclamation for Emancipation-Day we thought, if possible, even more beautiful than the Thanksgiving Proclamation.

At the close of Colonel Higginson's speech he presented the flags to the color-bearers, Sergeant Rivers and Sergeant Sutton, with an earnest charge, to which they made appropriate replies. We were particularly pleased with Robert Sutton, who is a man of great natural intelligence, and whose remarks were simple, eloquent, and forcible.

---

[12] John Celivergos Zachos (1820–1898) was a scholar and activist who studied the formerly enslaved person's literacy acquisition and developed curricula for their benefit.

Mrs. Gage also uttered some earnest words; and then the regiment sang "John Brown" with much spirit. After the meeting we saw the dress-parade, a brilliant and beautiful sight. An officer told us that the men went through the drill remarkably well,—that the ease and rapidity with which they learned the movements were wonderful. To us it seemed strange as a miracle,—this black regiment, the first mustered into the service of the United States, doing itself honor in the sight of the officers of other regiments, many of whom, doubtless, "came to scoff." The men afterwards had a great feast, ten oxen having been roasted whole for their especial benefit.

We went to the landing, intending to take the next boat for Beaufort; but finding it very much crowded, waited for another. It was the softest, loveliest moonlight; we seated ourselves on the ruined wall of the old fort; and when the boat had got a short distance from the shore the band in it commenced playing "Sweet Home." The moonlight on the water, the perfect stillness around, the wildness and solitude of the ruins, all seemed to give new pathos to that ever dear and beautiful old song. It came very near to all of us,—strangers in that strange Southern land. After a while we retired to one of the tents,—for the night-air, as usual, grew dangerously damp,—and, sitting around the bright wood-fire, enjoyed the brilliant and entertaining conversation. Very unwilling were we to go home; for, besides the attractive society, we knew that the soldiers were to have grand shouts and a general jubilee that night. But the Flora was coming, and we were obliged to say a reluctant farewell to Camp Saxton and the hospitable dwellers therein, and hasten to the landing. We promenaded the deck of the steamer, sang patriotic songs, and agreed that moonlight and water had never looked so beautiful as on that night. At Beaufort we took the row-boat for St. Helena; and the boatman, as they rowed, sang some of their sweetest, wildest hymns. It was a fitting close to such a day. Our hearts were filled with an exceeding great gladness; for, although the Government had left much undone, we knew that Freedom was surely born in our land that day. It seemed too glorious a good to realize,—this beginning of the great work we had so longed and prayed for.

L. and I had one day an interesting visit to a plantation about six miles from ours. The house is beautifully situated in the midst of noble pine-trees, on the banks of a large creek. The place was owned by a very wealthy Rebel family, and is one of the pleasantest and healthiest on the island. The vicinity of the pines makes it quite healthy. There were a hundred and fifty people on it,—one hundred of whom had come from Edisto Island at the time of its evacuation by our troops. There were not houses enough to accommodate them, and they had to take shelter in barns, out-houses, or any other place they could find. They afterwards built rude dwellings for themselves, which did not, however, afford them much protection in bad weather. The superintendent told us that they were well-behaved and industrious. One old woman interested us greatly. Her name was Daphne; she was probably more than a hundred years old; had had fifty grandchildren, sixty-five great-grandchildren, and three great-great-grandchildren. Entirely blind, she yet seemed very cheerful and happy. She told us that she was brought with her parents from Africa at the time of the Revolution. A bright, happy old face was hers, and she retained her faculties remarkably well. Fifteen of the people had escaped from the mainland in the previous spring. They were pursued, and one of them was overtaken by his master in the swamps. A fierce grapple ensued,—the roaster on horseback, the man on foot. The former drew a pistol and shot his slave through the arm, shattering it dreadfully. Still, the heroic men fought desperately, and at last succeeded in unhorsing his master, and beating him until he was senseless. He then made his escape, and joined the rest of the party.

One of the most interesting sights we saw was a baptism among the people. On one Sunday there were a hundred and fifty baptized in the creek near the church. They looked very picturesque in their white aprons and bright frocks and handkerchiefs. As they marched in procession down to the river's edge, and during the ceremony, the spectators, with whom the banks were crowded, sang glad, triumphant songs. The freed people on this island are all Baptists.

We were much disappointed in the Southern climate. We found it much colder than we had expected,—quite cold enough for as thick winter clothing as one would wear at the North. The houses, heated only by open fires, were never comfortably warm. In the floor of our sitting-room there was a large crack through which we could see the ground beneath; and through this and the crevices of the numerous doors and windows the wind came chillingly. The church in which we taught school was particularly damp and cold. There was no chimney, and we could have no fire at all. Near the close of the winter a stove came for us, but it could not be made to draw; we were nearly suffocated with smoke, and gave it up in despair. We got so thoroughly chilled and benumbed within, that for several days we had school out-of-doors, where it was much warmer. Our school-room was a pleasant one,—for ceiling the blue sky above, for walls the grand old oaks with their beautiful moss-drapery,—but the dampness of the ground made it unsafe for us to continue the experiment.

At a later period, during a few days' visit to some friends living on the Milne Plantation, then the head-quarters of the First South-Carolina, which was on picket-duty at Port-Royal Ferry, we had an opportunity of seeing something of Port-Royal Island. We had pleasant rides through the pine barrons. Indeed, riding on horseback was our chief recreation at the South, and we enjoyed it thoroughly. The "Secesh"[13] horses, though small, poor, and mean-looking, when compared with ours, are generally excellent for the saddle, well trained and very easy. I remember particularly one ride that we had while on Port-Royal Island. We visited the Barnwell Plantation, one of the finest places on the island. It is situated on Broad River. The grounds are extensive, and are filled with magnificent live-oaks, magnolias, and other trees. We saw one noble old oak, said to be the largest on these islands. Some of the branches have been cut off, but the remaining ones cover an area of more than a hundred feet in circumference. We rode to a point whence the Rebels on the opposite side of the river are sometimes to be seen. But they were not visible that day; and we were disappointed in our long-cherished hope of seeing a "real live Rebel." On leaving the plantation, we rode through a long avenue of oaks,—the moss-hung branches forming a perfect arch over our heads,—and then for miles through the pine barrens. There was an Italian softness in the April air. Only a low, faint murmur—hardly "the slow song of the sea"—could be heard among the pines. The ground was thickly carpeted with ferns of a vivid green. We found large violets, purple and white, and azaleas of a deeper pink and heavier fragrance than ours. It was leaving Paradise, to emerge from the beautiful woods upon the public road,—the shell-road which runs from Beaufort to the Ferry. Then we entered a by-way leading to the plantation, where we found the Cherokee rose in all its glory. The hedges were white with it; it canopied the trees, and hung from their branches its long sprays of snowy blossoms and dark, shining leaves, forming perfect arches, and bowers which seemed fitting places for fairies to dwell in. How it gladdened our eyes and hearts! It was as if all the dark shadows that have so long hung over this Southern land had flitted away, and, in this garment of purest white, it shone forth transfigured, beautified, forevermore.

On returning to the house, we were met by the exciting news that the Rebels were bringing up pontoon-bridges, and were expected to attempt

---

[13] Secesh was a colloquialism for a secessionist and his or her supporters.

crossing over near the Ferry, which was only two or three miles from us. Couriers came in every few moments with various reports. A superintendent whose plantation was very near the Ferry had been watching through his glass the movements on the opposite side, and reported that the Rebels were gathering in large force, and evidently preparing for some kind of demonstration. A messenger was dispatched to Beaufort for reinforcements, and for some time we were in a state of expectancy, not entirely without excitement, but entirely without fear. The officers evidently enjoyed the prospect of a fight. One of them assured me that I should have the pleasure of seeing a Rebel shell during the afternoon. It was proposed that the women should be sent into Beaufort in an ambulance; against which ignoble treatment we indignantly protested, and declared our intention of remaining at our post, if the Colonel would consent; and finally, to our great joy, the best of colonels did consent that we should remain, as he considered it quite safe for us to do so. Soon a light battery arrived, and during the evening a brisk firing was kept up. We could hear the explosion of the shells. It was quite like being in the war; and as the firing was principally on our side, and the enemy was getting the worst of it, we rather enjoyed it. For a little while the Colonel read to us, in his spirited way, some of the stirring "Lays of the Old Cavaliers." It was just the time to appreciate them thoroughly, and he was of all men the fittest person to read them. But soon came a courier, "in hot haste," to make report of the doings without, and the reading was at an end. In the midst of the firing, Mrs. D. and I went to bed, and slept soundly until morning. We learned afterward that the Rebels had not intended to cross over, but were attempting to take the guns off one of our boats, which they had sunk a few days previous. The timely arrival of the battery from Beaufort prevented them from accomplishing their purpose.

In April we left Oaklands, which had always been considered a particularly unhealthy place during the summer, and came to "Seaside," a plantation on another and healthier part of the island. The place contains nearly a hundred people, The house is large and comparatively comfortable. Notwithstanding the name, we have not even a distant glimpse of the sea, although we can sometimes hear its roar. At low tide there is not a drop of water to be seen,— only dreary stretches of marsh-land, reminding us of the sad outlook of Mariana in the Moated Grange,—

"The level waste and rounding gray."[14]

---

[14] From Alfred, Lord Tennyson's "Mariana" (1830).

But at night we have generally a good sea-breeze, and during the hottest weather the air is purer and more invigorating than in many parts of the island.

On this, as on several other large plantations, there is a "Praise-House," which is the special property of the people. Even in the old days of Slavery, they were allowed to hold meetings here; and they still keep up the custom. They assemble on several nights of the week, and on Sunday afternoons. First, they hold what is called the "Praise-Meeting," which consists of singing, praying, and preaching. We have heard some of the old negro preachers make prayers that were really beautiful and touching. In these meetings they sing only the church-hymns which the Northern ministers have taught them, and which are far less suited to their voices than their own. At the close of the Praise-Meeting they all shake hands with each other in the most solemn manner. Afterward, as a kind of appendix, they have a grand shout, during which they ring their own hymns. Maurice, an old blind man, leads the singing. He has a remarkable voice, and sings with the greatest enthusiasm. The first shout that we witnessed in the Praise-House impressed us very much. The large, gloomy room, with its blackened walls,—the wild, whirling dance of the shouters,—the crowd of dark, eager faces gathered around,—the figure of the old blind man, whose excitement could hardly be controlled, and whose attitude and gestures while singing were very fine,—and over all, the red glare of the burning pine knot, which shed a circle of light around it, but only seemed to deepen and darken the shadows in the other parts of the room,-these all formed a wild, strange, and deeply impressive picture, not soon to be forgotten.

Maurice's especial favorite is one of the grandest hymns that we have yet heard:—

> De tallest tree to Paradise
> De Christian calls de Tree oh Life,
> An I hope dat trumpet blow me home
> To my New Jerusalem.

CHORUS.

> Blow, Gabriel! trumpet, blow louder, louder!
> An' I hope dat trumpet blow me home
> To my New Jerusalem!

Paul and Silas jail-bound
Sing God's praise both night and day,
An' I hope dat trumpet blow me home
To my New Jerusalem.

CHORUS.

Blow, Gabriel! trumpet, blow loader, louder!
An' I hope dat trumpet blow me home
To my New Jerusalem!

The chorus has a glad, triumphal sound, and in singing it the voice of old Maurice rings out in wonderfully clear, trumpet-like tones. His blindness was caused by a blow on the head from a loaded whip. He was struck by his master in a fit of anger. "I feel great distress when I become blind," said Maurice; "but den I went to seek de Lord; and eber since I know I see in de next world, I always hab great satisfaction." We are told that the master was not a hard man except when in a passion, and then he seems to have been very cruel.

One of the women on the place, Old Bess, bears on new limbs many marks the whip. Some of the scars are three and four inches long. She was used principally as a house-servant. She says, "Ebery time I lay de table I put cow-skin on one end, an' I git beatin' and thumpin' all de time, Hab all kinds o' work to do, and such a gang [of children] to look after! One person could n't git along wid so much work, so it go wrong, and den I git beatin.'"

But the cruelty of Bess's master sinks into insignificance, when compared with the far-famed wickedness of another slave-holder, known all over the island as Old Joe Eddings. There seem to have been no bounds to his cruelty and licentiousness; and the people tell tales of him which make one shudder. We were once asking some questions about him of an old, half-witted woman, a former slave of his. The look of horror and loathing which overspread her face was perfectly indescribable, as, with upraised hands, she exclaimed, "What! Old Joe Eddings? Lord, Missus, he second to none in de world but de Debil!" She had, indeed, good cause to detest him; for, some years before, her daughter, a young black girl, maddened by his persecutions, had thrown herself into the creek and been drowned, after having been severely beaten for refusing to degrade herself. Outraged, despised, and black, she yet preferred death to dishonor. But these are things too heart-sickening to dwell upon. God alone knows how many hundreds of plantations, all over the South, might furnish a similar record.

Early in June, before the summer heat had become unendurable, we made a pleasant excursion to Edisto Island. We left St. Helena village in the morning, dined on one of the gun-boats stationed near our island, and in the afternoon proceeded to Edisto in two row-boats. There were six of us, besides an officer and the boats' crews, who were armed with guns and cutlasses. There was no actual danger; but as we were going into the enemy's country, we thought it wisest to guard against surprises. After a delightful row, we reached the island near sunset, landing at a place called Eddingsville, which was a favorite summer resort with the aristocracy of Edisto. It has a fine beach several miles in length. Along the beach there is a row of houses, which must once have been very desirable dwellings, but have now a desolate, dismantled look. The sailors explored the beach for some distance, and returned, reporting "all quiet, and nobody to be seen"; so we walked on, feeling quite safe, stopping here and there to gather the beautiful tiny shells which were buried deep in the sands.

We took supper in a room of one of the deserted houses, using for seats some old bureau-drawers turned edgewise. Afterward we sat on the piazza, watching the lightning playing from a low, black cloud over a sky flushed with sunset, and listening to the merry songs of the sailors who occupied the next house. They had built a large fire, the cheerful glow of which shone through the windows, and we could see them dancing, evidently in great glee. Later, we had another walk on the beach, in the lovely moonlight. It was very quiet then. The deep stillness was broken only by the low, musical murmur of the waves. The moon shone bright and clear over the deserted houses and gardens, and gave them a still wilder and more desolate look.

We went within-doors for the night very unwillingly. Having, of course, no beds, we made ourselves as comfortable as we could on the floor, with boat-cushions, blankets, and shawls. No fear of Rebels disturbed us. There was but one road by which they could get to us, and on that a watch was kept, and in case of their approach, we knew we should have ample time to get to the boats and make our escape. So, despite the mosquitoes, we had a sound night's sleep.

The next morning we took the boats again, and followed the course of the most winding of little creeks. In and out, in and out, the boats went. Sometimes it seemed as if we were going into the very heart of the woods; and through the deep silence we half expected to hear the sound of a Rebel rifle. The banks were over-hung with a thick tangle of shrubs and bushes, which threatened to catch our boats, as we passed close beneath their branches. In some places the stream was so narrow that we ran aground, and then the men had to get out, and drag and pull with all their might before we could be got clear again. After a row full of excitement and pleasure, we reached our place of destination,—the Eddings Plantation, whither some of the freedmen had preceded us in their search for corn. It must once have been a beautiful place. The grounds were laid out with great taste, and filled with fine trees, among which we noticed particularly the oleander, laden with deep rose-hued and deliciously fragrant flowers, and the magnolia, with its wonderful, large blossoms, which shone dazzlingly white among the dark leaves. We explored the house,—after it had first been examined by our guard, to see that no foes lurked there,—but found nothing but heaps of rubbish, an old bedstead, and a bathing-tub, of which we afterward made good use. When we returned to the shore, we found that the tide had gone out, and between us and the boats lay a tract of marsh-land, which it would have been impossible to cross without a wetting. The gentlemen determined on wading. But what were we to do? In this dilemma somebody suggested the bathing-tub, a suggestion which was eagerly seized upon. We were placed in it, one at a time, borne aloft in triumph on the shoulders of four stout sailors, and safely deposited in the boat. But, through a mistake, the tub was not sent back for two of the ladies, and they were brought over on the crossed hands of two of the sailors, in the "carry-a-lady-to-London" style. Again we rowed through the windings of the creek, then out into the open sea, among the white, exhilarating breakers,—reached the gun-boat, dined again with its hospitable officers, and then returned to our island, which we reached after nightfall, feeling thoroughly tired, but well pleased with our excursion.

From what we saw of Edisto, however, we did not like it better than our own island,—except, of course, the beach; but we are told that farther in the interior it is much more beautiful. The freed people, who left it at the time of its evacuation, think it the loveliest place in the world, and long to return. When we were going, Miss T.—the much-loved and untiring friend and physician of the people—asked some whom we met if we should give their love to Edisto. "Oh, yes, yes, Miss!" they said. "Ah, Edisto a beautiful city!" And when we came back, they inquired, eagerly,—"How you like Edisto? How Edisto stan'?" Only the fear of again falling into the hands of the "Secesh" prevents them from returning to their much-loved home.

As the summer advanced, the heat became intense. We found it almost over-powering, driving to school near the middle of the day, as we were obliged to do. I gave up riding, and mounted a sulky,[15] such as a single gentleman drives in at the North. It was exceedingly high, and I found it no small task to mount up into it. Its already very comical appearance was enhanced by the addition of a cover of black India-rubber cloth, with which a friend kindly provided me. Thus adorned, it looked like the skeleton of some strange creature surmounted by a huge bonnet, and afforded endless amusement to the soldiers we chanced to meet, who hailed its appearance with shouts of laughter, and cries of "Here comes the Calithumpian!" This unique vehicle, with several others on our island, kindred, but not quite equal to it, would create a decided sensation in the streets of a Northern city.

No description of life on these islands would be complete without a word concerning the fleas. They appeared at the opening of spring, and kept constantly "risin'," as the people said, until they reached at height the possibility of which we had never conceived. We had heard and read of fleas. We had never *realized* them before. Words utterly fail to describe the tortures we endured for months from these horrible little tyrants. Remembering our sufferings "through weary day and weary *night*," we warn everybody not gifted with extraordinary powers of endurance to beware of a summer on the Sea Islands.

Notwithstanding the heat, we determined to celebrate the Fourth of July as worthily as we could. The freed people and the children of the different schools assembled in the grove near the Baptist Church. The flag was hung across the road, between two magnificent live-oaks, and the children, being grouped under it, sang "The Star-Spangled Banner" with much spirit. Our good General could not come, but addresses were made by Mr. P.,—the noble-hearted founder of the movement for the benefit of the people here, and from first to last their stanch and much-loved friend,—by Mr. L., a young colored minister, and others. Then the people sang some of their own hymns; and the woods resounded with the grand notes of "Roll, Jordan, roll." They all afterward partook of refreshments, consisting of molasses and water,—a very great luxury to them,—and hard-tack.

Among the visitors present was the noble young Colonel Shaw,[16] whose regiment was then stationed on the island. We had met him a few nights before, when he came to our house to witness one of the people's shouts. We

---

[15] A small horse cart.
[16] Colonel Robert Gould Shaw (1837–1863) of Boston commanded the famed all-black 54th Massachusetts Infantry Regiment. He became a martyr for the abolitionist and Union causes.

looked upon him with the deepest interest. There was something in his face finer, more exquisite, than one often sees in a man's face, yet it was full of courage and decision. The rare and singular charm of his manner drew all hearts to him. He was deeply interested in the singing and appearance of the people. A few days afterwards we saw his regiment on dress-parade, and admired its remarkably fine and manly appearance. After taking supper with the Colonel we sat outside the tent, while some of his men entertained us with excellent singing. Every moment we became more and more charmed with him. How full of life and hope and lofty aspirations he was that night! How eagerly he expressed his wish that they might soon be ordered to Charleston! "I do hope they will give *us* a chance," he said. It was the desire of his soul that his men should do themselves honor,—that they should prove themselves to an unbelieving world as brave soldiers as though their skins were white. And for himself, he was like the Chevalier of old, without reproach or fear. After we had mounted our horses and rode away, we seemed still to feel the kind clasp of his hand,—to hear the pleasant, genial tones of his voice, as he bade us good-bye, and hoped that we might meet again. We never saw him afterward. In two short weeks came the terrible massacre at Fort Wagner, and the beautiful head of the young hero and martyr was laid low in the dust. Never shall we forget the heart-sickness with which we heard of his death. We could not realize it at first,—we, who had seen him so lately in all the strength and glory of his young manhood. For days we clung to a vain hope; then it fell away from us, and we knew that he was gone. We knew that he died gloriously, but still it seemed very hard. Our hearts bled for the mother whom he so loved,—for the young wife, left desolate. And then we said, as we say now,—"God comfort them! He only can." During a few of the sad days which followed the attack on Fort Wagner, I was in one of the hospitals of Beaufort, occupied with the wounded soldiers of the Fifty-Fourth Massachusetts. The first morning was spent in mending the bullet-holes and rents in their clothing. What a story they told! Some of the jackets of the poor fellows were literally cut in pieces. It was pleasant to see the brave, cheerful spirit among them. Some of them were severely wounded, but they uttered no complaint; and in the letters which they dictated to their absent friends there was no word of regret, but the same cheerful tone throughout. They expressed an eager desire to get well, that they might "go at it again." Their attachment to their young colonel was beautiful to see. They felt his death deeply. One and all united in the warmest and most enthusiastic praise of him. He was, indeed, exactly the person to inspire the most loyal devotion in the hearts of his men. And with everything to live for, he had given up his life for them. Heaven's best gifts had been showered upon him, but for them he had laid them all down. I think they truly appreciated the greatness of the sacrifice. May they ever prove worthy of such a leader! Already, they, and the regiments of freedmen here, as well, have shown that true manhood has no limitations of color.

Daily the long-oppressed people of these islands are demonstrating their capacity for improvement in learning and labor. What they have accomplished in one short year exceeds our utmost expectations. Still the sky is dark; but through the darkness we can discern a brighter future. We cannot but feel that the day of final and entire deliverance, so long and often so hopelessly prayed for, has at length begun to dawn upon this much-enduring race. An old freedman said to me one day, "De Lord make me suffer long time, Miss. 'Peared like we nebber was gwine to git troo. But now we's free. He bring us all out right at las.'" In their darkest hours they have clung to Him, and we know He will not forsake them.

> The poor among men shall rejoice,
> For the terrible one is brought to nought.

While writing these pages I am once more nearing Port Royal. The Fortunate Isles of Freedom are before me. I shall again tread the flower-skirted wood-paths of St. Helena, and the sombre pines and bearded oaks shall whisper in the sea-wind their grave welcome. I shall dwell again among mine own people. I shall gather my scholars about me, and see smiles of greeting break over their dusk faces. My heart sings a song of thanksgiving, at the thought that even I am permitted to do something for a long-abused race, and aid in promoting a higher, holier, and happier life on the Sea Islands.

Stewart's Works

21
Meditation VI and Meditation XII

Before we proceed any fa[r]ther, permit me to ask you, my Christian friends, in the name of the Lord Jesus Christ, what progress are you making in the divine life?[1] Are you bringing forth the fruits of righteousness, and proving to the world, by your own conduct that there is reality in religion, and a beauty in the fear of the Lord? Are you letting your light so shine before men that they may see your good works, and glorify your Father which is in heaven? Christ has said, that he is more willing to give his Holy Spirit to them that ask him, than earthly parents are to bestow good gifts upon their children; and that if two or three shall ask any thing in his name, believing that he is able to perform, it shall be done for them of their Father which is in heaven; and certainly the fervent, effectual prayer of the righteous availeth much. O, then, shall precious and immortal souls perish through our neglect?[2] Shall they stumble into hell over us, and rise up in judgment and condemn us? Is it not to be feared that many who profess the name of Jesus at the present day are much like the whited sepulchres,[3] which indeed appear beautiful without, but inwardly are full of all manner of uncleanliness? Do not many love the praise of man more than the praise of God? Have we not all been unprofitable servants? And is it not to be feared that at the great and terrible day of the Lord, he will arise and shut the door? and many will stand without, and begin to knock, and say, Lord. Lord, open unto us; but he will say, I know not from whence ye are: depart from me, ye workers of iniquity. And soon the summons will go forth against you, my unconverted friends; cut them down, for why cumber they the ground? Christ has been seeking fruit of you these

---

[1] The second-person address, rhetorical questions, and sequentiality mark the many elements of formal oratory that shape this and other Meditations. The Meditations often address God or Stewart's soul; several also apostrophize a human audience (e.g., "Christians" or "unconverted friends"). Half of the Meditations are accompanied by bracketed prayers.

[2] Stewart's paradigms of racial solidarity rest on notions of Christian ethics of community accountability and the individual's responsibility to be an agent of (Christian) change. This passage on Christians' failures reveals some of the religious origins of Stewart's invectives against successful black persons who divest from their communities. See her "Farewell Address" in Stewart, 91–99.

[3] Matthew 23:27. Literally a tomb painted white but idiomatically used to denote hypocrites. Stewart also uses it in the Masonic Hall address (see Stewart, 178–185).

many years, and lo, he hath found none. O, how can you go on, year after year, and month after month, sinning against a holy and a righteous God, who is constantly showering down the choicest of his blessings upon you? O, how can you see your friends dropping into the eternal world, and yet feel no concern for your never dying souls? Will not the terrors of death alarm you, nor the calls and invitations of mercy persuade you? Come, now, saith the Lord, and let us reason together; though your own sins have been as scarlet, they shall be made as wool; and though they have been red like crimson, they shall become whiter than snow. O, my friends, believe me or not, I have felt at times to exclaim with Moses: O, Lord God, this people have sinned a great sin; but now if thou wilt forgive them, blot me[4] I pray thee, from thy book. And the Lord said, him that sinneth against me, him will I blot from my book.

Meditation XII.

> Come, welcome death, the end of fear,
> I am prepared to die;
> I trust my soul will straight ascend,
> Up to the Lord on high.[5]

Alas! and am I born to die! O, my soul, wilt thou ere long take thy flight to realms of endless bliss, or to the shades of darkest night, and leave this frail tenement? Will these eyes be closed, a lump of cold and lifeless clay; these lips cease to speak, and this heart cease to beat? these hands and feet become inactive, cold, and stiff; and this form of mine become food for worms, and turn to dust! Alas, alas, how mournful is the thought! but, pale messenger, I fear thee not, with all thy grim and ghastly terrors, for my Redeemer lives. He lives, and he is able to disarm thee of thy sting, and no one is able to pluck me out of my Redeemer's hand. He will safely carry me through the dark valley and the shadow of death, and angels will convey me to heaven. Then

---

[4] Aligning herself with Moses, Stewart professes a messianic desire to take on the punishment for her sinful unconverted friends. See the "Address Delivered Before the Afric-American Female Intelligence Society of Boston" (Stewart 85 – 90) for more on how she understood the difficulties of her oratorical career in Boston and the Christian historical background she offers to legitimate her controversial public speaking and writing.

[5] This verse comes from a long poem reprinted in the *New England Primer* attributed to Protestant martyr John Rogers (d. 1554). According to the *Primer*, Rogers wrote the poem as advice to his children a few days before he was burned at the stake. Stewart routinely positioned herself as a martyr, especially during and immediately following her public career in Boston.

while my body lies mouldering here, my soul shall rest from all sorrows, and shall chant the praises of my Redeemer, till the last trumpet shall sound; then shall my sleeping dust awake, and my soul and body be reunited and fly with transport to meet my Saviour, when he shall come with ten thousand of his saints and angels, to take vengeance on his enemies.

> The trumpet sounds,
> Hell trembles,
> Heaven rejoices;
> Lift up your heads, ye saints, with cheerful voices,
> No more shall atheist mock his long delay.
> His vengeance sleeps no more.
> Behold the day!
> His guards are nigh;
> Tempest and fire attend him down the sky.
>
> When God appears,
> All nations shall adore him;
> Whilst sinners tremble,
> Saints rejoice before him.[6]

PRAYER.

Almighty God, it is the glorious hope of a blessed immortality beyond the grave that supports thy children through this vale of tears. Forever blessed be thy name, that thou hast implanted this hope in my bosom. If thou hast indeed plucked my soul as a brand from the burning, it is not because thou hast seen any worth in me;[7] but it is because of thy distinguishing mercy, for mercy is thy darling attribute, and thou delightest in mercy, and art not willing that any should perish, but that all should come to the knowledge of the truth as it is in Jesus. Clothe my soul with humility as with a garment. Grant that I may bring forth the fruits of a meek and quiet spirit. Enable me

---

[6] Part of an Isaac Watts hymn based on Psalm 50. See Joel Barlow's *Doctor Watts' Imitation of the Psalms of David* (1785).

[7] This focus on salvation via election rather than belief, goodness, or works echoes the predestinationist logics of Calvinists, the deeply influential founding sect of most New England colonies.

to adorn the doctrines of God my Saviour by a well regulated life and conversation, May I become holy, even as thou art holy, and pure, even as thou art pure. Bless all my friends and benefactors: those who have given me a cup of cold water in thy name, the Lord reward them. Forgive all my enemies. May I love them that hate me, and pray for them that despitefully use and persecute me. Preserve me from slanderous tongues, O God, and let not my good be evil spoken of. Let not a repining thought enter my heart, nor a murmuring sigh heave from my bosom. But may I cheerfully bear with all the trials of life. Clothe me with the pure robes of Christ's righteousness, and that when he shall come in flaming fire to judge the world, I may appear before him with joy, and not with grief; and not only for myself do I ask these blessings, but for all the sons and daughters of Adam, as thou art no respecter of persons, and as all distinctions wither in the grave.[8] Grant all prejudices and animosities may cease from among men. May we all realize that promotion cometh not from the East nor from the West, but that it is God that putteth up one and setteth down another. May the rich be rich in faith and good works toward our Lord Jesus Christ, and may the poor have an inheritance among the saints in light, a crown incorruptible that fadeth not away, eternal in the heavens. And now what wait we for? Be pleased to grant that we may at last join with all the Israel of God, in celebrating thy praise.

---

[8] Likely a veiled allusion to race, including Stewart's unswerving claim that black Christians more frequently lived true Christianity than white Christians, especially slaveholders.

22
The Negro's Complaint

FORC'D from home and all its pleasures,[1]
    Afric's coast I left forlorn;
To increase a stranger's treasures,
    O'er the raging billows borne.
Men from England* bought and sold me,
    Paid my price in paltry gold;
But though slave they have enroll'd me,
    Minds are never to be sold.

Still in thought as free as ever,
    What are England's rights, (I ask;)
Me from my delights to sever,
    Me to torture, me to task?
Fleecy locks and black complexion,
    Cannot forfeit Nature's claim;
Skins may differ, but affection
    Dwells in white and black the same.

Why did all-creating Nature,
    Make the plant for which we toil?
Sighs must fan it, tears must water,
    Sweat of ours must dress the soil.
Think, ye masters iron-hearted,
    Lolling at your jovial boards:
Think how many backs have smarted
    For the sweets your cane affords.

---

[1] The poem closes out *Productions of Mrs. Maria W. Stewart* (1835). The advertisement at the end is for purchase of the entire book.

Is there, as ye sometimes tell us,
    Is there ONE who reigns on high?
Has HE bid you buy and sell us,
    Speaking from His throne, the sky?
Ask him if your knotted scourges,
    Fetters, blood-extorting screws,
Are the means which duty urges,
    Agents of his will to use?

*England had 800,000 Slaves, and she has made them FREE! AMERICA has 2,250,000! and she HOLDS THEM FAST!!!

Hark! He answers—wild tornadoes,
    Strewing yonder sea with wrecks:
Wasting towns, plantations, meadows,
    Are the voice with which He speaks.
He, foreseeing what vexation
    Afric's sons would undergo,
Fix'd their tyrant's habitation
    Where his whirlwind answers—"No!"

By our blood in Afric wasted,
    Ere our necks receiv'd the chain;
By the miseries we tasted,
    Crossing in your barks the main.
By our sufferings, since ye brought us
    To the man-degrading mart;
All sustained with patience, taught us
    Only by a broken heart.

Deem our nation brutes no longer,
    Till some reason ye shall find
Worthier to regard and stronger
    Than the *color* of our kind!
Slaves of gold! Whose sordid dealings
    Tarnish all your boasted powers;

Prove that *ye* have human feelings,
Ere ye proudly question ours!

For Sale at the office of the Massachusetts Anti-Slavery Society, No. 46, Washington Street, Boston, by B.C. Bacon, Agent and Secretary; and by David Ruggles, No. 67, Lespenard Street, New York City.

23
The First Stage of Life

By Mrs. Mariah W. Stewart.

The writer of this article has become so very obscure in life, these late years, so much immersed in care and anxiety of mind. Away from home, in a land of strangers, away from those once loved, once honored, and once revered, and so far sunk in oblivion's dark shade, that she feels little or no disposition ever to aspire therefrom.[1]

Yet amid discouragements from the earliest ages of antiquity, there has ever been some individual, however humble, to contribute a straw as it were, if nothing more to aid the press, the minist[r]y, the church, and there ever will be.

All are not born to govern, there must be subjects to rule, all are not the favorites of fortune, and the poor will never cease out of the land, and our conditions in life, our dispositions and our different pursuits, after happiness in this world, are as varied, as the flowers of the field, the birds of the air, and the cattle upon a thousand hills, yet all are searching for one great point, all end in one termination, all finally blend together, and take their course, and wend their way, until they pour themselves into an ocean.[2] The ocean of eternity.[3]

In order to become a writer the mind must be stored with useful knowledge it requires study, deep thought, nay, more, it requires profound meditation, and fervent prayer. And how is this frame of mind to be acquired, this intellectual food obtained, amid the perplexing care of what shall I eat, and what shall I drink, and where withal shall I be clothed. But a whisper tells me, there must a sacrifice, be made unto God, on the altar of our time, if it is not performed until those dark, still hours, when deep sleep falleth upon man.[4]

---

[1] An allusion to Stewart's departure from Boston and migration southward after 1833. See her "Farewell Address" in Stewart, 91–99.

[2] See Deuteronomy 15, which calls for cancelling debts and freeing enslaved persons, and showing compassion and leniency toward the enslaved, poor, and indebted.

[3] Death.

[4] Self-referential exordia of this sort were not common in American short fiction of the time. But versions of what opens this story appear time and again in Stewart's corpus. Like the exordium here,

But my subject. The first recollection of little Letitia, (for by that name I shall call the heroine of my subject,) was, of her father taking her up in his arms, in consequence of some little excitement out of doors, and carrying her in the house, and placing her in the lap of her mother, she never saw him more, he was drowned, when and where, she knows not.[5]

The first time Letitia remembers of having her face and hands washed, was by her aunt Sarah, but not without the threat of rubbing all the skin off from her arms, if she did not behave herself, and the first sweet potato she ever saw, her aunt gave her, it was red.

The first time Letitia ever noticed the blue sky, and the light of day, she was sent with another little girl to get a pail of water, she climbed upon a ledge of rocks, she fell, and one of the rocks fell upon one of her limbs, she was wounded, she saw the blood flow. How she got home, or when she recovered, she knows not, she only knows that it was.

The first flowers Letitia saw, was a field of clover, enclosed by a fence. It was in full bloom, and the colors being pink and green, appeared beautiful to her infant vision. What caused the beautiful light of day, she could not imagine, she had never heard of, or seen the sun, and if she had, she had not sense enough to know it. And the first time Letitia was ever out in the sable orb of night, that she recollects her attention attracted by the light of the lamps. All was dark above, she saw no moon nor stars, she knew not what they were, and passing by a shop she saw a monstrous large boot, she was filled with fear, she thought it was God's boot, and walked away very softly.[6] This was the first idea Letitia ever had of God.

Thus Letitia passed away the guileless hours of infancy, like a butterfly in the sunbeams of a summer's day. Where she first saw the blue sky, the beautiful light of day, the field of tall clover elegantly arrayed in pink and green, or the hand that sustained her she knew not, she only knew that it was so.

And now the scene changes, and Letitia remembers that herself, her mother, and her step-father were all on their way, she knows not where, she knows not when this gentleman became her step-father, she only knew that he was her step-father, and when she comes again to her recollection,

they emphasize her humble beginnings, prophetic calling, and tremendous personal sacrifice in the face of great danger.

[5] Letitia's father taking her inside to protect from "excitement" in the street (i.e., disturbance) and his subsequent disappearance and drowning may be unrelated, but it could speak to the War of 1812 in which Stewart's husband, James Stewart, served.

[6] The prevalence of lamplight suggests Letitia is in a city in this episode.

she finds herself in a strange place, surrounded by the beautiful light of [d]ay,[7] the blue sky above her head, clouded with white, and herself disarranging a beautiful little baby house, the shelves all decorated with broken earthen ware, her little playmate was absent, she returns, she reproves Letitia gently. She was white, the first white face, Letitia ever saw, that she knows off [sic].

And now Letitia returns home, but the word home, she had never heard of, and what does she see. Her mother sick, propped up in the bed, supported by pillows, her step-father administering to the wants of her mother. And what does her mother say. She tells Letitia she is sometimes good, and sometimes bad. The first, and last reproof that ever sounded in the ears of Letitia, from the lips of that gentle mother.

And now what does Letitia hear. Her mother desires to go to the city, to die, at a dear friend's house, for by the light of Letitia's vision she must have been in the country, but the word country, she had never heard, she knew not what it meant. A cart was procured, and the bed put in it, and Letitia, her mother, and her step-father, drove off she knew not where. It was the first ride Letitia ever had that she knew off [sic]. And now when Letitia again recollects, she finds herself out doors at play, in front of an old brown house, with a flight of old brown steps, a woman comes to the door, she says, Letitia, your mother is dying. In an instant Letitia was at the foot of her mother's bed. She jumps, she screams, she cries, Oh! mother, what shall I do, I shall have no one to take care of me. Her mother extends her hand, the last breath is departing, she dies, and poor little Letitia is left an orphan.

Oh! Death, thou grim and cruel monster, how terrific thou must be in thy appearance, to frighten the infant-imagination at thy approach.

THE FIRST STAGE OF LIFE.
No. 2
BY MRS. M. W. STEWART.

"I WILL take care of you," said a woman who was standing by the bedside, taking Letitia by the hand, "I will take care of you, if no one else will." And she tried to soothe her aching heart and her throbbing bosom, and the poor little orphan began to dry up her tears.

---

[7] Originally printed as "pay."

Aunt Sally, for that was the name of Letitia's new aunt,[8] began to be very busy in making arrangements to lay her mother out, and among the articles collected for that purpose, the only thing that attracts her attention, is a pair of white cotton stockings, the first pair she ever saw in her life. And the next morning she steals into the room softly, uncovers her mother's face, takes the cents from her eyes, opens the lid, to try to bring her to life, sees they won't stay open, replaces the cents, kisses her clay-cold cheek, then leaves the room. It was the last time that she ever saw her mother, that she knows of.

And now the scene changes, and Letitia sees herself all dressed in black, the first black she ever saw in her life. And her step-father takes her by the hand, and they go, she knows not where, until they come to a house, the outside surrounded by a very large number of men, all dressed in black, and the inside crowded with women, all dressed in black, and by the light of her infant vision, it appears they had to sit in each other's laps. And then a tall man stood up, with a gown on: he must have been a minister, and he had something in his hand, it must have been a book, and then sweet sounds vibrated through Letitia's ears, the first she ever heard.[9] They must have sung a hymn. And then the tall man said something, she knows not what it was; it must have been a prayer. And then they all walk, she knows not where, the blue sky over their heads, and the brown earth, under their feet, until they came to a large hilly space, the hills covered with a little short, green grass here, and the naked earth there. And they walk until they come to the side of a fence. They stop; but her mind is wandering; she sees not what they are doing, till her eye catches a glimpse of a long, narrow space of fresh earth. She knows not what it is; but it must have been her mother's grave. And she turns away with her [step-]father, unconscious of her loss. And they all turn away, and leave Letitia's mother there to sleep, until Gabriel shall step one foot upon the earth and the other upon the sea, and swear by Him that liveth forever and ever, that time shall be no longer.

And oh, will Letitia recognise her mother, amid contending elements, when the sea is roaring, the earth quaking, the rocks rending, the graves opening, the dead arising, the the [sic] world on fire? Oh, will she have a part in the first resurrection, and is her name written in the Lamb's book of life?

---

[8] Aunt Sally is not actually related to Letitia but is called "Aunt" as a term of endearment and chosen kinship.

[9] Letitia's parents were not regular churchgoers, this passage suggests. See "The Proper Training of Children" in Stewart, 186–190 for Stewart's insistence on Christianity in childrearing and early education.

And will Letitia and her mother be caught up with God's elect from the four winds of heaven, to meet that innumerable throng, out of every nation and kindred, and tongue and people, who have come up out of great tribulation and washed their robes and made them white in the blood of the Lamb?

O! thou chiefest among ten thousand, the one altogether lovely. Thou bright and morning star, Thou only knowest.

THE FIRST STAGE OF LIFE.
No. 3
BY MRS. M. W. STEWART.

"Thou shalt by no means afflict my fatherless child. If you afflict them, and they cry unto me, I will surely hear their cry."

This command was among one of the first given to Moses, by God, on the mount. No doubt but what God saw, at that early period of time, and through all coming ages, the forlorn and helpless condition of the widow and the orphan, and, therefore, has ever made those the objects of his peculiar care who put their trust in him.

But to my subject. Letitia turned away from her mother's grave, with her [step-]father and others, but she knew not where they went; but the next day her aunt Sally took her somewhere, she knew not where; but the blue sky was over her head, and the brown earth was under her feet, and it appeared as if there was an old barn there, but no other buildings around. And Aunt Sally told Letitia that the tall man spoken of previously, was her cousin, and that he wanted to carry her off, and that she wanted to hide her, so that he could not get her. Letitia knew no better. She went into the barn, and her aunt covered he[r][10] up in the hay, in the box under the manger, and then left her, and the poor child went to sleep. It is not known how long she slept, but when she awoke her aunt was standing beside her, and told her she was rejoiced to see her open her eyes, for she thought she was dead. Search was made for Letitia, but she could nowhere be found, and the gentleman was obliged to go and leave her, who was afterwards ascertained to be a distinguished man of God. Aunt Sally became housekeeper for Letitia's step-father. And nothing much transpired till about one year after, when word was brought to Letitia that her [step-]father was dead, for she was not at home at the time.

---

[10] Originally printed as "het."

Thus Letitia was cast upon the cold charities of the world, with no one to care for her but her adopted aunt, and she was incapable of training her up as she ought to have bee[n].[11] However, she put her out in a family where they had one son, and he frightened her almost to death by telling her about the devil.[12] Letitia had never heard anything of the kind before, and she made those who had the charge of her afterwards an unaccountable sight of trouble in consequence. As it has been asserted that infants, birds and flowers retain the native innocence they possessed before man's fall, so Letitia was as artless and innocent as her sinful nature would allow her to be. She did not as yet know right from wrong. She was scarce six years old, but it appears that her intellect began to unfold and ripen, and she could recollect of picking up pears and apples under the trees, with Mr. Harvey Stanton, for he was the one that delighted to frighten her so.

But her Aunt Sally did not permit her to stay there long, for she took her away, and the child became almost a wandering gypsy, for her aunt had no settled home, and she taught Letitia all kinds of naughtiness, and became very unkind and cruel to her, and went away and left her in the street, without home and without friends. But Letitia did not cry unto God in her distress; she did not know he was; she had never been taught anything about him. But God knew who Letitia was, and directed her infant steps to an old man called Uncle Pete, and he told her to call on a certain lady and gentleman, and tell them that her aunt had gone off and left her in the street, and that she had no father or mother. She did so, and the lady and gentleman took the little stranger under their charge; and when her Aunt Sally came after her, they would not let her go. And now Letitia entered upon a new career. She was taught about God, to read, to pray, and was catechised; but she was almost a ruined child, she was so bad, and she told the other children in the family what Mr. Harvey had told her about the devil, and it was as much as the family could do to undo the evil that had been done, and pacify their minds.

Letitia spent her summers in working about the house, weeding the flower beds, and in going over the hedge, when her work was done, to pick

---

[11] Originally printed as "beeu."

[12] Letitia is hired out as a domestic to another family, most likely but not necessarily a white family. Orphaned, impoverished children across race were regularly subject to the intertwined practices of child indenture, domestic labor, and foster care. Yet the atmosphere of chattel slavery and its legacies exacerbated the experience for black children, even in non-slaveholding states. Harriet Wilson's semi-autobiographical novel *Our Nig* (1859) provides the definitive account from the period. Stewart was an orphan and put out to a family at about the same age as Leticia is; this suggests the story might be autobiographical.

strawberries, blackberries and whortleberries,[13] and in the short summer evenings used to sing and dance, and play till bed-time. And once Letitia robbed a bird's nest, but she was told it was so wrong, she never did so again. And in the fall she used to ramble in the woods during leisure hours, to pick up chestnuts and walnuts, and in winter her time was employed in knitting, spinning, and sliding on the ice—so much of a boy girl[14] was she, that she used to try to make sleds to slide on—and trying to see how nice she could put up the kitchen when the family were out visiting.

Letitia never liked to work very hard, and when she had to work harder than she felt disposed, she would cry, and make such a fuss, that they would send her to bed, or somewhere else, to get rid of her noise. Letitia was very fond of making boquets [sic] of the humble, modest blue violets in spring.

And now I must bring my story to a close, and the sequel is, that we must never despise the day of small things. And to show that the poorest little ragged boy may become an ambassador for Christ, and the pensive little maiden a mother in Israel. The first religious desire of Letitia was to be a good girl; and from being one of the most abject and despised, she became one of the most caressed and admired among her associates. And the last time I heard from her she was like a tree planted in the house of my God, towering like some of the tall cedars of Lebanon, considering all things as loss compared to the excellency of Jesus Christ—soaring aloft, as it were, on eagles' wings, amid the stars, to a city out of sight, whose builder and whose maker is God, leaving the world, with its pomps and vanities, beneath. Thus showing that the Lord He is God, for He setteth up one and putteth down another, and taketh the beggar from the dunghill, and setteth him among the princes.[15]

---

[13] Huckleberries.

[14] Letitia's active play and participation in masculine-coded sports leads Stewart to a phrase that resonates with the figure of the "tomboy."

[15] Stewart's emphasis on spiritual greatness arising from poverty and humility reflects her claims about African Americans' unique spiritual capacity for piety arising from their suffering.

24

Sufferings During the War

CHAPTER I.

It was on a beautiful Sunday morning in the month of—, in the year of—[1], between the hours of 10 and 11 o'clock. The bells were ringing; the people were going to and fro, and the officers were riding the streets with white scarfs on their arms. News had just reached Baltimore that the rebels had encamped five miles from the city. The churches were assembled, but were soon dismissed. All was commotion. Everybody who could think of such a thing was on the eve of flying.

> "And what are you going to do?" said a young lady to me.
> "O," said I; "I shall go with Mr. and Mrs.—."
> "But they may not want you to go with them," said the young lady.
> "Then I will go with so and so," I replied.
> "And perhaps they might not want you to go with them," replied she sarcastically.
> I answered indignantly: "O, God will take care of me, if He sends an angel to do it!"

And God did take care of me; for an order was passed that none of the poor people need pay their rent; so the money I had saved to pay my rent I took and paid my way to Washington.

Having lost my position at Williamsburg, Long Island, and hearing the colored people were more religious and God-fearing in the South, I wended my way to Baltimore in 1852. But I found all was not gold that glistened; and when I saw the want of means for the advancement of the common English branches, with no literary resources for the improvement of the mind

---

[1] Most likely September 1862, when the Confederate army launched its Maryland Campaign which culminated in the Battle of Antietam. Under federal martial law and still a slaveholding state, Maryland's populace was divided between Union and Confederate sympathies and the fears of secession were omnipresent.

scarcely, I threw myself at the foot of the Cross, resolving to make the best of a bad bargain. And there I lay; and then arose, in the strength of the Lord and in the power of His might, wrote my programme, printed and issued my circulars stating I would open school and would teach reading, writing, spelling, mental and practical arithmetic, and whatever other studies called for.

Not knowing the prices, I found myself teaching every branch for 50 cents per month, until informed by another teacher that no writing was taught for less than $1 per month. Bought wit is the dearest wit. I have never been very shrewd in money matters; and being classed as a lady among my race all my life, and never exposed to any hardship, I did not know how to manage. I had been teaching in New York and Williamsburg, and had the means of always paying my way. But when I came to teach a pay school I found the difference. But God promised that my bread and water should be sure; and having food and raiment I was content. I would make enough just to supply my wants for the time being, but not a dollar over. I did not make any charge for wood and coal. And always had that refined sentiment of delicacy about me that I could not bear to charge for the worth of my labor. If any loss was to be sustained the loss was always on my side, and not on the side of the parent or the scholar. But toward the commencement of the war times began to be hard, and I began to be poor, and had to resort to exhibitions and festivals to pay my rent;[2] and, getting sick, became discouraged. I went to a colored gentleman (a man of influence) and to a lady friend and stated my condition, telling the amount of rent I owed; and they expressed their sympathy for me in strong terms, and said if I would be willing to have it put on the programme that I was poor, they would get up an entertainment for my benefit. I consented.

They got up the festival with the help of others; made $300; gave me $30 to pay my rent; paid expenses, then divided the remainder among themselves, and then laughed ready to kill themselves to think what a fool they had made of me. I never noticed it, but quietly went on and did the best I could. They flourished like the green bay tree for several years, enjoying the good things of this life. But lo! they passed away and their places were no more to be

---

[2] It is probable that the need to raise money at exhibitions and festivals led to the publication of Stewart's 1860 "The Proper Training of Children" in Stewart, 186–190, which was originally delivered at a literary festival.

found. They left no sweet-smelling savor around them, no fragrance, no poor to embalm and bless their memory

> Little acts of kindness
> And little deeds of love.[3]

The children of this world are wiser in their generation than the children of light, sayeth the Scripture. I never could get along like some people, and was always struggling to keep my head above water; but I could never get money enough to carry me home, and would not go unless I could go looking as well in appearance as I did when I came away. Many were the bitter tears I shed to think I had left all my friends at the North and had come here among strangers. Oh! many were the tears I shed! But it was no use to cry for spilt milk; so I went on serving the Lord, turning neither to the right hand nor to the left; always attending church and Sunday school, trying to be useful in some way. It must be that I was kept by the mighty power of God through faith unto salvation, or I never could have surmounted my difficulties. I had brought letters of introduction to the minister of Saint James' Church, and had attended the services of the church regularly, but becoming dissatisfied, left and worshipped at Mount Calvary, and was never treated better in my life during my short stay among them, and was referred from that church to Trinity at Washington; and one of the motives that induced me to come to this city was to seek a habitation for my God to dwell in, not dreaming that I should ever own a house adapted to that purpose.

CHAPTER II.

During the rebellion, just before the candidacy of General McClellan to the presidency of the United States the different denominations of Christians issued an edict among themselves that they would establish their own schools and supply their own teachers. It was the general topic of conversation among all classes. Mrs. Stewart, going into her grocery store, heard the proprietor say to a gentleman referring to her, "She is an Episcopalian, and will lose her

---

[3] From Julia Abigail Fletcher Carney's "Little Things" (1845), a popular poem for children.

situation." Upon inquiry she found that the denomination of Christians to which she belonged were unpopular with the Government, and were going to have nothing to do with the colored school. Without further inquiry Mrs. Stewart replied: "Well, before I will give up my religious sentiments for dollars and cents I will beg my bread from door to door." And she did almost beg her bread, as the sequel will show.

At the September term the teachers of several denominations assembled in their respective churches and received their appointments, while our heroine was left out in the cold. There were four other distinguished Episcopalians, one gentleman and three ladies. But they hid their light under a bushel and kept on the side of dollars and cents. The weather began to grow cool, and our heroine rented a room and paid two months' rent in advance; and then went to work and set herself about trying to get scholars, but met with poor success, not getting enough to pay expenses. The weather growing colder, the funds low, encountering cross looks, and sometimes unkind words, the distress of our heroine became extreme, so she called upon Judge Day,[4] and he afforded her present relief for the time being.

Under all circumstances our heroine maintained a genteel appearance, and always attended the services of the church regularly every Sunday; but was a stranger in the city. Becoming acquainted with a colored lady belonging to the church of the Ascension, our heroine related her condition to her. The lady recommended her to go and see her minister, the Rev. Dr. Hall.[5]

"Oh! What can he do?" said the distressed one.
"Nothing beats a trial," was the reply.

So, in despair, after much persuasion, the two went together to see Dr. Hall; were kindly received; the tale of woe was told; Dr. Hall said he had no schools. The decision was the school was to be continued, if the supplicant could get scholars enough to supply her with food, which was almost doubtful. A Sunday school was to be established and a room rented at the expense of the church. The room was rented; a prayer meeting was formed; a Sunday school was established; a night school was opened, and a day school

---

[4] Likely George E. H. Day, a manager of the National Freedmen's Relief Association.
[5] Rev. Dr. Charles Hall, Episcopal minister of the Epiphany church in Washington, D.C. After the war, he helped establish an Episcopal church for black congregants in Foggy Bottom, which Stewart describes in Chapter IV. St Mary's Foggy Bottom later employed the theologian and political philosopher Alexander Crummell, friend and recommender to Stewart, as rector.

continued. Finally Christmas drew near; a five dollar bill was presented; a tree was purchased and dressed; benches were sent from the Epiphany. Forty persons were present at the celebration of the Saviour's birth. Dr. Hall was there, your heroine was there, and only one colored gentleman there to represent the colored Episcopalians in this city. This Christmas eve came on Saturday night. Notices were read in the different churches and put up on the east side of the house so they could be seen. Yet your heroine was a sufferer, with scarce the necessaries of life. The say was: "She belongs to white folks' church, let them take care of her." The curtain falls thus and ends the scene.

But to return to my trip to Washington. I had prayed to the Lord that there might be standing by the cars some lad to conduct me where I wanted to go, for I was a perfect stranger. And upon my arrival, there stood a young man looking as if he wished he had something to do; so when I alighted from the cars I went up to him and asked him if he was acquainted in the city. He answered yes. I told him if he would conduct me to where I wanted to go I would pay him for it; so we went on and passed the White House. I was told on my way that Washington had become a perfect Paradise for the colored people since President Lincoln had taken his seat.

I went to the city soon after the President had taken his seat. It was very dreary and dull, but I went on, trusting in the Lord, and found the minister's family I was looking for, and was welcomed and made myself useful in the family until next spring. There was a lady, Mrs. Keckley, I knew, formerly from Baltimore, who proved to be an ardent friend to me in my great emergency which took place afterward.[6] I also had a letter of introduction to another lady, Miss M. F. Kiger,[7] and got along very nicely, having no complaints to make, and was in the Nineteenth Street Baptist Church when the Emancipation Proclamation was read.[8] Spring came; the sun began to shine and the birds began to sing. I began to think about opening a school in the lower part of the city. And as I had promised to fight under Christ's banner against the world, the flesh, and the devil, and to be his faithful soldier and follower unto my life's end, I began to consider which church I should join.

---

[6] Almost certainly Elizabeth Keckley, a formerly enslaved woman who became a dressmaker and confidante to Mary Todd Lincoln. Keckley founded the Contraband Relief Association ("contraband" was colloquial at the time for escaped or rescued enslaved people), which grew into an important freedmen's relief and mutual aid society during the years she knew Stewart. Keckley later published a memoir titled *Behind the Scenes: Or, Thirty Years a Slave and Four Years in the White House* (1868), which was highly controversial for its discussion of the Lincoln family's private lives.

[7] Kiger was a black public-school teacher.

[8] A black congregation that is also the oldest Baptist church in Washington, D.C.

The minister of Trinity Church, Rev. Dr. Syle, was so much in sympathy with the South that an objection was raised by some of Episcopalian friends from Baltimore.[9] The colored people were not altogether please with the rector of St. John's Church, Rev. Dr. Payne, before Dr. Lewis' times; and although Dr. Hall was in sympathy with the South, he was considered the best man of the three; in sympathy with the South because he had resided there; it was thought natural that he should be. So I called upon Dr. Hall and placed myself under his parochial care. I saw by the papers Dr. Hall was very much spoken against. I said: "Doctor, the papers speak very hard of you." "Oh!" said he, "I do not read the papers." He lost is church; it was used for Government purposes. Having just put myself under his Christian care, I followed his flock to Williard's Hall, and there worshipped until he was against restored to his church. In the meantime I rented rooms, opened a school, and got along splendidly, until solicited by Judge Day and others to throw in my influence with theirs for the common good, and I should be paid by the month. I did so, and did it to my sorrow, as the sequel will show.

CHAPTER III.

But to return to the Christmas tree. The celebration of the Saviour's birth was celebrated in my school-room on Saturday night, which was rented of a man and his wife living in the same house; and the man said I could my Christmas as I liked. On the Monday evening after, he said he was going to have music and dancing. I was horrified at the thought, and made arrangements to leave the house for the night, and locked up my room and went elsewhere. The next morning I met an Irish lady. She said to me:

"Why don't you rent this nice little dwelling-house[?] It will cost you but little more than you pay now, and you ought not to live with such folks?"

"Why?" said I; "I did not know that you would rent the house to me."

"Yes I will," said she.

---

[9] Rev. E. W. Syle resigned after refusing to read a pro-Union prayer. The dominance of white pastors in Episcopal churches, including Southern and proslavery ministers, was an issue in many of the churches Stewart mentioned. Hall and other ministers, particularly pro-South ministers, had their churches commandeered by federal troops for various uses, especially housing injured troops.

"I shall want prayer meeting, Sunday school, day school, and night school," said I.

"Oh," said she, "you can do just as you like, and have no one to trouble you."

So I moved forthwith. The house contained two fine-sized rooms, one up stairs and one down, and I always kept the house clean and in order. Every morning at nine o'clock it was ready for school, except Saturday; that day was devoted in arranging for the Sabbath. Every Sunday morning the house looked inviting for the scholars—the floor, the benches, the steps, and windows were always as clean as they could be. The scholars and teachers would come and work; would commence and end in time to get to church in season. I recollect the prayer meetings commenced under very adverse circumstances. Before I could move into the other house nothing was inviting. I was poor in the extreme; my stove was very small—not large enough to warm the room. I do not know how I did get along and where I got food to eat and fire to keep me and the children warm, what few I had; yet I was compelled to work after school hours, trying to get scholars to come either day or night, and people to come to prayer meeting at night; and such was my extreme poverty that objection was raised to my having them at my room. No contributions were made to buy wood and coal. But Dr. Hall did his part; he paid the rent, supplied the books. I had only five scholars in the day and as many or more at night. And that whole work was supported from these scholars I had night and day.

Punctuality was always the life of business with me. One bitter cold night I prepared for prayer meeting, and made everything appear as cheerful as I could, but it began to grow so late I began to think nobody was coming. I had been after the only colored gentleman who took any interest in the matter, but he could not or would not come, although I told him Dr. Hall would be present; so I returned to my lone room disappointed and sad. The bench was close to the stove, and I believe my floor was covered with an old carpet I had bought when I first went to Baltimore; however, the fire looked dull, so I thought I would go and see the lady of the Ascension. But I had not gone far before I met Dr. Hall. The walking was very slippery, the ground was covered with snow and ice, it was a cold sleet. I thought Dr. Hall surely was a good man, or he would not be willing to come to so poor a person's house as were the people of whom I rented. I told him no one had come to the prayer meeting. He returned home, and called to tell the lady of the Ascension of my sorrow and disappointment.

CHAPTER IV

But to my new house. I cannot tell when the appointment was made to change the prayer meetings to the different houses of the members. But I do know that when I had my prayer meeting the room would be nearly full, for I would go all around among the people and beg them to come; and when the others had their prayer meetings they would not have any strangers, only their lone selves, and they did not appear to be so much better off than I was, either.

There was another dear, Christian brother who fell in with us and invited us to his house to prayer meeting. He belonged to our faith and order, anyhow. And when we met, the lady of the house and the rest of the family retired and left the gentleman of the house, her husband, Dr. Hall, and a few others of us in a great big parlor, nicely fitted up, with a good fire, to carry on the prayer meeting by ourselves. I felt embarrassed for Dr. Hall at that time. He said he had a Colored Church South, with four hundred communicants, and he wanted to get up one here for the colored people. And no matter whom he was in sympathy with he was the principal man in laying the foundation of Saint Mary's Church. In the first place it was chiefly composed of females. But our representative brother was always with us, and by degrees others fell in. The prayer meeting and the Sunday school were under the Church of the Epiphany. Dr. Hall paid $10 toward the rent of the house, supplied the school with books and benches. I was to pay $2. Dr. Hall paid $10 for the one room. After I moved, the sisters contributed small sums toward getting wood and coal for Sunday school, but not much. My house was in the parish of the Trinity Church. Dr. Hall had to ask permission of the then rector of Trinity Church. I was the bearer of the note. So they both co-operated together. The prayer meeting was at my house once a week; and so one minister would come one evening one week and the other minister one evening the next week. Thus the prayer meetings at my house were conducted by the rector of the Epiphany and the rector of Trinity. All went on well for a while, and it thus went so far that a proposition was to be made to the vestry of Trinity to let the people have the small church on the corner of N and Sixth streets.

And the rector of Trinity said I could teach school there; but an objection was made, for fear the boys would throw stones. And Dr. Hall said that if the colored people would not have a church in that part of the city, he would have one at the west end, and he would dare any boys to throw stones at any work he had anything to do with. It was afterward sold to the Lutherans. It was an elegant little church; it belonged to Trinity. A lady said to me: "When we were getting up our church, we met in the same room for one year, and then we moved in a body; but when you go from house to house, half of the persons do not know where the different places of meeting is."

Lent was about to commence. And the rector of Trinity was telling us how we must keep Lent and use a great deal of self-denial about our food, &c. We had thirty-two present when the notice was given for the next meeting. I told the audience what the lady had said, and asked them if they did not think it would be best to meet in one place until the body became consolidated. It was now in its embryo state. The lady of the Ascension, and one of the ladies of the Epiphany, and I do not know how many more, were highly incensed, and went right straight to Dr. Hall and told him I wanted all the praise and credit for getting up the work; and cast my name out as evil all over the city as far as their circle extended; and broke up the prayer meetings. Dr. Hall said he would never come to my house again, and withdrew his rent money. He never came to my house again. No tongue can portray my agony of mind. I did not know what I should do, or how I should get along. I do not recollect whether my school increased in numbers or not. Still I kept on, turning neither to the right hand nor to the left. Ash Wednesday came. I went to church just as if nothing had happened Oh! What a day that was. If I had had the wings of a dove I would indeed have flown to the utmost part of the earth. But I prayed God to show Dr. Hall in a vision that I was a clean woman before the Lord; and I believe he did, as the end will show. Be that as it may, I made up my mind twice. Rather than to ask for any further aid I would starve to death. But God prevented it both times. The say would be: "Don't say you are an Episcopalian." And at last I went to see the Rev. Dr. Garnet of the Presbyterian Church. He blamed me for belonging to a set of unfeeling Christians. But he gave me one dollar and sent me to Dr. Channing, a Unitarian minister.[10] I told Dr. Channing the circumstances in great distress of mind, walking the floor backward and forward. So he told me to come to him when the month

---

[10] William Henry Channing, a Unitarian minister who spent much of his life in England. Channing was a Christian socialist whose work helped shape transcendentalism.

was up and he would give me money to pay my rent or to go to my friends in New York. I went home. There were persons that were giving out to the poor. I did not go, for fear it would lessen the dignity of the Episcopal Church for it to be known that one of her members had to beg. It was a bitter cold night I had to go and get some coal. I met a man and begged him to carry it for me to my house, for the cold almost overpowered me.[11]

There were only two male members of the church that I knew anything about. They were like Peter; they stood afar off to see the end. They seldom attended the church; and there were only a handful of us poor lone colored women followers of the cross. More like the outcasts of the house of Israel than anything else. The proscription of the church at that time was awful. Sometimes she administered her communion to the blacks when they were at the table of the Lord, and sometimes she passed them by when they were at the table. My soul became filled with a holy indignation. I complained.[12] And the result was the organization of Saint Mary's Church. Still I clung to the church. And had I left, no one would have cared. But by grace I overcame; and to-day am one of those that John saw in a vision on the Isle of Patmos having harps in their hands. I have suffered martyrdom for the church in one sense; and rejoice that I now feel that I have a home not only in the Protestant Episcopal Church, but in the Holy Church Catholic throughout the world.

CHAPTER V

After I went to see the Rev. Dr. Garnet I think I began to get along better. But meeting the young lady (Miss M. F. Kiger) I brought the letter of introduction to, and looking poor in my apparel, I burst into tears and wept in the bitterness of my soul, and told her I did not think I should ever get along in Washington. She looked as if she pitied me from the bottom of her heart. I do not know what she said. But in three weeks' time I began to get along. All

---

[11] Stewart was about sixty years old at the time.
[12] Although Stewart moves pass this conflict quickly, her activism against racial segregation in Washington's Episcopalian church was vital to the establishment of St. Mary's Foggy Bottom, the first Black Episcopalian church in the city. St. Mary's quickly became an important hub of black social and political life in the region.

this suffering was in lent. Two Presbyterian ladies, Mrs. Slade[13] and Keckley, came to my help; and they did not say "Be ye warmed and be ye fed" without affording the means; and one of them was the lady I was acquainted with in Baltimore. The other was a resident here. A lady from the John Westey, Mrs. Tidball, was a staunch friend, and sent her child to school to me and paid in advance. The spring opened; my school increased. I went to see Dr. Channing at the time appointed. I told him I was beginning to get along so well I did not wish to leave Washington just then. He gave me $15. And a colored gentleman told me I must learn to manage, and said he wanted to pay my room upstairs. He paid me $6. I paid my rent; bought me a new shawl; went to the Church of the Epiphany every Sunday; kept my Sunday school, my day school, and my night school.

Dr. Hall sent the lady after me that had helped to make the fuss, but I think she had made an apology previously. And as I had committed my cause to Him who judgeth righteously, I said nothing about the past. She said Dr. Hall wished me to notify as many colored people as I could to come to the Church of the Epiphany on a certain evening named. He wanted to organize Saint Mary's Church. So I and thirteen night scholars went, and Dr. Hall said he would have the church organized right away. Two colored gentlemen present volunteered their services to help me teach the Sunday school, in order to forward the work. And when the church was consecrated we carried with us forty scholars and $2.50 the children had saved. Dr. Hall and Dr. Lewis were both waiting for us. And the services began after we entered the house.

Thus endeth my sorrows for the present.[14]

---

[13] Possibly the wife of William Slade, a steward and assistant for Abraham Lincoln and leader in D.C. black Presbyterian life. William Slade's employment in the White House would have overlapped with Elizabeth Keckley's, so her association with Mrs. Slade would be highly plausible.

[14] The 1879 edition of *Meditations* was published after her successful claim for her late husband's benefits for his service in the War of 1812. Stewart died shortly after its publication in December 1879 at the age of seventy-six.

Selected Bibliography

Abdy, Edward Strutt. *Journal of a Residence and Tour in The United States of North America, From April, 1833, to October, 1834* Vol. III. London: John Murray, 1835.
Beeching, Barbara J. "African Americans and Native Americans in Hartford 1636–1800: Antecedents of Hartford's Nineteenth Century Black Community Antecedents of Hartford's Nineteenth Century." Hartford, CT: Trinity College, 1993.
Beeching, Barbara J. *Hopes and Expectations: The Origins of the Black Middle Class in Hartford.* Albany: State University of New York Press, 2017.
Beirne, Francis. *The Amiable Baltimoreans.* 1951; Baltimore: Johns Hopkins University Press, 1994.
Cooper, Brittney. *Beyond Respectability: The Intellectual Thought of Race Women.* Champaign, IL: University of Illinois Press, 2017.
Cooper, Valerie C. *Word, Like Fire: Maria Stewart, the Bible, and the Rights of African Americans.* Charlottesville: University of Virginia Press, 2011.
Douglass, Frederick. *Autobiographies.* New York: The Library of America, 1994.
Easton, Hosea. *A Treatise on the Intellectual Character and Civil and Political Condition of the Colored People of the U. States; And the Prejudice Exercised toward Them: With a Sermon on the Duty of the Church to Them.* Boston: Knapp, 1837.
Fields, Barbara J. *Slavery and Freedom on the Middle Ground: Maryland during the Nineteenth Century.* New Haven, CT: Yale University Press, 1985.
Glaude, Eddie S. *Exodus!: Religion, Race, and Nation in Early Nineteenth-Century Black America.* Chicago: University of Chicago Press, 2000.
Grimke, Angelina. *Appeal to Christian Women of the South.* New York: American Anti-Slavery Society, 1836.
Harrison, Robert. *Washington During Civil War and Reconstruction: Race and Radicalism.* Cambridge: Cambridge University Press, 2011.
Hatch, Nathan O. *The Democratization of American Christianity.* New Haven, CT: Yale University Press, 1989.
Hinks, Peter P. *To Awaken My Afflicted Brethren: David Walker and the Problem of Antebellum Slave Resistance.* University Park: Pennsylvania State University Press, 1997.
Horton, James O., and Lois E. Horton. *Black Bostonians: Family Life and Community Struggle in the Antebellum North.* New York: Holmes & Meier, 1999.
Hutchinson, Enoch, and Stephen Remington, eds. *The Baptist Memorial and Monthly Record,* Vol. 8. New York: Hatch, 1849.
Jefferson, Thomas. *Notes on the State of Virginia.* 1787.
Lee, Jarena. *The Life and Religious Experience of Jarena Lee, Giving an Account of Her Call to Preach the Gospel.* Philadelphia, 1849.
Levesque, George A. *Black Boston: African American Life and Culture in Urban America, 1750–1860.* New York: Garland, 1994.

Lindhorst, Marie. "Politics in a Box: Sarah Mapps Douglass and the Female Literary Association, 1831–1833." *Pennsylvania History: A Journal of Mid-Atlantic Studies* 65, no. 3 (Summer 1998): 263–278.

McHenry, Elizabeth. *Forgotten Readers: Recovering the Lost History of African American Literary Societies*. Durham, NC: Duke University Press, 2002.

Payne, Daniel A. *History of the African Methodist Episcopal Church*. Nashville: Publishing House of the A.M.E. Sunday-School Union, 1897.

Payne, Daniel A. *Recollections of Seventy Years*. Nashville: Publishing House of the A.M.E. Sunday-School Union, 1897.

Rael, Patrick. *Black Identity and Black Protest in the Antebellum North*. Chapel Hill, NC: University of North Carolina Press, 2002.

Picquet, Louisa, and Hiram Mattison, 1811–1868. *Louisa Picquet, the Octoroon, or, Inside Views of Southern Domestic Life*. New York: 1861.

Shulman, George M. *American Prophecy: Race and Redemption in American Political Culture*. Minneapolis: University of Minnesota Press, 2008.

Stewart, Maria. *Meditations from the Pen of Mrs. Maria W. Stewart*. Washington, DC: Enterprise Publishing Company, 1879.

Stewart, Maria W., and Marilyn Richardson. *Maria W. Stewart, America's First Black Woman Political Writer: Essays and Speeches*. Bloomington: Indiana University Press, 1987.

Truth, Sojourner. *The Narrative of Sojourner Truth*. Boston, 1850.

Walker, David, and Peter P. Hinks. *David Walker's Appeal to the Coloured Citizens of the World*. University Park: Pennsylvania State University Press, 2000.

Waters, Kristin. *Maria W. Stewart and the Roots of Black Political Thought*. Jackson: University of Mississippi Press, 2022.

Index

For the benefit of digital users, indexed terms that span two pages (e.g., 52–53) may, on occasion, appear on only one of those pages.

Acts 8:21, 203
"Address at African Masonic Hall" (Stewart)
   on African origins of civilization, 182
   on blacks as objects of pity, 180
   on black self-determination through strict moral virtue, 183–84
   on blacks' need to overcome their fears, 181
   on building of schools and colleges for blacks, 184–85
   colonization movement opposed in, 184–85
   on hypocrisy and Christianity, 182–83
"An Address Delivered Before the Afric-American Female Intelligence Society of Boston" (Stewart), 87–92
Afric-American Female Intelligence Society of Boston (AAFI), xxxi–xxxii
African Baptist Church (Boston), xi, 169n.10
African Dorcas Association, xxxii–xxxiii
African Meeting House (Boston), xi
African Religious Society of Hartford, xiv–xv
Allen, Richard, xix–xx, 199–200, 199n.4, 202, 206–7
Appeal to the Christian Women of the South (Grimké)
   on the Bible and slavery, 25–26, 27
   on Catholicism and the Bible, 28
   on Christian fellowship with Southern white women, 23–24
   Declaration of Independence cited in, 24–25
   on imperative of emancipating slaves, 29–30
   on Northern attitudes toward slavery in the South, 24–25
   on obeying God rather than man, 29–30
   on sinful nature of slaveholding, 24–25, 28, 29–30
   on women's responsibility to ensure humane treatment of slaves, 28
   on women's responsibility to pray about slavery, 27–28
   on women's responsibility to read about slavery, 27
   on women's responsibility to speak about slavery, 28
   on women's responsibility to teach slaves, 28–29
Appeal to the Coloured Citizens of the World (Walker)
   African American political theory and, xvi
   on African origins of Greek culture, 112–13, 112n.4
   anti-Catholicism and, 113–14, 113n.6
   appeal to men of color to enlighten their brethren, 120–21
   on colored people in large cities, 114–15
   on education of colored people, 121–24
   on Haiti, 113–14, 113n.6
   on ignorance as cause of wretchedness of colored people, 112–24
   on Jefferson and racial theory, 116–20
   on Punic Wars, 112–13
   satisfaction with low employment denounced in, 85n.14, 120–21
   on slavery as cause of miseries of colored people, 109–10
   thwarted slave escape (1829) recounted in, 115–20

Appeal to the Coloured Citizens of the World (Walker) (*cont.*)
  on "wretched condition" of colored people in the United States, 107, 114–15
"Aunt Chloe's Politics" (Watkins Harper), 223

Baltimore (Maryland), xxxiv–xxxvii, 273, 277–78
Bascom, John, 62, 62n.12
Beecher, Henry Ward, 158n.13
Bethel African Methodist Episcopal Church (Baltimore, MD), xxxiv–xxxv
"The Black Woman of the South: Her Neglects and Her Needs" (Crummell)
  on black women school teachers, 49
  on the colored population's advantages over the black population, 44–46, 45n.1
  on descriptions of black women's tenderness, 50–53
  on establishment of sisterhoods among black women of the South, 53–55
  on family separations among slaves, 47
  on marriage-like relationships between masters and slaves, 45
  proposed establishment industrial schools for black women in Southern states and, 55–58
  on slavery's legacy for black women in post-Civil War era, 47–49
  on slave women as victims of sexual assault, 46
  on women's elevation in American society, 44
Blake, William, 82n.6
Boucicault, Dion, 174n.15
Brune, Frederick W., xxxvii
Butler, Fanny Kemble, 54, 54n.11
Butler, Thomas, 146
Byron, Lord, 65–66

Cain (Book of Genesis), 210–11, 210n.2
Carney, Julia Abigail Fletcher, 275, 275n.3
Cato, 12–17
"Cause of Encouragement" (Stewart), xxix, 177–79
Cennik, John, 202, 202n.7

Channing, William Henry, 50, 50n.6, 281–82, 281n.10
Charlemagne, 65
Chaucer, Geoffrey, 62–63, 63n.14
"The Church's One Foundation" (Stone), 63, 63n.15
Church Street (New York City), 210–12, 210–11n.3
Colored Methodist Episcopal Zion Church (CMEZ, Hartford, CT), xv
"Come Thou Fount of Every Blessing" (Robinson), 201, 201n.5
Congregationalists, 76
Cooper, Anna Julia. *See* "Womanhood: A Vital Element in the Regeneration and Progress of a Race" (Cooper)
Cornish, Samuel, xvii
Crawford, Adair, 13n.3
Crummell, Alexander, xxviii–xxix, xxxi. *See also* "The Black Woman of the South: Her Neglects and Her Needs" (Crummell)
Crumwell, Lucy, xxxii–xxxiii

Daniel 5-8, 201n.6
David (Old Testament king), 190
Day, George E. H., 276, 276n.4
Declaration of Independence, 24–25, 144–45, 147–48
Delany, Martin R., 70
de Staël, Madame (Anne Louise Germaine de Staël-Holstein), 60–61, 60n.7
Dickens, Charles, xxx
Douglass, Frederick, xxxv–xxxvi, 87n.1, 156n.11, 178n.3
Douglass, Sarah Mapps ("Zillah")
  on children's interactions with teachers, 128–29
  colonization movement rejected by, 81n.2
  Female Literary Association and, xxxiii–xxxiv, 126
  message for children who read *The Liberator* from, 133–35
  on Pennsylvania bill regarding migration, 127
  on proposals regarding black emigration from United States, 129

on slave mothers' relationship with their children, 130–31
on violence against female slaves, 131
Dred Scot v. Sanford, 32n.4
The Dunciad (Pope), 12–17, 14n.5
Dymond, Jonathan, 24–25, 25n.5

East Baltimore Mental Improvement Society, xxxv–xxxvi, 87n.1
Easton, Hosea, xv–xvi. See also *A Treatise on the Intellectual Character, and the Civil and Political Condition of the Colored People of the U. States; and the Prejudice Exercised towards Them: With a Sermon on the Duty of the Church to Them* (Easton)
Ecclesiastes 7:27–28, 91, 91n.6
"Elegy Written in a Country Churchyard" (Gray), 84, 84n.12
Emerson, Ralph Waldo, 61, 61n.9, 77
Epictetus, 12–17, 16n.9
Essays on the Principles of Morality and on the Private and Political Rights and Obligations of Mankind (Dymond), 24–25, 25n.5
Esther 4:13-16, 23
"Ethiop" (William J. Wilson), xxx–xxxi, 209–12
Evangeline (Longfellow), 233, 233n.8
Exodus 4:1-12, 206, 206n.11

"Farewell Address to Her Friends in the City of Boston" (Stewart)
conversion narrative in, 94–95, 94n.3
prophecy and, 94–95, 96–97
Saint Paul and, 96
on Stewart's reasons for leaving Boston, xxix, 98
Female Literary Association (FLA), xxxiii–xxxiv
Fields, Barbara, xiv
First Congregational Church (Hartford, CT), xiv–xv
First Regiment South-Carolina Volunteers, 242–43
"The First Stage of Life" (Stewart), xxxv, 266–72

Forten, Charlotte. See "Life on the Sea Islands" (Forten)
Fort Wagner, battle (1863) of, 253–55
Freedom's Journal, xvii–xviii
Fuller, Margaret, 83n.7

Garnet, H. H., 150, 150n.2, 150n.3
Garrison, William Lloyd, xxi–xxii, xxxiii–xxxiv, 94–95, 133n.20, 173–74, 177n.1
Genesis 30:30-43, 140, 140n.6
Gliddon, George R., 50–51, 51n.7
Goldsborough, Asa, xv
Gray, Thomas, 84, 84n.12
Grimké, Angelina. See *Appeal to the Christian Women of the South* (Grimké)
Guizot, François, 61–62, 61n.11

Haiti, 52, 90–91, 90–91n.5, 113–14, 113n.6, 173–74
Hall, Charles, 276–77, 276n.5, 279–81, 283
Hall, Primus, xi
Hall, Prince, 180n.1
Ham (Book of Genesis), 112n.4, 136n.1
Hannibal, 112–13
Hartford (Connecticut), xiv
Hatton, Louise, xxxix
Henry, Elizabeth, xxxi–xxxii
Higginson, Thomas Wentworth, 237–38, 237n.9, 243–44
Homer, 12–18
Howe, Julia Ward, 226n.5
Hunt, James, 50–51, 51n.7
Hunter, Henry, 137–38, 137n.5
Hymns for Those That Seek and Those That Have Redemption in the Blood of Jesus Christ (Charles Wesley), 204, 204n.9

Ignatius de Loyola, 73
Isaiah 65:1-2, 200–1

Jackson, Andrew, 144–46, 181
Jefferson, Thomas. See *Notes on the State of Virginia* (Jefferson)
"Jehovyah, Hallelujah" (hymn), 241
Jeremiah 29, xx, 85n.13

290 INDEX

Joel 2:28, 197
John 1:14, 74–75, 75n.21
John 5:1-8, 24n.3
"John Brown's Body" (hymn), 226, 226n.5, 232–33, 245
Johnson, Fanny, xxxvii
Joshua 9:23, 81n.4
Journal of a Residence on a Georgian Plantation in 1838-1839 (Butler), 54, 54n.11
Judges 13:4, 137–38
Judson, E.Z.C., xxx

Keckley, Elizabeth, 277–78, 277n.6
Kiger, M. F., 277–78, 277n.7, 282–83
Knapp, Isaac, xxi–xxii, 94–95

Ladies Literary Society of New York, xxxi–xxxiv
Lalla Rookh (Moore), 130, 130n.12
"Lecture at Franklin Hall" (Stewart), 81–86
Lee, Jarena. See *The Life and Religious Experience of Jarena Lee* (Lee)
Lee, Richard Henry, 144, 144n.7
"Letter to the People—No.1" (Shadd Cary), 156–59
The Life and Religious Experience of Jarena Lee (Lee)
  conversion narrative in, 198–203
  on Lee's call to preach the gospel, xix–xx, 206–8
  on Lee's childhood as a servant, 197
  on Lee's coming to know Jesus, 202–3
  on Saint Paul, 205–6, 207, 208
  on sanctification of the soul, 203–6
  on Satan, 198, 200–2, 205, 206
  suicidal thoughts in, 200–1
  on women's right to preach, 207–8
"Life on the Sea Islands" (Forten)
  on baptisms among Southern blacks, 246
  on Battle of Fort Wagner (1863), 253–55
  on Beaufort, 225–26
  on black children in liberated territories of the Confederacy, 225–26
  on black hymns at Sea Islands, 226, 228, 229–30, 240–41, 249–50
  on challenges of the Southern climate, 246–47, 253
  on children's singing and shouting, 235–36
  on Christmas celebrations, 239–41
  on Confederate advances near Port-Royal Island, 247–48
  on cruelty of Southern slave owners, 250–51
  on Edisto Island, 251–52
  on Emancipation Day (1863), 242–45
  on fears of Confederates raiding territories liberated by Union troops, 238–39
  on fleas in Sea Island, 253
  on Forten's arrival at Ladies Island, 226–27
  on Forten's arrival at Seaside plantation, 248
  on Forten's house at Oaklands, 227–28, 230–32, 234–35
  on Fourth of July celebrations, 253
  on Hilton Head, 224
  on homes of former white slave owners in Sea Island, 230–32
  on manners in Sea Islands, 234
  on marriages of freed slaves, 237
  on Port-Royal Island, 247
  on praise meetings under slavery, 249
  on Saxton's command in South Carolina during Civil War, 224–25, 224–25n.2, 236–38, 242–43, 244, 245
  on slave escape attempts during Civil War, 242
  on teaching in Sea Islands, 232–33
  on Thanksgiving Day celebrations, 237–38
"The Little Black Boy" (Blake), 82n.6
"Little Things" (Carney), 275, 275n.3
Longfellow, Henry Wadsworth, 233, 233n.8
Louisa Picquet, the Octoroon, or, Inside Views of Southern Domestic Life (Picquet and Mattison)
  on examination and auctioning of slaves for sale, 34–35
  on how one of Louisa's owners was her father, 32

on how one of Louisa's owners was the father of her children, 37
on Louisa being disciplined as a slave, 33
on Louisa being sold and moved as a slave, 32, 33, 34–36
on Louisa's African ancestry, 31, 32
on Louisa's brother, 33, 40–41
on Louisa's conversion to Christianity, 38, 38n.8
on Louisa's helping fugitive slaves, 39
on Louisa's husband, 38–39
on Louisa's inability go to church during slavery, 36
on Louisa's mother's appearance, 33–34
on Louisa's physical appearance, 31
on Louisa's restoring contact with her mother, 39–43
on Louisa's separation from her mother, 36
on Louisa's trying to buy family members out of slavery, 40–41, 42–43
Lowder, Charles, 55n.14
Luke 18:9–14, 201n.6
Luke 19:20, 179n.7

Macaulay, Thomas Babington, 61, 61n.8, 73
Macpherson, James, 125, 125n.1
Massachusetts General Colored Association (MGCA), xvii–xviii
Mattison, Hiram. See *Louisa Picquet, the Octoroon, or, Inside Views of Southern Domestic Life* (Picquet and Mattison)
McKane, Alice Woodby, 132n.18
Meditations from the Pen of Mrs. Maria W. Stewart (Stewart), xxi–xxii, xxxix, 259–61
Michelet, Jules, 51–52, 51n.8
Moore, Thomas, 130, 130n.12
More, Hannah, 130, 130n.14
"Moses in the Bulrushes" (More), 130, 130n.14

National Colored Conventions, 177n.1
"The Negro's Complaint" (Stewart), 263–65

Newman, William, 152–53, 153n.7
New York City, 209–12
Nineteenth Street Baptist Church (Washington DC), 277–78, 277n.8
"No Man Can Hinder Me" (hymn), 226, 226n.4
Notes on the State of Virginia (Jefferson)
on citizenship and naturalization, 9, 11
on criminal law punishments in Virginia, 18–19
on forced migration of emancipated slaves, 12–18
on Homer's reflections on slavery, 12–18
on inheriting slaves, 9–10, 11
on land acquisition, 10–11
on Native Americans, 12–17
on poor assistance in Virginia, 7–8
on public education in Virginia, 19–22
on public library in Virginia, 22
on racial theory, 12–18, 116–20
on slavery in the Roman Empire, 12–18
on transporting slaves convicted of offenses to Africa, 19
on Virginia's political structure, 5–7

The Octoroon (Boucicault), 174n.15
"Open Letter to Frederick Douglass" (Shadd Cary), 150–52
Our Nig (Wilson), 83n.9

Park, Mungo, 51–52, 52n.9
Pattison, Dorothy Wyndlow, 55, 55n.13
Paul, Thomas, xi–xii, 169n.10
Payne, Daniel, xxxiv–xxxv, 49
Pennington, James W.C., 212, 212n.7
Phaedrus, 12–17, 16n.9
Picquet, Louisa. See *Louisa Picquet, the Octoroon, or, Inside Views of Southern Domestic Life* (Picquet and Mattison)
Pilgrims, 85–86, 191
Pilmore, Joseph, 199, 199n.3
Pope, Alexander, 14n.5
"The Proper Training of Children" (Stewart), xxxv, 188–92
Proverbs 27:6, 183n.6
Provincial Freedom newspaper, 152–53, 152n.6

Psalm 8, 25–26
Psalm 10:17-18, 148–49, 149n.12
Psalm 50, 261, 261n.6
Psalm 68:31, 165–66, 165n.3, 177n.2
Psalm 119:18, 24n.4
Psalm 137:6, 92, 92n.7
The Psalms of David (Watts), 89n.2, 190, 190n.6, 198

Ramsey, Elizabeth (mother of Louisa Picquet), 40, 43
Randolph, John, 32, 32n.5
"Religion and the Pure Principles of Morality" (Stewart)
  on the African Baptist Church in Boston, 169, 169n.10
  on Christianity and true happiness, 167–68
  on Christianity and white supremacy doctrine, 164, 172–74
  on contradictions of desire for religious improvement and acceptance of slavery, 169
  on European revolutions, 173–74
  Garrison's publication of, xxi–xxii
  "Hymn" poem in, 175–76
  on mothers' responsibilities, 170
  on the need for black unity to overcome slavery, 165–66
  prayer in, 168
  on sin and ignorance, 169, 170–71
  on Stewart's childhood, 163
  on Stewart's conversion to Christianity, 163
  Walker (David) and, 164
  on Wethersfield "onion maidens," 171, 171n.11
The Repository of Religion and Literature and of Science and Art, xxxv
Richardson, Marilyn, xxviii–xxix
Ritualism, 55, 55n.12
Robinson, Robert, 201, 201n.5
Rogers, John, 260n.5
"Roll, Jordan, Roll" (hymn), 229–30, 253
Russworm, John, xvii

Sacred Hymns for the Use of Religious Societies (Cennik), 202, 202n.7

Saint Mary's Foggy Bottom Church (Washington DC), 280–81, 282–83, 282n.12
Sancho, Ignatius, 12–17, 15n.6
Saul (Old Testament king), 190
Saxton, Rufus, 224–25, 224–25n.2, 236–38, 242–43, 244, 245
Scott, William, 204
Second Book of Kings 2:23-24, 189n.3
Second Great Awakening (c. 1795–1840), xix–xx
Sewell, Willem, 127, 127n.7
Shadd Cary, Mary Ann Shadd
  Christian convention for colored people proposed by, 150–52, 151n.4
  on moral and intellectual debasement of the United States, 150–52
  Provincial Freedom newspaper, 152–53, 152n.6
  women's suffrage speech to Congress by, 153–56, 153n.8, 153n.9
  on workplace discrimination against blacks in Washington DC, 156–59
Shaw, Robert Gould, 253–55, 253n.16
Shelton, Wallace, 31–32, 38
Shulman, George, xx
"Sketches of the Fair Sex," 96–97
Slade, William, 283n.13
Stewart, James, xi, 93n.2, 163
Stewart, Maria. *See also specific works*
  on abolishing slavery in the District of Columbia, 185–86
  on ascent of a latter-day Ethiopia, xxi
  birthplace of, xiii
  black nationalism and, xii
  on black-owned businesses, xxiii–xxiv
  on black self-determination through strict moral virtue, xxii–xxiii, 90–91, 183–84
  on black women workers, xxiii–xxiv
  census records of, xxxiv
  childhood of, xii
  colonization movement rejected by, 81n.2, 184–85
  departure from Boston (1833) by, xxix
  humility in the writings of, xxvii–xxviii
  invective in the writings of, xxvi–xxviii
  the jeremiad and, xx–xxi, 87n.1

Ladies Literary Society of New York
and, xxxi–xxxiv
move to Baltimore (1852) by,
xxxiv–xxxv
move to Boston (1826) by, xii
move to New York City (1833) by, xxix
parents of, xiii–xiv
prophecy and, xx
racial solidarism, xxiv–xxvi
school in Baltimore operated by,
xxxvi–xxxvii
as school teacher, xxxi
self-education efforts of, xxxi
United States compared to Babylon in,
186–87
Walker and, xviii–xix
wedding of, xi
Stone, Samuel Johnson, 63, 63n.15
Stowe, Harriet Beecher, 53–54, 53n.10
St. Philip's Row (New York City), 211–12
"Sufferings during the War" (Stewart)
on Confederate advances near
Baltimore, 273
on Lenten observances, 281–82
on prayer meetings, 280–81
on pro-Confederate pastors in Civil
War Baltimore, 277–78
on religious denominations' decisions
to establish their own schools,
275–76
on Stewart's boarding house in
Washington, 278–79
on Stewart's move to Baltimore,
273–74
on Stewart's move to Washington,
277–78
on Stewart's teaching in Baltimore, 274
Sutton, Robert, 244
Syle, E.W., 277–78, 278n.9

Tacitus, 61, 61n.10
Talcott Street Congregationalist Church
(Hartford, CT), xiv–xv
Terence, 12–17, 16n.9
Travels in the Interior Districts of Africa
(Mungo), 51–52, 52n.9
*A Treatise on the Intellectual Character,
and the Civil and Political Condition
of the Colored People of the U. States;
and the Prejudice Exercised towards
Them: With a Sermon on the Duty of
the Church to Them* (Easton)
African American political theory and,
xv–xvi
on African origins of civilization,
136n.1
on American Revolution and slavery,
143–45
Article of Confederation cited in, 144–
45, 145n.8, 147
on blacks' service in the Revolutionary
War, 148–49, 149n.11
on "causes of apparent differences
between nations," 136–37
on conditions rather than genetics as
cause of slaves' inferiority, 138–40
Declaration of Independence cited in,
144–45, 147–48
on excuses for American hypocrisy,
148–49
on humans' constitutional uniformity,
xv–xvi
on hypocrisy of race in the United
states, xvi–xvii
on Jackson's address to free colored
people of Louisiana during War of
1812, 144–46
on political condition of colored people,
142–49
on psychological impact of violence
against slaves, 139
on recovery of fugitive slaves, 147–48
slavery compared to fatal disease in,
140–42
Turner, Nat, 187n.10
"Two Offers" (Watkins Harper), 213–22

Uncle Tom's Cabin (Stowe), 53–54, 53n.10

Vedius Pollio, 12–17, 16n.8

Walker, David, xvii–xix, xxii, 93n.2, See
also *Appeal to the Coloured Citizens of
the World* (Walker)
Washington, George, 189
Waters, Kristin, xiii

Watkins Harper, Frances Ellen
    "Aunt Chloe's Politics" and, 223
    "The Two Offers," 213–22
Watts, Isaac, 190, 190n.6, 198, 198n.2
Wesley, Charles, 204, 204n.9
Wesley, John, 73, 204n.10
Wethersfield "onion maidens"
    (Wethersfield, CT), 171, 171n.11
Wheatley, Phyllis, 12–17, 14n.5
White Cross League, 70–71
Whittier, John Greenleaf, 224–25, 224–25n.2, 236–37, 239–40
Wilson, Harriet E., 83n.9
Wilson, William J. ("Ethiop"), xxx–xxxi, 209–12
"Womanhood: A Vital Element in the Regeneration and Progress of a Race" (Cooper)
    on the A.M.E. Church, 72
    on black parishioners and white ministers, 74
    on blacks' status in American South, 67–69
    on black women and the black race's progress, 69–71
    on Christian churches' duties to black women, 76
    on Christian churches' duties to Southern blacks, 71–72
    on Christianity and women's status, 62–65
    on Episcopal Church in the South, 71–72
    on the feudal system and women's status, 61–62
    on Islamic societies and women, 59–60
    on Oriental societies and women, 59
    on potential for progress for women in US society, 60–69
    on Roman Empire's fall, 64
    on Turkey's "effete society," 60
    on women's responsibility to train children, 66
Woman in the Nineteenth Century (Fuller), 83n.7
Wordsworth, William, 52–53, 65–66
The Works of Ossian (Macpherson), 125, 125n.1

"Zillah." *See* Douglass, Sarah Mapps